AGNES LAKE HICKOK

Portrait of Agnes Lake, circa 1860.
Courtesy Kansas State Historical Society, Topeka.

AGNES LAKE HICKOK

Queen of the Circus, Wife of a Legend

Linda A. Fisher
and Carrie Bowers

UNIVERSITY OF OKLAHOMA PRESS : NORMAN

Also by Linda A. Fisher

(ed.) *The Whiskey Merchant's Diary: An Urban Life in the Emerging Midwest,* by Joseph J. Mersman (Athens, Ohio, 2007)

Library of Congress Cataloging-in-Publication Data

Fisher, Linda A., 1947–2006.
　Agnes Lake Hickok : queen of the circus, wife of a legend /
Linda A. Fisher and Carrie Bowers.
　　p. cm.
　Includes bibliographical references and index.
　ISBN 978-0-8061-3983-8 (hardcover : alk. paper)
　1. Hickok, Agnes Lake, 1826–1907. 2. Circus performers — United States —
Biography. 3. Circus owners — United States — Biography. 4. Horsemen and
horsewomen — United States — Biography. 5. Women entertainers — United
States — Biography. 6. Hickok, Wild Bill, 1837–1876 — Family. 7. Hickok, Wild Bill,
1837–1876 — Marriage. 8. Frontier and pioneer life — West (U.S.) 9. West (U.S.) —
History — 1860–1890.
I. Bowers, Carrie, 1980– II. Title.
CT275.H5955F57　2009
791.3092 — dc22　　[B]
2008024202

The paper in this book meets the guidelines for permanence and durability of the Committee on Production Guidelines for Book Longevity of the Council on Library Resources, Inc. ∞

1 2 3 4 5 6 7 8 9 10

To all the nineteenth-century circus performers whose names and accomplishments history has forgotten . . .

. . . and to Bertha Fisher and Chris Bowers, two mothers whose ceaseless love and support have allowed their own daughters to run off and follow their dreams

Tribute

Dr. Linda A. Fisher, a Board-certified internist, was researching historical documents for an article on the mid-nineteenth-century cholera epidemic when she happened upon the diary of Joseph J. Mersman, stored in the files of the Missouri Historical Society. She was fascinated by the entries, and so began to learn about Joseph and his life in the 1840s and 1850s. Many of the diary entries spoke with pride about Mersman's sister Agnes, and Linda came to realize that the story of this amazing woman was one that needed to be told. The biography of that life is this book, the story that Linda began, and that was so ably completed by Carrie Bowers and her other staff assistants.

Sadly, Linda Fisher succumbed to a long-term heart disease and, following transplant surgery, passed away in January 2006, shortly before the Mersman diary was published and while Agnes's story was still in progress. Linda's greatest work in life was as a physician and healer. Her greatest literary accomplishments were the biography of Agnes Lake Hickok, the volume you hold in your hand, and the Joseph J. Mersman diary annotation.

We miss her . . .

The circus is our most popular and the most democratic of all our institutions. There are no class distinctions among circus-goers. . . . The gaudy dresses, the witchery of horsemanship, the feats of strength and slight-of-hand [*sic*] tricks, all are gazed at with open mouthed wonder and admiration, and the clown has only to open his lips to spread a grin over a thousand faces. Great is the circus, with just enough spice of sin and folly to make it pleasant to everybody!

Portland (Maine) Transcript, June 9, 1860

That which thrills, arouses, and puts new vigor into sluggish nature [is] renewing, recreating, [and] rejuvenating. . . . Be jolly with the children and see how contagious it is. There's naught that fire the young blood like prancing horses, the glitter of gaudy trappings, the clangor of horns, the sight of beasts and the surging multitude of eager humanity racing after a show.

Scranton (Pa.) Daily Times, August 6, 1873

Contents

Illustrations

Preface

I first met Agnes Lake through the writings of her brother, Joseph J. Mersman. A prominent St. Louis businessman, Joseph kept a diary from 1847 through 1864 and mentioned his sister in over two dozen entries. Of his siblings, she was the one he enjoyed the most, and I, too, quickly decided that I wanted to know her better. According to Joseph, Agnes was attractive, talented, and restless. At a time when many women in her social circle longed to settle down with a prosperous merchant for a husband, Agnes had dared social convention and defied her family's expectations to wed a traveling entertainer, Bill Lake. Agnes visited every state and even ventured to new territories far to the west.

Over the decades, she transformed herself from a barefoot farm girl to a successful doyenne of the tent-show circuit. Agnes's marriage to the legendary Wild Bill Hickok once again brought her to the nation's attention and added another episode of high-profile glamour to her story. Agnes found love not once but twice in her many years. She lived to see her daughter achieve equestrian fame and to hold her great-granddaughter in her arms. Few mid-nineteenth-century women stand out in such sharp relief against the broad backdrop of American history: the waves of European immigration, the steamboat era, the Civil War, westward expansion, and the export of entertainment to Europe. Agnes Lake played a role in all those events.

To research Agnes Lake, I had to travel throughout America's heartland. Agnes had journeyed on steamboats, circus wagons, and railroad cars. I chose airplanes and automobiles — faster and more comfortable than any conveyance available to the circus star. Precious few documents Agnes wrote still exist, but I found traces of her life and work in archives from Florida to Maine and from New York to California. The trajectory of her life brought her into contact with accomplished individuals throughout America. Too often, the men in her life received most of the public notice. Even the Library of Congress has a photograph of Agnes Lake filed under "Buffalo Bill Cody."

But Agnes Lake's story was there for anyone who looked, and her life is pieced together in these pages for you to read. Notable American women of the nineteenth century were not only presidents' wives, writers, or artists. Agnes Lake's activities in the entertainment industry paved the way for other women — and men — in the field. As the first woman in America to own a tent show, she popularized entertainment trends introduced by others. At a time when transportation was difficult and communication limited, she brought dazzling performances to millions and wonder to ordinary lives.

Many details of nineteenth-century existence were grim or downright ugly. Epidemic disease, financial depressions, and harsh living conditions affected most people. For over three decades Agnes Lake brought entertainment and joy to audiences and launched a younger generation that continued the circus arts.

"*What is hope without a circus?*" asked one pundit. "*And what is America without hope?*"

Whether by steamboat, wagon, or rail, Agnes Lake delivered hope.

Linda A. Fisher
Annandale, Virginia

Acknowledgments

M any people and institutions helped me discover the facts of
Agnes Lake's life. I deeply appreciate all their help during the
years of work required to create this book.

I also wish to thank the National Library of Medicine (NLM),
the National Historical Publications and Records Commission
(NHPRC), and the State Historical Society of Missouri (SHSMO)
for providing funding that enabled me to finish the project. By
aiding my research on the diary of Joseph J. Mersman, the brother
of Agnes Lake, those supporters enabled me to track down information on both sides of the Atlantic Ocean and to carefully document
the life of the circus pioneer as well.

Reinhard Hennig provided translations of German-language
publications and manuscripts found in archives. He also gave sound
advice concerning research strategies. Dennis Northcott provided
research support in St. Louis, Ann Hambrecht in Cincinnati, Falk
Liebezeit and Sylvia Möhle in Germany, Jean Fisher in New Jersey,
Pat Fennerty in New Orleans, and Eugene Zepp in Boston. Research
assistants at newspaper archives included Betty Drucker (Alabama),
Marie Imus (Arkansas), Gwendolyn Lott (Georgia), Stacy Pratt Mc-
Dermott (Illinois), Richard Enochs (Indiana), Becky Thoms (Iowa),

Ann Cameron MacRae (Kentucky), Jeffrey Banas (Michigan), and Jayne Davis and Miriam B. Kahn (Ohio).

Stuart Thayer, William Slout, and Fred Dahlinger, Jr., generously shared their insights concerning nineteenth-century American circuses. Jerry Dalton, master distiller of the Jim Beam Brands Company, provided information about American whiskey making. Joseph G. Rosa and Robin Carmody offered suggestions regarding information about Wild Bill Hickok.

Several genealogists helped me trace the Mersman family from Oldenburg to America: Ann Carter Fleming, Elizabeth Shown Mills, Roger Minert, and Marion Wolfert provided advice and assistance. Other people who aided me included Rev. David Hoying and his mother, Rita Hoying, Allen W. Bernard, Simon Baatz, Martha Nodine, Don Heinrich Tolzmann, Jürgen Schlumbohm, Wolfgang Grams, Helmut Schmaul, Antonius Holtman, Rainer Schimpf, Stephen Rowan, Esther Katz, Candace Falk, Marianne Wokeck, Faye Dudden, Jane Censer, Renée Sentilles, Bonnie Fisher, and Allan Fisher.

Individuals at many libraries and archives helped me find source materials to document Agnes Lake's life: Anne B. Shepherd (Cincinnati Historical Society Library); Paul Immel (State Library of Ohio); Sylvia Verdun Metzinger, Claire Smittle, and M'lissa Kesterman (The Public Library of Cincinnati and Hamilton County); Juda Moyer (Troy [Ohio] Historical Society); Kathy Grillo and Melvina Conley (St. Louis Civil Courts Archives); Ronald Miller (Ancient Free and Accepted Masons of the Grand Lodge of Missouri); Steve Gossard (Milner Library, Illinois State University); Mary Ellyn Hamilton (Oscar Getz Museum of Whiskey History); Erin Foley (Circus World Museum and Library); Mark Levine (Brooklyn Public Library); Joan Kilpatrick (Texas General Land Office); Lila Fourhman-Shaull and June Lloyd (York County Heritage Trust); Gail Cassini (Historical Archives of the Chancery, Archdiocese of Cincinnati); Randy Bloomquist and Emily Jaycox (Missouri Historical Society); Ruth Hager (St. Louis County Library); Sandra Bender (City of St. Louis, Recorder of Deeds Office); Lucas Dennis and Annette Fern (Harvard College Library); and Charles Bean, David Kelly, Thomas Mann, and Travis Westly (Library of Congress).

A number of Pohlschneider and Mersman descendants assisted with establishing family pedigrees and finding photographs of ancestors; Fred Althoff, Trish Blakely (Scudder Association genealogist), William Carlson, Agnes Cromack, John T. Dilschneider, JoAn Dreahn, William E. "Jerry" Giraldin, Nancy Lindquist, George Petticrew, and Lori Steadman were especially helpful. The Johannes Pohlschneider family of Damme, Germany, showed me their community and shared warm hospitality.

Research assistants Veronica Fletcher, Christopher Robertson, James T. Garber, and Jason M. Beagle organized the records for this project and helped me produce the diary of Joseph Mersman, which led to this biography. Carrie Bowers helped with manuscript preparation, illustration scanning, proofreading, and many other tasks requiring computer skills. Andrea Myles of Washington University Medical Photography, Illustration, and Computer Graphics prepared the maps.

Bertha Fisher and Tove Post-Roberts provided encouragement; Christopher E. Byrne gave me technical assistance, moral support, and much love. A really big thanks goes to my personal physician, Edward Kasper, MD, who, when I feared that ill health might jeopardize my project, told me, "Write faster."

Linda A. Fisher
Annandale, Virginia

Coauthor's Note

I also first met Agnes Lake through the writings of her brother, Joseph J. Mersman. As a graduate student at George Mason University, I became a research assistant for a local physician-turned-historian, Linda A. Fisher, and in November 2004 I joined the crew that worked from her home. Linda was making the final push toward completing an ambitious documentary editing project: a full transcription of Joseph J. Mersman's diary, complete with annotation, maps, photographs, and contemporary advertisements. The result: Linda resuscitated the antebellum atmospheres of Cincinnati and St. Louis and revealed an overlooked niche of American history—mid-nineteenth-century bachelorhood.

During this process I learned about Agnes Lake, Joseph's younger sister who became a circus performer. Linda was excited to tell me more about his famous sibling, the subject of her second project—a biography of this amazing woman. She eventually secured a contract for Agnes's biography and was over the moon as she worked simultaneously on projects about both siblings. (The Joseph Mersman diary was awarded its own contract with a separate publisher in October 2005.)

Quietly, however, Linda's body had other plans. Despite the

efforts of a renowned medical team in a world-class facility, she died in January 2006 from complications following a heart transplant.

Stunned and grief-stricken, Linda's family was left with the difficult task of deciding the fate of her beloved Agnes project. Before Linda passed away, she had completed the necessary research, secured a publishing contract, and written approximately half of the manuscript. In April, Linda's family asked me to finish the manuscript. I was extremely honored to be asked to complete the work of the woman whom I had considered a mentor but was also a bit overwhelmed by the prospect of taking over such an extensive project. I carefully considered the options, and, with few reservations, I gladly accepted this unique opportunity. Despite my grief over losing Linda and some additional turmoil in my life, I kept returning to the same conclusion: Agnes's story needed to be told, and Linda's work needed to be completed.

Picking up where Linda had ended was no easy task. Although I was accustomed to her writing habits and style, it took weeks to familiarize myself with the plethora of research she had completed. Soon, however, I developed my own rhythm and the words began to flow as Agnes's life unfolded before my eyes. Agnes Lake was a fascinating woman, and although not all of her secrets are divulged here, I look forward to continuing the quest to discover all I can about her.

In the months that have passed since I officially started writing Agnes's biography, those whom Linda had previously contacted for assistance willingly reached out to me as well. In addition to those recognized by Linda, I extend my heartfelt thanks to those who have been instrumental throughout this process. Stuart Thayer, Fred Dahlinger, Jr., Fred Pfening III, and William Slout offered advice and provided additional illustrations of Agnes's circus career. Stuart also graciously allowed me access to a large body of his research, upon which the appendix is based. Joseph G. Rosa generously shared his knowledge of Wild Bill Hickok and provided suggestions to clarify the mysterious relationship between Agnes and Wild Bill. M'Lissa Kesterman and Anne Shepherd (Cincinnati Historical Society Library), Sylvia Verdun Metzinger, and Diane Mallstrom (The Public Library of Cincinnati and Hamilton County) provided immeasurable assistance via e-mail and photocopies by fax. AnnaLee Pauls assisted above and beyond the call of duty with the McCaddon Collection of the Barnum and Bailey Circus at Princeton University. Cynthia Rosinski graciously shared her family's history with both Linda and me. Jason Beagle photocopied books at the Library of Congress, and research assistant Tim Merrill in Utah provided exceptional research that enhanced Agnes's historical legacy. Christopher Robertson assisted with manuscript preparation and proofreading and conducted extensive research at both the Library of Congress and the National Archives.

I would also like to thank the University of Oklahoma Press, especially Chuck Rankin, Alice Stanton, and Steven Baker, for their support and patience in receiving this manuscript. In addition, Cheryl Carnahan provided encouraging copyediting. Linda's mother, Bertha, as well as her siblings and their families, offered encouragement, faith, and patience in allowing me to complete Linda's unfinished text. Christopher Byrne was always just a phone call away, and he provided insight and theories, edited several drafts, and contributed much-appreciated humor. A "gravy-eared" basset hound and two cats with fluffy tails displayed their paperweight expertise and supplied endless distractions and stress relief. Finally, my sisters Catherine and Lauren, and especially my mother, Chris, listened for months to stories about Agnes, the circus, and my frustrations while conducting research, and they read hundreds of pages of the manuscript; but most important, they provided an endless reserve of support and love.

Carrie Bowers

Editorial Note

To preserve the historical integrity of the documents reproduced herein—Joseph J. Mersman's diary, newspaper advertisements, and personal correspondence — the erratic spellings and inconsistent capitalizations have not been edited to reflect current orthography standards. In some cases, however, punctuation and brackets have been added to facilitate the reader's understanding when a misspelling might have altered the context or content of the original text.

When a relative's or performer's birth and death dates are known, they are included the first time the person is mentioned. In addition, alternate spellings of names are provided. Some of the entries in the appendix such as "Willard's" or "Britton's Mills" refer to places known at the time but whose names have been changed over the years.

AGNES LAKE HICKOK

Prologue
Deadwood, South Dakota

D espite the heat of the summer day, visitors sprint past the blinking slot machines and crowded restaurant tables to board the tour bus on Main Street. T-shirts and ball caps hint at the states they left to take this vacation: New York, Florida, California, Illinois, and others. They are excited to be in the Wild West and to see at last the historic town of Deadwood, South Dakota. They have read about the town for years, seen television shows and cinematic interpretations, and now they are actually here. The village, just a few streets at the bottom of a ravine, with hillsides rising steeply on both sides, has welcomed tourists for many decades. These pilgrims support the local economy: officials expect in excess of 1 million visitors annually, bringing an estimated $50–$80 million to the community through receipts from restaurants, hotels, shops, and gambling.[1]

The tour bus rolls past the old brick buildings and weathered storefronts with antique lettering that recreate the mood of 1876. The visitors need the bus to take them to Mount Moriah Cemetery — walking up the incline would leave many of them too breathless to talk about the discoveries there. Just inside the cemetery's gate, they spot the grave they have traveled so far to see: Wild Bill Hickok, who was gunned down August 2, 1876, while playing poker in a Deadwood saloon. His cards, legend has it, were black aces and eights—the "Dead Man's Hand."[2] The tour guide points to another monument nearby that marks the final resting place of Martha Jane Canary, better known as "Calamity Jane" — another character of the era who wore buckskin clothes, rarely bathed, and shot a rifle with the skill akin to many men. The proximity of the two graves suggests a close relationship in life.

"Where's Wild Bill's wife?" asks one man. He wants to make sure he gets his money's worth by seeing every sight.

"I don't know," says the guide. He shrugs and returns to his prepared speech, gesturing toward other graves. He knows Agnes Lake Hickok is dead *somewhere*—arithmetic makes that a certainty. But who was she, and what happened to her?

Wild Bill Hickok's widow, known widely by her stage name, Agnes Lake, also toured Deadwood in the summer of 1877.[3] Traveling on horseback from Cheyenne, Wyoming, in the company of friends, she visited Hickok's grave long before the town grew and forced the relocation of the coffin to a higher site on the mountain.[4] Agnes wed Hickok only five months before his death, following a courtship that had extended nearly five years, consumed stacks of stationery, and relied on the often unpredictable United States Post Office. Two individuals with dramatically different pasts, Agnes and James —as she called him—had hoped to create a new life together. When Hickok set out to make a grub stake in Deadwood, Agnes waited for him in Cincinnati. They planned to buy a ranch and settle down in the West.

That September day in 1877 when Agnes rode into Deadwood a year after his death, she confronted the problem of bringing Hickok's body back East so it would be closer to the people who loved him. The complicated loyalties and logistics that figured into her final decision elude modern-day tourists who gaze upon the marker. Today, Wild Bill Hickok sleeps eternally in Deadwood—alone. If Agnes Lake loved Hickok so much, why did she leave him buried in Mount Moriah Cemetery?

After her visit to South Dakota, Agnes Lake lived another thirty years. When she died in Jersey City, New Jersey, on August 22, 1907,[5] her obituaries indicated that she enjoyed national stature, not only because of her marriage to Hickok but also because of her professional and personal accomplishments. The various summaries of her life revealed some puzzling contradictions:

> "Mrs. Lake . . . the first woman to own a circus in the United States . . . was born in Doehme, Alsace in 1826. Her parents' name was Mersman. They came to this country when she was about four years old."
>
> *Evening Journal* (Jersey City, N.J.), August 23, 1907

> "born in Doehm, Alsace . . . her parents' name being Messman. Her parents came to this country shortly after her birth and settled in Cincinnati when she was about 16 years old."   *New York Times*, August 23, 1907

> "Mme. Lake, whose maiden name was Katterhorn, was born in Cincinnati."   *Billboard*, August 31, 1907

> "Great Slack Wire Performer and Skilled Rider — After First Husband, Old-time Clown, Was Killed by Desperado, She Managed Show, Made Fortune, and Lost It — Second Husband Also Slain."   *The Washington Post*, August 23, 1907

> "The career of . . . Mrs. Agnes Lake . . . was one of the most remarkable in the history of the circus in America. . . . Her husband's real name was Thatcher."
>
> *Indianapolis News*, August 24, 1907

Anyone trying to research Agnes Lake's early years quickly encounters difficulties: no town spelled "Doehme" or "Doehm" exists in France or Germany — or anywhere in Europe. Some accounts claimed that Agnes Lake was as young as fifteen at the time of her first marriage. Records that precede her obituaries, including passenger manifests and marriage licenses, subtracted years and even decades from her age, making her alleged birth and marriage dates seem about as insecure as loose sand. In the era of "confidence men and painted women,"[6] the public often witnessed such modifications of the truth, initially started by the performers themselves but proliferated through the years by the media. An uncertain birthplace and birth date, however, make it difficult to track the trajectory of a person's life. Attempting to backtrack, making the leap across the Atlantic Ocean to an unknown destination in nineteenth-century Europe, adds exponentially to the difficulty of the challenge.

Agnes Lake's older brother, Joseph J. Mersman (1824–92), provided the key to tracing the equestrian's past. Mersman, a St. Louis tobacconist and wholesale whiskey dealer, kept a diary from 1847 to 1864, recording details of his activities and frequently mentioning his famous sister. His bound volume, in the collection of the Missouri Historical Society,[7] describes his father and siblings, making it possible to follow the trail of the entire family back to Europe.[8] Mersman's diary leads directly to a village never mentioned by Agnes Lake: Damme, in Lower Saxony, about 100 miles southwest of Bremen. Parish registers, scrawled in Latin by Catholic priests, document the origins of Agnes and her family. Official records from the Grand Duchy of Oldenburg enable us to reconstruct the life Agnes and her family left behind. Placing Agnes Lake in context — with parents, siblings, husbands, and children — vastly improves our understanding of the woman and her amazing career.

The numerous records created during the nearly eighty-one years of Agnes Lake's existence reveal a series of surnames acquired through birth, custom, marriage, and artistic endeavors: Pohlschneider, Messman, Mersman, Lake, Thatcher, DeLonne, Hickok, and Carson. She traveled extensively throughout the Union's states and territories, leaving a trail in newspapers and official documents. Although her personal papers are limited to a few letters,[9] Agnes Lake's life is documented on microfilm, in filing cabinets, on index cards, and in record books all over America. She was married once in Louisiana and twice in Wyoming, owned land in Kentucky, died in New Jersey, and now rests beneath a granite marker in Ohio.

Fig. 1. Joseph J. Mersman, circa 1851, whose diary provided the key to unearthing information about his sister Agnes and her early years in the circus. From the collection of Linda A. Fisher.

In tracking her story, one uncovers an energetic woman who overcame gender bias to assert herself as a businesswoman and entrepreneur. A successful circus owner, Agnes Lake found love for the second time in middle age and married the man of her dreams.

It is a life story that deserves attention.

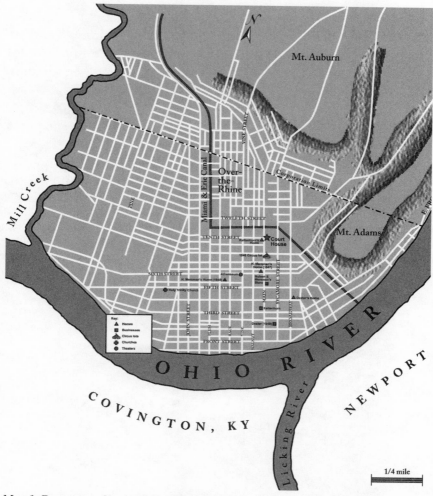

Map 1. Downtown Cincinnati as Agnes Lake knew it, with her family's and friends' homes and businesses indicated.

Map 2. The Mississippi River and its major tributaries. In 1852 and 1853, the *Floating Palace* visited the important river cities indicated. (West Virginia was formed as a separate state in 1863.)

CHAPTER ONE

Families, Farm Names, and the Great Migration

1800–1838

Agnes Lake's marriage to Wild Bill Hickok in 1876 once again brought her to the nation's attention. Nineteenth-century audiences expected the personal history of a theatrical performer to contain storybook romance and breathtaking adventure. Rising to meet those expectations, Agnes Lake fabricated a few glamorous fictions to her life's story and fed them to journalists. She embellished the details of her early years and created a European birth and childhood in a place hundreds of miles from her actual roots.[1] She claimed she was from Alsace, France, and subtracted four and sometimes up to twelve years from her age, a traditional practice for performers. The actual story of Agnes Lake's origins includes plenty of romance and adventure, but the elements that shaped her personality were not French as she claimed: Agnes was born in what is now northwestern Germany, more than four hundred miles from Alsace.

Agnes's future son-in-law, Gilbert Robinson, also a circus personality, included the story of Agnes Lake's emigration from "Doehm,

Alsace" in his memoir, *Old Wagon Show Days*, and it has been repeated in circus histories ever since. Robinson probably distributed the error-filled information used in her obituaries.

Since European archives have maintained records for centuries, the actual past of Agnes's family is carefully preserved for those determined to seek the facts. In the nineteenth century, the twin powers of Church and State created documents as fast as paper could record them. The essential records of government — tax rolls, census lists, and court documents — reveal details of Agnes's family that church registers augment. What emerges from those papers is an accurate picture of the life that shaped Agnes's personality. Furthermore, the documents reveal how and why her family came to America.[2]

The clues to track her family back across the Atlantic Ocean came from a diary kept by Agnes's older brother, Joseph J. Mersman.[3] Agnes was his favorite sibling, and Joseph mentioned her often in his record. In describing members of his Catholic family, Joseph provided the information needed to link his famous sister with the land of their birth. His 1865 naturalization papers document that he was born in the Grand Duchy of Oldenburg. A search of Catholic parishes in Oldenburg revealed only one family with five children of the ages Joseph described. Their surname, however, was not Mersman but Pohlschneider.

The Pohlschneider Farm in Damme provided Agnes's family with their original home and their first surname.[4] Damme lies approximately a hundred miles southwest of Bremen, in today's state of Lower Saxony. Situated just east of the Netherlands and surrounded by bogs, the land is perpetually so damp that farmers use drainage ditches instead of fences to divide the fields. They cut peat moss from the moor to burn as fuel and raise rye, not wheat, as the grain for bread.[5] A Gothic tower, built in 1435, stands in the center of the village and calls the faithful to Mass, as it has done for nearly six hundred years. Burned and rebuilt several times throughout the centuries, Saint Victor's Church itself symbolizes the resilience of the local Catholic congregation.

In the early nineteenth century, the parishioners faced a crisis of unprecedented proportions: Damme had too many people and too little land.[6] Virtually all 6,000 residents of Damme depended on agriculture for their livelihood.[7] The owners of farms — both large estates and smaller pieces of land — wielded more influence than laborers who owned no real estate. Improving one's position in society was nearly impossible because there simply was no unclaimed land. Landless workers were stuck at the bottom of the social hierarchy because farms usually changed hands only through marriage or inheritance. Custom called for the youngest son or a married daughter to inherit the family farm and for other children to receive cash.[8] This practice, called ultimogeniture, is found even today among the Old Order Amish families in America.[9]

In early-nineteenth-century Oldenburg, every generation of landowners produced offspring for whom downward social mobility was inevitable. Numerous children, commonly ten to twelve in a family, resulted in a growing population, even after childhood deaths took their toll. Since the parcels of land had been subdivided over centuries, some farms were so tiny that they barely supported the families who worked them.[10] Further subdivision was impractical, even illegal.

At the beginning of the nineteenth century, one-third of male farm workers from Damme took seasonal employment in the Netherlands — far from their homes — harvesting hay or peat moss. The cash bought essential commodities and bolstered Damme's economy. That infusion of support kept people from starving, but it created a tenuous lifeline, dependent on another country's favorable economic and agricultural climate.[11]

The Pohlschneider Farm consisted of only 12 acres in a chain of disconnected fields, some as small as a half acre.[12] By comparison, nineteenth-century farmers in the eastern United States often farmed contiguous land comprising 40 to 100 acres. In the western United States, many farmers worked farms with a minimum of 140 acres.

Located about two miles outside the village proper in a little hamlet called Borringhausen, the Pohlschneider Farm consisted of a farmhouse, a bake house, and a *Heuerhaus*, the residence for hired

Fig. 2. Heuerhaus similar to the one in which Agnes's family lived before emigrating to the United States in 1833. Her father, Friedrich Messman, was a hired farmhand when he met Catharina Pohlschneider, the farmer's daughter he married in 1811. Courtesy Museumdorf Cloppenburg, the Netherlands.

farmhands (*Heuermann*). The Heuerhaus sheltered animals as well as the farm laborers in an architectural design characteristic of the region.[13] Typically constructed of bricks, the Heuerhaus was a long barn with a dirt floor and few windows. The damp chill of the Oldenburg air penetrated the building throughout the year.

Larger estates might have several such dwellings, but the Pohlschneider Farm had only one Heuerhaus, which provided up to twenty people with a place to sleep. The design of the structure had remained unchanged for four centuries. An open fire burned peat for cooking, but there was no chimney, so the interior was frequently filled with smoke. In the summer, the acrid haze discouraged insects, but in winter the pollutants made eyes weep. Most of the Heuerhaus was given over to one large room: stalls for horses, cattle, sheep, and pigs lined three walls, with two large doors at the end of the building that opened out to the yard. Chickens roosted

Fig. 3. Interior view of a typical Heuerhaus, showing cattle stalls at left and the cooking fire without exterior ventilation. Courtesy Museumdorf Cloppenburg, the Netherlands.

in the rafters.[14] The humans claimed the other end of the building, where the fire burned, but no barrier separated the animals from the human residents. Family members slept in closet-like alcoves that conserved heat but also facilitated the spread of contagious diseases. Vegetables were stored under the platforms on which the people slept because the ground was too damp for cellars.

When Agnes's father, Friedrich Messmann,[15] first came to the farm in the early 1800s, he lived in the Pohlschneider Heuerhaus with the other hired workers. Friedrich was the third of eight children from a landless family. He, his parents, and his brothers migrated from farm to farm, boarding in each farmer's Heuerhaus.[16] Once in their teens, the Messmann boys joined the army of youths in Damme seeking employment on neighbors' farms.

The widow Pohlschneider, formerly Anna Margarethe Hellebaum,[17] needed help with her crops, and she hired Friedrich Messmann to live and work on her farm. Her husband had died in April

1800 at age forty-four, leaving her with six children and many debts. Just two months after her husband's demise an infant son died, leaving her with only one son, six-year-old Johann Friedrich. Her daughters — Anna, Elisabeth, Catharina, and Angela[18] — ranged in age from nine to sixteen and helped with the gardening, milking, and baking, but many farm tasks required a man's strength.[19] Friedrich Messmann joined the crew in the Pohlschneider Heuerhaus, providing labor in exchange for a place to live and a share of the harvest.[20] For a decade, the widow depended on the workers to help her eke out a living from the tired land. When crops failed, she borrowed cash using the farm as collateral, and she gradually sank deeper into debt. On her own at age forty, she never remarried.

Friedrich Messmann soon played an important role in the Pohlschneiders' life. He and the other laborers worked beside the widow and her family and walked with them to church in the village each Sunday. At festivals they shared food, laughter, and folk dancing. Messmann saw the girls grow from children to young women. Anna, the oldest, died in 1807 at age twenty-two,[21] and everyone on the farm mourned her passing. But early deaths were an ugly fact in the bucolic life of Oldenburg. The average life expectancy was less than forty years: communicable diseases, childbed tragedies, and farm accidents took an enormous toll. One-third of the children died before age fifteen.[22]

As the Pohlschneider daughters matured, they found their marriage prospects limited. In Damme, laborers outnumbered farm owners by a factor of four.[23] Faced with a short supply of eligible men of equal or higher social status,[24] each of the girls married a Heuermann — thus descending the social ladder. Such matches were typical, however, for most women thought it was preferable to be the wife of a Heuermann rather than a spinster. The Pohlschneider girls looked no further than their own parish for mates. Following tradition, they married in the order they had been born: first Elisabeth (January 11, 1809), then Catharina (April 24, 1811), and then Angela (September 3, 1811).[25]

Messmann courted Catharina and married her when he was twenty-nine and she was twenty-two. On their wedding day, Catha-

rina moved from her mother's farmhouse to join Friedrich Messmann in the nearby Pohlschneider Heuerhaus. Marriage to the
owner's daughter secured Messmann's place on the farm, and he
began using Pohlschneider, not Messmann, as his surname, indicat-
ing that he and his wife regarded the Pohlschneider Farm as their
permanent residence.[26] Even though he had married into the owner's family, Agnes's father experienced no dramatic change in his
financial status. His teenage brother-in-law, Johann Friedrich Pohlschneider, seemed destined to become the property's eventual
owner. Catharina quickly became pregnant and gave birth before
the year was out.

By the autumn of 1811, all three Pohlschneider daughters were
married. They all lived on farms within a few miles of their mother's
house, so she could easily visit them.[27] Death, however, cut short the
family's joy. In February 1812 the Widow Pohlschneider died.[28] The
surviving sisters made arrangements to care for the seventeen-year-
old Johann Friedrich, but he died less than four months after his
mother. When the three sisters and their husbands discussed sharing
the estate, they recognized that title to the Pohlschneider Farm was a
mixed blessing. The liens against the property totaled nearly twice its
appraised value, which was only 1,000 thalers (about $21,600 in 2005
U.S. dollars).[29]

Despite the debts, Friedrich Messmann Pohlschneider wanted to
own the land. He and Catharina already resided there and used the
Pohlschneider surname. Confident that he could make the farm
support his family, Friedrich offered his two sisters-in-law a small cash
settlement, just 76 thalers paid over several years. In exchange, he
and his wife would assume ownership of the farm, in addition to the
associated liabilities. Elisabeth and Angela accepted the deal, which
maintained the integrity of the Pohlschneider Farm, and they continued to live on other farms with their husbands.[30]

In August 1812, Friedrich Messmann Pohlschneider and his
wife assumed title to the property. Thus, Agnes's father became a
landowner, a step up in social status, albeit a small one since the
farm was so tiny. The young married couple moved into the farmhouse; a wooden floor and a chimney made it vastly more comfort-

able than the Heuerhaus. Over the next seventeen years the family grew with the births of ten children, all baptized with the surname Pohlschneider.[31]

Catholic custom required that a saint's name, often Johann or Maria, be a child's first name, so families commonly used the middle name to address the individual. The day-old daughter baptized "Maria Agnes Pohlschneider" on August 26, 1826, was called Agnes by those who knew her. The ninth child of the family, Agnes was only the second daughter to survive infancy.

In that era, married women usually produced one child every two years. Births were numerous, but infectious diseases such as smallpox, measles, diphtheria, and tuberculosis devastated the youngsters.[32] Four of the Pohlschneider's ten children — two boys and two girls — died in childhood, leaving two girls and four boys to reach adulthood. From oldest to youngest, their names were Elisabeth,[33] Friedrich, Heinrich, Joseph, Agnes, and Franz.

Agnes's maternal aunts both succumbed to childbirth complications: Angela died at twenty-two and Elisabeth at thirty.[34] Their widowers soon married again, for they needed help caring for their young children. Such serial monogamy, common in Oldenburg where families and farms depended on the skills of two parents, produced many step- and half-siblings.[35] It was no wonder that families took farm names as their surnames whenever possible. Land had far greater permanence than individuals.

When Agnes was born, her mother, Catharina Pohlschneider, was the sole survivor of her birth family. Agnes's earliest memories doubtless consisted of a rural life among a network of extended relatives and close friends. Her daily routine of household tasks brought her into contact with people who had known her parents and grandparents for years. Agnes's father, Friedrich Messmann Pohlschneider, whose marriage had changed both his name and his economic status, now hired others to help him with farming. Some of Agnes's paternal uncles bunked in the Pohlschneider Heuerhaus with other workers. Additional relatives lived on neighboring farms, and everyone attended the same church on Sundays.[36] Few Protestants lived in Oldenburg, and everyone Agnes knew spoke a dialect of German called *Plattdeutsch*, or Low German, in contrast to the *Hochdeutsch*, or High German, spoken in the mountainous regions.

Agnes grew up in constant contact with animals, since the Pohl-schneider Farm raised all the livestock necessary to feed the people who lived there. They used oxen, not horses, for plowing fields and pulling wagonloads of hay. Only the wealthiest farmers had horses for riding, but many other creatures surrounded her: cows pro-duced milk for drinking and making cheese, and sheep provided wool for clothing. Hogs produced the ham, bacon, and lard for the best meals; and geese, ducks, and chickens provided eggs and some-times meat. Even domesticated house pets had a purpose: cats helped keep the rodent population under control, while the family dog provided protection and powered the butter churn.[37]

To supplement his income from farming, Friedrich Messmann Pohlschneider made cigars, which gradually became the preferred method for smoking tobacco as the century progressed.[38] Men and some women throughout German-speaking lands took up smoking. Working at night on the same table his family used for meals during the day, the part-time tobacconist rolled cylinders of leaves imported from Maryland, Virginia, and Kentucky, since tobacco from America was the most popular type. By 1830, when Agnes was four, the holds of vessels sailing east from Baltimore to Bremen were crammed with tobacco, a more profitable commodity than rice, cotton, or whale oil.[39] Dealers in Bremen purchased one-quarter of North America's entire tobacco crop, and workers such as Pohlschneider processed it for retail sales. Wholesalers brought bales of tobacco to workshops and homes throughout the northern communities and later dis-tributed the finished cigars to shops in the region.

In Damme, other families commonly wove fabric from linen to supplement their incomes, but Agnes's family did not own a loom.[40] Instead, the tobacco leaves, ranging in color from gold to almost black, strewn on the worktable, filled the farmhouse with their pun-gent aromas. Agnes's father became skilled at rolling cigars and taught each of his children to help by checking the bales for insects, cutting the veins out of the leaves, and sorting piles of tobacco. Even as a small child Agnes would have replenished the piles of tobacco or stacked cigar molds for her father. Cigar making provided the cash that pulled the Pohlschneider family out of debt in Oldenburg and later got them started in commercial ventures in America. Making cigars occupied every free moment. Each batch of cigars filled baskets for the wholesaler to collect, and the same man who delivered the bales of tobacco leaves would drive off with baskets of cigars in his wagon.

Many inhabitants of Damme traveled no further than within a five-mile radius in their entire lives. But Friedrich Messmann Pohlschneider was more adventurous than his neighbors, more willing to try new things, and more determined to see his children have a better life. His ambition would take him and his family out of the little orbit of Damme. Agnes's family played a small part in international commerce, and the shiploads of tobacco grew larger with each passing year. Owners of the vessels searched for something to fill the holds during the return voyage to maximize their profits. By 1832, the ships that imported tobacco were returning to America with human cargo: emigrants.[41]

*   *   *

Gottfried Duden was the man of the hour. Residents of Damme and many other German communities were talking about his books, rereading and sharing copies until the bindings nearly fell to pieces from use. *Report on a Journey to the Western States of North America and a Stay of Several Years along the Missouri (during the Years 1824, '25, '26, 1827)* was a long title, sixty-nine syllables in German, but his audience read every word and discussed the contents with friends, wondering how much to believe.

First published in 1829, Duden's report described his travels on the Ohio and Mississippi rivers and his farming on the banks of the Missouri River. Written for Germans hoping to emigrate, the book included a supplement filled with detailed observations and practical advice: "Cincinnati is called the most beautiful city of the entire West. . . . There is probably no city in America where one can live more pleasantly and at the same time more cheaply."[42]

Duden made Cincinnati sound like a bargain, and he described

Missouri as "the Garden of Eden."[43] He encouraged German immigrants to establish farming communities in America. He estimated that a family of five would need about 1,000 thalers to emigrate to the New World; buy land, farm animals, and equipment; and establish a household. He raved about the friendliness of Americans, claiming "no foreigner needs to fear the rudeness in North America."[44] The soil surrounding Cincinnati and environs was "romantic" and very "fertile."[45] Duden quelled safety concerns by reassuring readers that thieves find "no receiver[s] for stolen goods and everyone helps track [them],"[46] while many homes were left unattended without locks.

Duden included a few paragraphs about New World hazards that were small in size, minimal in number, and totally avoidable. Many of the hazards were familiar nuisances to German immigrants, but with variations. Rattlesnakes and sand fleas were new varieties of familiar pests that frightened foreigners, with deadly consequences. Duden also noted a greater abundance of bats, ticks, and bedbugs that annoyed immigrants and animals alike.[47] He gave details about traveling arrangements: "In general the freight [charge] in America is not very high. A seat in the mail coach from Philadelphia to Pittsburgh costs about twenty dollars, from Baltimore to Wheeling about sixteen dollars."[48]

Sounding very much like the author of a guidebook written today, Duden told travelers how to stretch their finances and get the most out of every thaler. Because of the high cost of tailors in America, he recommended that immigrants outfit themselves with enough underwear for several years, as well as with ready-made woolen outer clothing.[49] Duden noted that many items were less expensive on the East Coast than in the country's interior, but in Cincinnati food was amazingly cheap: "The best beef costs two and a half to three cents [a pound], pork one and a half to two cents, smoked ham four to five cents, a tame fat turkey cock twenty cents, a fat chicken eight cents, a dozen eggs three to four cents. There is a similar abundance of fish and game."[50]

The mention of food caught everyone's attention. Duden's list sounded especially appetizing because of the terrible economic con-

ditions raging throughout Europe, where prices of cash crops had
fallen while populations kept increasing. By 1830, hay farmers in
the Netherlands stopped employing migrant workers from German-
speaking lands, subsequently terminating the infusion of foreign
cash into Oldenburg. Since the small farms of Damme had never
been self-sustaining, the 1830s were a decade of distress. Anxious
Heuermann discussed their prospects and reached the same inevitable conclusion: they owned no land and none was available, even if
they had money. They and their families faced starvation unless they
took drastic steps.

Influenced by Duden's book and similar works by other German
authors, a young schoolteacher and bookbinder from Damme
named Franz Joseph Stallo emigrated to Ohio in 1831. A widowed
father of five children, Stallo followed Duden's advice carefully. After getting a job in a Cincinnati print shop, he wrote letters home
and urged others to make the trip. Thus, Stallo became the first link
in a long chain of migration from his village. Over the next twenty
years, one-third of the population of Agnes's hometown—around
2,000 persons—emigrated to America. Transplanted to the New
World, many residents of Damme, mostly hired hands or small farm
owners (*Kötter*), met again on the west side of the Atlantic Ocean
and created communities in Ohio. Agnes's father, Friedrich Messmann Pohlschneider, read Duden's book and Stallo's letters and
then made plans of his own.

Agnes's family, along with the villagers of Damme, became part
of a great migration from Europe. Between 1833 and 1843, nearly
200,000 Germans entered the United States, primarily through the
ports of Baltimore, New York, Philadelphia, and New Orleans.
Thousands traveled to Cincinnati, where the northeast quadrant of
the city became an ethnic enclave. To reach that neighborhood,
pedestrians and horse-powered vehicles crossed short bridges span-
ning the Miami and Erie Canal, which locals jokingly referred to as
"the Rhine." As a result, the entire district became known as the
"Over-the-Rhine" neighborhood. Encompassing nearly one hundred city blocks, the area grew steadily to include churches, schools,
markets, beer gardens, and residences. By the time of the 1850

federal census, one-quarter of Cincinnati's population had been born in German states.

Back in the hamlet of Borringhausen, members of the Pohlschneider, Messmann, Puthoff, Kramer, Tebbelmann, and Tangemann families made plans. Emigration was a complicated process that subjected each traveler to rigorous government scrutiny. First, the emigrant had to obtain permission to depart from the Grand Duke of Oldenburg. Second, the emigrant had to sell all of his or her possessions, frequently at low prices because buyers and cash were limited. Third, the emigrant had to agree never to return, even if the American adventure turned out to be a terrible mistake. Faced with such bureaucratic hassles, some Oldenburgers left illegally, without permission or documentation. Friedrich Messmann Pohlschneider, however, enlisted the cooperation of his extended family to organize his household's departure from Damme and thus left a trail of papers documenting the complex arrangements.

Agnes's parents called on aunts and uncles to help them shed personal property and sell farm animals, knowing that eventually many of those family members would join them in America. The family used a plan replicated by dozens of other households: the oldest children — eighteen-year-old Elizabeth and fifteen-year old Friedrich — would leave first, travel to Bremen, and then sail on a tall-masted vessel across the ocean to Baltimore. From there, they would go west to Ohio and wait in Cincinnati for their parents and the younger children to follow, using the same route. Elizabeth and Friedrich could send letters to the rest of the family, tell them about any needed supplies, and alert them to pitfalls of the journey. The Pohlschneiders expected that friends such as Stallo would look out for the teenagers. Word had reached Damme that Stallo was organizing a settlement society, and the immigrants planned to purchase land together and establish a German-speaking community about a hundred miles north of Cincinnati.

In the autumn of 1832, Elizabeth and Friedrich Pohlschneider left Damme forever. Records indicate when they departed from Oldenburg, but there is no record that Friedrich ever reached the United States. Perhaps he died on the ship; bad food, crowded conditions, and the absence of hygiene took an enormous toll on travelers. One observer called the trans-Atlantic ships "floating coffins."

Under the best of conditions, the crossing took between six and eight weeks. Gottlieb Mittelberger's personal account of his Atlantic Ocean crossing details the ghastly conditions passengers endured: "[I]n the vessels an awful misery, stink, smoke, horror, vomiting . . . fever, purgings, headaches, sweats, constipations of the bowels, sores, scurvy, cancers, thrush and the like" plagued the travelers.[51] While his account was written nearly a century before Agnes's family made their crossing, little had changed in the trans-Atlantic voyage. Lice and rats filled the cramped holds below the deck. Fresh air was accessible only through small portholes or when the weather was calm enough to allow passengers to congregate on the deck. The holds were terribly overcrowded, and there were no separate quarters for sick passengers — a situation that facilitated the spread of deadly bacteria and contagious diseases. Cholera, a worldwide epidemic in 1832, spread easily aboard ships and may have ended Friedrich's young life. The details of what happened to him are unknown, but we do know that only Elizabeth reached the relative safety of Cincinnati. There, she waited for her family to join her.

Meanwhile, Agnes's father struggled to sell the family farm in Damme, as well as all the family's personal property. Depressed land values and unexpected legal problems encountered in selling the farm slowed the process.[52] Even worse, on February 27, 1833, Catharina Pohlschneider died, leaving Agnes (six) and her three brothers — Henry (twelve), Joseph (eight), and Frank (three) — without a mother.[53] Nevertheless, six weeks after her death, the family finally traveled to Bremen and obtained passage on a ship. As Duden had recommended, they set sail in early May: "May and June are considered excellent calm months on the ocean between Europe and North America. . . . I would think that the beginning of Spring would be the best time for one's departure. One would then also be able to get to the Ohio [River] in plenty of time [to avoid low water]."[54]

After braving the horrific conditions on the ship, Agnes's family disembarked in Baltimore at the end of June 1833. Now thousands

Fig. 4. Cincinnati riverfront landing, 1848. This image is one of eight daguer-
reotype plates made in 1848 that show the entire length of the Cincinnati, Ohio,
riverfront. Courtesy The Public Library of Cincinnati and Hamilton County.

of miles from the Pohlschneider Farm near Oldenburg, they abandoned the Pohlschneider name. Ever after, the family used Messmann or its derivative, Mersman, as their surname, although careless clerks and typesetters commonly omitted one of the terminal
"Ns." Occasionally, former neighbors from Germany called them by
the farm name, but legal documents in America used Messmann
(or some misspelling thereof). The ship manifest further identified
them with anglicized given names.[55] Henry, Joseph, Agnes, Frank,
and their father, fifty-one-year-old Frederick, got off the ship and
probably traveled on the National Road (present-day U.S. Route
40), the most direct overland road westward.

The five travelers reached Wheeling, Virginia (now West Virginia), and then took a boat nearly four hundred miles down the
Ohio River to Cincinnati. The city that greeted them was indeed as
dazzling as Duden had claimed. At Cincinnati, the Ohio River, one-
third of a mile wide, had been christened "*La Belle Riviere*" (the
beautiful river) by French explorers. On the north bank of the placid
water, the city spread out on a plateau surrounded by tree-covered
hills about three hundred feet high. With a population of nearly

25,000 in 1830, Cincinnati boasted around 1,300 buildings and nearly two dozen churches. River craft of all kinds moored at the landing. In 1816, Cincinnati had constructed and launched its first steamboat; but rafts, flatboats, and keelboats continued to transport heavy cargo and even passengers on the downstream route from Pittsburgh and Wheeling. In 1833, three hundred steamboats plied the western waters of America — and on any given day, about five of them were moored at the Cincinnati landing.

Agnes's family may have spent a few days recuperating in Cincinnati, but the presence of cholera in the city prompted them to continue their journey. No one knew what caused the illness, but many blamed miasmas, foul-smelling vapors from rotting produce and butchers' waste that were more common in cities than in rural places. Even though Cincinnati looked beautiful, the countryside was safer during a cholera outbreak.[56]

Frederick Messmann took his four young children and continued north to Stallotown, Ohio, the community that had been founded in the fall of 1832 and named for Franz Joseph Stallo, formerly of Damme. Agnes's family probably traveled by packet boat on the Miami and Erie Canal as far as Dayton and then proceeded by wagon until they reached the settlement in the thick forests of Mercer (now Auglaize) County.

When the Messmann family finally arrived in late summer of 1833, they found the community of a hundred residents in the midst of turmoil. Acting for the group, Stallo had purchased 640 acres in the wilderness, at $1.25 per acre. Since each person had contributed $8.00 to the purchase fund, the immigrants had drawn lots to select sites for their homes and had begun to clear the land. However, Stallo died suddenly of cholera on July 23, 1833, leaving Stallotown without a leader and the residents with a legal mess: Stallo died without a will before deeding the property to the community. As a result, the settlers found themselves in court, with Stallo's five orphaned children — all minors — as their adversaries. Many of the immigrants thought Stallo had intentionally planned to swindle the group or, at the least, had been extremely careless with their money and his record keeping.

It took several years to straighten out the ownership of land in Stallotown. By that time, even the town's name engendered negative feelings, and the residents considered other options. In 1836, after rejecting "New Damme" and "New Oldenburg," they renamed the town Minster, an anglicized version of Münster, a German region they remembered fondly from their homeland.[57]

Meanwhile, Agnes's family began to establish themselves in the wilderness community. Minster consisted of a cluster of log cabins, each housing several families, with a single log church that also served as a schoolhouse and community meeting place. Two of the Messmann sons, probably Joseph and Frank, attended the school, where they learned to read and write English.[58] Henry, at twelve, was old enough to work and contribute to his family's income. Agnes was probably looked after by female neighbors while her father and brother worked all day. Under her caretaker's tutelage, Agnes learned the domestic chores that would teach her valuable skills and prepare her to be a farmer's wife, just as her mother and grandmother had been.

Life in Minster was more difficult than most of the immigrants had anticipated. Clearing the land of trees and undergrowth was rougher than farming the ancient fields of Europe. Potable water was scarce, and, in the early years, crop failures were alarmingly frequent. Provisions and farming equipment had to come from other settlements or from traveling salesmen. The settlers repeatedly confronted food shortages. The unexpected hardships in rural Ohio made the familiar drudgery of Oldenburg seem less odious in retrospect. Many immigrants expressed their anger to anyone who would listen. With Stallo dead, they blamed Duden for exaggerating the ease of farming in the new land and referred to him as "Duden, *der lüger Hund,*" or "Duden, the lying dog."[59] Immigrants who had made the trans-Atlantic journey wrote back to friends and family, warning them to "read him carefully, and take nothing lightly. Eliminate . . . some of the picturesqueness [*sic*] . . . from his account, and you will have the plain truth."[60] The ease of farming and leisurely pace of life Duden promised would come only after years of farming the land.

Herman Steines and two companions, "full of a certain yearning and with beating hearts," visited Duden's famous homestead in Missouri and recorded the scene in his diary: "Now we saw the hut in which *he* . . . had lived . . . the field and . . . the forest so fantastically described in the 'Report.' Everything was very much neglected. The fence had decayed . . . the field was full of weeds, and a garden was nowhere to be seen."[61] Frederick Steines reiterated the general ill will and noted, "That man has much to answer for, he has led many people into misery."[62]

Shrewdly, Agnes's father did not rush to join the ranks of Minster landowners. While Frederick Messmann assessed the situation and learned the ways of his new country, he worked as a day laborer. He earned enough to support his family but did not become bound to the land. He helped others clear their land and tend their crops, but Frederick never bought real estate in Minster.[63] By 1837, Messmann's older sons, Henry and Joseph, had jobs on the Miami and Erie Canal construction project. Work on the waterway, being extended north from Dayton to Piqua and beyond, paid laborers thirty cents a day (about seven dollars in 2005 values). By pooling their wages, the Messmann family accumulated enough capital for the boys to consider other options.

Agnes's older sister, Elizabeth, probably never lived in Stallotown. While waiting for her father and siblings to arrive from Oldenburg, she had met a merchant, Arnd Kattenhorn, who was born in Bremen. The pair married in 1834, when Elizabeth was twenty-one and Kattenhorn was twenty-four. They made their home in Cincinnati, where Kattenhorn prospered as a grocer. In that era, every grocery stocked whiskey, and liquor produced Kattenhorn's greatest profits. He was soon investing in property around the city. Within three years the Kattenhorns had two daughters, Louisa and Sophia, the start of a family that eventually numbered six children. The growing family gave the other Messmanns good reason to make the journey to Cincinnati for periodic visits.

Since their mother's death, Elizabeth had taken on a motherly role with respect to her younger siblings. She had them visit her in Cincinnati for weeks at a time, the custom in that era. In addition to

Fig. 5. Arnd Kattenhorn, a prosperous grocer who married Agnes's sister Elizabeth, typified the staid German American community Agnes left behind in Cincinnati. From Maurice Joblin, *Cincinnati Past and Present: Its Industrial History as Exhibited in the Life-Labors of Its Leading Men* (1872).

helping Elizabeth care for her young daughters, Agnes and Frank had the opportunity to enjoy attractions that Minster sorely lacked. Street life, streetlights, and even streets were absent in the wilderness community. Cincinnati's many shops displayed goods transported from distant manufacturers. Milliners featured the latest fashions, and booksellers offered literary classics as well as popular fiction. Tailors and shoemakers produced ready-made and couture apparel to suit their customers' measurements. Tobacconists made cigars in workrooms located behind their retail shops. As the city grew, all kinds of personal services became available: barbershops, public baths, and hairdressers. Apothecaries, an assortment of licensed doctors, salesmen drumming bogus cure-alls, and dentists advertised their expertise on signs, in newspapers, and in city directories.

The Over-the-Rhine district grew dramatically during the first decade Agnes's family was in the United States. Germanic-style writing on storefronts and beer gardens with waiters in long aprons made the neighborhood seem like a part of Europe. The Kattenhorns did not reside in the Over-the-Rhine neighborhood, but many old friends from Damme did. Each month brought more and more Puthoffs, Kramers, Tangemanns, and Tebbelmanns to Cincinnati. Other members of the Messmann family also made the long voyage to America. Many of the new arrivals did not go on to Minster but remained in Cincinnati, where they could practice their trades, see old friends, and enlarge their social network with other German immigrants.

While Cincinnati offered theaters, concert halls, and other performance venues, Minster, with a population of only a few hundred, was far too small and geographically remote to host even a traveling menagerie, let alone a performance troupe. Instead, the circuses played in larger towns nearby, and the residents of the farming community traveled to see them. Circus Day outdid the Fourth of July, Christmas, and May Day rolled into one grand celebration. The event featured delights for the eyes, ears, and stomachs of all. For Agnes, her family, and their neighbors, the wait for such festivities was well worth it.

Circus Day began with a parade of the visiting troupe through the chosen community. The troupe's band — a bass drum, cymbals, brass horns, and perhaps a piccolo — provided marching tunes. The performers urged onlookers to follow them to the lot where the tents stood. The audience had time for a picnic lunch and an opportunity to purchase penny candies and lemonade. Then, a single afternoon show thrilled the crowds. Twenty-five cents bought entrance to the show; seats might cost extra. A sideshow had its own admission charge. In the solitary ring, equestrian acts dominated the program, while clowns and acrobats added to the fun. Band music helped create the magic.

By four o'clock the entertainment had ended. The lack of an evening show eliminated the need to provide lighting after dark. The crew packed up the tents, loaded the wagons, and traveled to the next venue, which might be ten or twenty miles away. Six days a week, such itinerant wagon shows, called "mud shows" by those in the business, brought delight to audiences far removed from centers of civilization. When the weather was dry, transportation over deeply rutted roads was cumbersome. When the weather was rainy, the wagons stuck in the mud like insects on flypaper. Long detours around flooded creeks often delayed the troupe's arrival in the next town. The performances, however brief, gave isolated communities a break from the monotony of pioneer life and fueled the imaginations of individuals far from America's bustling cities.

On October 23, 1838, when Agnes was twelve, A. Hunt & Company's Menagerie and Circus played in nearby Sidney, Ohio.[64] Posters and newspaper advertisements announced the show for weeks in advance. Even though the day was a Tuesday and the sixteen-mile trip to the Shelby County seat took Minster residents three or four hours by wagon, the Messmann family was sure to have attended the show.

To give the crowds some excitement before the main event, a sideshow was open in a smaller tent near the Big Top. Inside on display were paintings, wax figures, an anaconda, and a black-face minstrel company that sang and played tunes on banjos, guitars, and bone castanets.[65]

The circus program began with a saddled elephant providing

rides around the ring for spectators. An animal act featured a lioness and a lion, a pair of leopards, and a trainer who dared to enter their cages and command them to follow his orders. Next, four riders with magnificent horses raced around the ring, demonstrating their prowess. Spencer Q. Stokes was the name of one of the equestrians. A dog act, an India-rubber man, a vaulter, and three clowns added to the fun.[66]

A high point of the afternoon was a young fellow, just getting started in the business, who performed a comic song to great applause. Born William Lake Thatcher, he was known professionally as Bill Lake.[67]

CHAPTER TWO

Transplanted, but Not Uprooted

1838–1846

M r. Dickens and Lady arrived in our city yesterday morning and have taken rooms at the Broadway Hotel. We understand they will be at home today from 11 o'clock until 3 o'clock," reported the *Cincinnati Daily Republican* on April 5, 1842. Tactfully, the newspaper omitted mentioning that his countryman, Edmund Dexter, a prominent merchant who lived on the corner of Broadway and Fourth Street, would honor Charles Dickens and his wife, Catherine, with a private reception because the city's leading residents had already received their invitations.[1]

The city that welcomed the celebrated English couple had doubled in size since Agnes's family first saw it a decade earlier. Now with nearly 50,000 residents, Cincinnati had become the "Queen City of the West" and was the sixth largest city in the United States.[2] In 1830 only 5 percent of the population was of German origin, but by 1840 the Germans comprised 23 percent.[3] Five German-language newspapers competed with the ten English-language newspapers published daily and weekly.[4]

Dickens, just thirty years old but already famous for having written five best-selling novels,[5] reported what he saw:

Cincinnati is a beautiful city; cheerful, thriving, and animated. I have not often seen a place that commends itself so favourably and pleasantly to a stranger at the first glance as this does: with its clean houses of red and white, its well-paved roads, and footways of bright tile. . . . The streets are broad and airy, the shops extremely good, the private residences remarkable for their elegance and neatness.[6]

Some jokingly called Cincinnati "Porkopolis" because its prosperity resulted from the fact that it led all other American cities as a packer of hogs.[7] In 1842, Cincinnati butchers processed about 230,000 squealers, three times the number processed just ten years earlier. Products such as flour, tobacco, and whiskey reached Cincinnati by way of two waterways that terminated there: the Miami and Erie Canal and the Whitewater Canal. The first, built between 1825 and 1845, provided passage from Lake Erie to the Ohio River, a distance of 249 miles. Passengers and freight traveled from Cincinnati to Dayton, Troy, Piqua, Minster, and Toledo on horse-drawn packet boats. The second canal, constructed between 1839 and 1843, reached Brookville, Indiana, ninety miles west of Cincinnati. Both canals stimulated trade, and some of the freight continued on steamboats and flatboats to markets as far away as New Orleans.

Cincinnati's waterfront, the center of commercial activity, sparked the city's growth. On most days, twenty or thirty three-story steamboats jammed the wharf, smokestacks fuming like towering metal cigars.[8] In 1842, a total of 450 steamboats plied the western waters, making the Ohio-Mississippi-Missouri-Illinois rivers network the major thoroughfare for interstate commerce. Because of its location halfway between Pittsburgh and Cairo, Illinois, where the Ohio River joins the Mississippi, Cincinnati became a principal site for building steamboats, second only to Pittsburgh.[9] The Queen City's boatyards launched more than 800 steamboats between 1830 and 1860.[10]

The average steamboat, however, survived only four years. Flimsy construction, gross overloading, and careless handling made the vessels dangerous. Navigational hazards and boiler explosions took an alarming toll of property and human lives. One notable case was the destruction of the *Moselle* on April 25, 1838. Built in Cincinnati, the *Moselle* was a 150-ton side-wheeler that ran the Cincinnati to St. Louis route. On its first trip to Missouri, the steamboat had made remarkably good time, and the young captain was determined to remain unsurpassed. When another steamboat challenged his boat, the captain ordered full steam. Only two miles downstream from Cincinnati, all four boilers blew up and 150 passengers lost their lives.[11] Charles Dickens knew of the tragedy before he boarded the steamboat *Messenger* in Pittsburgh. He wrote: "Passing one of these boats at night and seeing the great body of fire . . . that rages and roars beneath the frail pile of painted wood . . . under the management of reckless men, one feels directly that the wonder is, not that there should be so many fatal accidents, but that any journey should be safely made."[12]

Fortunately, Dickens's trip down the Ohio River went without incident. The author arrived safely in Cincinnati and stayed for two nights. Edmund Dexter hosted a reception in his magnificent red-brick dwelling in Dickens's honor, before the author continued his journey to St. Louis.

Later, Dickens published his observations as *American Notes for General Circulation*. Of all the cities he visited—including New York, Boston, Washington, D.C., and Pittsburgh—Cincinnati received his most favorable comments. No doubt some of Dickens's positive experience was directly related to Dexter, who gave the author a warm welcome.

A middle-aged merchant, Dexter extended friendship not just to visiting celebrities but also to promising entrepreneurs and enterprising immigrants, like Agnes's family. Originally from Leicester, England, Dexter was certainly among those who encouraged the Messmann family to move to Cincinnati. Dexter had been in Cincinnati since 1829 and was well established by the time the Messmann family appeared. He was one of the most successful whiskey rectifiers in the Ohio Valley and operated a store with a still on Lower Market Street, close to the landing and only three blocks from Arnd Kattenhorn's store. Wholesalers such as Dexter bought barrels of the raw liquor and "rectified" it by distilling the liquor a second time, thus removing any contaminants and transforming the raw whiskey into a palatable beverage. The finished whiskey was distributed to saloons, brothels, groceries, and other retail establishments.

*   *   *

Attracted to the growing business opportunities and social advantages Cincinnati offered, Agnes's family began the transition from farm life to city life. Their visits to the Kattenhorn household became longer and more frequent, until the family finally moved their belongings into a flat on the corner of Main and Eighth streets, just five blocks north of Kattenhorn's store and the residence above it. The household consisted of Frederick Messmann, his three sons, and thirteen-year-old Agnes. As the sole female of the household, Agnes assumed the domestic chores, especially cooking and cleaning for four men. Within a few years, however, her brothers Joseph and Frank were residing in local boardinghouses. As time wore on, the Messmanns began to fancy the city's amusements, the growing numbers of friends there, and the greater opportunities to make money.

Agnes's older brothers, Henry and Joseph, soon ventured into the world of commerce. In January 1839, Joseph began a ten-year apprenticeship with Edmund Dexter, learning the secrets of rectifying and minding the store when Dexter was away on business. This opportunity cultivated Henry and Joseph's own success in tobacco and whiskey. Henry struck up a friendship with Anthony Nulsen, a German immigrant his own age from Hanover whose large family had been tobacco wholesalers for thirty years in Europe.[13] Three Nulsen brothers — Francis, Anthony, and Clemens — aimed to make tobacco their primary business in America. Francis had a shop on Main Street near Kattenhorn's store, and the two younger brothers helped him.

Faced with the need to establish a business identity when he partnered with Anthony Nulsen, Agnes's brother Henry urged his family to change their surname once again. This time "Mersman" replaced "Messmann." Perhaps the name first resulted from a typographical error, because initiating the change was not consistent among all family members.[14] Eventually, Agnes's family relinquished the ancestral Messmann in favor of Mersman as their last name. Henry's business with partner Anthony Nulsen, styled as Nulsen & Mersman, stenciled its logo on signs and boxes in Cincinnati and became well-known over the next twenty years. By 1849, Joseph had assumed that surname when he and Clemens Nulsen established their own liquor and tobacco business in St. Louis, also called Nulsen & Mersman.

Further changes to the Mersman family occurred in April 1842 when Henry married Mary Imsicke, a girl from Damme whom he had known since childhood. Now age sixteen, Agnes was one of the witnesses. Unfortunately, Mary died in childbirth just two years later. In August 1845, Henry, then twenty-five, married seventeen-year-old Adeline Tebbelman, the sister of a local tobacconist, also from Damme. When they moved out of the Mersman family home, the burden of running the household again fell to Agnes.

Despite the move to Cincinnati — now a major metropolis — and their growing success in the business world, life for the Mersman family was still dictated by the people and customs of their German heritage. By the beginning of 1846, nineteen-year-old Agnes was in the rut common to unmarried women of her time and place. She spent her days close to home, doing the cooking, cleaning, shopping, and sewing for her father and two brothers, twenty-one-year-old Joseph and seventeen-year-old Frank. Every Sunday at midday the entire family, including Henry and Adeline, gathered at the Kattenhorn's home for dinner. The Mersman family spoke German with each other and their friends, but Joseph, Agnes, and Frank also spoke English fluently. They interpreted newspapers and letters for their father, whose mastery of English was never good.

Although the Mersmans had settled in Ohio, Agnes and her family's social and business networks swelled from the effects of chain migration. Within two miles of Agnes's residence lived two dozen relatives — aunts, uncles, and cousins — and many friends, including tailor Frank Puthoff, tavern keeper Henry Wellman, and tobacconist John Tebbelman, all of whom had known Agnes's family in Oldenburg.[15] Their new friends — the Nulsens, Wagners, and Werners — were all Germans, too.[16] Henry had twice married hometown girls, and Elizabeth also married a German immigrant.

Agnes and her family's recreational activities revolved around their German friends or were organized by Holy Trinity Catholic Church, the first German-speaking parish in Cincinnati. From his diary, we know that Joseph Mersman participated in the Liedertafel,[17] a German singing group that sponsored picnics and balls, and Agnes likely joined as well. Organized by Fritz Tappe, the Liedertafel was Cincinnati's first amateur singing society and lasted from 1839 to 1855. Its regular meetings at the Rising Sun Saloon provided opportunities for Germans to socialize. Agnes also played the guitar and enjoyed music. Joseph took dance lessons from a band leader, Monsieur Ernst, and learned the polka steps that were all the rage. Since evening balls provided opportunities to meet eligible men, Agnes also likely mastered the popular quadrilles, reels, and waltzes.

Agnes was the age at which many of her friends and contemporaries were getting married, and she was certainly feeling her family's pressure to settle down with a nice, German-born merchant and start a family. Her family likely wanted her to marry a grocer like John Kattenhorn, Arnd's brother, or a former neighbor from Damme, with whom one of her brothers could form a business partnership in tobacco or liquor. But Agnes soon met William Lake Thatcher, and her life was changed forever.

*   *   *

William Lake Thatcher, an East Coast native, had been in the circus business for about a dozen years when he met the young Agnes Mersman. Nothing is known about his childhood, but at age seventeen he had joined Matthew Buckley's troupe, the Mammoth Circus & Gymnastic Arena Company. The circus claimed in 1834 that it was one of the largest in the nation, with "thirty-nine men and thirty-eight horses."[18] They played in New York, Philadelphia, and Baltimore amphitheatres, then took their eight wagons on a route that included Poughkeepsie, New York, and Newton, New Jersey.[19] Billed as "Master Thatcher" early in his career, between 1834 and 1840 the young man performed a variety of equestrian acts with multiple traveling companies. His work in the ring received no special attention, but he became acquainted with Spencer Q. Stokes and John Robinson, two riders who went on to long careers as proprietors in the circus world. His friendships with them lasted many decades.

However, like many equestrian performers, Thatcher faced potentially life-threatening physical risks performing daring stunts on horseback. Thatcher may have suffered a severe injury that forced him to retire from equestrian feats. He dropped his real surname, Thatcher, and called himself Bill Lake.[20] Although he was never featured as a rider after 1841, many equestrian performers credited him with their training, and some assumed his surname as homage.[21]

In 1838, he traveled throughout Ohio with the A. Hunt & Company's Menagerie and Circus. When the firm folded and put him "at liberty," Lake signed on with other shows. He learned to put up the canvas, make the ring, and load wagons—anything to stay on the road with a circus. Over the next eight years, Lake appeared as a clown throughout the Mississippi River Valley. He worked with multiple companies;[22] between 1841 and 1846 Lake was billed as an actor, a plate balancer, and a juggler. He soon focused on witty clown routines, at which he was exceedingly popular with audiences. He also developed a routine with his two dogs, Bibo and Rolla. Lake's first known printed billing as "Master of the Arena" was in November 1847,[23] and he continued as "Master" or "Director" for the next twenty years.

The circus was a high-risk business. Companies folded often when overhead costs made it impossible to continue planned tours, and performers' salaries were never guaranteed. His experience with many productions, however, introduced Lake to an ever-widening circle of performers and managers. Lake developed a reputation as an entertainer and became increasingly known to fans as well as to potential employers.

In the spring of 1846 a curious series of advertisements muddies the trail of the meeting and developing relationship between Agnes Mersman and Bill Lake. The first advertisement for the Great Western Circus, in the *Cincinnati Daily Commercial* on March 25, 1846, proclaimed that the circus would open on April 1 on the corner of Sixth and Vine streets, about four blocks from Agnes's home.

MESSRS. STONE & MCCOLLUM would respectfully announce to the citizens of Cincinnati that they have in the most costly manner, fitted out a superb and extensive Equestrian Establishment, which will be known as the SOUTHWESTERN CIRCUS, for 1846. It will be under the direction of S. Q. Stokes, whose whole attention, during the past winter, has been devoted to the training of horses and getting up of the requisite appointments, and he is confident that the Company will surpass anything of the kind that has ever visited the West.[24]

In subsequent advertisements throughout April, the name of the circus was changed to the Great Western Circus, and the opening date was pushed back to April 15, then the eighteenth, and finally the twenty-third.[25] Evidently, Stokes had some difficulty recruiting and organizing his cast. Beginning on April 1 and continuing until April 23, Bill Lake's name appeared among the featured performers. When the show finally began its season near the end of the month, any mention of Lake and his trained dogs abruptly ceased. Reviews of the show included no comment about Bill Lake. The Great Western Circus played through May 2, 1846, in Cincinnati, and then went to Louisville. The show returned to Cincinnati during the Fourth of July holiday, from June 30 to July 4, 1846.[26]

An account of Lake's first meeting with Agnes Mersman appears in Gil Robinson's book, *Old Wagon Show Days*.[27] Using information possibly supplied by his future mother-in-law, Agnes Lake, Robinson wrote:

[Agnes] was an Alsatian, and was brought to this country by her parents in 1829 when she was three years old. The family

settled in Cincinnati. Life passed uneventfully for her until
her sixteenth year, when the Robinson & Eldred's Circus
exhibited in Cincinnati. The tents were pitched a few blocks
from her home. "Bill" Lake was the star clown of the show;
one day in passing her residence, he saw Agnes swinging in
the yard. It was a mutual case of love at first sight; he sought
and secured an introduction and begged her to marry him;
despite the opposition of her parents, she consented, but
her youth was so evident that it was impossible to get anyone
to perform the ceremony. It was decided that she should
elope and go to St. Louis and make an effort to get the
marriage knot tied[,] only to again suffer disappointment.
Neither clergymen nor justice of the peace would marry
them, the young people determined to go to New Orleans.
But even there marrying powers were obdurate. Finally in
the little town of Lafayette, La., ten miles from New Orleans,
they were joined in wedlock.[28]

In 1846 it took at least a week to travel from Cincinnati to New
Orleans by steamboat. Therefore, a plausible interpretation of the
documentary evidence is that Bill Lake arrived in Cincinnati at the
beginning of April 1846 and planned to open the circus season with
Stone & McCollum's company and participate in the scheduled
tour. Showmen he had known for years, including Spencer Q.
Stokes, Joe Clavau, and Eaton Stone, also signed on with the company. While the show was in rehearsal, Lake encountered Agnes
Mersman. He sought an introduction and then courted her for a
few weeks.

Robinson's version contains several errors. He subtracted years
from Agnes's true age and suggested that the wedding occurred in
the early 1840s. In addition, her birthplace, the presence of both
her parents, and the name of the circus that featured Lake are all
incorrect.[29] Agnes was nineteen years old when she married Lake in
1846, hardly a child bride. Based on the naturalization papers of her
brother Joseph, Agnes was born in Damme, Oldenburg, not Alsace;
her mother died in 1833 prior to Agnes's immigration when she was

six years old; and Lake was employed by the Great Western Circus, not the Robinson & Eldred show.[30] While there is no documented roster for the Robinson & Eldred circuses between 1845 and 1847, Lake was ostensibly employed by other circuses: John Mateer's Southern Circus (or American Pavilion and Circus) (1843–44),[31] Samuel P. Stickney's New Orleans Circus (1846),[32] and Rockwell & Co. New York Circus (1847).[33] A shadow is cast over Lake's whereabouts during 1845, however. Neither Rich's Circus (or the Rich & Rowe Circus) nor William Lake appears in any of Thayer's documented rosters in 1845. Robinson, however, provides an explanation with events that occurred after Lake's marriage: "Lake joined Rich's Circus for a winter season in Mexico, leaving his wife in New Orleans. This was in the perilous period culminating in the war with Mexico, and Americans were exceedingly unpopular in the cities south of the Rio Grande. Rich's Circus was confiscated by the Mexican authorities and Lake[,] hidden in a cellar by a friendly priest[,] narrowly escaped with his life."[34] Lake allegedly returned from Mexico with nothing but the clothes on his back, collected his new bride, and joined the "reorganized Rich Circus" for two years.

Stuart Thayer notes that in spring 1844 the Rich & Rowe Circus departed for South America. Bill Lake may have joined them, since his recent employer, John Mateer's Southern Circus, ceased operations on January 17 of that year.[35] U.S. archives failed to yield information about Lake's activities during 1844–45, but a trip to Mexico could explain his absence from circus rosters in the United States prior to his marriage to Agnes Mersman.[36] Robinson seems to have several pieces of the puzzle; however, he has likely arranged them in the wrong order. There is no evidence that Bill left Agnes to go to South America right after their marriage, especially since America was at war with Mexico and both Bill's and Agnes's presence are noted in rosters and advertisements throughout the summer of 1846.

Robinson's account of Agnes and Lake's romance and subsequent wedding does contain truthful elements. The location of the couple's first encounter (Cincinnati), the location of their marriage (Louisiana), and the mutual attraction that captivated them are all correct. The couple eloped, and therefore Lake failed to open the season with the Great Western Circus in Cincinnati. Robinson's flawed account of that fateful meeting is not entirely his fault. In a newspaper interview with the *New York Morning Telegraph* in 1906, Agnes herself proclaimed that she had met Bill Lake while he was performing in Cincinnati in 1842 and married him in Lafayette, Louisiana, later that year.[37]

At present, the only reliable documentation found to help distinguish fact from fiction includes an application for a marriage license in Jefferson Parish, Louisiana, dated May 1, 1846, for William Lake Thatcher and "Mary Agnes Mersmann" [*sic*].[38] Two dozen newspaper advertisements printed in the *Cincinnati Daily Commercial* and the *Cincinnati Enquirer* herald the arrival of the Great Western Circus that played in Cincinnati from April 23 to May 1, 1846, and document Lake's presence in the city. Advertisements for Stickney's New Orleans Circus that appeared in newspapers in Virginia, Pennsylvania, Ohio, and Mississippi later that year contradict Robinson's chronicle of Lake performing in Mexico after he and Agnes were wed.

To reach New Orleans and fill out the marriage license on May 1, the couple would have had to have left Cincinnati no later than April 23, if they traveled directly to New Orleans. In Robinson's account, however, the couple traveled first to St. Louis, and when they were denied a marriage license they continued on to Louisiana. That journey would have taken at least fifteen days, requiring a departure from Cincinnati somewhere between April 12 and April 14, when Lake's name was printed daily in the newspapers.

Although Agnes was not a child bride, as Robinson claims, her sudden elopement with Bill Lake likely resulted from her father and brothers' concerns and objections regarding Lake as an acceptable suitor. A professional clown was not seen as a desirable husband by most young people of that era.[39] Lake, an unschooled vagabond with no family, contrasted dramatically with Arnd Kattenhorn — who was German, had stable kinfolk, a conventional lifestyle, and a steady income.[40]

After Agnes and Bill Lake were married in Louisiana, Lake sought employment with new troupes, taking his bride with him. In May, he and Agnes joined Samuel P. Stickney's New Orleans Circus. They began the season in Memphis on May 23 and then went north.[41] On June 25 the Pittsburgh *Morning Post* reported that William Lake and his dogs, Bibo and Rolla, were performing with Stickney's troupe.

Lake, however, still owed a debt to the Great Western Circus, the company he had left in the lurch on opening day. Also, he needed to make peace with Agnes's family. As a result, when the Great Western Circus returned to play for Cincinnati audiences over the Fourth of July weekend, Lake performed with the show for three days.[42] That maneuver repaired his relationship with Stokes because his name on the advertisements increased the size of the audiences. That same weekend, Lake somehow made peace with Agnes's family because Joseph's subsequent diary entries indicate no animosity toward his brother-in-law. Lake delighted the circus fans and, between shows, visited Agnes's family. According to newspaper accounts, the Lakes rejoined Stickney's New Orleans Circus as it continued the tour to Circleville and Chillicothe, Ohio, and beyond.[43]

Agnes and Bill Lake had begun a life together — and Agnes had finally escaped the village of Damme.

CHAPTER THREE

Itinerant Showmen
"From the Haunts of Profligacy"
1846–1851

When Agnes married Bill Lake and developed a circus career, she began a lifestyle that had its own language and customs. Agnes once again found herself an immigrant in a new world. This time she left behind her traditional domestic housekeeping routine for an unscripted life with the circus. Agnes had to learn the history of her new environment, its customs, and language — an undertaking similar to her first months in Ohio after emigrating from Germany.

The U.S. entertainment industry was in its infancy in the nineteenth century, but it grew rapidly as communities took hold in the new republic. Theaters and other amusements sprang up as entrepreneurs sought to capitalize on the public's clamor for diversion. The earliest circuses performed in cities that had indoor arenas and enough people to form sizable audiences.

In 1793, Philadelphia provided the setting for the first equestrian display in America called a circus, which featured a man balancing on a bareback horse as the animal cantered around a ring. Even George Washington was impressed.[1]

In those days, horses were the primary adjunct to human talent. Other animals that could follow commands—dogs and mules—sometimes appeared in the center ring, but only to "relieve the monotony" of horse acts.[2] Horses without riders, called "liberty horses," displayed their ability to prance and bow at a command from a nearby trainer. Performers demonstrated skills of balancing and leaping while the horses circled the ring. The mastery of men over horses was a common theme of the events. Acrobats, wire walkers, jugglers, and clowns augmented the featured acts in the hippodrome.

Although the first elephant in America was exhibited in 1804, displays of exotic animals had traveled to various U.S. cities as early as 1716.[3] During the first three decades of the nineteenth century, proprietors transported a few cages of beasts—perhaps a lion, a tiger, a peacock, and some monkeys—and set them up in barns or other buildings where they could charge admission to view the animals. By the end of the 1830s, these static displays no longer captivated the public, and most traveling animal shows were connected with circuses.[4] It was only in the late 1850s that circuses routinely featured elephants, for these animals were as expensive to maintain as they were fascinating to audiences.[5]

For the initial three decades of their history, circuses were limited to U.S. population centers, namely, cities on the East Coast. For example, one show in 1825 played in only four locations—Washington, D.C., New York, Philadelphia, and Baltimore—for runs of up to three months in each city.[6] Between the stands, there was downtime when the circus traveled and generated no income. The country was growing, however, and the creation of additional states increased the number of potential audiences. The towns of Louisiana (which became a state in 1812), Indiana (1816), Mississippi (1817), Illinois (1818), Alabama (1819), and Missouri (1821) tempted the owners of traveling shows. Residents of Arkansas (1836), Michigan (1837), Texas (1845), Iowa (1846), and Wisconsin (1848) would pay good money to see the wonders circuses offered, so traveling showmen developed ways to transport their productions.

In 1825, Joshua Purdy Brown of Somers, New York, presented

his show in a canvas tent and demonstrated that he could reach audiences outside the urban centers.[7] The use of a tent permitted circuses to reach new markets in towns located between bustling cities. Brief runs of a day or two eliminated the dead time between larger places. Canvas pavilions enabled shows to play continually to capacity audiences and to generate income six days a week. Since the human and animal performers had to be fed and housed regardless of whether they were producing, any innovation that increased audience size improved a circus's bottom line.

By the 1836 season, all twelve of the circus companies in the United States used tents. The result of this change was twofold: first, reliable transportation became critical to the success of each production, and second, the advertising support for each show assumed new importance. Instead of dealing with a handful of venues, circus owners had to contend with an average of 150 locations annually. Each site posed its own challenges: licensing the show, feeding and housing the performers, and controlling the crowds. Throughout the 1840s and 1850s, circuses kept devising new and innovative methods for bringing entertainment to the masses, and their organizations grew in response.

In their early years as circus entertainers, Agnes and Bill Lake performed in circus tents that held from 800 to 2,500 people. By the late 1840s, crude seats were routinely provided, although newspapers commonly reported bleachers collapsing. Canvas tents held another danger, that of a "blowdown":

> "A blow-down" is like an avalanche in the Alps or a storm at sea. The winds rise and the great canvas is lifted in the air, swinging quarter poles fifty feet in length like the lightest flails in the hand of the thresher. About they go, dealing death and destruction to all within their reach. Man tramples upon man in his hurried flight and the loosened steeds gallop at random through the frightened throng, while the tent seats are hurled in the air, dashing the fleeing ones to the ground, adding fatality after fatality to the scene of confusion.[8]

Wagons provided transportation for the majority of circuses until the 1860s. Drays, about five feet wide and ten feet long, carried the heavy baggage each show required. Separate wagons were modified to meet specific needs and carried each component of the venue: the canvas, support poles, bleacher seats, and tent stakes. The property wagon carried tables and other props; the candy stand wagon dispensed peanuts, candy, lemonade, and other treats. The ticket wagon served as the office, the bandwagon carried instruments and band members for the parades and performances, and hacks transported the performers and staff. Crew members rode with the baggage.[9] The number of wagons was directly related to the size of the show, and advertisements commonly publicized the tallies to draw crowds to see the "bigger and better" shows.

Agnes soon learned the unique language of the circus. Since most roads were unpaved, the convoys came to be called "mud shows."[10] The travels between performances were "jumps."[11] Townspeople were "rubes," "clems," "gillies," or "towners." To "blow a date" was to fail to show in a booked town. To "burn up" meant to kill the business in a place because of poor performances, crooked business practices, or both. To "crack the nut" was to make the show's daily expense. The "holdback," a portion of an employee's pay held by the circus office, was paid to the individual if he or she completed the season. These were just a few of the words and phrases that comprised the language of circus people. As the years went on, more and more circus slang came into use, such as "chump heister," or Ferris wheel; to add "flash" meant to add decorative touches to a drab tent, and a "sawbuck" was a ten-dollar bill.[12]

In the 1840s, a few circuses each season made steamboats their primary mode of transportation. Water transportation was less expensive than overland movement, and a chartered steamboat, instead of local hotels, could provide lodging for circus personnel.[13] In 1840, however, only fifteen cities on navigable rivers had populations of 2,500 or more, so audiences were limited. Shows that played their entire season on water would commonly stop in many towns twice — once when going upstream and a second time when returning.[14] Because of its central location, with overland routes and prime waterways, Cincinnati was blessed with more circus visits than any other city in antebellum America. Agnes Lake's story is filled with occasions when she "popped in" to see her family in the Queen City while en route to a performance elsewhere.

Using the waterways had drawbacks, however. First, the size of a steamboat limited the size of the circus, for all the personnel and equipment had to fit onboard. As a result, most circuses on steamboats tended to be smaller shows. Second, droughts, floods, and fog commonly disrupted river traffic. Steamboats altered their schedules to accommodate river conditions, but mishaps such as running aground sometimes caused traveling shows to miss dates.[15]

*   *   *

Agnes Lake's circus debut came one year after her marriage. For the 1847 season, the Lakes signed on with Rockwell & Company's New York Circus. Henry Rockwell, an orphan who had worked in circuses since age twelve, had managed shows since 1839 and been a proprietor since 1842. His Mammoth Circus opened in Indianapolis on April 26, 1847, and played at more than one hundred venues, traveling by wagon through Kentucky, Ohio, Indiana, and Illinois. Tickets sold for seventy-five, fifty, or twenty-five cents. Throughout the season, Agnes performed as an equestrian and also as a singer.[16] "Mr. Lake and his two wonderful dogs, Bibo and Rolla," delighted the crowds. He also took the role of "Director of the Circle," or ringmaster, from time to time.[17]

The show wintered in St. Louis, leased the St. Louis Theater, and gave daily performances from November 15, 1847, through January 21, 1848, including Christmas Day.[18] The best seats cost seventy-five cents; the second tier was fifty cents, and the third tier sold for twenty-five cents. St. Louis had about 60,000 residents, a large enough population to support the long run. In an effort to change the program constantly, the performers tried out new acts on the audiences. One evening Agnes and Bill Lake appeared together singing a comic duet,[19] an act they repeated months later in Cincinnati.

On Friday, January 28, 1848, Rockwell & Company returned to

Fig. 6. William Lake Thatcher began his circus career as an equestrian and general performer but gained enormous popularity for his clown performances. Eventually, he was a successful circus owner. This undated photo shows him in a typical nineteenth-century clown costume, around the time he met and married Agnes Mersman. From Gilbert Robinson, *Old Wagon Show Days* (1925).

Cincinnati, to the joy of the entire Mersman family.[20] They gathered at the Kattenhorn residence for dinner and welcomed Agnes and Bill Lake home. Joseph confided to his diary: "Agness looked very nearly as handsome as ever in fact to her husband I believe she looks more so, for the good and to him very satisfactory reason that she is in the 'Familly Way[,]' a very bad way by the bye, but one in which it seems most Women will fall into. Well! I hope it may be a boy. If it should be I will make him my Hair in case I should die an Old bachelor."[21]

Following Agnes's marriage, her father moved in with the Kattenhorn family, and the two unmarried Mersman brothers, Joseph and Frank, lived in boardinghouses, as many bachelors their age did. The family gave every indication of having completely forgiven the couple for their elopement. Joseph, who often attended theater performances and sought to cultivate a cosmopolitan outlook, now took delight in having a sister who gave public performances.[22]

During their stay in Cincinnati, before the start of the 1848 season, Agnes and Bill Lake visited with the Mersmans, attended theatrical performances, and perfected their acts for the next season during evening preview performances.[23] Agnes sought a larger role in the circus, beyond that of a member of the equestrian corps. On Saturday, March 25, 1848, the entire Mersman family attended the circus to watch Agnes debut her new act. Joseph wrote,

> Wm Lake my brother in law had a benefit[24] this Evening at the Circus. It proved to be a real benefit. When I came in, about 1/2 past 7[,] the House was nearly filled and kept filling till it was the best House that has been there this winter excepting the Clown's benefit. The performance was the best and most pleasing I have ever seen in any Circus. Agness on the Slack wire did very well. She fell off 3 times, but on the whole she made a very favorable impression on the Audience. She had presents thrown in the ring to the value of 40$.[25]

In addition to her equestrian and vocal skills, Agnes Lake unveiled a slack wire routine.[26] Such a performance calls for a wire to be secured between two vertical supports, but unlike the tightrope, the slack wire is not pulled taut between its supporting pole tents. This allows the rope to "hang like a shallow crescent."[27] The artist walks between the two ends — balancing objects, jumping rope, and in other ways demonstrating superior coordination — while the wire swings back and forth. Circus historian Stuart Thayer noted that the performer swung "in great arcs" and that the demonstration was akin to the modern trapeze.[28] In the ring, Agnes wore a shortened skirt that exposed her legs, although she was always modestly dressed outside performances.

On April 2, 1848, Rockwell & Company's circus left for Louisville, traveling by steamboat. Spencer Q. Stokes, the company manager, featured William Lake as the clown. The program included Lake singing a comic song and putting his three dogs, Napoleon, Rolla, and Bibo, through their paces. Agnes was on the bill as an equestrian and a wire walker. The circus played in Louisville for ten days and then headed up the Ohio River, aiming for Pittsburgh. The company performed at a few smaller towns along the way including Maysville and Covington, Kentucky.

When Agnes and Bill Lake returned to Cincinnati on April 23, they shared some bad news with their family. While in Louisville, Agnes had given birth to a stillborn baby, perhaps a premature infant. Joseph reported, "The Accouchement confined her only some 5 or 6 days. She has allready commenced taking her part in the performance, as though nothing had happen'd."[29] It is unclear whether the stillbirth was a natural occurrence or was caused by her circus acts, but either was a likely scenario.

Agnes returned to the ring without delay and performed throughout the season. Rockwell & Company's New York Circus traveled by steamboat to stands on the Arkansas, Missouri, and Mississippi rivers. The show performed in Cincinnati again for a week beginning June 4, 1848, giving Joseph a chance to talk with his sister about the Lakes' plans: "Poor girl. She half Complained of her Husband. Say's that he Commences to drink again and is Cross to her sometimes. I consoled and advised her as much as was in my power. Lake has been talking of going to South America. I have done all I could to dissuade him from doing so. These people are so unsteady that one is totally at a loss how to advise."[30]

To American showmen, South American audiences presented a large, underserved market and an opportunity to amass great wealth. Perhaps Lake wished to build on the experience he had gained with Rockwell & Company's New York Circus.

In the following months, however, the Lakes did not depart for South America but instead stayed with Rockwell & Company for the entire season. Agnes was pregnant again, which might have affected Lake's decision. Her condition did not affect billing for her performances, however. The show played in river towns throughout the Mississippi Valley, and newspaper advertisements regularly included both Agnes and Bill Lake. A second show organized by Rockwell & Company traveled by wagon to inland cities, but the Lakes stayed with the steamboat troupe.[31]

"Mrs. Lake will appear on the slack wire and introduce and perform many difficult feats in which she stands without a rival," reported the Missouri *Liberty Tribune* on September 1, 1848. From there, they traveled south into Arkansas.[32] Further south, in Vicksburg, Mississippi, in November, another newspaper further praised Rockwell & Company: "In addition to a large number of the best male performers, Rockwell & Co. can boast of *five* graceful, daring and accomplished female equestrians, one of whom (Mrs. Lake) is also distinguished for her performances on the slack-wire. Altogether Rockwell's Circus, if at all equal to its fame, must be an unusually pleasant place of resort."[33]

If the advertisements can be believed, Agnes performed on the slack wire throughout her pregnancy and also appeared with the equestrian corps. The circus was so small that every performer was needed.

The 1848 season came to a close with the Lakes in New Orleans. Rockwell & Company played in the Crescent City from December 22, 1848, to January 11, 1849, but since Agnes was preparing to give birth, she did not appear on the list of featured performers. A cholera epidemic had struck the city, and the Lakes were caught up in the disaster.

*   *   *

Cholera is a devastating illness that strikes with alarming speed. Spread by food and water contaminated by human waste, cholera causes profound diarrhea and death from dehydration. Without treatment, once cholera symptoms begin, a previously healthy person can die within twenty-four hours. We now know that a microbe, *Vibrio cholerae,* causes the disease, but that was only discovered in 1881.[34]

Early-nineteenth-century doctors debated over what caused cholera. Some believed in contagion, the concept that disease spreads from one person to the next. Everyone knew of cases of smallpox and measles, which clearly attacked a person after contact with a sick person. Cholera, however, did not appear to spread in that manner. Many cases occurred among people who had no face-to-face contact with other cholera victims. Many informed practitioners believed cholera was caused by miasmas, foul-smelling vapors that came from the bowels of the earth or were produced by rotting garbage. Some blamed God, and others blamed dietary indiscretions for the disease. The epidemic reinforced anti-immigrant feelings because immigrants often became ill.[35] Fresh vegetables, fish, ice water, and certain combinations of foods came under attack. Even physicians were convinced that the Irish diet of potatoes and whiskey and the German favorites, beer and sauerkraut, were lethal combinations.

Nineteenth-century cholera treatments were universally ineffective. Bleeding and purging, popular remedies prescribed by medical practitioners, actually made patients' conditions worse. Whiskey, tonics, and other alcohol-based nostrums may have calmed the doomed but did not prolong their existence. Doctors enthusiastically promoted medicines such as opium, pepper, castor oil, camphor, and capsicum, although they had no proven benefit.

Cholera was an emerging infection in the nineteenth century, and in 1832, 1849, and 1866 major outbreaks occurred in the United States.[36] Imported from Europe by ships, the spread of cholera was fostered by human migrations in 1849; famine in Ireland, political unrest in Germany, and the Gold Rush in California all encouraged the movement of large numbers of people. Two factors contributed to the resulting epidemic: carriers of cholera transported the germs to distant places, and travelers were often especially vulnerable to the illness.

Americans read about the cholera outbreak approaching ever closer from Europe. U.S. cities saw the epidemic as bad for business; individuals inflicted with the malady saw it as a poor reflection of their character. In many places, cholera was considered a disease of the lower classes, a cause of shame.

In the autumn of 1848, newspaper reports mentioned cholera in Europe. Since New Orleans was an international port, cases were reported there early in the outbreak. By January 1849, the Crescent City was overwhelmed with illness.

Steamboats unknowingly continued to transport passengers with cholera up the Mississippi River to other towns. Infected passengers rapidly spread the illness to others, for sanitary facilities onboard were limited. In January, the *Cincinnati Daily Commercial* reported that steamboats were arriving in Cincinnati with dead bodies onboard.[37] Many individuals who died during voyages were thrown into the river or buried in shallow graves onshore.

The first cases in St. Louis were reported on January 6, 1849, but an especially cold winter froze the river and slowed traffic during February. The outbreak there reached epidemic proportions during the warm months of May, June, and July 1849.[38]

The outbreak in New Orleans continued during the first four months of 1849. A total of 3,501 people died, a rate of 30 deaths out of every 1,000 residents. Public health authorities recommended burning pitch to cleanse the air, picking up garbage to eliminate miasmas, and holding a day of prayer to beg for God's help,[39] but these actions had no effect on the mortality rate. Only when the epidemic had run its course and every susceptible person had been tested by the illness did the dying cease.

Among New Orleans casualties in January 1849 was a twelve-day-old boy born to Agnes and Bill Lake at the start of the New Year. There were so many other cholera deaths that week that the baby received little notice. In a manner typical of the era, New Orleans newspapers did not waste the ink to publish an obituary of the infant, although his uncle, Joseph Mersman, documented the child's demise in his diary.[40] There was no time to mourn the loss of their son because the troupe was moving again, and the Lakes needed the income. Physically and spiritually drained, they continued to perform in the river towns along the Mississippi River.

*   *   *

While Agnes and Bill Lake traveled the great rivers of America, Joseph Mersman had completed his apprenticeship with Edmund Dexter in February 1849. Soon thereafter, he relocated to St. Louis, Missouri, and started a tobacco and whiskey-rectifying business with Clemens Nulsen. They called their partnership Nulsen & Mersman, the same name their brothers had used for their business in Cincinnati. With their own savings and borrowed funds from family members, they constructed a new building on Third Street in St. Louis and outfitted it with rectifying apparatus, liquor, and cigars.

The cholera epidemic, which had traveled upriver from New Orleans, hit St. Louis in May, June, and July 1849, killing 7,000 people. Thousands fled to the countryside to escape danger, leaving the downtown desolate. "Business is suspended except what appertains to sickness and Death," Joseph wrote in his diary.[41] A theatrical performance he attended had only two women in the audience. "Fortunately, good looking specimens," he noted, but the summer was otherwise grim.[42]

Amid the chaos and nationwide panic, Agnes and Bill Lake suddenly appeared in Joseph's St. Louis shop on July 13, 1849, while traveling by steamboat with Spencer Q. Stokes's South-Western Circus. The Lakes had lots of news: Rockwell & Company's New York Circus had gone out of business earlier that year, taking seven hundred dollars of the Lakes' withheld wages. The Lakes had signed on for the 1849 season with their old friend Stokes, but he owed them three hundred dollars as well.[43] It was common in the circus business for employers to withhold a portion of a performer's wages until the end of the season as insurance that the employee would complete the entire term of a contract. However, that meant performers faced a financial crisis when a show failed. Mersman agreed to help the Lakes sue Henry Rockwell for their back wages, but he could do little else for them.

Agnes's life as a circus performer was emotionally and physically hard. Thinking of the physical danger and strenuous activities circus work required, Joseph wrote: "The poor Circus Women! How they do have to suffer through their profession."[44] Joseph believed Agnes's choice of work put her at risk of an early death. Each time he wrote a will, Joseph left a bequest for Agnes, believing she would need financial assistance more than the other siblings.[45] "[R]eligious prejudice, the elements . . . fires . . . other 'acts of God,' "[46] steamboat explosions, faulty equipment, and contagious diseases were just some of the hazards Agnes and Bill Lake faced every day. Dan Carlyon noted that a "majority of the towns were rough towns," and a circus had to be an "efficient fighting unit" to physically defend itself. Shows were sometimes followed to the next stand "to be attacked anew."[47] Drunkenness fueled townspeople's anger toward and resentment of these transient performers. Eager crowds pushed their way into the tents, tent ropes were sliced, and canvasses were burned — scenarios all too familiar to circus folk and which often resulted in serious injuries and even death.

During the 1849 season, Stokes's circus traveled on the Mississippi River as far north as Prairie du Chien, Wisconsin, and Guttenberg, Iowa.[48] That year, every river town lost scores of residents to cholera: Cincinnati had 4,774 deaths (38 per 1,000 residents), Louisville 200, and Memphis 100.[49] The illness was especially devastating to children — cholera had claimed Agnes and Bill Lake's newborn son — and sometimes the bacteria wiped out entire families. Notable circus performers were among the thousands who perished: James Buckley (1823–49) was the principal rider with the Spencer Q. Stokes show and died in New Albany, Indiana. Compounding the tragedy for the Lakes, Henry Rockwell (ca. 1814–49), the circus owner, died in Cincinnati.[50] The Lakes never recovered the money they had lost by investing in his circus or their withheld wages. The highs and lows of the circus dictated Agnes and Bill

Lake's lives. Although Agnes had escaped a life as a farmer's or a merchant's wife, she was constrained by circus owners and bankrupt companies; it would be almost a decade before the Lakes achieved financial security.

As might be expected, the epidemic had a negative effect on the circus business. Many people were afraid of crowds, where they might be exposed to contagion, so audiences were much smaller than the tents' capacity. Mourning rituals affected virtually everyone, even after the outbreak passed. Everywhere the South-Western Circus traveled, spectators were wearing black, the mood was somber, and it was difficult to get a laugh. On November 22, 1849, Stokes's show was in New Orleans, where it played for several weeks and then disbanded for good. Agnes and Bill Lake were at liberty again.

For the next circus season, 1850, the Lakes traveled to Indiana and signed on with Samuel B. Burgess. His American Circus opened in Lafayette on April 16, 1850.[51] It was a small show, able to fit on a steamboat, and "the great AMERICAN CLOWN, Bill Lake, that most inimitable Jester," received prominent billing.[52] Agnes performed as an equestrian and also walked the slack wire.[53]

The circus played mostly in Illinois and Missouri but stopped in Cincinnati for performances on June 17 and 18. The Lakes took that opportunity to spend a weekend with their relatives. Joseph Mersman was also in Cincinnati visiting, so all five Mersman siblings and the spouses of Elizabeth, Henry, and Agnes gathered with the family patriarch for Sunday dinner. "The whole familly was assembled under one roof, a reunion that may never take place again in this World. I enjoyed to the full the rarity of the occurrence," Joseph wrote in his diary.[54]

Agnes and Bill brought happy news: they planned to adopt an eight-year-old child from Portsmouth, Ohio, and call him William.[55] Such adoptions were common among circus folk, who wished to add young talent to their acts, and were sought by single biological parents (often unmarried or widowed) who hoped their children would learn the circus business.[56] The child was still with Agnes and Bill three months later, in September, when the census enumerator counted them in St. Louis,[57] but William disappeared soon thereafter. Whether he returned to Portsmouth or died is not known; he was with the Lakes only briefly and never performed with them.

Burgess's American Circus was the scene of unexpected violence during the run in Cincinnati. On Tuesday evening, June 19, 1850, two well-known constables, Peter Davidson and Alexander Dalzell, were stabbed by an intoxicated John C. Walker, who was trying to get "too near the arena for the comfort of the performers or the audience." The men's injuries were so great there was little hope of their recovery.[58] This type of crime made circuses undesirable to many communities. Although the performers and crews were not necessarily rowdy, the shows attracted drinkers, fighters, pickpockets, and other shady characters. The reputation was earned by only a few shows, but it affected the entire circus industry. Along with many of their colleagues, Agnes and Bill Lake were constantly struggling to overcome the negative stereotype much of the population held toward circuses and traveling entertainments.

In October 1850, Burgess's American Circus, which had suffered from cash-flow problems since its beginning, ceased operations. A month earlier, Agnes and Bill had left the show because of a pay dispute.[59] The Lakes had invested in the show, and when it failed they lost their capital. That autumn, Joseph Mersman helped the Lakes sue Spencer Q. Stokes for wages owed from the 1849 season. A court in New Orleans awarded them $150, but whether they ever collected is unknown — although unlikely.[60]

In November 1850, Bill Lake invested in another enterprise, with John Winn as his partner, getting a small show on the road with himself as performer-manager.[61] Vague information exists about the project: during the few weeks of the show's run it played in Memphis and then in New Orleans. By Christmas, the production had folded, and Lake had lost his capital once again.[62]

The first four years of marriage for Agnes and Bill Lake were filled with personal and professional triumphs often overshadowed by personal and professional tragedies. They had performed with five different circuses and received prominent billing but lost their jobs repeatedly when each of the shows went bankrupt. They were blessed with and then lost three sons and had teetered constantly on the brink of personal bankruptcy.

Agnes's family had good reason to worry about her. Agnes and Bill continued to struggle financially in the unconventional path they had chosen.

*   *   *

In 1851, after years of working with smaller circuses, Agnes and Bill Lake signed on with a new company, initially called Spalding, Rogers & Van Orden's People's Circus. Created with the performers and equipment from three defunct touring shows owned by Dan Rice, Stone & McCollum, and Sam Burgess,[63] the People's Circus went on to enjoy solid success. For the next six years, the Lakes enjoyed relative stability in their professional lives. They performed in thirty states and participated in innovative changes in the American circus.

Gilbert Spalding (1812–80), formerly an apothecary in Albany, New York, had entered the circus business in 1844 when he took possession of Samuel H. Nichols's Great Western Circus as payment for a debt.[64] His business partner, Charles J. Rogers (1817–95), had been in the circus business since age five and had been a premier rider. A performer in Spalding's circus in 1847, he became a partner the following year and worked with Spalding for nearly two decades.[65] Wessel T.B. Van Orden, Jr. (ca. 1820–77), the husband of Caroline Spalding, Gilbert's sister, had completed a college degree but went into circus management with his brother-in-law in 1844. The three men brought organizational talent to the business that made them wealthy.

Agnes and Bill Lake were among the leading performers of the People's Circus in 1851. "Madame Lake, the great Creole Gymnast and Crescent Wire Equilibrist," read the advertisements.[66] The description suggested that Agnes had a French heritage, which at the time was more desirable than a German background. Nativism was an active political force in America, and itinerant performers did not want to antagonize any faction that might make trouble. A French background in a country that admired General Marquis de Lafayette and followed Parisian fashions had a certain cachet. During that season, Agnes crafted a counterfeit ancestry and began circulating the bogus story that she had been born in Alsace and that French was her native language. Agnes even claimed that Johnster, her "celebrated imported French dancing horse," had come from Paris.[67]

"Bill Lake, the celebrated Shakespearean jester,"[68] appeared on the roster with two other clowns. Men and women riders, a strongman, and a leopard act kept audiences gasping in amazement. The show also featured "a whole troop . . . of trained, performing War Horses and Lilliputian Trick Ponies, more than brute and little less than human."[69] The show opened on April 16, 1851, in Cincinnati and followed a route primarily in Ohio. Toward the end of the season the troupe toured by steamboat and spent a month in St. Louis before traveling as far north as Keokuk, Iowa. The year ended with a month in New Orleans and environs.

In many ways it was a typical wagon show, with equestrian performances providing the main entertainment. There were no elephants, no menagerie, no sideshow. The circus got into the rhythm of itinerant production and completed all its dates. In Steubenville, Ohio, the People's Circus gave performances at 2 and 7 o'clock; admission was twenty-five cents. One novelty was "a brilliant Drummond light (used for illuminating outdoor spaces), which [was] displayed outside of their huge pavilion."[70] In town after town, the circus performed to cheering crowds. In Louisville, the *Morning Courier* reported, "The circus was again crowded to overflowing last night."[71]

The growing religious fervor in the United States, however, placed amusements such as theatres and circuses under fire. One newspaper editor wrote:

The Circus. This grand theatre of moral pollution made its appearance this morning and proceeded to make preparations for the exhibition. About noon were seen hastening to the spot all grades of individuals, from the Christian to the clown. There were blended in one common mass the profession Christian, the moralist, the skeptic and the confirmed infidel. On beholding the scene we were astonished and amazed to see persons who make a loud profession of religion, and who at the same time would not give half the amount requisite to purchase a ticket, for the support of the gospel, or to feed the needy poor, rushing with eager haste to cast their mite as it were into the treasury of Satan, thus robbing the Almighty of the goods he had placed in their hands for the benefit of their fellow man, to consummate the designs of the enemy of all good.[72]

Spalding and Rogers often encouraged local clergymen and their families to attend performances free of charge as long as they left their calling cards with the doorman. Spalding and Rogers compensated these influential community members so the troupe could prove to the community that the show was crafted for the public's taste and free of crude humor, offensive clowns, and scandalous women.[73]

As a performer, Agnes Lake refined her routines and honed her showman skills. Her wire acts, usually a precursor to the main entertainment under the canvas, were almost always mentioned as a featured exhibition in newspaper advertisements. Agnes's "crescent wire" and acrobatic skills received myriad reviews that heralded her talents among her greatest contemporaries.

CHAPTER FOUR

The *Floating Palace*
"Stirring up the Monkeys
Is a Profitable Business"
1852–1858

For three decades beginning in 1822, showmen used steamboats to travel the rivers of North America, bringing performers and equipment to towns with waterfront access.[1] At each location the shows hired local draymen to haul the canvas and other paraphernalia from the landing to the lot that served as the show's site. Crews set up an arena, seating, and tents in each town, then dismantled the venue at the end of the run, usually the next day. During this time-consuming process the performers sat idle, generating no income for the business.[2]

To address this problem, Gilbert Spalding introduced an innovation to the circus world: a traveling theater composed of several vessels. He commissioned a Cincinnati boatyard to create a showboat, a two-story amphitheater with permanent seating around a single, forty-two-foot ring (figures 7, 8). The craft, a barge without an engine, was transformed when Spalding added sumptuous de-

Fig. 7. In 1852 and 1853, Agnes and Bill Lake performed with Spalding & Rogers's *Floating Palace*, with 2,500 seats. Towed by a steamboat, the barge offered circus performances in up to three towns a day. *Gleason's Pictorial Drawing Room Companion*, February 19, 1853. Courtesy Library of Congress, Prints and Photographs, LC-USZ62-2643.

cor. At the time, circuses were thought to be an inferior variety of entertainment, "given in rude and uncomfortable surroundings," yet Spalding delivered "elegance and prestige to his floating establishment."[3] He christened it the *Floating Palace*. Agnes and Bill Lake signed contracts with Spalding for the 1852 season and traveled roughly 5,000 miles with the vessel, appearing with some of the best circus performers of the day.

The second ship in Spalding's circus flotilla—a 242-ton sidewheel packet called the *North River*—towed the barge, carried the gas supply for illumination, and provided sleeping accommodations for fifty persons, the performers and crew.[4] The five-year-old boat, renamed the *Circus Fleet*, stayed in service for only three years.[5] A third boat, the steam-powered *Humming Bird*—just thirty-five feet

Fig. 8. Interior view of the *Floating Palace*. The center ring was surrounded by two levels of box seats covered in rich fabrics. An ornate chandelier provided ambience and glamour to the covered arena. Courtesy The New-York Historical Society, Negative no. 36805.

long, lightweight, and fast — carried the advance crew, who placed advertising, secured supplies, and made arrangements for the show.[6]

The performers engaged by Spalding & Rogers had started the circus season in New Orleans on March 13, 1852. Although the company did not have the barge on hand, the circus advertised that it was going north to collect the *Floating Palace* and would return with the made-to-order amphitheater. Traveling upriver by char-tered steamboat, the performers played in tents in Baton Rouge, Natchez, Vicksburg, Memphis, Nashville, Clarksville, and Louisville. When they got to Cincinnati, the circus opened for ten days (April 29–May 8) in a canvas pavilion on the corner of Race and Thir-teenth streets, in the Over-the-Rhine district.[7]

Fig. 9. This 1852 broadside from New Orleans bills Agnes Lake in her debut as an equestrian and wire walker and Bill Lake as a clown. Courtesy Somers Historical Society, Somers, New York.

Then, the Lakes and other cast members had three additional weeks to visit friends and relatives in the city while the final touches were put on the vessel and additional performers arrived. The human and animal talent practiced in the new venue and adapted their acts to suit the space. Finally, the *Floating Palace* was ready for service.

About two hundred feet long and sixty feet wide, the *Floating Palace* drew only twenty-five inches of draft when a crowd was aboard. The theater could travel to previously unreachable towns on the Ohio and Mississippi rivers, as well as tributaries in the country's interior. Advertisements emphasized the lavish furnishings: "The *Palace* is a vast amphitheatre, surpassing all American Theatres in elegance, spaciousness, sumptuousness and comfort, with 1100 arm chairs, 500 cushioned settees, and 1000 Gallery seats, and an elaboration of luxury in all its appointments, involving the expenditure of a Princely Fortune."[8]

In addition to the areas open to the public — the arena, a small museum, drawing rooms, and saloons with refreshments — the *Floating Palace* contained stables for twenty horses, dressing rooms for performers, and offices for the managerial staff. Gaslights, mirrors, paintings, and carpets embellished the decor. Heralding the vessel's arrival were "the chimes of twenty bells" and an immense cathedral organ "with a vast forest of pipes" that obviated the need for a circus band.[9]

Departing from Cincinnati with tremendous publicity on May 29, 1852,[10] the *Floating Palace* and its sister ships traveled upriver, passing throngs of people on the banks. Called by some "one of the seven wonders" of the world,[11] the theater opened for its first performance in Pittsburgh on June 1, 1852. The *Pittsburgh Chronicle* enthusiastically reported:

We doubt whether any structure has ever been more appropriately named than the Mammoth Floating Amphitheatre moored at the foot of St. Clair street. Last night it was first opened to the public, and we have never heard such a unanimous expression of admiration. Elegance and refinement, convenience and comfort, pervade the entire establishment. Beautiful as it is, apparently beyond improvement, the proprietors courteously pointed out to us the progress of still greater beautifying and ornamenting, upon which scores of gilders and ornamental artists are busily engaged, so that every half-hour metamorphoses the interior into a still more fairy like [place].[12]

For the first time in American circus history, the performance hall was as much an attraction as the show itself. On Saturday, June 5, 1852, the Pennsylvania Railroad Company ran a half-price excursion train from Turtle Creek to Pittsburgh, a distance of twelve miles, bringing additional customers from the countryside to see the marvel.[13] The *Pittsburgh Chronicle* could not contain its praise:

There are better accommodations in this circus than in any theatre we have ever been in, comfortable arm chairs for each person, sufficiently elevated to command a view of the whole performance, everything wearing the appearance of a well-furnished parlor. The great obstacle heretofore in visiting these places on the part of ladies and children, has been the absence of order, cleanliness and character, in canvass exhibitions. All these are combined in this Palace, and the dress circle last evening [attested to] the truth of our remarks. Of the brilliant performances by the extensive troupe engaged, we have nothing to say, further than they are out of all comparison superior to any thing we have ever witnessed.[14]

Admission to the dress circle of the *Floating Palace* was fifty cents; children under ten paid half-price. Segregated boxes and gallery seats were available for "colored" audience members. The *Floating Palace* opened for three performances a day—10:00 A.M., 2:30 P.M., and 8:00 P.M.—sometimes in as many different locations.[15] Since a show usually lasted between two and three hours, there was time to cast off and go to the next town on the schedule. When moored at a large community such as Cincinnati, where audiences were crowded, the circus squeezed in *four* shows in a single day—at 9 A.M., 12, 3, and 8 P.M.[16]

The exhausting pace continued six days a week, except in New Orleans, where the troupe performed on Sundays as well. Everywhere, the *Floating Palace* received praise: "The circus can now be enjoyed without physical tortures. Instead of hard boards, exposure to the weather, and cramped seats, we are to participate in equestrian and gymnastic sports secure from rain, fanned by the river breezes, ensconced luxuriously in arm chairs, or lounging on cushions."[17]

The talent, two dozen top performers, "were selected . . . from the European Amphitheatres, as well as culled from the elite of Home Stars."[18] Madame (Agnes) Lake and Bill Lake were listed among the acts from America.[19] "European" stars included the rider, Benoit Tourniaire (born in Germany but billed "from Vienna"); his wife, "Madam Benoit" (actually the U.S.-born Rosaline Stickney); and the acrobat, Lavater Lee (born in Valparaiso, Chile, but billed "from London and Paris").[20] Double-billing performers and misrepresenting their origins were common ploys in circus advertising, and fans did not question the roster once they were in their seats.[21] They wanted to see breathtaking performances, and Spalding & Rogers gave them all that and more.[22] With calliope music and chimes to attract crowds,[23] the troupe capitalized on the unique setting of the *Floating Palace*. There was no daily parade, so performers outside the theater stimulated business.

One July day, John Gossin, a clown, somersaulted from the deck of the *Floating Palace* moored at Cincinnati and disappeared from sight in the murky water. His planned gymnastics had been announced in the morning newspaper, and crowds had gathered to see the fun. As the minutes ticked by, observers feared for his life when he did not reappear. Someone called for a search party to look for Gossin's body in the river. When the excitement became unbearable, the trickster, who had swum under the boat and boarded from the opposite side, revealed himself from his dressing room window.[24]

The *Floating Palace* played for fifteen months—from June 1852 through the end of August 1853—without a break, reaching towns in twelve states (see map 2, following the prologue). Next, the flotilla steamed along the Ohio River, playing in towns on both sides of the river, such as Steubenville, Ohio, and New Martinsville, Virginia (now West Virginia). The circus completed runs in Cincinnati and Louisville, then steamed upriver on the Mississippi, stopping in St. Louis, Missouri, and Keokuk, Iowa. Next, the *Floating Palace* played to audiences in Missouri and Illinois on its way south to the Arkansas River. After engagements in Little Rock, the vessels stopped in Memphis, Vicksburg, Natchez, and Baton Rouge. A ten-day run in New Orleans at the end of October 1852 was followed by a tour of Louisiana towns on the Ouachita and Red rivers.

By December, the *Floating Palace* was bouncing through the Gulf of Mexico to audiences along the Alabama River. In early 1853, travel up the Tombigbee and Yazoo rivers brought the show to communities in Alabama and Mississippi that seldom saw itinerant showmen. In March 1853 the company sailed north on the Mississippi River from New Orleans and played in smaller towns such as Vidalia and Fort Adams, Mississippi. In April it traveled the Cumberland River to Nashville and Clarksville, Tennessee. Later that month it navigated the Wabash River in Indiana.[25] Finally, the circus flotilla journeyed back to Cincinnati for a triumphal final show at the end of August. Altogether, the *Floating Palace* journeyed at least 7,500 miles; had it traveled in a straight line due west from Cincinnati, the circus would have reached China.

In September 1853 the *Floating Palace* returned to the Cincinnati shipyard for repairs and refurbishment. Outfitted to carry animals displayed by the Van Amburgh Menagerie, the barge was not used for circus performances for several years. At the start of the Civil War, its travels ended permanently when Confederate authorities seized it in New Orleans and converted it into a military hospital.[26]

*   *   *

Meanwhile, back in the spring of 1853, Agnes and Bill Lake had left the boat. They were offered another opportunity by the same employer. Spalding & Rogers owned a second show, the North American Circus, which traveled by land. In 1853, "Mrs. W. Lake, the brilliant Creole Gymnast," and "Bill Lake, the great New Orleans Clown," began traveling with the "colossal dramatic equestrian circus" that set out for towns in Michigan, Ontario, Quebec, New Hampshire, Massachusetts, and Connecticut.[27] The Lakes traveled over rocky hillsides and through pine forests, terrain completely different from the river valleys of the Midwest and southern United States.

The circus had a spectacular parade wagon, the Apollonicon, which Spalding had first introduced in 1849.[28] Originally designed to hold a pipe organ, the twenty-foot-long and six-foot-wide wagon was pulled by forty horses, ten spans of four horses each. Promoted as a colossal demonstration of humankind's mastery over animals, the Apollonicon by itself created the daily street parade. The mammoth vehicle did not have ornate carvings like other wagons in the circus parade. Instead, the flat sides were "embellished with panel pictures of deities of mythology. . . . [A] border in lavish colors separated each picture, and in this border scheme was a fretwork of holes to allow the passage of sound."[29] By 1853 the organ had been removed and a circus band occupied the vehicle, providing stirring music.

The following year, the 1854 season, Spalding & Rogers had only one circus on tour. Both "M'lle Agnes, the Celebrated Creole Gymnast," and "Mrs. Lake, the intrepid Horsewoman," appeared in the advertisements — another example of padding the roster. Bill Lake, "the Great New Orleans Clown," had top billing and the title "Principal Clown."[30] The route took the company to the East Coast, from Maine to South Carolina — thirteen states and the District of Columbia. The *Richmond Daily Dispatch* noted: "Spalding & Rogers' Circus will exhibit on Council Chamber Hill this afternoon and tonight. All who have visited this place of amusement agree that it is the best Circus that ever visited Richmond. The horses are very fine, and the performers excellent. . . . [T]he performance on a wire, by a lady, is really astonishing."[31] That lady, of course, was Agnes Lake.

*　　　*　　　*

The 1855 season continued with more of the same. Agnes and Bill Lake traveled with Spalding & Rogers's circus to eight states. During the cold months they played in Georgia, Alabama, and Tennessee.

At the end of March, they were in St. Louis for three days. Joseph Mersman's wife, Claudine, whom he married in 1851, had given birth to the couple's second child, Frederick, just two weeks earlier, and the rope-walker aunt and clown uncle likely paid a call on the merchant's household.

The 1855 circus season ran into the 1856 season almost without a break. Traveling with Spalding & Rogers's Two Circuses, Bill Lake, a featured clown, teased audiences into laughing at his witticisms and antics. Billed as "the Prince of Jesters," Lake was called "that embodiment of fun."[32]

Agnes was billed as two performers — "Mademoiselle Agnes, the rope walker," and "Mrs. William Lake, the intrepid *Maitres d'Cheval*" (roughly, the "mistress of horseback").[33] The 1856 show traveled across nine states and Ontario, Canada. When cold weather set in, the troupe performed in southern towns and wintered in New Orleans.

For at least half the season, Agnes appeared free of charge as an outside exhibition, designed to drum up business. According to advertisements, every day about 1 P.M., just before the opening of the tent (weather permitting), the "beautiful and daring Mademoiselle Agnes" ascended a wire two hundred feet long from the ground to the top of the center pole.[34] One newspaper reporter said, "We attended yesterday afternoon the exhibition of this *truly* magnificent circus. The feat of Madame Lake was performed to the utmost satisfaction of the outside spectators. Truly she is a wonder, in any latitude."[35]

Agnes had begun the decade traveling onboard a wonder — the *Floating Palace* — and in only five seasons had become recognized as a wonder herself. Synonymous with boffo performances, Agnes Lake was on the verge of achieving national celebrity.

No less important than the Lakes' professional accomplishments during this period were the changes in their personal life, as Agnes and Bill welcomed three children into their family — Alice, Emma, and "Little Willie." In 1858 an adopted child named Alice Lake, said to be seven years old, began appearing as a rider with Agnes and Bill Lake.[36] Her background is a mystery, but Alice was

Fig. 10. By 1856, Agnes Lake was a leading performer with Spalding & Rogers's Three Consolidated Circuses. In addition to her ascension act, which drew large crowds, she was also a popular equestrian and was often billed twice, as both "Madame Agnes" and "Mrs. Lake." From the *Memphis Daily Appeal*, October 24, 1856.

probably born between 1849 and 1851.[37] An undated photograph (circa 1863) of her with Agnes and Emma (figure 12) shows her as a poised adolescent.

A second daughter named Emma also begins to appear on circus rosters with the Lakes as early as 1857, as a little girl dancing a hornpipe.[38] In 1866, Bill Lake became the legal guardian of a child named William O. Dale (1859–1932), the seven-year-old son of William Owen Dale, a colleague of Bill's and a rider who had lost his vision and died in Cincinnati that same year.[39] The boy quickly became part of the Lake family's equestrian act and first appeared with them in 1866. Billed as "Little Willie," he performed alongside Agnes, Alice, and Emma in the ring on horseback and earned a reputation as a stellar performer.

Fig. 11. Emma Lake, undated photograph, started her circus career with the Lakes in approximately 1857. From the collection of Agnes Cromack.

Fig. 12. Agnes Lake with her daughters Emma and Alice, undated photograph. Courtesy The York County Heritage Trust, PA.

Agnes and Bill's decision to accept responsibility for three children, despite their itinerant and unpredictable lifestyle, fits well with the known practice of parents signing their children over to the circus when they could no longer care for them, in the hope that the child would learn a trade or craft to sustain its livelihood. Circus families desired and valued the arrival of children, since several circus acts depended on youthful performers. For example, one news-

Fig. 13. A Spalding & Rogers's advertisement, circa 1857, capitalized on both Agnes's daring athleticism and her feminine grace and prominently featured her wheelbarrow ascension act to promote attendance. From the collection of Linda A. Fisher.

paper, commenting on the Spalding & Rogers show in 1852, noted: "Another Family Fete is given at the big circus this afternoon. Their peculiarly chaste and rare style of representations, as well as the great number of their children performers, and ponies enables them to produce an entertainment especially adapted to the young."[40]

The Lakes capitalized on this desire for wholesome family entertainment, and by the start of the 1857–58 season Alice had joined Agnes and Bill Lake as one of the top-billed performers with Spalding & Rogers's circus. The owners called it "Three Circuses Combined" because the repertoire included acts that had previously appeared with the *Floating Palace*, the North American Circus, or their third company, the New Railroad Circus, organized in 1856. With 102 people and 109 horses, the consolidated troupe claimed to

Fig. 14. Lithograph, circa 1854, specifically illustrating "Madame Agnes Lake" and her abilities as the "celebrated Creole gymnast" with Spalding & Rogers's Two Circuses. Courtesy Pfening Archives, Columbus, Ohio.

be the "largest traveling show in the world."[41] A caravan of twenty-five wagons transported the tents, equipment, and performers to the approximately 150 locations where they played over the course of eight months. After opening in Vincennes, Indiana, on April 20, 1857, the circus traveled through Illinois, Iowa, Wisconsin, Pennsylvania, and Ohio. At the end of the season, they journeyed on the *Floating Palace* to New Orleans, where they performed throughout December and January 1858.

As was typical for such shows, an advance agent traveled three or four weeks ahead of the circus—leasing the tent site, paying license fees, contracting for animal fodder, and making other preparations at each stand. About a week or two before the circus arrived, posters and handbills appeared in each town center. The local newspaper printed circus advertisements, often two columns wide and an entire page long. The list of acts began with this publicity:

> "Wait for the Wagon!"
> THE FORTY HORSE WAGON!!
> Make Room for the Grand Ascension!!!
> SPALDING & ROGERS'
> THREE CIRCUSES
> *Consolidated this Season will be Exhibited at*
> (here the name of a town and performance
> dates were inserted)
> Everybody Admitted Free!
> If the Forty Horse Team is not Driven by ONE MAN, or if the great Creole Gymnast MAD'LLE AGNES does not trundle a wheelbarrow up a half inch wire 200 feet long to the top of the center pole, except when the weather renders the feat revolting to humanity or, if in personal and material, people and horses, and equipages, this triple establishment is not the most perfect and extensive that has ever appeared in the United States.
> "The Only Company that Performs everything on the Bills."[42]

In town after town, the triple show played to capacity audiences, up to 3,000 people at a time. Crowds at each venue clamored to see the circus parade that included the fabulous equine display, the forty-horse hitch Apollonicon, and the circus band and other waving performers riding in circus wagons. The acts inside the ring surpassed the expectations of even the most demanding spectators. In Youngstown, Ohio, the *Mahoning County Register* reported:

> On last Friday, our town was almost evacuated by the male population, and by a fair deputation of the female, to see the great three-barreled circus at Youngstown. . . . We "see'd" the beautiful Creole [Agnes Lake] wheel her barrow on the slender wire to the top of the tent — a feat worth

going miles to see. We see'd the boy throw the back sum-
mersets on horseback—the man on the high pole—the
men on the ladders—the lady on the slack wire [Agnes
Lake]—the little girl dance a hornpipe [Emma Lake] and
the little girl ride [Alice Lake]; and we heard the funny jokes
of the funny clown [Bill Lake], and the crowd seemed to
enjoy it all, and the popular voice said it was good, and all
went "merry as a marriage bell," and altogether it was about
the best show we have had along lately. Our population were
all at home safe by next morning.[43]

In most places, Agnes Lake was billed as both "Madame W.
Lake, the great Creole Gymnastic Equilibrist," *and* "the beautiful
French Ascensionist, MD'LLE AGNES, the original, of whom all others
are but feeble copyists."[44] Thus, her presence padded the list of
performers beyond the actual number. Her wire-walking act routinely took up to a half hour, compared to the seven to ten minutes
contemporary circus performances last.[45] Observers were uni-
formly amazed. "She must have more courage than discretion,"[46]
wrote one newspaper, referring to her abbreviated costume that
revealed much of her legs to spectators.

In the 1840s, some circuses had gone so far as to assure the
public that they had no female performers, for such "painted
women" were considered as immoral as actresses, prostitutes, and
dance hall hussies. Several male circus performers appeared in pet-
ticoats, notably Omar Samuel Kingsley, who performed as "Ella
Zoyara," and William Painter as "Miss Paintero."[47] Circus historian
Stuart Thayer noted, however: "Immodesty was the main description of female performers. This alluded to their costumes. While
tights, or leotards, did not appear on females until after the Re-
bellion, they did wear knee length skirts over long stockings. . . .
[E]ven the sight of a stockinged leg as high as the knee must have
excited the rural lads, who ordinarily saw nothing of a woman's
limbs above her shoe-tops."[48]

Thayer also commented on a performance petition submitted
by John Robinson in Connecticut, which was denied in 1852 on the

premise that the "legislature thought that the sight of a woman in tights was an awful thing. . . . [A]fter [Robinson] promised that the women of his show should wear long skirts . . . and the men would wear puffed and frilled shirts and knee breeches," however, the petition was granted.[49] But as the years progressed, circus proprietors recognized that sex appeal sold tickets to adults, no matter what the clergy said.

Agnes Lake dressed as an attention-getting performer when she was in the ring, but her clothing and demeanor outside working hours were reserved and modest. She maintained a reputation for being a respectable woman as well as a talented performer throughout her career. The circuses she performed with (and eventually owned) consistently offered wholesome family entertainment. Her work was free from downright crude and lascivious activities, although it was often shockingly daring.

Halfway through the 1857 season, Agnes added an exciting component to the way she opened the show: she invited a member of the audience, someone who weighed no more than 125 pounds, to sit in the wheelbarrow she trundled ahead of her up the wire incline. The circus advertised that if she and her passenger failed to reach the top, free admission would be granted to all. Astonished audiences gasped at Agnes's strength and audacity. Whether there were any accidents or any instances of whole towns admitted without charge because of her failure to deliver a stunning performance remains unknown but unlikely. Agnes may not have been French, as she claimed, but she certainly was a star.

As might be expected, however, not everyone was pleased with Spalding & Rogers's Three Circuses Combined. An editorial from Waynesburg, Pennsylvania, revealed the prejudice all antebellum circuses periodically confronted:

> The show was here on Monday, and had quite a large audience. Madamosella Agnes (but whether a man or a woman, we could not tell at our distance) did walk up the wire, with her wheelbarrow, to the no little astonishment of the admiring crowd. . . . One thing is quite certain, this fandango cost

the people of Greene county several thousand dollars, and we have no doubt many who were present could have spent their means to far better purpose. If they had been called upon to give to the suffering poor or any other charitable purpose, they would not have had a dime to spare — many of them, at least. But such is the strange perversity of human nature. The usual amount of drunkenness and debauchery was also attendant upon this gathering.[50]

Traveling tent shows, totally cash businesses, attracted the ire of many community leaders. While most of rural America used bartering for everyday purchases of goods and labor, circuses extracted hard currency from every town they visited. Anticipating a tent show and amused at their own wit, newspaper editors wrote, "Boys, Look Out! Get your dimes ready!" But the undeniable truth was that circuses siphoned all available cash from townspeople's pockets. Even in 1857, a year of national economic crisis, some itinerant companies continued to see profits. Nineteenth-century American life was so tedious in most places that the majority of folk enthusiastically anticipated circus visits and willingly traded their limited coins for the ephemeral pleasures of performance art.[51]

At the same time, social conservatives — often the clergy — railed against the waste of time and resources on mere amusements. Preachers condemned not only the performers but also the hangers-on: idlers, drinkers, rowdies, and pickpockets, all of whom gravitated to circus grounds like iron filings to a magnet.[52] Although Agnes Lake drew sizable crowds to her amazing performances, some newspaper editors criticized the Spalding & Rogers show:

Sensible enjoyments — amusements of any kind which do not partake of immorality — are well enough. . . . People need recreation. They should occasionally get away from the hum-drum of every day life, and give themselves up to rational pleasures. It conduces to health and gives them fresh vigor for the performance of the duties surrounding them. But a circus is not the place. Of all exhibitions allowed to travel, it is at once the most useless, ridiculous and immoral. Every boy and girl who attends one, goes away with his [sic] mind poisoned to an alarming extent. . . . They see drunken brawls, they hear frightful oaths, and in their enthusiastic conception of things every performer is a hero whose dexterity they covet as a rare endowment. They go away from such a place carrying impressions which will last all their lives. Nothing else is talked of among the children in all the country round about for many months after. . . . Thus the circus moves through the country, an immense engine of evil, casting its degrading influences broadcast over the land.[53]

One way cities and towns attempted to control circuses was by issuing licenses. Prior to selling any tickets, each show had to secure official permission to offer a public amusement. Fees varied widely among communities: in 1858, a one-day circus license in Davenport, Iowa, cost $25, while in Jersey City, New Jersey, the fee was double that. In Easton, Pennsylvania, the charge was $150, an indication that the town wanted to discourage tent shows.[54] Advance agents frequently negotiated lower fees, pleading hardship to get charges reduced or trading free tickets to clerks and officials who cut the companies a break.[55]

In some places, tent shows and theater performances were forbidden. Sometimes circuses played in unincorporated locations, outside of towns, to avoid outrageous charges or constraining ordinances. In the summer of 1858, Agnes and Bill Lake found themselves in the middle of a dispute with the conservative government of Lynn, Massachusetts.

After seven years with Spalding & Rogers, the Lakes joined Nixon & Kemp's Great American Circus. The show capitalized on its bi-national origins, for it united the Great American Circus, organized by one-time acrobat James Nixon (1820–99), and the Mammoth English Circus, put together by the British clown William H. Kemp (1817–91). To promote audience involvement in the show, each American performer wore a blue ribbon on the left shoulder, and each European performer wore a red ribbon attached to the right shoulder.

The two companies' acrobats performed gymnastic feats in the ring at the same time, and the colored ribbons let audience members easily identify their nationalities. The proprietors announced a competition that would last the season: a prize of fifty dollars for the best acrobat and one hundred dollars for the best rider. The cash bonuses would be awarded at the end of the season, based on audience applause for the performers.[56]

In addition to Agnes and Bill Lake, the list of talent included a "Grand Cavalcade of Ladies": Alice Lake, once again billed as "the child rider"; Amelia Butler, a "lady clown"; and Madame Mason, a forty-horse chariot driver. Male performers included scores of equestrians,[57] as well as Monsieur Gregoire, "the strongest man in existence"; William Libby, "the American Hercules"; and Kemp himself as the principal jester.[58]

After opening in Indianapolis on May 1, the route took the circus north through Michigan, Ontario, Quebec, Maine, New Hampshire, Rhode Island, Massachusetts, and New York and concluded with a one-month run in New York City in November. The season got off to a good start, but the advance agent, Charles W. Fuller (1826–88), ran into trouble when he sought to make arrangements for the circus's August performances in Lynn, Massachusetts, a seacoast town with a population of approximately 3,000. In the spring, the Lynn committee on licenses had voted to refuse exhibits by all circus and theatrical companies.[59] The chairman, a devout Methodist, championed the decision, which prompted a response published in the local newspaper in July. "What one man should have a right to say . . . [that a circus may not] exhibit?" read the letter to the editor, signed by "P," perhaps for "Tom Pipes,"[60] in all likelihood a pseudonym for Fuller.

Instead of being put off by the controversy, Nixon & Kemp used the public debate as a means to generate business. Still on schedule, the circus crew pitched tents in Salem, Massachusetts, a town of 2,000 citizens five miles to the north. Fuller negotiated with the Eastern Railroad to have additional trains run on circus day and transport residents from Lynn, ostensibly for an open discussion about the issue.[61] Fresh from a print shop in Boston (ten miles south of Lynn) and clearly not the work of a Lynn resident, notices of a gathering were tacked up prominently in Lynn's public places:

MASS MEETING of the CITIZENS OF LYNN
TO BE HELD AT SALEM!
On Tuesday Afternoon and Evening August 24th [1858]
The object of this meeting is to ascertain the sense of the good people of Lynn, respecting
PUBLIC AMUSEMENTS!
Whether it is their will that half a dozen pharasaical [sic], narrow-minded, bigoted, leather-handed fogies, shall dictate to the industrious working men in what manner they may employ their few leisure hours, or how they shall spend their money, or what recreations or indulgence they or their families may enjoy.
THE VOICE OF THE MEN OF LYNN,
Will be heard on this interesting subject around the Arena of
NIXON & KEMP'S GREAT AMERICAN CIRCUS!
Where the CLOWNS, KEMP AND LAKE, will Address the Meeting.

How long, O people of Lynn, will you suffer these sanctified antediluvians to abuse your patience and trample on your liberties? How long shall their daring insolence baffle the energies of genus, and prohibit rational amusements to the working classes?
In order to ensure a full & general
Expression of Public Sentiment,
The Proprietors of the Circus will make arrangements for an
Extra Train between Salem and Lynn
during the Day and Evening of Tues August 24th
Vox Populi, Vox Dei[62]
Assemble [sic] is your might. Let there be a full attendance. Let all those who begrudge a few moments of cheerful and innocent amusement to the toil-worn operative, be degraded from the high position they now so unworthily oc-

cupy, and good, faithful, liberal, unbigoted, practical men of the present age be put in their stead.

Tom Pipes

Of the St. Lawrence Flotilla, and Boatswain's Mate on board the Commodore's Flag Ship.[63]

Bill Lake, William Kemp, and Charlie Fuller based their strategy on the assumption that any spectator who traveled an hour round-trip by train to argue about personal rights would probably stay for lemonade and entertainment — and they were right. On August 24 the *Lynn News* published a letter claiming that "an abundance of amusements may be found without resorting to circuses or theaters,"[64] but Lake and Kemp found their pre-show rally packed with outspoken residents. It was more of a warm-up act for the circus performance than a town hall meeting. Popular as a clown, Bill Lake made fun of the stuffy churchgoers of Lynn. In that era, clowns interacted with the audience, sang comic songs, and provided social commentary. Lake was right at home, reciting a familiar poem that started,

Lynn, Lynn, city of sin:
You never come out the way you go in.

He made up verses to ridicule the pomposity of town officials, much to the delight of the audience members, who howled with laughter. More important, the crowd packed the Big Top for both performances. The lawmakers of Lynn had their way; but the railroad profited from the extra trains, Salem benefited from the additional commerce, and Lake and Kemp laughed all the way to the bank.

Soon after the Salem performance, the Nixon & Kemp circus ceased advertising the competition between its blue and red teams, and no record survives of who won the prizes. Three dozen people had competed for the equestrian award, but in terms of newspaper coverage, no rider received more attention than "the astonishing juvenile equestrienne"[65] Alice Lake. By the time the company opened in the Palace Garden in New York City on October 25,[66] Alice was the favorite performer of both adult and children's audiences.

Agnes Lake, who perfected her wire-walking act in 1858, had a full season of outstanding performances with Nixon & Kemp. The company's advertisements described her as "the only Wire Volante upon this continent [who] will give numerous and vivid illustrations of her matchless skill and graceful Exercises, Evolutions and Dances upon the Flying Wire."[67] In New York City, Agnes debuted a new wire act on November 8, but she gave only a few performances before her prominent billing was dropped in favor of Mademoiselle Loyal, a Parisian equestrian who had performed before royalty in Europe.[68] Having foreign-sounding credentials could be a major plus in the world of circus arts.

In the later part of the run, Nixon & Kemp mounted an equestrian version of *Cinderella*, with a corps of fifty amateur children and a chariot drawn by four Shetland ponies. The "fairy spectacle" targeted children's audiences, and the show received positive reviews. When the season ended on November 27, the circus disbanded completely.

Agnes and Bill Lake and their children were at liberty once again.

Southern Men, Southern Women, Southern Horses, and Southern Enterprise against the World

1859–1862

In 1859, Agnes and Bill Lake achieved their long-term goal: they had amassed enough capital to enter the ranks of circus proprietors. At the time, there were only about thirty itinerant tent shows in the United States. In the previous fifteen years, the Lakes had seen more than two dozen companies disappear because of financial problems.[1] They were tired of suffering from the whims of bosses who left performers with nothing when their circuses failed. The Lakes, veteran troupers, thrived on the excitement of circus life and had no desire to join the "towners" of the world, with their stay-at-home lives and predictable domestic chores. The Lakes wanted to own their own troupe and stay on the road for long seasons, making money all the while.

Organizing a circus required a sizable infusion of capital. Circus historian Stuart Thayer has estimated that starting an antebellum tent show called for a minimum of $8,000 cash, the equivalent of about $193,000 today. Bank loans were not available to circus folk, and the R. G. Dun Company did not even rate the credit standing of such unstable firms.[2] The only way to raise money was to recruit partners with cash they could invest in an operation.

Horses and related equipment constituted the single largest expense for a road show. Baggage horses, which could not be used for riding acts, cost about $100 each, and ring horses cost about $250. A medium-sized show traveling in wagons might require ten ring horses and two dozen baggage horses, or a total of $5,000 spent on equine support alone. Wagons, hitches, saddles, and trappings for horses might cost an additional $1,000. Canvas tents and seating could easily consume $1,000. Routine promotional costs — posters, handbills, and newspaper advertisements — accounted for another $1,000. Even before hiring performers or outfitting a menagerie, a show would likely require all the Lakes' savings just to get it on the road.[3]

Therefore, Agnes and Bill Lake sought a partner to share the financial risk and assist with the complexities of managing a show. They were acquainted with virtually everyone in the business and eventually settled on joining with a circus-owner friend they had known since the 1840s.

John Robinson (ca. 1807–88) of Cincinnati, a circus performer since childhood and a proprietor since 1842, needed an infusion of cash for his show.[4] Renowned as a horseman, Robinson had teamed up with clown performer Gilbert Naziah Eldred (1813–85) and established Robinson & Eldred's National Circus.[5] From 1845 to 1856, they had traveled primarily south of the Mason-Dixon Line, performing almost continuously to maximize profits. The wagon show reached many small towns other itinerant companies missed. In the winter months, the circus had long runs in warm cities such as Charleston, South Carolina, and Savannah, Georgia.

As the slavery issue gradually rose to the forefront of American politics and North-South friction increased, Robinson became increasingly identified with the South.[6] Beginning in 1851, Robinson

& Eldred called their enterprise the "Great Southern Circus." Their banners defiantly proclaimed "Southern Men, Southern Women, Southern Horses, and Southern Enterprise against the World."[7]

Called "Old John" or "Uncle John" by his friends, Robinson had a fiery temper, an iron will, and a widespread reputation for using profanity.[8] "He generally had his own way, and when he went after a thing he usually got it," observed his son Gilbert Robinson, who had been named for Eldred.[9] Robinson was reportedly verbally abusive to his wife, his three brothers (Alexander, James, and Boyd, all of whom were in the circus business), his six children (John, Gilbert, James, Frank, Charles, and Kate, all of whom worked or performed in the family show), and his colleagues. Robinson and Eldred ended their partnership of eleven years after a bitter argument left bad feelings on both sides.[10]

The seeds for another split — Robinson's temper and his politics — were present from the beginning of his partnership with Bill Lake. Nevertheless, Robinson and Lake launched their "Great Southern Menagerie and Circus" at the beginning of the 1859 season. They opened the show in Ohio and played in Cincinnati from April 18 through April 20. The circus caravan then headed into Dixie, touring Kentucky, Tennessee, Virginia, the Carolinas, and Georgia throughout the summer and autumn of 1859. While Gil Robinson later simplified Bill Lake's role in the partnership as that of "assistant manager," the show's appellation clearly included Lake as a co-proprietor during the next few seasons.[11]

The Lakes brought talent as well as capital to the partnership. The show's newspaper advertisements prominently featured "two great families," for Robinson and Lake were the surnames of the majority of the performers. "Mlle. Alice [Lake], the very incarnation of beauty, grace, daring, dashing effect, style and fascination," played a prominent role as an equestrian and also performed several ballet numbers.[12]

"Mlle. Agnes [Lake], the charming magic wire figurante," performed an act that was "astonishing, chaste, and beautiful." She also appeared on horseback as "Madame Agnes," showing off her "marvelous trained horses, Don Juan and Johnster."[13] Bill Lake, "the

Southern Clown," led a trio of jokesters who provoked laughter from even the toughest audiences. "All his jokes and queer doings tell upon an audience," reported the *Cincinnati Enquirer*. "He is too much the gentleman to introduce vulgarity into the circle, too mirth-provoking to become prosy, and too modest to *bore* his auditors."[14]

The brilliant artists in the Robinson family outnumbered the Lakes, even counting Agnes as two performers. Old John performed on his Arabian horse, Abdallah, and led a trained Russian elk through its paces. His wife, Madame Robinson (nee Elizabeth Frances Bloomer, 1825–79), demonstrated *manège*, elegant sidesaddle riding; and his brother Boyd delighted the crowds with gymnastic feats. His daughter, "La Farie Kate" (1851–74), danced duets with Alice Lake. Robinson's oldest son, billed as "Master John Robinson" (1843–1921), added to the list of equestrians. "A chip off the old block," reported the *Cincinnati Enquirer*, "he now ranks as one of the best principal riders in Europe or America."[15]

The show also included a small menagerie. A performing zebra appeared in the ring; and Eugenie de Lorme, a "lady lion-tamer," entered the big cats' cages and displayed her fearlessness. The menagerie, which could be seen for an additional charge, included a "magnificent collection of rare living animals": lions, tigers, monkeys, birds, and ostriches. The exotic animals on display impressed many spectators, although it is unknown what species was described as "the horned horse, the wonder of the age." Admission to the main show was usually fifty cents; "servants" (enslaved persons) and children were charged half-price.[16]

Throughout the South, Robinson & Lake's circus won enthusiastic praise as wholesome family entertainment. "We are glad to state that there was entire freedom from vulgar and obscene remarks—a too noticeable feature in most shows of the kind," reported the Augusta, Georgia, newspaper.[17] "Strict order is preserved and enforced," reported the *Charleston Daily Courier*.[18]

With the start of the New Year in 1860, the Robinson & Lake show entered Florida. Traveling and performing daily six days a week without a break, the performers did not change their program during the 1860 season. Robinson & Lake had developed a successful formula, and they did not tamper with the recipe. Programs generally followed this standardized format:

> [First, there was the] Grand Entry, which consisted of eight mounted people on horseback in a sort of drill, making figures and winding up with a circle around the ring. After this there generally followed a clown song, in which most of the people with the show, including workingmen and all who could sing, would join in the chorus. Then some wire act or aerial trapeze or contortionist, and when the riding act came it was announced something after this fashion: "Ladies and gentlemen: We take pride and pleasure in next introducing Mr. or Miss So and So, who will accomplish the wonderful feat of riding three times around the ring [standing] erect upon a horse's back!"[19]

In the summer and fall of 1860, the Robinson & Lake circus made the long trek back north through Georgia, the Carolinas, Virginia, and Washington, D.C., performing in different stands than the previous season. Throughout October, as the dark clouds of war were gathering, the circus played in the rural towns of Ohio where Agnes and her family had first settled when they arrived in America. Performances on October 4 in Wapakoneta and October 10 in Sidney were the closest Agnes had come to Minster in fifteen years. Some old friends from Minster (a ten-mile journey from either place) likely attended Robinson & Lake's show because members of the Tangemann, Kramer, and Hellmann families (all from Oldenburg) still lived there. After fifteen years in show business, however, Agnes Lake bore little resemblance to the young girl they may have remembered. By 1860 she was a sophisticated, even glamorous, performer who had traveled extensively and had a daughter (or two).

The circus returned to Cincinnati in time for Election Day, November 6, 1860. Throughout December and January the troupe was scheduled to play a winter show in a Queen City theater. Meanwhile, the world as they knew it began to fall apart.

The results of the national vote made war inevitable: Abraham Lincoln, the first Republican president of the United States, would take office in March 1861. The Southern states, alarmed at what they feared would be an oppressive federal administration, sought to escape. South Carolina seceded from the Union on December 20, and within two months six other states — Mississippi, Florida, Alabama, Georgia, Louisiana, and Texas — had formed a separate country.

While Robinson and the Lakes planned a route for the next season that would take them far from hostilities, the armies of the two nations gathered. News of political struggles as well as battlefield reports filled the newspapers, but there was still room for advertisements for all types of amusements, including circuses.

Despite the onset of the Civil War, Robinson and the Lakes kept their focus on their business. They were too old to serve in the military themselves (Robinson was in his early fifties and Lake was about forty-five), and "one hundred and seventy men (and women) and horses"[20] depended on them for their livelihoods. The overhead costs of the circus — feeding and housing animals and humans — continued even when the show was not performing. Therefore, circus owners were continually under pressure to generate income.

The 1861 show had many of the same acts as the previous two seasons. However, the proprietors made a change that sprang from political necessity: they dropped "Southern" from the name and called the show "Robinson & Lake's Great Menagerie and Circus." Robinson's sons moved into key administrative roles: John Jr. (1843–1921) served as the doorkeeper, Gil (1845–1928) worked as assistant doorkeeper, and James (1847–80) was boss canvasman. When it came to setting up the tent, "everybody had to work, and even the performers had to carry poles and seat planks and help put up the 'big top.' "[21]

Throughout 1861, the show followed a route far from the battlefields of Virginia, Kentucky, Missouri, and Oklahoma Territory. Kentucky, Indiana, Michigan, Wisconsin, Ohio, and Illinois were the only states Robinson & Lake's circus visited that year.[22]

In Pontiac, Michigan, in July 1861, the circus added a thirteen-year-old orphan named James Anthony McGinnis (1847–1906), who wanted to work posting bills. Enterprising and energetic, the young-ster immediately found his place among the circus folk. Since he reported to the advance agent, Frederick H. Bailey (1814–81), the teenager began appropriating the agent's surname as his own. He eagerly learned all he could about promoting a traveling show and made himself indispensable to the Robinson & Lake circus. In a series of unexpected twists, his life continued to be intertwined with the adventures of Agnes and Bill Lake over the next decade. Even-tually, as "James A. Bailey," he became a partner of P. T. Barnum (1810–91) and a stellar showman, the "Bailey" in Barnum & Bailey.[23]

The company traveled for just six months, from May to the beginning of November, a marked reduction from the pre-war schedule. Incomes suffered compared to the halcyon days of 1860. Not only was the season shorter, but audiences were smaller than usual because the nation was mourning the terrible losses resulting from the war. Some spectators, however, attended the circus for a brief diversion from the horrifying realities of daily life.

The second year of the war began badly and grew progressively worse as the weeks wore on. As just one example, on April 6, Confed-erates attacked Union forces at Shiloh, Tennessee, resulting in a two-day battle with combined losses of around 24,000 troops.

Despite these depressing developments, the Robinson & Lake circus opened its season in Cincinnati in late April. The troupe traveled only five months during 1862. During the previous year, other tent shows had taken routes to the north or the west in an effort to escape the war. In 1862, after several stands in Ohio, Robin-son & Lake's circus went to Michigan and then to the Canadian province of Ontario. At the end of summer the troupe returned to the United States, playing in Indiana in September, including a week-long run in Indianapolis. They arrived back in Cincinnati the first week of October.[24] The newspaper headlines there were filled with reports of the Battle of Antietam (near Sharpsburg, Mary-land), where casualties had reached 23,000 on a single day. Lincoln promptly issued the Emancipation Proclamation, which would take effect on January 1, 1863, freeing all slaves in areas rebelling against the United States.

Gil Robinson, seventeen years old, had traveled to Cincinnati ahead of the rest of the troupe. On September 2, 1862, the circus magnate's second son enlisted as a corporal in the 2nd Ohio Reserve Infantry, much to the consternation of his father, who was still with the circus in Indiana. Gil's active duty lasted only thirty days. He was mustered out on October 4, probably because his father paid for a replacement, not wanting to risk losing his son in the conflict. Gil never drew the wage of $3.50 that was due him, apparently chalking up the experience as payment enough. Ever after, Gil claimed that during the Civil War he had served in the Union Army, proof of his patriotism. He often referred to himself as "Major" or "Colonel" Robinson.[25]

The stress of the war took a toll on the Robinson & Lake circus. Faced with the challenging task of moving humans, horses, and equipment through potentially dangerous areas, the tough-minded owners argued over their strategy for the next season. Their differences of opinion proved insurmountable. They dissolved their partnership on January 12, 1863, in Cincinnati, and each made plans to go out on the road separately.[26]

CHAPTER SIX

Nashville

1863–1864

In the spring of 1863, Agnes and Bill Lake launched a show —
"Lake & Company's Great Western Circus" — that gave them
greater public attention while distancing them from their previous
connection with "Old John" Robinson.[1] As the nation was beginning the third year of the Civil War, the Lakes sought to take a
politically neutral position. For years, Robinson had linked his circus — and his performers — with Southern sympathies.

The "& Company" referred to two new partners: Horace Norton (dates unknown), a horse trainer from Chicago, and Levi J.
North (1814–85), a bareback rider who had known Bill Lake for
nearly twenty years.[2] Using his associates' money as well as his own
capital, Lake purchased the horses, wagons, and other equipment
that had belonged to the Antonio Brothers' Circus, a tent show that
had gone out of business after the 1862 season.[3] Only five months
after the Robinson and Lake partnership dissolved, Agnes and Bill
Lake were back on the road with ambitious plans for the season
ahead.

Levi North, the manager of the new circus, worked with the
Lakes to schedule the route. They came up with a daring scheme,

one that would require all their ingenuity to accomplish successfully. The show's ultimate destination was Nashville, Tennessee, the first Confederate state capital to fall into Union hands. Occupied by federal troops since February 1862, Nashville was a major transportation center: from its position on the south side of the Cumberland River, railroad tracks went north to Louisville and south to Chattanooga. Trains had brought thousands of federal casualties to the city from the western battlefields, and at least fifteen buildings — including the Masonic Hall, three factories, and half a dozen schools — had been converted into hospitals.

Nashville's pre-war population of nearly 30,000 had swollen to double that size — exclusive of soldiers.[4] Civilian employees of the federal government and their families — most of whom worked in the quartermaster's department, in railroad operations, or in river transport — accounted for a sizable number of the newcomers. White refugees heading north, black freedmen from surrounding areas, and camp followers of all descriptions added to the mix. Military units awaiting deployment, wounded soldiers under care, and rebel prisoners in custody stayed only briefly but drained the community's resources.[5]

Andrew Johnson (1808–75), the future president, served as the federally appointed military governor of Tennessee. An additional provost marshal governed the city of Nashville. A majority of the native residents, supportive of the Confederate cause, despised the federals and referred to the Yankees as invaders.[6] The secessionist sympathizers generally stayed close to home and avoided unnecessary contact with federal officials. The city's two theaters, however, held nightly performances — staging everything from melodramas to operas — and both were always "filled almost to suffocation."[7] Off-duty soldiers, government employees, loyal citizens, freed slaves, and secessionists scrambled for seats. One journalist, visiting from Cincinnati, described the rage for entertainment as "among the extraordinary developments of the present extraordinary times." He wrote, "If [General] Hood were to bring up his ragged legions to Nashville tonight, and hurl his shells and cannon balls into the heart of the city, it would have no effect on diminishing the numbers of the vast throng rushing to see 'the play.' "[8] His words proved prophetic.

Nashville had not seen a circus since the start of the hostilities. During the previous two seasons, Agnes and Bill Lake had remained in the north, far from the battlefields, as had most U.S. traveling shows. Now, the Lakes planned to bring their show south, to play for federal soldiers and civilians who had both the hard currency and the free time to attend performances of the Great Western Circus.

Lake & Company started the 1863 tenting season in Springfield, Illinois, on May 5 and ended the regular tour five months later with a five-day run in Cincinnati, Ohio, October 12–17. The circus traveled by wagon and performed at stands in Missouri, Iowa, Illinois, and Indiana, far from the sounds of gunfire. As described in the *(Springfield) Illinois Journal*, "The Star Troupe of 1863" promised to delight the crowds with its roster of performers:

LITTLE ALICE [LAKE], the best Female Equestrienne in the World, and the only one who has accomplished backward riding.

MADAME AGNES [LAKE], the Model Equestrienne, will introduce her highly trained and thorough-bred horse JOHNSTER.

LA BELLE JEANETTE [PERRY], the Beautiful Sylph of the Circle.

LA PETITE EMMA [LAKE], with her patriotic Songs and Dances.

MADAME AGNES [LAKE], in her Great Wire Act.

MR. E. W. PERRY, the Famous Two and Four horse rider.

MR. H. MARKS, in his varied scenes of Equitation.

MAST. THOMAS PERRY, the daring Hurdle Rider.

MR. WILLIAM LAKE, the greatest Wit, Satirist and Clown now in the ring.

THE LAZELLE BROTHERS, in their thrilling and beautiful acts of Groupings, La Trapeze, &c.

WM. LESTER, the Greatest Contortionist of the age.

CHARLIE CLONEY, the great modern Gymnast.

THE AFRICAN FLYING TRICK MULE, introduced by Mr. LAKE.

THE PERFORMING HORSE DON JUAN, introduced by Miss LAKE.

The Great Western Silver Cornet and String Band will execute at each exhibition.[9]

The small cast depended primarily on equestrian skills: the Lake family and their animals accounted for at least seven of the fifteen acts listed. The equestrian director, Eben Wood Perry, and his children were three of the other billed performers. Several seasoned performers — Hiram Marks (1832–1910), a clown and bareback rider; Fred Lazelle (dates unknown), a gymnast; and William Lester (d. 1872), a contortionist — had worked previously with Levi North.

Despite the limited number of acts, the Great Western Circus delighted spectators at every stand. The *Illinois Journal* reported, "[T]he performance of the troupe was as good as usually seen in New York and Boston."[10] The *Indianapolis Daily Journal* raved, "This great circus was witnessed by a large number of our citizens who pronounce the performances unsurpassed by any circus company that ever exhibited here."[11]

In town after town, the Great Western Circus played to cheering audiences. The *Canton (Illinois) Weekly Register* noted, "This city has not been favored with a visit from a circus for a year or two, and the citizens have almost forgotten the ways of the clown, trick ponies, etc."[12]

When the circus played in Cincinnati at the end of the season, J. J. Justice (d. 1880), an agent who had worked for the Antonio Brothers the previous three seasons, stepped in to manage the show. Thus, Levi North and Benjamin M. Stevens could travel to Nashville in advance of the rest of the troupe. Since long-distance communication was problematic, agents had to make many arrangements for the circus in person.[13]

Before the performers were allowed to board the train from Louisville to Nashville, they had to secure permission from the military command to perform in the occupied city. Traveling ahead of the show, North and Stevens negotiated with federal authorities, obtained the necessary papers, and competed with supply officers for logistical support. They secured fodder for the circus animals, found lodging for the performers, leased a suitable lot for the tent, and paid for a license to perform. They arranged to run advertisements in the newspapers and to post bills on fences.

On November 1, 1863, three Nashville newspapers contained notices about the show; no one could overlook the announcements. Although no handbills have been preserved, accounts indicate they were posted all over town. Even illiterate residents were intrigued by the images. The Great Western Circus played for more than three weeks — from Tuesday, November 3, through Saturday, November 28 — giving two performances every day except Sundays. Admission was fifty cents; "servants" and children paid twenty-five cents.

Since the tent (which held 2,500 spectators) was packed at every performance, the run was financially successful. Disappointed customers, turned away because of a sellout, were urged to come earlier for the next show. Soldiers and civilians flocked to the canvas erected on the corner of College and Jackson streets, two blocks from the river. The *Nashville Daily Press* reported:

> Last evening Madame Agnes treated her numerous admirers to a display of her skill on her French imported dancing horse Johnster, the most beautiful as well as most learned horse at present known. Madame Agnes sat upon him in his leaps and plunges, with perfect confidence in her skill and ability; and we have no hesitancy in saying that Madame A. stands to-day without a rival. Mr. Lake introduced his celebrated trained mule again, who is all, and more than all, that has been said of him. Little Emma appeared in a new character, and delivered an oration, which showed her to be possessed of much ability, and one destined to occupy a high position among the world's celebrities. The rest of their admirable troupe excelled themselves.[14]

Day after day, the newspapers contained descriptions of the performances and the size of the audiences. Despite a week of gloomy weather, crowds braved the wind and rain.[15] The *Nashville Union* reported that the training of horses is Mr. Lake's particular pleasure, and his system of education of the horse as well as mule is certainly an accomplishment few can boast of. Mad. Agnes as usual appears in her startling but fascinating positions on the floating wire. Little Alice, so beautiful in figure, and so accomplished, holds the audience in breathless silence during the difficult positions she appears in on her highly trained horse. Go early, as the seats are always full.[16]

Fourteen-year-old Alice Lake particularly charmed the spectators, who felt "admiration, wonder and fear" at the sight of the diminutive equestrian.[17] "We have never seen better [riding], and doubt if even as good. She is indeed a perfect phenomenon, and has already established herself in the affections of all that have seen her," concluded the *Nashville Daily Press*.[18]

Despite the distraction of the performances, neither the circus troupe nor the residents of Nashville could long forget the war. Meat was scarce, and other foods were expensive.[19] Accounts of horse theft, disorderly conduct, and accidental shootings filled the newspapers.[20] Reports of violent deaths and property seizures squeezed out commercial news. The presence of both Confederate and Union spies added to the pervasive atmosphere of intrigue.

As might be expected, a city full of whiskey, soldiers, and firearms created a milieu in which all types of criminal behavior flourished. On Saturday night, November 14, the total receipts for the evening's circus performance ($1,500) were stolen from the show's cash box. Military authorities arrested nine individuals and prosecuted two.[21] The money was never recovered, but the show continued twice-daily performances with increased security.

On November 16 the circus moved to the corner of Broad and Spruce streets in an effort to reduce expenses, since the new site was outside corporate limits and therefore subject to reduced fees. Within a few days, however, the circus had returned to its original site, where it remained for the rest of the run.

Meanwhile, another problem compounded Nashville's troubles. An outbreak of smallpox erupted, which some blamed on the refugees and freed slaves arriving in droves from the surrounding countryside. The mayor urged vaccination for all those susceptible, and dozens lined up for inoculations. The *Nashville Daily Union* reported this calamity, next to the reports of military actions. Juxtaposed with accounts of war and pestilence, circus news contrasted to the point of absurdity.

For example, on November 24, the *Daily Union* reported the dedication of the cemetery at the Gettysburg battlefield (now Gettysburg National Military Park) and published the complete text of President Lincoln's memorable address delivered five days earlier. The same edition noted that the crowds at the Great Western Circus were large and advised townspeople to arrive early to obtain seats. Three days later, with playful exaggeration, the newspaper suggested that circus spectators risked dying from laughter because the clowns were so funny. Unfortunately, that weak humor foreshadowed a tragedy at the circus in which death came another way.

On Friday, November 27, a group of soldiers belonging to the 5th Kentucky Cavalry, probably under the influence of alcohol, charged the circus tent at showtime. Two guards stationed there attempted to stop the assault. A fight ensued, with rifles and pistols fired. When the smoke cleared, Corporal Davis of the Provost Guard was dead; a cavalryman and one of the circus roustabouts were wounded.[22]

The Lakes may have sought to leave the city before another ugly incident occurred, but limited space on trains prevented them from doing so. Besides, they were obligated to provide one more evening performance. On the final night, the clown Hiram Marks demonstrated his cat piano, much to the amusement of the crowd. Twenty-five felines were caged separately in an apparatus that exposed each tail to a sharp needle attached to a keyboard. Depressing one note drove a needle into the tail of one cat, eliciting a screech from the animal. The clown created a cacophony by accompanying his singing with "playing" the piano.[23] According to observers, the audience roared with laughter at his contraption, first designed about four hundred years earlier.[24] While a modern audience might be outraged at the animal abuse, spectators of the Civil War era saw the cat piano as a humorous invention. Compared to the horrors of the war around them, the injury inflicted on the cats may have seemed minor indeed.

Agnes and Bill Lake considered the show's run in Nashville a great success. With their cash in hand, the proprietors of the Great Western Circus headed back north by train, stopping to give performances in Kentucky and Illinois. While the Great Western Circus wintered in Cincinnati, Levi North dropped out of the partnership.[25]

When the Lakes compared their experience with that of other shows, they discovered that the 1863 season had been especially lucrative for the entire amusement industry. After the initial shock of war had worn off, people all over the country sought diversion. Soldiers provided a new audience for traveling shows.[26]

As a result, Agnes and Bill Lake planned to return to Nashville the following year for a month-long engagement. They calculated that four weeks at one location — even in the proximity of pestilence and rowdy troops — produced better returns than four weeks on the road, where audiences might prove more variable in size and temperament.

*   *   *

The 1864 tenting season started in familiar territory for the renamed "Lake & Company's Mammoth Circus." After opening in Kentucky in April, the show played in Cincinnati for a week in May. The Lakes added new performers to the talented group who had played the previous year. The troupe was joined by a juggler, Silas D. Baldwin (1825–67); an animal trainer, Willis Cobb (1841–1913); and two clowns, John Lowlow (1841–1910) and Clark M. Gibbs (dates unknown). Three new gymnasts — Charles Coreil, James Larus, and Harry Blood — augmented the talented Lazelle Brothers and the Perry family's equestrian acts.[27]

After he recruited Lowlow and Gibbs, Bill Lake skipped his clown routines and displayed his skills as an animal trainer instead. He demonstrated the sagacity of two mules, Sancho and Paul Pry.[28] Following Lake's cues, the mules appeared to count as well as answer "yes" and "no" questions.

Agnes Lake performed as both a wire walker and a rider. She directed her prize horse, Johnster, as he performed a series of tricks with her mounted on his back. He pranced, bowed, and laid down on command. Horses were a major mode of transportation, so audiences of the era especially appreciated equine talent. One newspaper review called Willis Cobb's horse, F. H., "one of the most splendid specimens of a horse that ever appeared within an arena."[29]

Cincinnati had grown so much in the eighteen years since Agnes Lake had started her career that the 1864 circus lot was now situated on the corner of Eighth and Baymiller streets, farther north and west than earlier sites.[30] Crowds nevertheless thronged to see the performances, and the *Cincinnati Enquirer* gushed: "The equipoise performance of Madame Agnes upon the slack wire is really marvelous, and the tumbling, somersaults, and gymnastic feats . . . have never been excelled in this city. The clowns display wit devoid of vulgarity and there is originality in their drollery. Altogether this is one of the best circuses that has ever visited Cincinnati."[31]

The Mammoth Circus traveled for six months, reaching towns in Ohio, Michigan, West Virginia, and Pennsylvania. Bill Lake led the wagon show to communities that were hungry for entertainment, and he avoided contact with the military. Lake was a showman earning a living by doing what he loved.

The Lakes' circus finished its regular 1864 season tour in Zanesville, Ohio, with performances on October 24–25. Bill Lake announced that henceforth he would be the sole proprietor of the show and that the circus would winter in Zanesville.[32] Leaving their wagons and baggage stock behind,[33] the Lakes and their best acts hurried to Cincinnati to join long-term friends arriving from Chicago. Agnes and Bill Lake had big plans for the following month, but unbeknown to them, the plans set them on a collision course with the military.

Meanwhile, the Civil War had continued to rage throughout the South. In February 1864, the U.S. government had instituted a draft to conscript an additional half-million men for three years of service. Confederate forces also suffered terrible losses and were less able to replenish their ranks. The grim realities of the war—tens of thousands of casualties and widespread property damage—weighed heavily on both sides.

*   *   *

After nearly a one-year interval, Agnes and Bill Lake returned to Nashville by train with a host of talent. Opening night, Monday, November 14, 1864, revealed a show organized under the banner of Horace Norton and Frank J. Howes (1832–80), an accomplished rider and circus proprietor. Resources from three organizations—Lake & Company's Mammoth Circus, Robinson & Howes's Railroad Circus, and Howes & Norton's Circus—had created a unique exhibition that played in the occupied city for a single, four-week run. Called "Howes & Norton's Champion Circus," the show featured the most daring acts of the era both inside and outside the ring.

Conditions in Nashville had deteriorated since Agnes and Bill Lake's previous stay. Even with the provost marshal issuing directives, lawlessness reigned. "Robbers and assassins infest our city," complained the *Nashville Dispatch*.[34] "Scarcely a night passes but what we hear of a burglary, a knock down or a robbery of some description, and it has actually become dangerous for a man to appear upon the streets at night," reported the *Nashville Daily Press*.[35] The newspapers were crammed with lists of deserters, accounts of mayhem, and notices of public hangings. Agnes was undoubtedly concerned for the safety of her family, especially her two young daughters, as they entered the city of intractable citizens.

The provost marshal attempted to control public inebriation by closing the taverns when duty demanded sobriety—for example, on Election Day—but generally the Recorder's Court stayed busy prosecuting drunkenness and other misdemeanors. Dr. Coleman's "dispensary for venereal diseases" advertised in 28-point type on the front page of the *Nashville Dispatch*, suggesting that the physician's services were in great demand. Describing the city, one soldier from Ohio wrote, "No city in the United States ever had so bad a population as the city of Nashville. . . . The thieves, gamblers and disreputable of both sexes, swarmed in from all over the country."[36]

Howes & Norton's Champion Circus raised its canvas on the corner of College and Jackson streets, the same lot previously used by Lake & Company. The show charged higher fees compared to 1863: admission was seventy-five cents, fifty cents for children under twelve. Afternoon performances began at 2:00 and evening shows at 7:30.[37] As expected, the circus attracted thousands of spectators, and virtually every performance was sold out, despite weather that started soggy and then remained below freezing for a week.

The three females from the Lake family topped the roster of acts, and Alice received the most ink from reviewers. "Little Alice, the fairy equestrienne, is the wonder of the circle; how one so young can accomplish so many daring feats with such evident coolness is the astonishment of all beholders," wrote the *Nashville Dispatch*. In addition to appearing on horseback, Agnes Lake performed her wire-walking routine. The newspaper referred to her as an established favorite: "Madame Agnes' performance on the slack wire is always well received."[38] Emma, now about nine years old, sang patriotic songs and rode around the ring with her mother and sister in various equestrian acts.

An enlarged cast of four clowns added to the fun: Bill Lake, John Lowlow, William T. Aymar (1830–83), and John L. Davenport, Sr. (1836–1916). The show featured three gymnasts: George M. Kelley (1841–1921), Charles S. Burroughs (d. 1901), and William Donavan (d. 1873). Also on the bill were Silas D. Baldwin, "Illusionist and Prestidigitator Extraordinaire"; William Lester, contortionist; and Professor Peters's Silver Cornet Band.

The backbone of the show, billed as "the Hippo-Arenic Model of the Age,"[39] was definitely the equestrians. The traditional opening for every performance was the grand entrée, which called for eight horses with riders moving in patterns around the ring. Although baggage men could substitute for professional riders, there was no substitute for the equine talent.[40] The Howes & Norton's Champion Circus featured some of America's best horsemen and women of the day: Charles Fish (1848–95), John R. Glenroy (1828–1902), Madame Elise, the Lakes, Frank Howes, Horace Norton, James Madigan, and Jeanette Perry — all of whom rode expertly.

Animals named on the bill included two comic mules, Broad Gauge and Beau Hackette; Agnes's favorite mount, Johnster; and a blind horse called General Grant. On December 3, 1864, the *Nashville Union* mentioned the horse's impaired vision. Far from being disabled, a blind horse would not be spooked by flashes of light or fabric waved in front of its face and could perform well in a circus arena. The average cantering steed circled a forty-two-foot-diameter ring in sixteen paces. A consistent rhythm provided the ideal mount for a gymnast turning somersaults or leaping onto the animal's bare back. In addition, the show had a fine cast of at least seventeen other horses.

The circus opened to capacity crowds, and the rainy weather did not deter spectators the subsequent week. It was the only tent show to reach Nashville that season, and fans craved the entertainment. The gaslights at evening performances revealed that many seats were filled with soldiers.[41]

The troupe modified the "countryman act," a classic circus routine, to feature a supposedly intoxicated enlisted man. The ringmaster offered a sum of money to anyone in the audience who could ride a horse in the ring. A drunken soldier sitting in the crowd took the offer and stepped into the ring with an unsteady gait. After bantering with the clown, the volunteer undressed, taking off at least a dozen vests. Following a few missteps, the "soldier" rode the horse around the ring, performed a number of stunts, and then took off his trousers — revealing that he was a fully costumed member of the troupe.[42] Nashville audiences loved the joke.

One week into the run, on November 21, the circus moved to a site on Market Street, a stone's throw from the Louisville & Nashville Railroad Depot. The new location was closer to the river and the center of town.[43] The site was more convenient for customers, for pavement provided access all the way to the tent. In addition, it was further from the anticipated front lines. Even if the troupe considered escaping the city, travel by rail was impossible because the Federal Army was using all available trains to transport men and supplies.[44]

On November 26 the *Nashville Union* gushed, "This really fine organization of wonderful horses, graceful gymnasts, daring riders, with juggler, contortionist and other host of attractions[,] still continues to draw large crowds." The next day the newspaper reported that a soldier attending a performance exclaimed, "[expletive], wouldn't our cavalry regiment like to have them hosses!"[45] What may have been a joke at the time soon became reality.

The signs of an impending battle were unmistakable. Confederate forces, which numbered about 24,000, led by General John Bell Hood (1831–79), were advancing toward Nashville from the south, and Union soldiers under General George H. Thomas (1816–70) were digging trenches in the fields close to the city.[46]

Nashville and the armies continued to prepare for battle. On December 2, the Union provost marshal ordered all saloons closed by 8:00 P.M. nightly. Two days later he closed them completely and kept them shuttered until December 20.[47] Next, the authorities cut off civilian travel from Louisville to Nashville.[48]

While General Thomas readied the 70,000 troops at his command, the circus continued twice-daily performances. "The soldiers patronize the circus so much that . . . part of the tent looks like a blue-berry patch," reported the *Nashville Union*.[49] Equipping the cavalry posed the greatest challenge because many units required fresh horses. Of 12,000 mounted troops, one-quarter had nothing to ride.[50]

On December 6, Thomas advised General Grant that as soon as he had sufficient mounts, he would attack the rebels. Federal soldiers thereupon commandeered all the horses found on Nashville's streets — even farm stock and dray horses. Abandoned wagons littered the city.[51] On December 7 the soldiers impressed eighteen horses from the circus, including Johnster and General Grant, and paid $1,800 for the lot — a paltry sum, considering their value as performers. Only the two mules and Charles Fish's mount, which had gone lame, remained to perform with the show.[52]

On December 8, the *Nashville Union* and the *Nashville Daily Press* reported the loss of the circus animals but assured readers that the show would nevertheless go on as scheduled. The acrobats and clowns did their best to fill in for the equestrian acts, but there was no grand entrée. That same day, an icy storm of sleet and snow blanketed the city, making the hills around Nashville too slippery for the armies to move. Spectators nevertheless made it to the circus tent.

A circus without horses! It would be easier to envision the night sky without stars. Several versions exist of what happened next. John Lowlow's, the *Nashville Daily Press*'s,[53] and John Glenroy's published memoirs provide independent accounts that contain similar themes. Both sources allege that Alice Lake staged one of the best performances of her career to secure the release of the ring stock. Lowlow claimed she called on General James H. Wilson (1837–1925), who was in charge of the cavalry corps, and made the case for returning the show animals. Whether she pleaded, cajoled, or cried is not known; somehow, though, Alice convinced Wilson to order the return of the animals. Lowlow added that the mounts were unsuitable for military use:

> The horses, you know, were all trained for ring service, and most of them, including the stallions, were trained to dance to the music, and to fall upon the knees and sides upon being touched upon the haunches with a spur or the whip. Our whole bunch was turned over to a military band as their mounts, and the orderly told me that during the four days that the band was mounted on our beasts there was not an hour when one of them was not dancing around . . . or rolling on the ground . . . the musician[s] having unwittingly given the horse his lying down cue.[54]

The newspaper report says that Alice convinced a lower-ranking officer who had led the confiscation to release the horses and that he acquiesced to her pleas.

A second version of the story comes from another eyewitness, John Glenroy, who published his memoirs, *The Ins and Outs of Circus Life*, in 1885. Glenroy claimed Frank Howes complained to General Thomas about his loss. When Thomas refused to intercede, Howes spoke with the Tennessee military governor, Andrew Johnson, the vice president elect. Johnson communicated with President Lincoln, who suggested that the circus animals be released on the condition that the showmen find substitutes. It took considerable searching, but Howes & Norton had their horses back even before the replacements were obtained.[55] It is difficult to imagine Lincoln's involvement with this issue, and a more likely scenario is that the dispute was worked out on a lower level. The indisputable fact is that on December 11, 1864, the *Nashville Union* reported that all of the horses had been returned to the circus troupe. Three days later the *Nashville Daily Press*, attempting to be humorous, noted, "Notwithstanding the inclemency of the weather, the Horse Opera continues to be largely attended. Uncle Sam went into the Circus business for a few days, but the institution didn't pay, and the horses being returned, the management have been enabled to revive the Grand Entree, which is one of the most attractive features of the entertainment."[56]

On December 14 a warm rain melted the ice, enabling the men in blue and gray to move through the mud and meet their destiny. The Battle of Nashville began at dawn on Thursday, December 15, and lasted two days. The fighting took place in the fields and hillsides to the west and south of the city. No townspeople were casualties, and no buildings in the city were significantly damaged. Low-low described the scene Thursday evening under the Big Top:

That night, while the city was full of wounded men and prisoners, and while the guns were booming like thunder, our show was jammed. Whether the people came to meet each other and to hear the news or whether they wanted the fun in the ring to relax their tensely strung heart-strings, I can't say, but it is certain that on Thursday and Friday while the battle was in progress in easy hearing — there, almost on the battlefield — the people and strangers in Nashville came to the circus in great crowds, and laughed like children.[57]

On Friday, December 16, as the battle continued, the circus gave another evening performance, this one to benefit the poverty-stricken residents of Nashville. Despite editorial mention in the *Nashville Dispatch*, attendance was down and the take was only $526.50.

With expenses of $471.77, the balance was $54.73. "The proceeds would undoubtedly have been larger had it not been for the inclemency of the weather," noted the *Nashville Dispatch* in an effort to save face for the community.[58]

Weather, of course, had little to do with the low turnout. By December 16, many members of Nashville's civilian population were tending the wounded from both armies. The Union Army had crushed the Confederate forces. General Thomas reported that 387 federal soldiers had been killed and 2,562 wounded. General Hood lost about 40 percent of the men he had led into battle. Nearly 4,500 rebels, including three generals, were taken prisoner, and Confederate casualties numbered 5,500.[59]

After the Friday night performance, the canvas men struck the tent and packed the equipment. On Saturday, December 17, the circus troupe boarded a northbound train. During the brief engagement, Howes & Norton's Champion Circus had provided a ray of hope, or at least a measure of distraction, in a city besieged by war.

The fighting officially ended on April 9, 1865, with the Confederate surrender at Appomattox Court House. The end of the Civil War marked the start of a new phase in the life of Agnes Lake. As the country began rebuilding, industrial developments unknowingly jettisoned the progress of traveling exhibitions, affecting Agnes for the next decade.

Agnes also faced changed circumstances in her personal life. Her father, Frederick Mersman, had died of general infirmities in Cincinnati a year earlier, at age eighty-three.[60] Her oldest brother, Henry, died in Cincinnati on October 12, 1864, at age forty-four, probably from complications related to alcoholism.[61] He left a widow and five children ranging in age from eighteen to a few months, as well as investment property and his tobacco business.

Agnes's younger brother, thirty-six-year-old Frank, never married and worked as a tobacconist in Cincinnati. He suffered from consumption, and doctors feared he would not live much longer. Agnes's sister, Elizabeth Kattenhorn, who had six children, cared for Frank as another of her dependents. Frank, who depended on his two sisters, also stayed at the Ninth Street address.

In addition, Agnes's beloved brother Joseph Mersman, the St. Louis whiskey merchant, was suffering from incurable eye problems and was losing his vision — a consequence of contracting syphilis at least fifteen years earlier. By then the father of six children, Joseph continued his activities as a capitalist for many more years, investing in real estate and other businesses, but concerns about his health weighed on the entire family.

Faced with these changes in her family, Agnes took stock of her own life. Thirty-nine years old, the equestrian still hoped to add another success to her accomplishments. In that day, many performers boasted of having appeared "before the crown heads of Europe." Receiving approval from royalty carried great weight with the American public. As long as the Civil War raged, travel abroad was out of the question, but with the end of hostilities, a trip to Germany became not only a possibility but Agnes's professional goal. *Mazeppa* could be her ticket to recognition as a celebrity in Europe and could also enhance her status in America.

CHAPTER SEVEN

Mazeppa Enters the Ring

1865

S ex sells. Each generation makes that discovery anew, although the truth of the statement has been abundantly clear since the dawn of civilization. Horses have an innate sexual mystique, and their basic theatrical appeal was seen in the circus and the legitimate theater. Agnes Lake was certainly aware of the value and allure of horses in her circus life and planned to make the connection even more prominent. The theatrical production known as *Mazeppa* was sweeping across European and American theatres but is virtually unknown today.

In the early nineteenth century, the poet Lord George Gordon Byron (1788–1824) created rhymed verse that thrilled the English-speaking world. His themes influenced artists throughout Europe; music, painting, and literature reflected his poetry. An outrageous lifestyle contributed to both Byron's fame and his early death at only thirty-six. Rumors of incest, homosexuality, and extramarital affairs in his personal life made him one of the most talked-about personages of the era. Among the poems he created was a long narrative titled *Mazeppa*, published in 1819.

The poem was based on a true story from the seventeenth century. Byron used iambic tetrameter verse to relate the tale of Ivan

Mazeppa, a page in the court of the Polish king.[1] The youth fell in love with a nobleman's wife, and his unbridled passion led to secret trysts. Finally discovered, Mazeppa received punishment that fit his crime: the count made Mazeppa the victim of forces beyond his control, strapping him naked to a wild horse that was then set free to run. Mazeppa suffered from the elements as the stallion galloped for days, east toward its homeland, Ukraine. When it finally reached the land of its birth, the steed collapsed. Weak from fatigue and hunger, Mazeppa was rescued by peasants who cared for him until he re-covered his strength. He eventually married a Cossack's daughter and became a chieftain. The poem ends with the motto, "*Nil desper-andum* (despair at nothing)."

Byron's poem had many ingredients that fascinated nineteenth-century audiences: love, sex, violence, and uncontrolled forces. Other creative minds latched onto the legend for inspiration and interpreted it in various media. Artists like Eugene Delacroix and Louis Boulanger created images that depicted Mazeppa's wild ride. Alexander Pushkin and Victor Hugo wrote their own adaptations about Mazeppa. Influenced by various poems, Karl Loewe and Franz Liszt set the epic to musical compositions. Peter Ilyich Tchai-kovsky wrote an opera titled *Mazeppa*, which he based on Push-kin's verse.

Theatrical versions brought Byron's characters to the stage in Paris as early as 1825. Horse drama or horse opera—that is, a pro-duction that included equine talent—was a popular gimmick be-ginning in the 1820s in both Europe and America, and theater owners sought original plays to feed the public's voracious appetite for novelty. In 1830, Henry M. Milner, reworking a play by John Howard Payne, wrote *Mazeppa; or The Wild Horse of Tartary*, which premiered in London the following year. A horse drama in three acts, Milner's version modified the tale by eliminating the adultery but keeping the sex appeal and adding dramatic serendipity.

In the first act, the hero appears as Casimir,[2] a Tatar adopted by a Polish nobleman after he was found on a battlefield. The hand-some young man has fallen in love with Lady Olinska, betrothed against her will to the evil Count Palatine. Casimir defeats the count in a duel, but Olinska's father orders harsh punishment. By some coincidence, he has a wild horse on hand. Olinska pleads for Casimir's life but is unsuccessful. The act closes as Casimir is unclothed and bound to the untamed black stallion. The horse rushes off and is subsequently seen climbing three ranges of hills, repeating a zigzag from left to right across the stage, ascending higher and higher. The curtain drops with the glare of torches in the foreground lighting Lady Olinska, who has fainted; her father, and Count Palatine.

In the second act, Mazeppa continues his wild ride. In the midst of a thunderstorm, the wild horse and Casimir come into view, crossing over the hills until he reaches the front. The horse is chased by wolves, is pursued by a vulture, fords a river, and finally comes ashore. Shepherds rescue the exhausted stranger. By a stroke of luck, the wild stallion has carried Casimir back to his own country, where the King of the Tatars recognizes him as his long-lost son, Mazeppa. The act ends as Mazeppa and his father mount their horses, planning to attack the Poles.

In the third act, Prince Mazeppa returns to Poland to find his true love. Riding the now-tamed black stallion, Mazeppa avenges himself against those who kept him in servitude. By the final curtain, Mazeppa stands with his arms around Lady Olinska. Defeated Poles and triumphant Tatars fill the scene, which is lighted by a forest fire. All ends happily, with the main characters fully dressed in regal costumes.

Milner's play, well-received by British audiences in 1831, premiered in New Orleans in February 1833. Two months later, it opened for audiences in New York City. By 1836, smaller cities, such as Louisville, Kentucky, had staged productions, and in April 1838 *The Wild Horse of Tartary* reached St. Louis. The Mazeppa vogue spread throughout the country in the 1840s and finally reached California in 1851. At one point, five different productions of the play were showing in San Francisco.[3]

Over the years, numerous male actors and their horses won recognition in the role, including Mr. Lewellen and his horse Timon and William Derr and his horse Don Juan. In some cases, the animals became better known than the actors.

Frequently, *Mazeppa* was staged with a mannequin tied to the back of the horse to prevent injury to actors who lacked equestrian skills. Treadmills and moving panoramas created the illusion of passing scenery. The "untamed steed," commonly played by a mare or a gelding, generally cantered or walked through the wild ride of Acts I and II. In time, the *Mazeppa* spectacle became so familiar that it gave its name to the elevated platform and the zigzag, which subsequently appeared in many other horse operas. Everyone called this the "Mazeppa run."

In the 1850s, numerous Mazeppa burlesques poked fun at the play. Two popular versions were subtitled *The Fiery Untamed Rocking Horse* and *The Wild Steed of Williamsburgh*. By 1861, *Mazeppa* was a well-worn melodrama in dire need of revitalization. A fresh approach came in the form of Adah Isaacs Menken, a young American actress who pursued celebrity status with single-minded dedication. From her debut on a New Orleans stage in 1857, Menken became a national figure in just a few years, famous for being famous. As in Lord Byron's case, Menken's unconventional — some would say scandalous — personal life only increased the trajectory of her professional career. In June 1861, Menken transformed the hackneyed play by taking on the title role of Mazeppa in Albany, New York.

Although other women had played the Tatar prince before her, Charlotte Cushman and Charlotte Crampton among them, Menken set a precedent by having her manly attire torn from her body onstage and having herself lashed to the horse. Cushman and Crampton had avoided portrayals that resembled bondage and had kept their breeches on, limiting exposure of their skin. In contrast, the semi-nude Menken appeared supine on the horse's back in a sexually provocative pose.

Menken's timing was fortuitous: the combination of sex and danger captivated audiences of the Civil War era, and the role became an international sensation. For the next few years Menken traveled widely, performing Mazeppa and other roles that called for cross-dressing. Historian Renée Sentilles has thoroughly analyzed Menken's appeal and the popularity of gender-bending art forms during the mid-nineteenth century. If one reads Sentilles's biography of Menken, the reader will find many contrasts between Menken's brief life, which ended in 1869, and that of Agnes Lake.[4]

Because of her interest in theatrical uses of horses, Agnes Lake probably saw a Menken performance when the actress played at Wood's Theatre in Cincinnati from December 9 through December 21, 1861. Agnes often attended theater performances when she was in Cincinnati with her family.[5] "[Menken] draws like a magnet, and fascinates like a siren," reported the *Cincinnati Daily Commercial*.[6] During the run, Menken appeared in numerous productions that featured her in male roles: *The French Spy, Dead Shot, Jack Shepphard, Black-Eyed Susan*, and *Joan of Arc*.

Menken appeared in at least thirteen different plays during twelve days of performances, a demanding schedule. She did not perform *Mazeppa*, however, primarily because she had not brought a horse. *The Wild Horse of Tartary* required a fierce-looking animal that nevertheless behaved dependably—a well-trained creature that would not be startled by loud noises or flickering lights. The logistics of transporting a four-legged performer — problems circus troupes routinely solved—were more difficult for an inexperienced actress traveling without an entourage. Menken was primarily an actress, so an equine costar was of minor importance to her and her fans.[7] Unlike the case with her predecessors in the role, advertisements for her performance never mentioned the name of the horse.

Although Mazeppa was Menken's most famous role, it did not become her principal role until late 1862.[8] That year, Menken played in Cincinnati once more. The National Theatre engaged her from October 13 through November 8. Although Cincinnati audiences clamored to see her as the Tatar prince, she had not brought a mount. Where could Menken find a trained horse on short notice?

According to the *New York Clipper*, it was "Old John" Robinson, Bill Lake's former partner, who loaned Adah Isaacs Menken a horse.[9] For five performances, October 20–25, Cincinnati audiences saw the signature play. "Unquestionably, Mazeppa is the most brilliant and fascinating role in which Miss Menken has yet appeared. There was a great rush to see her last night and the crowd will be still bigger this evening," reported the *Cincinnati Daily Commercial*.[10] Even if she did not provide the stallion, Agnes Lake was in Cincinnati and probably witnessed Menken in the legendary role.

Menken finished the Queen City engagement, then left for tours in Maryland, California, England, and France,[11] where she played the Tatar prince to crowded theaters. Critics attacked her dramatic talent, but audiences turned out to see the scandalous actress.

In the wake of Menken's success, other women with various levels of equestrian and acting talent played Mazeppa. One even called herself "Adah I. Montclain," obviously hoping audiences would confuse her with the more famous actress.[12] Kate Vance (1840–67) built a countrywide career with the play. Lizzie Wood gave top billing to her horse, Black Bess, who apparently had more training than the actor. One accomplished equestrian, Kate Fisher (c. 1840–1918), rode the Tatar horse during a career much longer than Menken's. Among her nationwide appearances was a two-week stint in the Nashville Theatre beginning November 9, 1863, while Lake & Company's Great Western Circus played on the lot nearby.[13] The theater did a booming business every night, and Agnes Lake could not fail to notice the reception the show received. In March 1866, in Zanesville, Ohio, where Lake's circus wintered, Kate Fisher, riding Minnehaha, performed *Mazeppa* during a sold-out six-night run at the Zanesville Theatre-Music Hall.[14]

Like Agnes's feats in the circus ring, playing Mazeppa in a theater had dangers: Fisher fell from her horse on November 20, 1863, and missed the final performance of the Nashville run.[15] Actors often suffered onstage mishaps and were seriously injured, and at least one female Mazeppa, Leo Hudson, perished as the result of a performance-related accident.[16] Even the seasoned performer Adah Isaacs Menken sustained broken fingers, a torn ear, and a concussion from falling while performing the title role.[17] Horses fared even worse: Black Bess and a string of other mounts suffered fatal injuries during their stage careers.

Females playing Mazeppa were not the only ones to provide a reinterpretation of the old play. Male actors also introduced new sexuality to the drama. One of the best male equestrians to play Mazeppa was Robert E.J. Miles, who rode his horse Hiawatha. Miles enjoyed his success in the theater and later became a circus proprietor. A new round of burlesques, such as *The Wild Steed of Bohoken*, played off the Mazeppa craze after Menken breathed new life into it. *Mazeppa* went on to become "the most frequently acted drama in the world apart from Punch and Judy."[18]

One classified advertisement in the *New York Clipper* on May 27, 1865, showed how much Menken and her contemporaries had revitalized horse operas:

WANTED

AN ACTRESS FOR THE EQUESTRIAN BUSINESS,

For Mazeppa and other equestrian dramas. Good looking and good form. Send carte de visite with particulars. Salary good and sure for one year.[19]

*   *   *

In 1865, Agnes Lake began to adapt *Mazeppa* to fit her own style. Agnes and Bill Lake had prided themselves on providing wholesome family entertainment. Journalists had always described the Lake circus as "chaste" and "free from vulgarisms," so adapting the provocative play was not only a risk but a drastic change of pace. Although Agnes wore shortened skirts for her wire-walking performances, they were never shorter than the knee. Off the circus lot, she always dressed like a lady, wearing a corset and hoop skirt that created a fashionably smooth silhouette while keeping her body rigidly incarcerated.

Contrary to the perception of performers leading scandalous lives, Agnes Lake's personal life lacked anything that would raise eyebrows: she had been married to the same man for nearly two decades — in contrast to Adah Isaacs Menken, who had gone through at least four husbands and several high-profile liaisons in about half that time.[20] Approximately ten years older than Menken,[21] Agnes Lake was the hardworking mother of two children (Alice and Emma) and a wife who devoted her energies to helping her husband run the family business.

With a biography that lacked titillating details, Agnes approached *Mazeppa* in her own manner, emphasizing her athletic skills rather than sexuality. Agnes learned and performed the Milner play as a conventional stage production. While Menken considered her horse an afterthought in preparing for her role, Agnes Lake trained her animals carefully. Menken borrowed horses for brief runs of *Mazeppa*, but Agnes Lake always traveled with her own mounts that were schooled to respond to the cues she gave them. Whereas Menken raised her visibility with highly publicized photographic sessions, Agnes rarely sat still long enough to create a picture. Menken mastered the art of publicity while Agnes worked to perfect her artistry. Finally, the production was ready, and Agnes planned to tackle Europe with a publicist, one other equestrian, William Jason Smith (d. 1874), and her horses.[22]

*   *   *

Agnes and Bill Lake opened the 1865 tenting season in Zanesville, Ohio, on April 20. They had painted, refitted, and repaired their wagons for the grueling season ahead.[23] Newspaper advertisements indicated that "Lake & Company" were the proprietors of the "Hippolympiad" (spelled with one "o"), a coined word intended to combine the elements of "horses" and "outstanding athletic accomplishments."[24] (Although many alternative spellings appeared in print, "Hippolympiad" and "Hippoolympiad" among them, this book will use Hippo-Olympiad in subsequent references to the Lakes' circus.)

By this time "& Company" was Agnes, every bit her husband's partner in show business, although it was not until 1867 that she was recognized with the title "Manageress."[25] The circus lumbered along roads in Ohio, Michigan, Indiana, and Illinois, playing six days a week, two shows a day. Along the way, they spent a week in Louisville and a week in St. Louis. By mid-October the season was over, and the show was back in Zanesville for the winter.

Although Agnes Lake started the season as a rider and wire walker, by August she had vanished from the bills, leaving Bill Lake and the children to finish the tour and bed down the circus stock in

MAMMOTH PAVILION
CIRCUS!

Fifth Street, between Pine and Chestnut, rear of the Planters' House.
WM. L. THATCHER, sole Proprietor.   WALTON RICH, Director.

☞ **THERE WILL BE A GRAND**
DAY
PERFORMANCE,

THIS DAY, commencing at half past 2 o'clock.

SATURDAY EVENING, AUGUST 10,

The performance will commence with a Grand Entree, entitled, the

SONS OF FREEDOM!

COMIC SONG, - - BY THE CLOWN.

GROUND AND LOFTY TUMBLING!

BY THE NUMEROUS ARTISTS.

Grand Principal Act of

HORSEMANSHIP,

BY MR. MATEER, *without Saddle or Bridle.*

Mr. LAKE AS

THE CHINESE DELPH SPINNER!!

PEASANT'S FROLIC!!

By Mr. SHAY.

After which, the performance of

THE REAL VIRGINIA MINSTRELS.

MR. SMITH, one of the first Equestrians of the day, will appear, as the

SHIPWRECKED MARINER.

The whole to conclude with an amusing Afterpiece, called, the

GOLDEN FARMER!!

☞ Doors open at 8, and performance to commence at half past 8 o'clock.   ☞ No Ladies admitted unless accompanied by a gentleman.   ☞ No Smoking allowed in the Pavilion.

Fig. 15. Poster for the Mammoth Pavilion Circus for performances in August 1865, with William Lake listed as the sole proprietor. Agnes Lake was not billed because she was in Europe. Courtesy Missouri Historical Society, St. Louis.

MAZEPPA, - - MADAME AGNES LAKE.

Fig. 16. Agnes adapted the traditional stage play, *Mazeppa*, to her one-ring circus. She performed in Germany before Prince Karl in 1865 and kept the adaptation as part of her circus repertoire until 1873. Detail, *The Weekly Tribune,* July 31, 1869. Used by permission, State Historical Society of Missouri, Columbia.

Zanesville for the winter. Readers of the entertainment trade newspaper the *New York Clipper* had to wait several months for an explanation of her sudden disappearance.

Meanwhile, Agnes arrived in Prussia on October 27, 1865, accompanied by William Jason Smith, a thirty-year circus veteran who planned to direct and perform in the German production of *Mazeppa.* Traveling with them was a string of horses, including Linden, a new mount carefully trained for the role of the Tatar steed. Matthew V. Lingham (1832–81), an American actor, served as Agnes's agent and negotiated a contract for her to open at the Victoria Theater in Berlin. "Great preparations are being made for her debut," reported Lingham in a letter to the *New York Clipper.* "The piece will be played without any curtailment, and the beautiful scenes which have been omitted by all the Mazeppas in the States will be retained, and a tilt on horseback will be introduced by Mrs. Lake and Mr. Smith."[26]

On December 13, 1865, Agnes Lake debuted in the title role of

Milner's play. "Miss Agnes Lake will speak her role in German," the newspaper announced.[27] Curious to see the guest performer "from New York,"[28] a crowd of over 1,400 in formal attire filled the Victoria Theater. The performance was honored by the presence of His Royal Highness Prince Karl,[29] as well as a number of Prussian elite. A review of the proceedings appeared in Berlin's *Deutsche National-Zeitung* two days later:[30]

Berlin. Day before yesterday, an American, Miss Agnes Lake, performed in the Victoria Theater, presumably her début in Germany, to present herself both as an actress and equestrienne. Apparently, she is more secure in the saddle than in the buskin, which no doubt has to do with the fact that Miss Lake is able to use the German language only with difficulty[,] speaking with a heavy accent, thus depriving herself of the best effect. Although the audience showed great leniency, it was unable to follow the act properly, especially since the performer was obviously suffering from fear and shyness. The piece in which she exhibited herself is a "melodramatic play with songs," entitled *Mazeppa*. It gives the performer in the role of Casimir (Mazeppa) the opportunity to show her skills as an equestrienne. Her very first entrance is on horseback, likewise her appearance in the first act during the contest with her partner Mr. Smith. The riding contest is followed by a duel in which Miss Lake presented herself as a daring and skilful [*sic*] swordsman. But the main effect is produced at the end of the first act by the flight of the well-trained desert horse with Mazeppa tied onto its back. A second effect is made by the swimming horse in the second act. The theater management hosting this event left nothing undone to show the effects in the best light, the highpoint being Mazeppa's flight over the approximately 40-foot high bridge that was specially built for this purpose. There was no lack of encouraging applause for the guest performer. At times, the applause even rose to calls for encores. The cooperation of the theater members who did their best to contribute to the success of the play must be acknowledged with gratitude. We recognize the ladies Berl, LeSeur, the gentlemen Hänseler, Tietz and Guthery.[31]

The observation that Agnes Lake's German words were unintelligible may surprise the reader. Agnes had been speaking German all her life with her family and friends, but it was the dialect of Oldenburg, akin to *Plattdeutsch,* or Low German. The citizens of Berlin spoke *Hochdeutsch,* or High German, and had difficulty understanding the lines spoken by the "New York" native.

Far more difficult to understand is the comment that Agnes Lake displayed "fear and shyness." After all, Agnes was a well-seasoned ring artist. With Lake & Company's circus she routinely performed death-defying feats without a safety net and interacted constantly with audiences of all sizes and ages. Unfortunately, no other German critiques exist to compare with the single review presented here. Perhaps the writer misinterpreted hesitation as fear when complications with the staging caused delays in the action.

Agnes Lake's interpretation of *Mazeppa* focused on her skills as an athlete. The costume she wore in Act I (figure 17) was an abbreviated tunic, certainly not shocking. Daily attire for women at the time commonly called for about eight yards of fabric fashioned into skirts six feet in diameter, so many nineteenth-century audience members would have considered Agnes's *Mazeppa* attire daring. Even when she was lashed to the horse, Agnes's emphasis was less on exposing her body and more on her ability to stay on the steed through its stage cues. While Menken used her racy reputation and suggestive portraits to stimulate the sale of theater tickets, Agnes maintained an air of decorum in her trip abroad without her husband. If there was some conflict between the Lakes that prompted Agnes to attempt her solo act or a romantic link with William Smith, Agnes never raised those possibilities in public.

Although some audiences called for extended engagements, Agnes Lake's *Mazeppa* ran for only thirteen performances in Berlin. By Christmas 1865, Agnes and Smith were at liberty, casting about for other opportunities. Although Lingham attempted to obtain

Fig. 17. Agnes Lake as Mazeppa, circa 1865. Her show ran for two weeks in Berlin, where critics praised her swordplay and equestrian talents. From Gilbert Robinson, *Old Wagon Show Days* (1925).

other bookings, his extensive advertising proved unsuccessful in prolonging the performances. The *New York Clipper* printed portions from a letter from Lingham on February 24, 1866, in which he reported that Mrs. Lake and company would start for home about the middle of February, and they would be there in time to start the tenting season. Although she may have been disappointed with the lack of opportunities in Prussia, Agnes salvaged the trip by turning it into a purchasing expedition. When she returned to the United States, she brought additional animals for the show. The horses Zadd, D'Yalma, and Apollo were souvenirs of her trip to Berlin.[32]

Despite the cool reception in Berlin, Agnes could now honestly claim to have performed before royalty in Europe. She sailed home from the harbor in Bremen, the same port her family had left many years before, adopting Mazeppa's motto as her own: *Nil desperandum*.

On March 31, 1866, the *New York Clipper* reported on "Lake's Hippolympiad":

> Extensive preparations have been made by Mr. Lake for this season. He will turn out with some of the best broken trick horses, pad horses and ponies in the business. Mrs. Lake will shortly arrive from Berlin, Prussia, with several valuable horses. His baggage wagons and carriages (with but two or three exceptions) are entirely new, built by Mr. Clancy, of Zanesville. The Dolphin Chariot is one of the handsomest "band wagons" in the country. The company comprises the following: William Lake . . . Alice Lake, Mrs. Lake, Emma, Laura[33] and Master Willie Lake, [and] John Wilson.[34]

In addition to the human talent, Lake's advertising named key animal performers: the Spanish spotted mule, Don Carlos; the thoroughbred dancing horses, White Cloud and Spot Beauty; the highly trained ponies, Romeo and Juliet; and the German trick horse, Zadd.

Lake's Hippo-Olympiad and Mammoth Circus began its season on April 30. The show opened in Zanesville and continued on to Ohio, Indiana, Illinois, and Missouri. A week-long run in Cincinnati

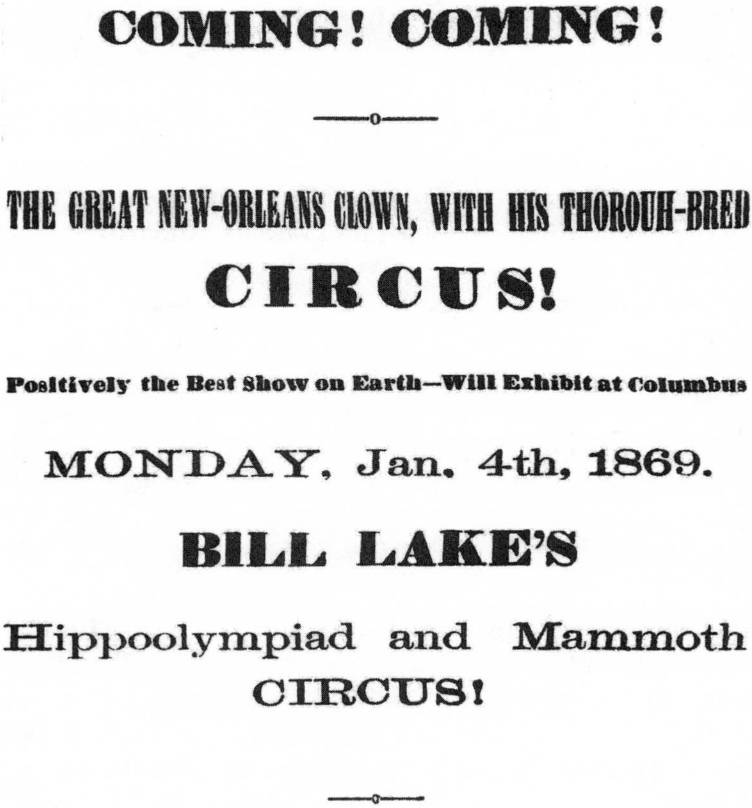

COMING! COMING!

———o———

THE GREAT NEW-ORLEANS CLOWN, WITH HIS THOROUH-BRED

CIRCUS!

Positively the Best Show on Earth—Will Exhibit at Columbus

MONDAY, Jan. 4th, 1869.

BILL LAKE'S

Hippoolympiad and Mammoth CIRCUS!

———o———

Fig. 18. By 1869, Bill Lake's Hippo-Olympiad and Mammoth Circus was one of the largest traveling tent shows in the United States, with 240 men and horses. From the *Daily Sun* (Columbus, Ga.), January 3, 1869.

and four days in St. Louis gave the Lakes a chance to see their relatives.

With each season the show developed a finer reputation, and the Lakes strove to introduce a new act each year. The circus did not have elephants or other exotic animals; it primarily featured horses, with a few mules for variety. What better way to celebrate horses than with *Mazeppa*?

Nevertheless, it took another year before Agnes had translated her *Mazeppa* performance to a format suitable for the circus ring. Beginning with the 1867 season, the Lakes used *Mazeppa* in their advertising:

MAZEPPA

Or the Wild Horse of Tartary

From Lord Byron's Poem, arranged for the ring expressly for Wm Lake, Esq.

Mazeppa ------ Mad. Agnes Lake

(As played by her over 100 nights at the *Victoria Theatre, Berlin, Prussia*) where she achieved a most unparalleled success both as *an Actress and Equestrienne* in which she will introduce her beautiful and thoroughly *Trained Horse Apollo*, the same used by her in Berlin.

Madame Lake will be assisted by a full and efficient company of *Dramatic and Equestrian Artists*, such as have never before been combined in One Show, and every effort will be made to render this the most interesting and exciting performance of the present age.[35]

The addition of the *Mazeppa* act paid off well for the Lakes, and their circus featured it every season until 1872. Even though the reception in Berlin had been far less enthusiastic than the advertising copy suggested, how was anyone to know?

No other circus in America had a segment based on the horse opera. Agnes showed her version of *Mazeppa* in at least twenty-one states and one territory,[36] in towns too small to have theaters, where Milner's play could never be offered as a stage show. Since the capacity of the Lakes' Big Top was about 2,500 people, at the rate of two shows a day and 150–200 stands per year, a conservative estimate is that at least 2 million people saw Agnes Lake as Mazeppa — a far greater number than those who saw Adah Isaacs Menken. Indoor theaters were commonly smaller than circus tents, with capacities of 1,500 or less. In addition, Menken never maintained the grueling pace of twice-daily Mazeppa performances for six to ten months a year typical of Agnes Lake's circus schedule. By reaching the masses with her performances, Agnes boosted the tale's popularity and helped make "Mazeppa" a household word.

*   *   *

While Agnes was working hard to promote her Mazeppa act at home and overseas, an untimely, although not entirely unexpected, death struck her family. Her youngest brother, Frank, died January 11, 1866, at age thirty-eight at the Kattenhorn residence at 10 West Ninth Street. After years of chronic illness, tuberculosis finally claimed him. While Agnes was in Prussia, her older sister, Elizabeth Kattenhorn, cared for Frank during his last days. When Agnes returned from Europe in March, she traveled to Cincinnati to mourn and to help settle Frank's meager estate. Before beginning the 1866–67 circus season, Agnes visited Frank's grave in the cemetery where he had been buried near their father.

Among his siblings, Agnes may have been uniquely affected by Frank Mersman's death because of the possibility of a direct link between them in the person of Emma Lake. Specifically, the authors speculate that Emma was not the biological daughter of Agnes and Bill Lake but of Frank Mersman and possibly a woman named Margaret Simmons.

The belief that Emma Lake was not Agnes and Bill's biological daughter is not immediately obvious, especially since they never referred to Emma as an "adopted child," as they did with Alice and, later, "Little Willie," the children the Lakes adopted during their marriage. However, closer inspection of certain legal documents and photographic evidence opens questions about Emma's parentage and suggests an alternate scenario in which Agnes and Emma were not mother and daughter but actually aunt and niece. Unfortunately, no definitive documentation of Emma Lake's birth has been located, and Agnes's accuracy regarding birthdates, as shown in so many instances, was unreliable. Born before the introduction of birth certificates, Emma might have been baptized in a Catholic church, just as Agnes had been, but no record has been found.

One source that raises questions about the nature of the relationship between Agnes and Emma is the U.S. Census. In 1870, Agnes and Emma Lake were entered in the census enumerator's log within minutes of each other while living on their property in Kentucky. Agnes clearly lists Prussia as her place of birth, yet Emma claims her mother was native-born and her father was foreign-born. These contradictory statements, presumably made in each other's presence before the census enumerator, appear to eliminate the likelihood not only of Agnes as Emma's biological mother but also of Bill Lake as Emma's biological father, since he was not foreign-born but had presumably been born in New Jersey. Assenting evidence appears in the 1900 Census, when Agnes, living with Emma and her husband, Gil Robinson, stated that she had no living children.

Another document that may shed light on Emma Lake's true origins is an indenture agreement signed February 12, 1866, by one William Lake assuming custody of a seven-year-old girl named Emma from her mother, Margaret Simmons. Before adoption procedures were standardized, such an agreement could have been used by a parent to consign a child to another family's care:[37]

> Indenture of Emma Laura Simmons
> from Margaret Simmons to William Lake
> Received and Recorded March 16th 1866
> This indenture witnesseth, that Margaret Simmons of the City of Cincinnati Hamilton County Ohio and mother of Emma Laura Simmons (the father of said Emma being dead) herewith binds out her child whose age is seven years to serve as a servant unto William Lake for the space of eleven (11) years as provided by an act concerning apprentices and servants passed March 8, 1831, and other laws upon this subject to serve him said Lake until the first day of January 1877 at which time she will be eighteen years of age should she be living, and the said Margaret Simmons hereby covenants to make herself individually liable for any and all such service done by said child. And the master William Lake hereby covenants to raise the said child with care and kindness and further covenants that he will furnish the said

child with the proper necessaries of life including medical attendance and medicines as her necessities may require during the term of service and will at the expiration of the term of service aforesaid furnish the said child with a new Bible and at least two suits of common wearing apparel one of which shall be new and suitable for church garment and the said William Lake further covenants with the said Margaret Simmons that he will and in all other respects comply with the acts entitled as aforesaid and all other laws upon this subject passed as to be passed and will teach endeavor to teach or cause to be taught to read and write and so much arithmetic as shall include also the first four rules of arithmetic and the said William Lake further covenants with the said Margaret Simmons to secure to and for the sole use and benefit of said minor any money or moneys that may come into his hands during said term of service that said minor may be so entitled to Witness our hands and seals at Cincinnati this twelfth (12) day of February AD 1866.

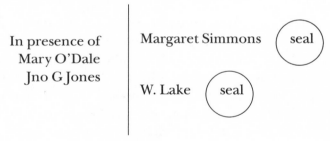

In presence of
Mary O'Dale
Jno G Jones

Margaret Simmons   (seal)

W. Lake   (seal)

Jno. G. Jones was a notary, Mary O'Dale's identity is unknown, and no further information about Margaret Simmons has been found. No William Lake other than the circus performer was listed in the 1866 Cincinnati city directory. If this is indeed an agreement regarding the future Emma Lake, it provides valuable information about her birth name, the identity of her biological mother, and how she came into Agnes and Bill Lake's care. The timing of the document, drawn up less than a month after Frank Mersman's death, may be significant. However, despite this circumstantial evidence, it is impossible to say with certainty that this indenture agreement refers to the same man who married Agnes Mersman and swept her into a life with the circus.

If the suggestion that Emma was not the biological daughter of Agnes and Bill Lake is accepted thus far, the question remains of why Agnes's brother Frank is connected to the story. The answer begins with visual comparisons of photographs that show physical similarities between Agnes and Emma striking enough to suggest that the two were biologically related in some way. Moreover, obvious similarities can also be found in pictures of Agnes's brother Joseph Mersman, the only one of Agnes's siblings of whom photographs have been found. Using imaging software, scanned photographs of Agnes, Emma, and Joseph were digitally superimposed upon one another. The result revealed a surprising number of similarities. The unique sloping of their eyes, the distances between the pupils, their brow lines, and their mouths aligned almost perfectly, despite the fact that the pictures were taken at different stages of their lives — Agnes was about thirty-three, Emma was forty-six, and Joseph was twenty-seven when the various photographs were made. Notably, when a digital image of Bill Lake replaced the image of Joseph for comparison, no significant similarities between Emma and Bill were identified.

Given photographic evidence that suggests a potential biological link to Agnes's family, the most likely candidate for Emma's father would be Agnes's younger brother, Frank. Agnes's older brothers, Henry and Joseph, are unlikely because of geography and their business standing within their respective communities. No evidence suggests that Frank ever married, but based on what is known about him through Joseph's diary, which indicates that Frank was socially and financially unstable, it would not be out of character for him to father a child out of wedlock. Furthermore, if Frank's family became responsible for raising his child after his death, his sister Agnes was a logical choice for a guardian. Henry predeceased his youngest brother in 1864, and Agnes's older sister, Elizabeth, may have been too old or unwilling to care for Emma. Joseph had lost his vision by 1864 and was undoubtedly suffering other effects of the syphilis that eventually killed him in 1892.

If the indenture papers signed in February 1866 between Margaret Simmons and William Lake are indeed connected to this family, a fuller picture of the situation may be coming into focus. If Margaret Simmons and Frank Mersman were Emma's biological parents, it is impossible to know the extent of their relationship, but one can deduce that after his death in January 1866, any financial support he may have provided for the care of their daughter would have ceased, prompting Margaret to seek alternative means of support — such as the indenture agreement with Emma's uncle, William Lake.

This theory of Emma Lake's origins is complicated by conflicting information about her date of birth. Gilbert Spalding claimed Emma had been born on the *Floating Palace*,[38] which would indicate a timeframe between June and December 1852 or early 1853. Emma's death certificate states that her birth date was February 22, 1855, and that her parents were Agnes and Bill Lake.[39] The completion of such a document, however, depends on the deceased person's survivors, who may have no firsthand knowledge of the facts. More tenuous evidence comes from circus rosters, which indicate that as early as 1857 a girl named Emma was appearing with the Lakes, dancing a hornpipe.[40] In 1876, while corresponding with Polly and Celinda Hickok, Agnes wrote: "Emma was Born on the 22nd of February Washington's Birth Day; only not the same year she was born [in] 1856."[41] Finally, the 1866 indenture agreement mentioned earlier indicates that the girl in question was born about 1859. Although the newspaper and the indenture contract may or may not refer to our Emma Lake, her age might have been misstated on any of these documents for numerous reasons, including professional ones.

Clearly, one challenge in researching circus people is sorting through the misinformation they and their managers created to enhance their images and heighten the public's curiosity. Josephine De Mott Robinson (ca. 1870–1920), an equestrian who dazzled audiences with her performances in many circus rings, noted: "Circus people never know how old they are, for their ages are usually shifted ahead, so that the authorities will let them alone. In fact, unless there is a birth certificate to prove the thing, some circus people never do know just how old they are."[42]

Shaving a few years off a young performer's age might enhance the wonder to audiences; in other cases, adding years might increase the attraction. P. T. Barnum claimed Tom Thumb, actually born in 1838, had been born in 1831, to make his small size more impressive to the throngs who came to see him.[43] Similarly, Barnum advertised Joice Heth, "George Washington's nurse," as a 161-year-old woman when she was actually half that age.[44]

While a definitive account of Emma's curious genesis has not been found, the explanation outlined here is plausible based on the vague information discovered thus far. However, beyond any preexisting biological or legal relationship between the two women, it is clear that Agnes and Emma developed a strong mother-daughter bond, as they were nearly constant companions until Agnes's death.

CHAPTER EIGHT

Building an Empire

Tempests, Triumphs, and Tragedies

1865–1869

Circuses clearly attracted some unsavory elements. The situation seemed to get worse in the years after the Civil War. Whenever a tent show raised its canvas, every good-for-nothing loafer in the county showed up for a day of amusement and gain. Petty criminals flocked to circus lots looking for ways to fleece the crowds. Circus workers referred to the gawkers who came to watch the canvas men set up and take down the show as "lot lice." Additional uninvited followers simply showed up at stands and made their living from their dealings there. Crooks with shell games often set up tables near the circus tents, offering opportunities to make bets. They palmed the peas, thus guaranteeing that the gamblers would never win. Card sharks shuffled their decks for a variety of wagers, all calculated to strip the unwary of their cash.

Pickpockets had a field day: while onlookers were distracted by the wonders of the show, nimble fingers removed their wallets and the contents of purses. In Springfield, Illinois, in the summer of 1865, a character who gave his name as James Foutch was arrested at the Lakes' circus after a foiled attempt to steal a soldier's wallet.

"The soldier, finding somebody's hand in his pocket, thought it [was] one of his comrades attempting to play a trick upon him, but on turning round discovered the person to be a stranger and immediately knocked the fellow down several times," reported the Springfield *Illinois Journal*.[1] The soldier rescued his $175 in cash, and Foutch was prosecuted in the local court a few days later. Such experiences were common when tent shows came to town.

Worst of all, violence became an uninvited patron at tent shows. Bullies and loudmouths directed their aggression against circus folk, who were transients. Without local contacts to protect them, canvas men and hostlers dealt with physical assaults and even gunfire. When unexpected violence erupted, circus folk summoned help from their comrades with the shout "Hey Rube!"

The brutality often had no specific inciting factor. At the start of the 1866 season, the John Robinson Circus was exhibiting in Crittenden, Kentucky. On March 25, 1866, a gang of ruffians attacked the circus troupe, using fists and firearms. Among the casualties were two sons of the owner, James D. Robinson and John Robinson, Jr., and a nephew, John Alec Robinson, who died of his gunshot wounds in Cincinnati a month later.[2]

Nine months later the *New York Clipper* reported another episode of ruffianism. Winona, Mississippi, was the scene of an attack on Mike Lipman's Colossal Combination Circus, a troupe with about sixty members. In the dead of night, several hundred towners ambushed the train carrying the show and fired guns into the windows. One band member was killed, and several were injured.[3]

Because the circuses attracted petty criminals and scam artists, it is not surprising that newspapers printed their distaste for the traveling shows. Before Agnes's troupe arrived in Sandersville, Georgia, in December 1869, one editor printed his revulsion for circuses and wondered why people flocked to them:

> We cannot understand why it is people are so anxious to see these great humbugs. . . . [E]very one that comes along has something that has never been seen before in America. . . . It would no doubt, be a benefit to the morals of the country, if

every paper in the State would adopt that rule [not to advertise the circus]. . . . One circus in a community will do more
harm, leave more low, vulgar sayings behind it after one performance, than anything that could be brought into it; and yet
everybody, almost, patronizes them. It is strange but true.[4]

One editor directed a caveat to the citizens of Bainbridge, Georgia,
hoping to dissuade them from attending the upcoming circus: "We
hope our people will keep away from it. No institution of the EVIL
ONE is in our judgment, more demoralizing, corrupting, destructive
of the best interests of society than a circus. Do not go; we entreat
both the young and old not to go to the circus!"[5]

Even with such savagery threatening circuses and town leaders
loathing their arrival, the Lakes were undeterred. Although they
encountered hostilities at various places, they never turned back
from their scheduled routes.

*   *   *

On April 20, 1867, Lake's Hippo-Olympiad and Mammoth Circus
commenced its season in Columbus, Indiana. The route took the
troupe through seven states, from Indiana to Nebraska to Arkansas.
By Christmas 1867, they were still on the road in eastern Texas.

The complexities of moving a circus by wagon through eight
states in as many months called for specialized jobs for company
members. In addition to the performers, the Lakes' circus employed a manager, treasurer, boss canvas man, boss hostler, and
watchman. Although there were a score of canvas men (who han-
dled the tents) and as many hostlers (who cared for the stock and
drove the wagons), male performers might be called on to help with
tasks that required additional strength.

Preparing the way for the company took a skillful advance team.
In 1867, no women undertook these assignments for any show, so
male pronouns are appropriate in this description of the routine.[6]

An advertiser, traveling with a horse and light buggy, started
fifteen or twenty days ahead of the company. His duties were to

secure a lot, obtain a license, and make arrangements to board the humans and horses.

The paste brigade followed a day later with a wagon full of pictorial bills. He posted the town with notices about the upcoming performance(s).

The writer arrived about ten days in advance of the show and contacted the newspapers with advertising copy and short bits suitable for local news sections.

On the day of exhibition, the canvas wagon entered the town. Canvas men then set up the tent and prepared the ground for the ring.

The agent arrived an hour before the rest of the troupe, assigned accommodations for performers, and checked preparations for horses at the stables. If there was no hotel large enough to accept sixty-plus guests, individuals might be lodged at private homes whose owners were pleased to have the extra income.

When the company arrived at the outskirts of the town, the performers prepared for a parade through the streets. First came the bandwagons, then performers in light wagons, then the luggage vans. Following the procession, performers might have time for a nap. The midday meal was at noon. The afternoon show began at 2 P.M. and lasted two hours. Supper was at 6 P.M., and the second performance began at 7 P.M. By 9 P.M. the show was over, and the canvas men immediately began taking down the tent.

The distance to the next stand (or town) determined the time for breakfast and departure the next morning. The heaviest wagons, which traveled only four or five miles per hour, carried the canvas and almost always started at midnight to make sure they would reach the destination on time. The rest of the troupe might have breakfast at 3:30 A.M. and be on the road an hour later. Occasionally, if the route was long and the roads in bad condition, the performers would start as soon as the show ended and travel all night.

The treasurer was generally the last person to leave the town. His task was to pay lodging bills and any other remaining expenses.

Traveling rapidly in a horse and buggy, he could catch up with the rest of the company and open the ticket wagon in time for the first show in the next town.

Wagon shows commonly visited towns about twenty or twenty-five miles apart and spent only one day in the small communities. The rigorous schedule resulted in endless fatigue among the workers. Although travel by moonlight on summer nights could be pleasant, rainstorms turned the unpaved roads into molasses. One member of Lake's company reported his experiences in the summer of 1867 to the *New York Clipper*:

> We have been stuck in the mud up to the hubs of the wagon wheels and been caught in three big rain storms. We started from Princeton, Ill., at four o'clock in the morning May 21st, for Toulon, and got stuck nine times. It is a seventeen mile route. We arrived at Toulon at seven o'clock in the evening of May 21st, too late to show, and as the roads were so bad we skipped the next stand, Victoria, and started for Galesburg, where we arrived at 10 o'clock on the morning of the 23rd. We pitched [the] tent and opened to a big house. The teams and men looked tired after going through a two days and one night's drive through some of the worst mud I ever saw. The mud in Illinois is like glue, it sticks tight to everything it touches.[7]

In 1867, the roster for Lake's Hippo-Olympiad and Mammoth Circus listed Agnes Lake as the show's manager, assisted by Dan Rhodes. Listed performers included Agnes, Bill, Emma, and Master Willie Lake (Little Willie) — but Alice, their oldest child, was absent.

Now eighteen, Alice had begun to pursue a career apart from the rest of her family. For some time she had been the star of her parents' circus; the *New York Clipper* called her "one of the most beautiful equestriennes in the business."[8] As a child, she was called the "Fairy Queen of the Arena," despite the fact that she was under ten when she received the title. As a six-year-old child, her riding was called "graceful and accomplished."[9] She won the admiration of

Fig. 19. Alice Lake, adopted by Agnes and Bill Lake, began giving daring performances on horseback in 1857. This undated photograph shows her circus costume, abbreviated to facilitate movement. Courtesy Harvard Theatre Collection, Houghton Library, Harvard College Library.

hundreds of fans and dozens of glowing reviews for her daring and bold equestrian skills. Her bareback riding act called for jumping through hoops while the horse circled the ring. Alice dazzled audiences with her poise and self-confidence and was a prize addition to any circus roster. For the 1867 season, Alice signed a contract with John Robinson's Mammoth Circus and Egyptian Caravan, and she was billed as "Mademoiselle Alice."[10]

The loss of Alice from the Lake's circus roster was likely a blow to her family, but it did not result in any obvious strain or animosity. Like her famous mother, Alice left her family and started a new life because she was in love.[11] The object of her affection was John Wilson (1844–1922),[12] a talented bareback and four-horse rider who had once been employed by her family's circus. A native of Cincinnati about five years older than Alice, Wilson had begun working for Robinson & Lake's Great Menagerie and Circus in 1862, so Alice had known him for several years. After the Robinson-Lake partnership dissolved, Wilson often worked for "Old John" Robinson, and in 1867 he was the show's equestrian director.

Details about Alice's wedding — the exact date and location — are not known. Her next mention, in the January 17, 1868, issue of the *New York Clipper*, is a report of an unexpected tragedy:

> Mrs. Alice Wilson, better known as Alice Lake, the adopted daughter of Wm. Lake and lately attached to John Robinson's Circus, fell overboard from the steamer *Laura*, on its passage from Mobile to New Orleans on Dec. 28th, near Grant's Pass,[13] and was drowned. Every effort possible to rescue the lady from a watery grave was made by the company, and officers of the boats, but all to no purpose. Mrs. Wilson had, just previous to the occurrence, lost overboard a valuable diamond pin, purchased in Mobile by her husband, and she was much affected in the consequence. It is supposed that she was looking over the side of the vessel, and becoming dizzy, tumbled overboard. She was a very clever equestrienne, and was well known in and out of the profession. She had been married but a short time.[14]

Neither the newspapers in Mobile nor the New Orleans press provided coverage of the accident. Circus people did not want negative publicity attached to their show. John Robinson's circus kept its schedule and opened in New Orleans without missing a beat. Distraught at the loss of his bride, John Wilson hired a small craft a few weeks later and searched the channel for Alice's body—he found it about twenty miles downstream from where she fell overboard.[15] Alice Wilson was buried in Spring Grove Cemetery in Cincinnati, Ohio, on April 6, 1868. Wilson mourned his loss, but eventually he married twice more. Although Alice was the daughter and the wife of two famous families, she has evaporated from circus history.

The death of her eldest daughter was not the first premature death Agnes had endured, but it was more distressing than the losses of her brothers Henry and Frank, whose deaths—related to alcoholism and tuberculosis, respectively—were slow and somewhat anticipated. The circus world lost a great equestrian when Alice Lake Wilson died, and Agnes suffered the first of several tragic deaths she would endure over the next ten years.

*   *   *

Agnes and Bill Lake started a new phase in their business strategy for the 1868 season. Outfitted with plenty of wagons, performers, and a small menagerie of animal entertainment, the Lakes began an ambitious twelve-month season rather than limiting their performances to the traditional itinerant season, usually April through October. Since the new business scheme kept the company moving, a steady stream of cash flowed into the treasury. The southern and western states offered thousands of venues and infinite travel itineraries, allowing the company to stay in southern states a month at a time. The company spent the winter months in the South to escape the frozen Midwest, while many contemporary circus shows spent the early months of 1868 reorganizing their rosters and refurbishing their equipment.

The Lakes traveled a grueling pace across Texas and Louisiana from January through March. In April, Agnes and Bill Lake turned north from Jackson, Mississippi, and visited smaller towns like Canton and Granada, traveling a route parallel to the modern-day I-55. After a three-day run at Memphis, the troupe followed the Mississippi River to riverfront towns in Illinois, including Cairo, and then traveled overland to Du Quoin and Mattoon. The ensemble headed west for a month in Missouri, including a week-long engagement in St. Louis, where Agnes and Bill undoubtedly visited friends and the Joseph Mersman family.

James A. Bailey, the young orphan who had joined Agnes and Bill Lake's troupe in 1861 and was now about twenty, was employed as general agent for Lake's Hippo-Olympiad. His name appeared often in the pre-show announcements, in reviews of performances, and—in 1868 and 1869—at the bottom of many circus advertisements.

WAIT FOR THE BOSS!
BILL LAKE'S HIPPO-OLYMPIAD!
—and—
Mammoth Circus.
Organized 27 Years Ago. And added to every year until it has become THE LARGEST AND BEST CIRCUS ON EARTH, Comprising 240 Men and Horses! . . . The only Traveling Exhibition in the World that Do What They Advertise![16]

Performances were held twice a day, at 1 and 7 P.M. Admission was fifty cents; children paid twenty-five cents. The advertisements promised stars culled "from the Prominent Companies of Europe and America" and stated that the show would go on, rain or shine. "The most astonishing mules," goats, and Shetland ponies delighted the crowds. "The sagacity of the trained dogs and monkeys is truly astonishing," one journalist reported.[17]

Agnes and Bill Lake created an aura of fantasy and excitement with a mile-long "Grand Procession" that was "headed by the Golden Dolphin Chariot," from which Professor Lutyen's Silver Cornet Band announced the arrival of the "Company mounted on thoroughbred Horses, arranged as Persian Cavalry and Knights of two hundred years ago."[18] The imagery surrounding the troupe — "the

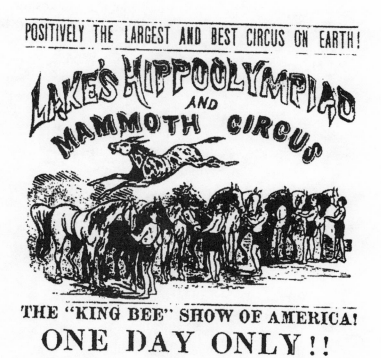

Fig. 20. In 1869, Lake's Hippoolympiad and Mammoth Circus played throughout Missouri. Detail, *Weekly Tribune* (Jefferson City, Mo.), July 31, 1869. Used by permission, State Historical Society of Missouri, Columbia.

days of Chivalry" and "the splendors of the Field of Gold" — drew on the Victorian audiences' fascination with the revival of medieval themes prevalent in the decorative arts and literature in the late 1860s. Romanticizing the "Persian Cavalry" and leaving a stream of "Gold and Glitter" added mystery and magic to the pomp and ceremony that awaited each audience.

After nearly a month in Missouri, the Lakes turned their wagons north to riverfront towns in Iowa. In July, Lake's Hippo-Olympiad traveled south, parallel to the Mississippi River, visiting Warsaw, Macomb, and Prairie City, Illinois. August was divided between Illinois and Indiana, and in September the troupe headed south again, reaching towns in Kentucky and Tennessee by the end of

October. By November the pace had slowed and the Lakes took a much-needed break, playing once in Florence, Alabama, and for two days in Columbus, Mississippi.[19] On December 14, the *Montgomery (Ala.) Daily Advertiser* ran an announcement that boasted of the famous Agnes Lake and her successful run in Berlin:

MAZEPPA.

OR THE WILD HORSE OF TARTARY

From Lord Byron's Poem, Arranged for the Ring,

Expressly for William Lake, Esq.

MAZEPPA,

MADAME AGNES LAKE

As played by her over 100 nights at the Victoria

Theater in Berlin, Prussia, where she achieved a most

unparalleled success, both as an

ACTRESS and EQUESTER

In which she will introduce her

BEAUTIFUL AND THOROUGHLY

TRAINED HORSE APPELLO,

The same Used by her in Berlin.[20]

In the grand tradition of celebrity, Agnes had exaggerated the number of her performances and the magnitude of her success in Europe. In Agnes's day, there was no equivalent to our contemporary mass media and hyper-vigilant paparazzi that could readily contradict her claims. What mattered to American audiences was not the exact number of performances but that she had in fact performed before royalty.

Ending 1868 in Montgomery, Alabama (December 18–19), the performers in Lake's Hippo-Olympiad, no doubt exhausted, were granted a short Christmas furlough. On January 2, 1869, the troupe performed in Crawford, Georgia, more than 230 miles from Montgomery. Despite the cold drizzle and subsequent flooding in Columbus, Georgia, that preceded the arrival of Lake's Hippo-Olympiad, Agnes and Bill Lake managed to thrill audiences as well as the editor of the *Daily Sun*: "Lake's Hippo-Olympiad. — Notwithstanding the flood, Lake's circus made a long and imposing procession on the streets yesterday morning. Two excellent performances were given in the afternoon and at night. Good audiences attended. They had to go through slosh, mud and pools to do so. Nothing [is] so attractive as a good circus troupe like Lake's."[21]

During the first five months of 1869, the Lakes trekked across Georgia, from Varnell to Cairo and from Augusta to La Grange. Joining Bill Lake, "the veteran Son of Momus," two other circus veterans headlined as clowns — Hi Marks, "the Humorist and Shakespearean Clown," and Al Aymar, the "Wit and Philosopher."[22] Both Marks and Aymar had performed alongside Bill Lake in the past. Marks had been a part of the troupe since 1867, while Aymar had been employed when Lake was still partnered with "Old John" Robinson.[23]

The newspapers that heralded their arrival reminded readers that "this establishment . . . is positively the Largest as well as the Best Traveling Exhibition on the face of the Globe."[24] Wherever Lake's Hippo-Olympiad traveled, their good reputation preceded them, as another journalist noted:

The great "Napoleon of Showmen" comes among us . . . in all the glory of his pageantry. . . . He comes favorably endorsed as having the "greatest, finest, and most wonderful exhibition" that ever visited the South. . . . [T]he Press speak unhesitatingly of its merits in the most wonderful terms. . . . Come, everybody, and give old BILL LAKE a welcome. The people *will* have fun and amusement, it is part of life, and there is nothing so pleasing as a Circus, with their Clowns' jokes and witticisms and the grand and lofty tumbling and somersaulting of Nature's children.[25]

In July of that year, the Jefferson City, Missouri, *Weekly Tribune* encouraged readers "not [to] confound this Mammoth Organization with the many different Shows that are perambulating the country, and style their inferior Circuses a Circus."[26] To ensure that every possible patron had a chance to attend their shows, Agnes and

Fig. 21. Lake's circus advertised in German-language newspapers wherever large populations of immigrants were found, such as Jefferson City and St. Louis, Missouri. Detail, *Der Fortschritt* (Jefferson City, Mo.), July 31, 1869. Used by permission, State Historical Society of Missouri, Columbia.

Bill Lake ran several simultaneous ads in *Der Fortschritt*, Jefferson City's German-language newspaper.

In Sandersville, Georgia, one journalist quipped, "If the people are as anxious to get to heaven as they are to attend places of amusement, Satan will have a small crowd in his domain."[27] The journalist continued his critique of the troupe's repertoire and noted that "Master Willie" and "one lady . . . [who] rode as well as any female performer" were highlights of the show. He also noted the audience's disappointment when neither "Madame Agnes" nor her prized mount Apollo performed in *Mazeppa*, especially "when so many hundreds . . . were so anxious to see her."[28] There is no explanation as to why Agnes did not perform as Mazeppa, although two months earlier, in Columbus, Georgia, the newspaper editor noted that *Mazeppa* was omitted because of "the sickness of the actress."[29] A similar malady probably prevented Agnes from performing her popular feat in Sandersville as well.

Even with all the positive reviews praising their performances, editors and journalists in Bainbridge, Georgia, continued to criticize the showmen's chosen lifestyle: "We enjoy a laugh — have a favorable opinion of one always in a good humor; but we think a man might be more profitably employed than to occupy his time and talents in making others laugh, or proving his agility by turning summer saults, or otherwise exercising his animal gifts in a circus ring. Immortals should aim at something higher, nobler and more useful."[30]

In March, while still in the midst of their Georgia route, advertisements reflected a change in Agnes and Bill's roster. John Lowlow replaced Aymar as the "Wit and Philosopher" for part of the month, and Professor Eckhardt took command of the Silver Cornet Band. Performances continued twice a day, in the afternoon and evening. Admission for the shows had increased to one dollar for most patrons, fifty cents for children under ten. The increased admission probably reflected higher lot-rental fees and other necessary costs to keep the show operating. Agnes and Bill Lake's "MAMMOTH THREE CENTRE POLE PAVILION" seated over 4,000 spectators and covered over an acre of ground.[31] Agnes's adaptation of Mazeppa with her horse Apollo remained one of the headlining acts, alongside the equestrian talents of "Master Willie" and Emma, "the Belle of the Arena."[32]

In late May the troupe turned north to Tennessee and was entertaining en masse in Kentucky by June. Before the show opened in Nashville in May, a new shipment of "wagons, horses, harness &c.," made by Hoblitzelle & Cousland of St. Louis, was delivered to Agnes and Bill Lake.[33] According to the *Missouri Republican*:

> This harness is what is known in the trades as the "Concord Stage Harness," and being silver-mounted and [with] letters, it presents a splendid show in a caravan of great length like that of Lake's immense concern. On the sidestraps of each wheel-horse's equipment, in large silver letters, you read, "Lake's Hippo-Olympiad," and on the pads, in similar letters, "Lake." On the blinds of the bridles the name "Lake" appears. There are ten sets of pony harnesses. Messrs. Hoblitzelle & Cousland got up no less than seventy sets of this splendid harness, ten of which was [*sic*] for the horses of the head wagon.[34]

The few advertisements that remain from June 1869 do not include *Mazeppa* as part of the featured acts. Perhaps it was an oversight at the printers, or Agnes may have sustained an injury during a previous engagement. In July the troupe headed west toward habitual stands in Missouri, where audiences were anxious for circuses after their annual hibernation. A week-long run in St. Louis brought Agnes and Bill Lake back to familiar ground. The circus set up at the corner of Twelfth Street and Washington Avenue for shows at 2 and 8 P.M. The lateness of the evening show was no doubt a result of the week-long engagement in the same lot, and the troupe also took advantage of longer daylight hours in the apex of summer. Advertisements for the circus were usually full of mirth, as this one, which testified to the humor and wit Bill Lake brought to the ring:

> On the swift wings of steam,
> Brightest Arenic dream

That was ever seen,
will be here:
Evoked by the will
And the magical skill
Of him, who is still
Without Peer.[35]

Poetic advertisements beckoned citizens from surrounding environs to enjoy the show:

Come — for a feast of unequaled delight
is presented for all at the circus to-night,
With a brilliant display of Olympian revels,
And all that can serve to dispel the blue devils.
Served up in a form, most delightful to take
By the Doctor of Momus, the famous Bill Lake![36]

In August, Lake's Hippo-Olympiad added Johnny Foster (1830–1906), "The Funniest Man Alive," and Ned Ainsley (dates unknown), "The English Trick Clown," to Bill Lake's clown roster. Foster and Ainsley filled the vacancies left by Aymar, Lowlow, and Sam Lathrop (d. 1870). Agnes resumed her *Mazeppa* act with Apollo. Hoping to quell the public's distaste toward itinerant shows, the Lakes assured audiences that "Polite Ushers [will be] in attendance to Seat Ladies and Children."[37] Creating an atmosphere suitable for ladies and children was paramount to Agnes and Bill as they endeavored to keep their circus free from vulgarity. The Lakes did not want their production confused with the troupes whose clowns told smutty jokes or that employed scandalous performers.

At long last, Agnes and Bill Lake were on the verge of achieving financial security and entertainment immortality. Lake's Hippo-Olympiad had a solid reputation as a world-class ensemble that provided daring yet wholesome family entertainment. The future was bright and promising. Under Agnes's constant tutelage, Emma and Little Willie began to achieve their own fame as equestrians. Agnes and Bill yearned for land near Cincinnati on which they

Fig. 22. William Lake Thatcher, shown here later in life, married Agnes
Mersman in 1846. The two used "Lake" as their surname for professional
appearances. Courtesy The York County Heritage Trust, PA.

could raise horses and continue their equestrian training between seasons. Agnes's adaptation of *Mazeppa* had been seen by tens of thousands and was highly praised. Newspapers all over the South and the Midwest declared that Lake's Hippo-Olympiad was the "King Bee" of shows, and Bill Lake was proclaimed "The Napoleon of Showmen!"[38]

*   *   *

After a summer of successful shows and high praise, the Lakes and their company traveled to Granby, Missouri, a remote hamlet in southwestern Missouri, about eight miles northeast of Neosho. Granby was visited infrequently by traveling showmen, so the town eagerly awaited the circus's arrival. The company arrived and the pre-show routines commenced: the canvas was erected on the dusty lot, the horses were watered and harnessed in their recital tack, and the performers slipped into their costumes and waited for the show to begin.

Agnes and Bill Lake surveyed the scene, proud that their perseverance and shrewd business sense in a fickle industry had at last paid off. They had even bigger plans for the future that included buying a horse farm in Kentucky, right across the river from Cincinnati, and seeing Emma and Little Willie succeed at their trademark feats.

Their dream was suddenly shattered, however, on a hot August night in Granby when violence changed the future of the show swiftly and permanently:

HORRIBLE TRAGEDY!
William Lake, Proprietor of the famous
Lake's Hippo-olympiad and Mammoth
CIRCUS
SHOT & INSTANTLY KILLED
BY A DESPERADO,
Who Escapes. A most wanton, cruel, cowardly Murder. Intense excitement among the PEOPLE. The community aroused and horror-struck. Parties after the MURDERER.[39]

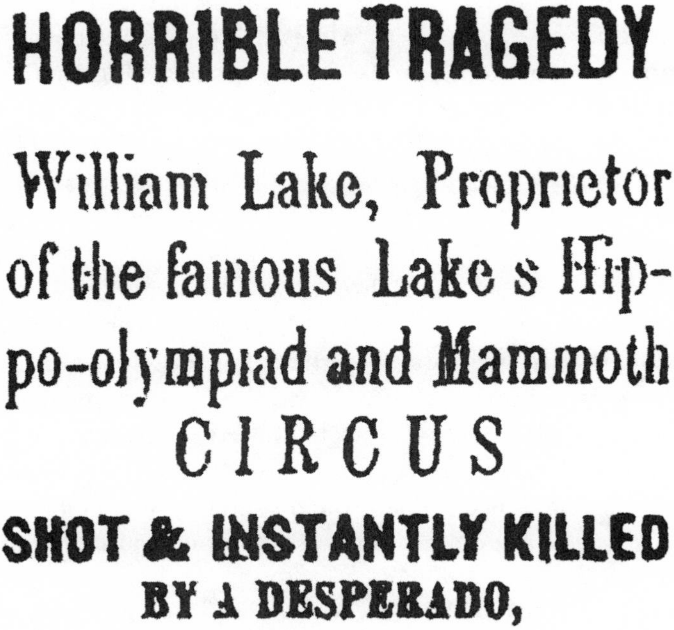

HORRIBLE TRAGEDY

William Lake, Proprietor of the famous Lake s Hippo-olympiad and Mammoth CIRCUS

SHOT & INSTANTLY KILLED
BY A DESPERADO,

Fig. 23. The murder of Bill Lake on August 21, 1869, in Granby, Missouri, made headlines in many states because Lake was well-known throughout the United States. Reports of his murder, Jacob Killian's flight from justice, and his murder trial in 1874 were published in newspapers from New York to Granby. From the *Spring River Fountain* (Mount Vernon, Mo.), August 26, 1869.

In the subsequent days, myriad newspapers in Missouri and as far away as the *New York Clipper* reported the shocking news of Bill Lake's murder. According to witnesses, the trouble began after the evening's regular performance on August 21, when ushers began clearing the canvas of patrons who had not paid to see the minstrel show, a bonus feature after the main event. A man named Jacob Killian (also spelled as Killyou, Killyon, and Killen) was found "secreted under a seat."[40] Bill Lake was summoned, and he grabbed Killian by the collar and ordered him to vacate the premises immediately or pay the extra admission. Killian "drew his revolver, which was immediately wrenched away from him and he was put out at the door of the canvas."[41] Killian stayed at the entrance for a few minutes, cursing and threatening to kill Lake "if he could get a revolver."[42]

A few minutes after the initial encounter, Lake went back behind the canvas to attend to business. Killian returned to the front door and told the doorkeeper that "he was not a quarrelsome man, and was willing to pay to go in." As Killian was paying the fare, he saw Lake return from inside the canvas and ducked behind other patrons, avoiding Lake's detection. Meanwhile, Deputy Marshal Bailey had been summoned and was informed that a revolver had been drawn. He inquired after the weapon's whereabouts, and Bill Lake replied that it was in his possession and he would relinquish it to the proper authorities in the morning. An article in the *Sedalia (Missouri) Weekly Bazoo* recounted what happened next:

> While they were talking, Marshal Bailey and a Mr. Thompson were standing facing Mr. Lake, not three feet from him. Killyon again approached from behind Thompson, and throwing his revolver over Thompson's right shoulder, shot Mr. Lake, the ball entering about three inches above the right nipple, coursing, apparently downward towards the heart. Mr. Lake staggered a few yards and then fell down on his hands and said "My God, boys, I am killed; carry me home." He was immediately carried to his room in the Southwestern Hotel, but expired almost as soon as it was reached.[43]

In the wake of the gunfire, "panic seemed to infect the bystanders and they all scattered."[44] In the chaos, Killian reportedly tripped and fell, accidentally discharging his weapon a second time before he disappeared into the night.

Agnes offered a reward of $1,000 cash for the "apprehension and delivery of the said Jacob Killian to the proper authorities of Granby."[45] The *New York Sun* later reported, "[I]t is rumored that [Agnes] was not nice about requiring that [Jacob] be delivered alive."[46] In September, Missouri's governor, Joseph W. McClurg, "by the virtue of the authority in me vested by law, for good and sufficient reason appearing," offered an additional $300 reward for Killian's apprehension.[47] Newspapers ran descriptions of Killian, and nearly every citizen of Missouri appeared to hunt for the "cowardly murderer," known by some newspapers as "A Republican Desperado":[48] "Jake Killyon is about 24 or 25 years of age; about 6 feet 1 or 1½ inches high; slim in figure, with light brown hair, florid complexion, and is blind or nearly so in his right eye, the socket of which is sunk deep in his head, and is badly disfigured."[49]

While there is no mention of her being present at the scene of Bill Lake's murder, Agnes rushed to her husband's deathbed. Moments later, Bill Lake died, having had one last look at his wife and the troupe he had made successful.

Agnes made funeral arrangements "under the auspices of the Odd Fellow's Lodge, of which order Mr. Lake was a member."[50] The Odd Fellows of Granby swathed their lodge room in mourning crepe, and the members of Lodge 113 donned the sartorial badge of mourning on all public occasions for the next month.[51] Bill Lake was buried on August 23, 1869, in Granby, Missouri.

The futures of Agnes, Emma, and the entire circus company were uncertain. Agnes was suddenly a widow at age forty-three, with two children, Emma and Willie, and a troupe of performers — unsure of her next move — depending on her. Agnes, although grief-stricken, was undeterred. She took command of the troupe and pressed on — continuing the dream she had started with Bill Lake.

CHAPTER NINE

Madame Agnes Takes Charge

1869–1871

Mourning rituals in nineteenth-century America dictated a strict set of guidelines that enabled the upper echelons of society to dramatically mourn their loved ones without offending "good society." Influenced by Queen Victoria's "fashionable mourning," books, pamphlets, and a variety of magazines — including *Godey's Lady's Book* and *Harper's Bazaar* — defined proper mourning etiquette for middle- and upper-class ladies. Rigorous dress, fabric, and jewelry specifications for each stage of mourning were carefully outlined. Authoritative articles espoused how to receive visitors during one's social confinement and how to carefully choose acceptable black-edged stationery for condolence messages. Women from wealthy families were expected to sequester themselves away from society for six months to two years, without attending social functions, while they quietly "honored" their deceased child, parent, or husband. These stringent conventions were expected of decent ladies. Men, however, were exempt from the majority of these rules because their business dealings could not be placed on hold while they retreated into an imposed year-long confinement.

Americans witnessed a grand spectacle of Victorian mourning during the funeral of President Abraham Lincoln in 1865. The funeral processions President Lincoln received in many cities were elaborate displays of Victorian America's mourning culture and rituals. Horses were capped in black plumes that bounced in the air, the caisson and carriages were draped with black bunting, and hundreds of mourners lined the streets. Men stood solemnly in black tailored suits and crepe shoulder sashes, and women wept behind mourning veils. Bill Lake's funeral in August 1869 was much less grand, but the shock waves from his death spread far and wide.

The circus community was stunned at the sudden and untimely death of Bill Lake on August 21, 1869. Lake's résumé included nearly a dozen companies during his thirty-five-year career, and he was finally enjoying the success of his own venture. News of his murder spread quickly. Headlines such as "BRUTAL MURDER," "HORRIBLE TRAGEDY," and "A SHOWMAN KILLED" were stamped across newspapers for weeks after his murder. Citizens in the towns near Granby were outraged at this wanton and unprovoked act toward Lake, and they vowed to catch Jacob Killian. The citizens of Sarcoxie, Missouri, were so livid upon hearing the news that they formed a committee and drafted "Resolutions of Respect to the Late William Lake, Esq.":

> The Committee reported the following for the action of the audience, which was read and unanimously adopted. WHEREAS, The citizens of Sarcoxie and vicinity, announce the killing of Mr. Lake a wanton, cruel, and cowardly murder, without the slightest provocation, thereby depriving the country of a well known and highly esteemed citizen; and furthermore, we hereby tender our heartfelt sympathies to the bereaved family and excellent Company, and assure them that we will use our utmost endeavors to bring to justice the cowardly assassin; and, furthermore, RESOLVED, That we kindly transmit a copy of these Resolutions to Mrs. Agnes Lake, and also a copy each to the MISSOURI DEMOCRAT, MISSOURI REPEBLICAN [sic], WEEKLY TIMES, Cincinnati, Ohio, and the CARTHAGE BANNER, Carthage, Mo., for publication. GILBERT SCHOOLING, Pres. H. HUBBARD, Sec'y.[1]

Unexpectedly widowed, Agnes was on her own for the first time in her life and was solely responsible for Emma, Little Willie, and hundreds of employees. Miles away from her sister Elizabeth in Cincinnati and her brother Joseph in St. Louis, Agnes drew strength from her circus family. She was surrounded by people she had known for twenty years, and together they honored Bill Lake's life and legacy.

Agnes contemplated her future as a proprietor; since she had so many employees depending on her for their livelihood, Agnes could not abide by society's protocol for mourning and quietly retreat into the Victorian conception of widowhood. The day after she buried Bill Lake, Agnes assumed sole command of Lake's Hippo-Olympiad. According to Gil Robinson, she gathered her employees and announced her plans: "Although Mr. Lake is dead . . . I intend to carry on his circus just as though he were here with us. If any of you think I am incapable, all I ask is that you will give me two weeks' notice and I will endeavor to fill your places. I am determined to keep the show on the road and I shall succeed."[2]

It is not known if any employees refused to work under Agnes's management and had to be replaced. Some accounts claim that all of her employees vowed to remain and that Agnes broke down upon hearing of their loyalty. Printing costs consumed an enormous amount of the budget, so editing and resubmitting newspaper advertisements proved too costly for Agnes's circus; as a result, Bill Lake was mentioned as one of three headlining clowns throughout the remainder of the season. Or perhaps Agnes was so grief-stricken that she could not bear to remove his name from any part of the circus.

Agnes was determined to keep her circus alive, and she buried her grief in its managerial duties. She kept the show on the road and produced an amazing season. Throughout the fall and winter of 1869, Agnes led the ensemble to nearly one hundred stands and never missed a date. The company traveled throughout Missouri in September, where the *Morgan County Weekly Banner* in Versailles printed advertisements announcing that Agnes's "Indomitable Acrobats" and "Dashing Horsemen" would soon arrive. Performances were at 1 and 7 P.M., and admission had increased to one dollar for most patrons, fifty cents for children under ten.[3] The increased admission reflected the general uncertainty in response to the financial panic known as "Black Friday" that had rippled across the country,[4] as well as Agnes's fiscal precautions in case the show suddenly dissolved.

Agnes Lake's Hippo-Olympiad left Missouri and trekked across Arkansas in October. By November the ensemble had reached the warmer climates of Texas and Louisiana. According to the posters and handbills, Johnny Foster and Ned Ainsley were still conducting their clown routines. Reviews of the show failed to mention if a third clown was hired to replace Bill Lake. Professor Lutyen resumed his place at the podium and conducted the Silver Cornet Band during the Grand Procession.[5]

Meanwhile, the hunt for Jacob Killian continued. Physical descriptions of Killian were printed in dozens of newspapers all around Granby and throughout the state. Citizens from a wide area vowed to catch him for murdering their beloved showman, Bill Lake. On September 2, 1869, both the *Sedalia Democrat* and the *Carthage Weekly Banner* in Missouri reported that Killian had finally been captured nearly three hundred miles away in St. Charles, northwest of St. Louis. The *Carthage Weekly Banner* wrote that "a man with all the features and marks described [was] loitering on the outskirts of the town."[6] The paper also noted that "the man had come down the Missouri River in a skiff, and all his movements were suspicious."[7] The *Sedalia Democrat* confirmed that "he was found in a skiff, fast asleep" and demanded that Killian be given a "speedy trial . . . and let an example be made of the murderer."[8] Although Killian was captured in September 1869, his murder trial was delayed for five years for undisclosed reasons and will be examined in chapter 12. Redress for Agnes and the circus community was delayed until 1874.

The 1869 season ended in Memphis with a show two days before Christmas. Gil Robinson praised Agnes's ability as a manager, writing in his memoir: "Mrs. Lake's success as a circus owner and manager was remarkable and the show became a gold mine under her direction."[9] The *Missouri Republican* in St. Louis remarked that under her direction the troupe had "made the tour of Arkansas, Mississippi, and part of Tennessee, clearing over $20,000" (about $298,000 today).[10]

Agnes left the circus to winter outside Memphis. In January she returned to St. Louis to make preparations to have Bill Lake's body exhumed and brought to Cincinnati for a second funeral and burial, again under the auspices of the Independent Order of Odd Fellows. In addition to preparing the details of his funeral, the Odd Fellows escorted Lake's body from Granby, Missouri, to Cincinnati. They conducted the funeral and burial services in full regalia according to their own rituals in honor of their fallen benevolent comrade and friend.

Bill Lake's second funeral received extensive publicity from St. Louis to Cincinnati. The journey of Lake's coffin was chronicled in several newspapers, allowing the public to pay their final respects as the entourage traveled by steamboat or solemnly marched through the streets. Newspapers in St. Louis and Cincinnati printed announcements that the funeral "will take place to-morrow, at his late residence, No. 10, West Ninth Street."[11] The *Cincinnati Daily Commercial* printed short obituaries on January 12 and 13, 1870. The Odd Fellows printed a separate death notice for Bill Lake on January 13. Lake was reburied in Spring Grove Cemetery, where a rose granite obelisk marks his final resting place. On January 14, Cincinnati newspapers printed descriptions of Lake's grand funeral:

> The funeral of Mr. William Lake, the veteran showman, was largely attended, yesterday, by members of the profession, public officers and friends. The funeral was conducted by the Odd Fellows of Ohio Lodge No. 1. Mr. Lake was one of the oldest showmen in the country, being connected with circuses for the past forty-three years. . . . [He] was murdered by a drunken ruffian, in Southern Missouri. There were over forty carriages in the procession.[12]

Although hardly as grand as the publicity for Lincoln's funeral five years earlier, the media coverage of the transport of Lake's body

from Granby to Cincinnati was unprecedented for a circus performer. No accounts have been recovered that describe Lake's funeral in further detail, but Victorian trends would certainly have
been evident in the design of and detail on his coffin, black bunting
and crepe would have been abundant, and the horses were probably
capped with black plumes. The presence of forty carriages in the
procession is evidence that Lake was respected and deeply mourned.
Even the obelisk — representing the spiritual connection between
death and the afterlife — that marks his final resting place is an iconic
symbol of Victorian funerary art.

*   *   *

In February, while the circus troupe was still wintering in Memphis,
Agnes Lake realized that with "240 Horses and Men" depending on
her, she was gambling with too many careers and personal fortunes.
Even though Agnes had the expertise and stamina to run her own
show, women's second-class legal status handicapped her business
dealings. Despite her initial success after Bill Lake's murder, Agnes
decided to start the 1870–71 season with a scaled-back program
featuring only the best horses and a simplified roster. Agnes returned to Memphis, where she held an auction at the old race track
near Elmwood Cemetery. "GREAT SALE AT AUCTION OF HORSES &
CIRCUS PROPERTY Belonging to the late Wm. Lake, deceased," announced the newspapers.[13] The auction began on February 21 and
lasted several days. Extra cars of the Hernando Street railway line
were readied to transport the buyers and expected throngs of curious browsers.

Circus historian Thomas P. Parkinson documented the items at
auction, "suitable for a first class outfit," as reported to him by George
A. Huff, a circus proprietor who attended the event. Items for sale
included the Dolphin Chariot and the couture silver-trimmed har-
nesses recently purchased from Hoblitzelle & Cousland in St. Louis.
The list continued:

40 ring horses, 80 baggage horses, 1 band chariot, 1 ticket
wagon, 2 box wagons suitable for trunks[,] properties,

cages; 9 baggage wagons (including 1 pole wagon); large assortment of band, baggage & carriage harness[es]; 110' round top canvas; 40-foot dressing room canvas; seats, poles. . . . All wagons, harness and outfit were new the previous May (1869) and are in first rate order. The wagons were made by A. Wright of St. Louis and are "the best and handsomest ever placed on the road."[14]

A faded blue, lightly stained original auction catalog is located in the McCaddon Collection of the Barnum & Bailey Circus at Princeton University. Some of the ring stock for sale was labeled as the favorite mounts of some of the most popular performers: Billy Muggins, trained for bareback riding, had been ridden by Willie Lake for four years; and San Antoine was a thoroughbred "partly broken for dancing" by Agnes. Young Emir had been trained and ridden by Emma Lake for nearly two years, and Agnes's "celebrated [*Mazeppa*] and trick horse 'Apollo' " were also available at the auction.[15] It is unclear if all the horses were sold at the time because the same names appear in subsequent circus advertisements and reviews over the next four years. Other miscellaneous items included "12 spangled banners," chandeliers, saddles, bridles, plows, and sledgehammers.[16]

The auction was a success and helped Agnes Lake finalize the purchase of an eighteen-acre farm in Kentucky. Campbell County land records document a deed of sale dated January 22, 1870, from John and Elizabeth Ewing to Mary Agnes Thatcher.[17] The property named "Sunnyside" was supposed to have been the first home Agnes and Bill Lake purchased together. Their home in Cincinnati at 10 West Ninth Street was leased from Agnes's brother-in-law, Arnd Kattenhorn, but the dwelling was inside the city, and there was no room to board or train their horses. Agnes and Bill wanted more space to raise horses and practice riding during the circus season's interim.

Veteran showman Louis E. Cooke (1850–1923) wrote a series of articles for the *Newark Evening Star* in 1915 and 1916 in which he described many aspects of circus life. In his commentary published on October 7, 1915, Cooke explained that many circus performers preferred to live on farms and in quiet communities, "where they can get away from the noise and bustle their business keeps them in" throughout most of the year.[18] Seeking solace and rejuvenation away from crowded cities, Agnes and Emma settled on their new farm, located just across the river from Cincinnati, near Covington, Kentucky. The property featured a large, two-story farmhouse with weathered planks and black shutters. The columns and portico on the side of the house, shaded by a second-floor balcony, echoed traditional southern architecture. A sizable covered pavilion served as a training ring. Agnes still owned seventeen horses and planned to raise and train them on the spacious grounds. Emma honed her equine skills in the training ring during winter months when the circus was on hiatus. Pictures of the house, Emma's training pavilion, and Agnes, Emma, and Agnes's granddaughter and great-granddaughter, Daisy and Emma, were printed in the December 7, 1901, issue of *Billboard* magazine.[19]

The farmhouse, where Agnes and Emma resided, was the ninth dwelling the census enumerator visited in John's Hill Precinct, Campbell County, on July 15, 1870. Agnes Lake stated that she was a "Retired Show Woman" and was born in Prussia. Agnes's personal property and real estate were valued at $49,000, approximately $730,000 today. Emma Lake documented that she was born in Ohio and entered "at home" as her vocation. Little Willie was not listed with Agnes and Emma in Kentucky because Agnes relinquished her guardianship of the boy on January 26, 1870. Frederick H. Bailey, an old friend and longtime business associate of Agnes's, was appointed eleven-year-old Little Willie O. Dale's new guardian.[20] Now billed as "Master Willie," the youngster soon ventured out on his own. Over the next few years he joined several circuses and became a notable equestrian.

Also on the property were Andrew Levi, Horace Nichols, and William Hindley. Sixty-year-old Levi was a veteran showman and had been a rider, tumbler, and "general performer" employed by more than a dozen shows over a thirty-year period. Listed as a "servant" at

Sunnyside, Levi managed the stables and acted as the overseer when Agnes traveled with the circus. Nichols was another veteran rider, equestrian director, and ringmaster for numerous shows, including the Lakes' in 1869. Hindley has not been identified.[21]

Agnes and Emma Lake remained on the farm throughout the spring of 1870, preparing for the imminent season. Details of the 1870 season are scarce. It is possible that having buried Lake and sold much of the equipment, the Hippo-Olympiad did not perform until December. The roster is largely unknown, and only a few newspapers have survived that provide a glimpse of Agnes's activities. We do know that Agnes Lake added a new element, however, as reported by the *Times-Picayune*: the "grand balloon ascension, which in itself will repay [patrons] for the visit."[22]

Traveling through the southern states during the autumn, the condensed troupe performed across Louisiana before reaching New Orleans just after Christmas for a four-day engagement, December 29 through January 1, 1871. The *Times-Picayune* reported that Lake's Hippo-Olympiad and Mammoth Circus had erected its tent at the corner of Orleans and Bourbon streets, a few blocks from the Mississippi River. The newspaper confirms the dates and location in New Orleans but fails to mention the roster. Only *Mazeppa* was mentioned as one of the featured acts. The circus advertisement that ran on December 30 in the *Times-Picayune* was small and featured none of the familiar stock illustrations that had become associated with the Lakes' advertisements. A few words were set in bold font, but otherwise it garnered no special attention.

In previous seasons and in countless newspapers, advertisements for Lake's Hippo-Olympiad ran several columns wide across a page, included several detailed illustrations, listed featured acts and performers, and contained various font styles and sizes. The richly visual notices were designed to set their circus apart from rival companies, especially since newspapers printed several circus companies' announcements simultaneously. Agnes and Bill Lake had published fliers that promised a wealth of entertainment in their programs. By comparison, the lackluster notices in New Orleans

LAKE'S
Hippo-Olimpiad and Mammoth Circus.

Fig. 24. This unique 1871 advertisement for Lake's Hippo-Olympiad and Mammoth Circus under Agnes's management features a grotesque figure characteristic of a nineteenth-century clown in contemporaneous costume and facial makeup and is possibly homage to the late Bill Lake's popularity. Courtesy Pfening Archives, Columbus, Ohio.

blended into the rest of the newspaper. Was Agnes managing funds more conservatively, or did she believe that a show with a glowing reputation like hers needed no extra flash from the press?

Agnes Lake and her troupe celebrated the New Year in Mobile, Alabama, with a three-day exhibition, January 2–4, 1871. During the early months of the year the circus stayed in the South, reaching stands in Alabama, Georgia, and Florida. Traveling sometimes by boat but mostly in conventional circus wagons, Agnes Lake's Hippo-Olympiad navigated familiar terrain and visited established routes. Local newspapers reported:

> Madame LAKE, in rendering a grateful recognition for the manifold and of repeated favors she has received at the hands of the Southern people the many seasons the
> ### "HIPPO-OLYMPIAD"
> has exhibited in the South, is pleased to be enabled to assure her patrons that she visits them this season with a Troupe of the Leading Artists of the Day.[23]

Agnes Lake's advertisements started returning to their former glory, running nearly the length of the page and illustrated with the recognizable fonts and stock images of clowns, equestrians, and acrobats. Agnes recruited Robert E.J. Miles as general director to handle many of the logistics for booking performances. Miles was previously an educator and an actor, starring in his own theatrical adaptation of *Mazeppa* for a number of years. Before acting as general director for Agnes's enterprise, Miles had purchased and operated the DeHaven & Company show in 1870.[24]

That season, 1871–72, the *New York Clipper* reported a robust roster for Madame Lake's Hippo-Olympiad that included Emma Lake and Minnie Marks as riders, Charles Lowery, Don Ricardo, and the Lazelle Brothers as tumblers, and Hi Marks and John Davenport as the "jester" and "trick clown."[25] Emma Lake introduced Lone Star, a horse she had trained herself, and incorporated Young Emir into her performances. Agnes Lake performed in the manège act, the "high school" type of riding akin to dressage, on her familiar steed Robert E. Lee, alongside several performers on horseback.

Agnes guided her company to familiar stands without any delays. The season officially ended for Agnes Lake's Hippo-Olympiad on February 24, 1871, with a performance in Atlanta. Agnes and Emma Lake then returned to Sunnyside. During March, Emma practiced in her riding pavilion for several hours every day, perfecting her vaulting and manège routines. Many performers from the recent season, like Hi Marks and his daughter, Minnie, as well as John Foster, had placed notices in the *New York Clipper* advertising their availability for the upcoming season. Later that month "a number of circus managers" converged on Cincinnati and engaged veteran performers, "gobbling up variety talent for side shows"[26] in preparation for the approaching season.

During 1871, twenty-six circuses, including John Robinson's Great Combination Circus & Menagerie and Isaac Van Amburgh's Menagerie, were making the rounds of American towns. Agnes was the only woman leading a troupe. John Robinson's and Van Amburgh's rosters were swollen with talent recently employed by Agnes Lake. Hi and Minnie Marks, John Lowlow, and Eddie Trainor toured with Robinson. Van Amburgh had acquired Horace Nichols and Charles Lowery. Young Willie O. Dale, Agnes and Bill Lake's former charge, was a star equestrian in Van Amburgh's troupe. Also joining Van Amburgh's roster was the famous trick mule Mungo Park, purchased at Agnes's Memphis auction a year earlier.

Agnes Lake's roster was the smallest she had ever employed, only fifty men and women and thirty-two horses. Although small in number, the roster was anything but diminutive in talent or reputation.[27] Levi North remained as the equestrian director, and Emma Lake was joined by John Saunders, the "English rider and leaper,"[28] and by Master Orrin.[29] Joining the equestrian corps was Curly, "the only dog ever trained to do a principal act on the back of a horse while coursing at full speed around the arena: leaping over banners, through balloons, somersaulting, pirouetting, etc., with the ease of [a] practical equestrian."[30]

The 1871–72 show season started in April, and over two dozen companies fanned out across the nation in a race to entertain the masses. The "20th Annual Tour of Lake's Hippo-Olympiad," as it was now billed, started in Dayton, Ohio, on April 13, at the corner of Madison and Erie streets. Throughout April and during the first two weeks of May, Agnes and her troupe kept a steady course in Ohio and Illinois.

Agnes Lake continued to present her company's exciting new feature: the balloon ascension, which was free to the public prior to the main event. Circus historian Bob Parkinson studied the additions of balloon ascensions in circuses after 1870. Referencing Howard Scamehorn's *Balloons to Jets*, Parkinson noted that balloon ascensions gained popularity in traveling shows when postbellum circus crowds demanded newer and more exciting exhibitions. Circus historian William Slout remarked that balloon ascensions replaced the "traditional wire-walking act" before each show[31] — the same slack wire-walking act for which Agnes had become famous early in her circus career.

The earliest documented "manned" balloon was exhibited for the sole entertainment of Louis XVI in September 1783, when Joseph and Jacques Montgolfier placed a duck, a sheep, and a rooster inside the basket. Steering the vessel was awkward and often impossible because primitive ballooning flights were at the "mercy of the shifting winds."[32]

Some American outfits were established for the sole purpose of exhibiting balloon ascensions, including O. K. Harrison's Balloon Ascension and the Ericsson Hydrogen Balloon Company, which toured in the 1850s.[33]

Parkinson believed balloon ascension was suddenly reinvigorated in late 1870 when Paris was invaded by Prussian armies. French statesman Léon Gambetta escaped from the city by balloon in an attempt to raise an army in southern France to assist struggling troops in Paris. Gambetta's flight spawned immense publicity as the first balloon excursion with a predetermined destination and influenced dozens of American circuses the following year.[34] French-inspired names adorned balloons in nearly every circus — the James Robinson Circus labeled its balloon "The City of Paris" — and the

MONDAY, JULY 24, 1871.

LAKE'S HIPPO·OLYMPIAD
— AND —
MAMMOTH CIRCUS.

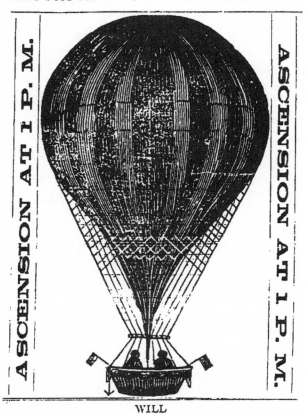

ASCENSION AT 1 P. M.

ASCENSION AT 1 P. M.

WILL

EXHIBIT AT CHEYENNE,
FOR ONE DAY ONLY

Fig. 25. During the 1871 season, Lake's Hippo-Olympiad and Mammoth Circus featured a hot-air balloon ascension as pre-show entertainment to attract curious bystanders. From the *Cheyenne Daily Leader*, June 19, 1871. Courtesy University of Wyoming Library, Laramie.

vast majority of the aeronauts' names were prefixed with "Mons." or "Monsieur."

Parkinson noted that nineteenth-century balloons were operated with hydrogen gas — "for greater safety and endurance" — that was carted in wooden tanks, cooled by passing copper pipes through water, then purified by lime. The balloons featured release valves at the top that were usually sealed with paraffin or beeswax.[35]

Agnes Lake, like her colleagues, was acutely aware of current entertainment trends and the public's persistent hunger for thrilling exhibitions, and she eagerly added this spectacle to her circus. Spread out on the circus lot, a giant canvas — "a real Paris balloon" — was carefully inflated.[36] The aeronaut would climb into the basket and release the ropes securing the vessel, and the balloon would gently ease into the sky, up to a few hundred feet above the amazed spectators. Under the navigation of Agnes's "celebrated aeronaut" Professor Miles (her manager Robert E.J. Miles), "who [had] made a thousand aerial voyages," the balloon would gently float "among the little stars" before descending to earth, landing as soft as a feather.[37] That was the plan, anyway.

Unfortunately, there were dozens of balloon mishaps. The majority of reports detailed only minor calamities, such as an incident in Quincy, Illinois: "After a great deal of waiting and watching and speculation as to whether the thing would be much of an affair, after all, during which time the canvass was being made red hot, the balloon made a 'go' of it, sailing upward a short distance. . . . Inside of five minutes that 'air ship' came down in a heap in a pond of water three feet deep. . . . And that was all."[38]

A similar incident occurred when Agnes and her circus were performing in Manhattan, Kansas, and the balloon was reported as "busted" after failing to take flight during the afternoon show. After successfully taking off later the same evening, it careened into "Sarber's woods, about half a mile from the place of ascension."[39] The crowds were not impressed. On another occasion, the "acrobatic aeronaut" introduced his gymnastic feats but "was violently thrown upon his side by the wiggling of the balloon, disjointing his arm and injuring him severely."[40] The "acrobatic aeronaut's" identity is unclear; it is unlikely that it was Miles, since he was about forty years old at the time and was never considered a gymnast or a tumbler.

Professor Miles, however, did have his share of disconcerting moments as the "celebrated aeronaut." In one instance in Kansas, Miles was not even in the basket when "the balloon seemed to shoot off before there was a good ready. The 'ship of air' turned a complete somersault . . . and caught fire. The Fire was speedily extinguished; so was the balloon."[41]

Other companies, eager to attract crowds, presented their own balloon ascensions. G. G. Grady's Great Three Tent Show had integrated an ascension act into its program and experienced the same misfortunes Agnes Lake and Professor Miles suffered. Grady's aeronaut, Professor Torrey, had raised the ante by performing on a trapeze suspended from the basket of the "air ship." During a performance in Dayton, Ohio, on April 21, 1871, Torrey "had a narrow escape" when the balloon "caught fire near its mouth and continued to burn during its ascent." When the fire went out the balloon descended rapidly, but "fortunately it came in contact with a willow tree." Torrey's fall was broken by the branches, and he escaped with only a sprained ankle.[42]

Some balloon mishaps turned into devastating catastrophes. The *New York Clipper* reported a tragedy in Nebraska City, Nebraska, that occurred on May 12, 1871. As Lake's Hippo-Olympiad prepared for the balloon ascension, "one of the supporting poles fell, striking Charles Knutson on the head smashing his brains out and killing him instantly."[43] Knutson was a patron, and a coroner's inquest "exonerated the circus company from all blame."[44]

Even though the balloon sometimes failed to inflate properly, flew off course and crashed, and occasionally injured and even killed aeronauts or patrons, these were risks Agnes and other proprietors were willing to accept. The novelty of a colossal balloon exhibited free to the public was a marketing maneuver that paid off handsomely in the day's profits, and Agnes continued to employ it through the rest of the season.

CHAPTER TEN

Westward by Rail

Agnes Meets Wild Bill Hickok, "Western Hero"

1871

While Agnes had trekked through the eastern half of the United States and crisscrossed the Atlantic Ocean, she had only ventured a few hundred miles west of the Mississippi River — no further than Dallas and environs. Although her travels were no small feat to her contemporaries, Agnes knew there were great opportunities to make money in the West. She made arrangements to take her circus west by harnessing the power of the railroads.

Just a few months before Bill Lake was murdered, dignitaries and officials from the Union Pacific and Central Pacific railroads had met in Promontory Summit, Utah. Together, the two companies drove a golden spike into the ground, and the two coasts of America were united by rail. The ink had barely dried on the freshly printed maps of the new territories when several circus companies, including Agnes's, arranged to visit the abundant stands in the West by rail.

By 1850 there were over 30,000 miles of track in the United States, but the railroads did not possess standardized equipment or track gauges for several more years. Instead, the nationwide railway system was a mélange of metal and wood that snaked from city to city, the locomotives belching thick smoke and ash. The lack of suitable train cars for circuses made loading and unloading the equipment strenuous and challenging, especially when the show's site was not next to the depot.[1] This created the "gilley show" and required the use of "manual labor, usually augmented by knock-down or rented dray wagons," to transport the equipment from the train to the show's site.[2] Some trains were forced to stop frequently to load their cars onto platforms designed for a particular variety of gauge. This often delayed the troupe's arrival at the next stand. Still, travel by train allowed the human and animal talent more time to rest between shows than did travel by wagons over rutted roads and in variable weather conditions.[3]

Rosters of antebellum railroad circuses were streamlined to fea-ture only the most profitable acts, since railroad travel was often unpredictable. Menageries and sideshows were eliminated because they added too many unpredictable factors to the nascent transporta-tion structure. The lack of a parade, museum, menagerie, and side-show led some to believe a railroad circus presented a production inferior to the traditional overland circus. In 1870, only a few circuses attempted to use the railroads as their sole conveyance during the circus season. To reassure potential markets, several overland troupes added "This is no Railroad Show" to their advertisements.[4]

Circus historian Fred Dahlinger, Jr., published a four-part study titled "The Development of the Railroad Circus" in four issues of *Bandwagon* between November 1983 and June 1984. Dahlinger studied the economic rewards and logistical challenges that beset the circuses that attempted to complete an entire season by rail. Dahlinger theorized that a railroad show may have cost less than a mud show because there were no baggage horses to stable and feed and hotel bills were drastically reduced, since performers could sleep while the train rolled into the next town.[5] The reduced num-ber of long-term expenditures made a railroad show appealing to its owners. Without a menagerie or sideshow to generate additional income, however, the railroad shows were completely dependent on large audiences for their revenue. Early railroad shows were an enormous gamble as circus companies ventured into the West, where population centers were sporadic.

Standardized equipment, developed after the Civil War, guided the trajectory of the railroad and traveling exhibition industries and generated greater efficiency when the "circus army" marched across the continent.[6] Specialized train cars were designed to accommodate circuses' unique baggage. Spearheaded by the "paramilitary fashion" of William Cameron "W.C." Coup in 1872, railroad circuses defined the various labor tasks and assigned them to particular workmen.[7] The arduous labor of loading and unloading the hundreds of trunks, bleachers, yards of canvas, and other circus equipment soon began to run like clockwork.

Dan Castello's Circus & Menagerie is credited as the first troupe to commence a bicoastal season by train. Beginning in Frederick, Maryland, Castello's entourage reached the shores of the Pacific Ocean just weeks after the famous golden spike was hammered into Utah's soil in May 1869. Castello's transcontinental circus traveled in eight railroad cars and included a small menagerie with two elephants. He even conducted a small parade before the main event, with "costumed performers on horseback."[8] Although he attempted to defy the stereotype that railroad shows gave inferior performances, Castello suffered financially and sold his enterprise just weeks after reaching California.[9]

Janet M. Davis examined "the circus's rising ubiquity [as] a symbol of national expansion and consolidation during the Gilded Age."[10] After the historic meeting in Utah in 1869, the railroad industry rapidly standardized track gauges to facilitate railroad travel. This meant circuses and menageries no longer had to sacrifice the parade, museum, or sideshow — commodities once deemed superfluous for railroad shows. As railroad travel became easier with unique circus specifications and labor disbursement, the overland wagon show consequently became obsolete within a few years.

Although the railroad circuses were able to reach towns from coast to coast, their itineraries focused on the cities closest to major railroad stations because they were usually the most profitable locales as well. Expansion of circus routes meant the smaller hamlets in Middle America were eliminated because they were now considered out of the way and financially unjustified. Dahlinger argued that U.S. towns and cities became "divided into a two tier system": "The larger population centers became the province of the big flat car circus with its ability to make long jumps and entertain patrons on a grand scale. The smaller towns were left to the overland and smaller gilley style rail shows which could not compete with the larger railroad shows."[11]

Agnes was aware of the promising fortunes to be made from towns in the West and made plans to transport her show. She carefully read several newspaper accounts of the West to guard against pitfalls—the climate, the characters, the strange indigenous beasts and vermin—just as her father had read Duden's accounts of America forty years earlier. Although Agnes prepared her troupe for the new season as she normally did, with advance agents and local logistical support, she was not prepared for what awaited her in the West—the foundations of a new life and a new love.

*   *   *

By mid-May 1871, Agnes Lake's Hippo-Olympiad was "traveling by railroad through Nebraska . . . and [had] done a fair business," reported the *New York Clipper*.[12] As always, Agnes's solid reputation preceded her, although she often faced tough critics as well. A two-day performance in Omaha was reduced to one day after poor audience attendance. A few weeks later, in Junction City, Kansas, one editor pronounced that while the "circus performance was good," the "entire affair would have been splendid had the opening scene, founded on Byron's poem, been omitted. The rendition of [*Mazeppa*] was horrible."[13] Agnes Lake received her first dismal review of *Mazeppa* since her cold reception in Germany. Undaunted by the criticism of one sour performance, Agnes kept *Mazeppa* as her circus's opening act.

A few poor reviews did not diminish the overall favorable impression of her organization. The *Fort Dodge (Iowa) Times* declared that Madame Lake's Hippo-Olympiad "was the most respectable and orderly Circus that has ever visited. . . . [I]t was not accompanied by the usual army of gamblers, thieves, pickpockets, prostitutes and vagabonds that generally follow a Circus."[14] Agnes Lake continued to pride herself on producing family entertainment, free from vulgarity. After Bill Lake's death, Agnes was determined to make her circus legitimate and "honorable [as] an occupation, [such] as the museum or drama,"[15] or she would abandon it.

Few respectable business opportunities were available to women in the nineteenth century, and Agnes did not want to be pitied because she was a widow. Instead, she wanted to prove that a woman could operate a business outside the widow's traditional milieu (such as running a boardinghouse) without having her morals questioned. The *Neosho (Mo.) Times* reminded readers that "the many traditional vices connected with exhibitions of this kind found no favor in the eyes of the Madam."[16] Agnes did not tolerate these unwelcome extras and took precautions to distance herself from tramps and vagabonds. Many "nefarious operations" allowed swindlers and gamblers certain concessions on the circus lot to practice games of chance and "the running of jewelry cases" for a percentage of the profits. "With Mrs. Lake's exhibition nothing of this kind is allowed," declared the *Neosho Times*; her only revenue was derived from ticket sales.[17]

Because some circus troupes and other traveling variety shows tolerated swindlers and gamblers, all circus companies and traveling exhibitions faced prejudice throughout the country. The residents of Greeley, Colorado, who "don't drink anything much stronger than ginger pop and lemonade," discouraged any outsiders who might pose a threat to the tranquility of their hamlet or who might corrupt their youth. Citizens of the town particularly deterred residents from neighboring towns from joining them on Sunday picnics because they "pollute the fair soil of Greeley colony, by drunken revelries over the supposed whisky these supposed barbarians bring with them to drink." Lake's Hippo-Olympiad had been scheduled to perform in Greeley, but the troupe was forced to exhibit at Evans, a small town four miles south of Greeley, because any circus was considered "an abomination to the Greeleyites."[18]

To discourage the licentious activity and seedy characters known to trail a circus, some cities started increasing the price of performance licenses. Memphis increased its fees for circuses to four hundred dollars per day for licenses within the city limits. While thousands of people might attend each show, each ticket cost only twenty-five or fifty cents. After the hotel and restaurant bills, as well as feed and stabling for horses, four hundred dollars in license fees quickly ate away at the day's profits. The *New York Clipper* commented that "we are of the opinion that few circuses will exhibit there this season."[19] For the first time in years, Memphis was not a destination on the itinerary of Madame Lake's Hippo-Olympiad.

Circuses faced additional prejudice and resentment in Kansas. In Topeka, circuses and menageries were charged one hundred dollars per day, while any show other than a circus or menagerie was charged a paltry five dollars. The city was determined to remove brothels, bawdy houses, circuses, and menageries to maintain order and reduce drunken disturbances.

Throughout May and June, the troupe traveled by railroad across Nebraska and Colorado. Even though the trains prevented access to much smaller towns, hundreds of people traveled to the nearest venues when they heard Madame Lake was coming. According to the 1870 census, Idaho City, Colorado, had only about 700 residents, yet nearly 2,000 people came out to see Agnes Lake's circus in June 1871.[20]

Circus Day provided a break in the tedium of frontier chores, and Agnes Lake experienced this from a different perspective in the West. She could remember from her days as a small child in rural Ohio the splendor and excitement that surrounded Circus Day. She remembered the colors, sounds, and tasty goodies that made that day special. Just as she had seen when she was a child, "[F]armers and ranchmen [came into town] with their families. Old ladies [brought] babies and knitting work, and youngsters [devoured] any amount of gingerbread and peanuts."[21] Now, with a show of her own, Agnes created similar Circus Day memories for children growing up in the rural West. The circus remained a community-wide event, even if some local authorities discouraged it. The *Cheyenne*

Daily Leader reported that even the "high-toned gentry will come out with their wives and sweethearts."[22] The newspaper in Salina, Kansas, reported that "a circus draws a bigger mass of beings than a fourth of July celebration, Henry Ward Beecher, or Cady Stanton."[23] The editors delighted in noticing that many "stately and dignified" citizens—who had no doubt lambasted the circus's arrival a few days earlier—entered the arena "with hats slouched over their eyes," afraid to be recognized.[24]

Despite the negative opinions that saturated newspapers and the disapproving looks from town leaders, hundreds of citizens— even "Greeleyites"—made their way to the closest venues on Circus Day. Lake's performance in Evans, Colorado, had been attended by "almost the entire population of Greeley," despite the obvious disgust at such shows from newspaper editors.[25] Colorado was especially profitable for Agnes Lake and her show, generating about $15,000 (about $255,000 today) in June alone.[26]

Lake's Hippo-Olympiad next traveled by "special train" and enjoyed rave reviews during a week-long engagement in Salt Lake City. Famed equestrian Wooda Cook joined the troupe and performed "the exceedingly difficult operation of a back [somersault] from a horse, while traveling around the ring."[27] George Mankin appeared to be entirely "composed of india rubber" as he stretched and contorted his body into astonishing poses. Henry Jennings was a beast of a man, but he completed a "succession of [somersaults] with such surprising rapidity that he appeared like a huge revolving wheel."[28] The residents of Salt Lake City were treated to a smorgasbord of entertainment on the Fourth of July that year. There were two grand processions during the day and two fireworks displays, "enough to satisfy any one," in addition to the entertainment provided by Madame Lake's company.[29]

*   *   *

In Victorian America, women were considered the "light of the home," the keeper of morals, and the family's religious conductor. Janet M. Davis noted that circuses "celebrated female power" and represented "a startling alternative to contemporary social norms."[30]

Despite the negative attitudes surrounding circuses, Agnes Lake — by managing her own show — challenged the Victorian stereotype but was not censured for it. Rather, she was redeemed as a phoenix rising from her desolation to overcome the hardships of being a widow while not faltering from the standards of Victorian womanhood. Agnes's status as a circus owner began to eclipse the average woman's ranking as a second-class citizen. The *Topeka Daily Commercial* published a social commentary on women, hailing Agnes Lake's fortitude:

> There are few women, we imagine, who labor under the delusion that they could manage a circus. We know the fair sex have an idea that they can do anything within the range of human possibilities, and confidently refer us to the examples of Joan of Arc . . . [or] Dr. Mary Walker[31] . . . to show how equally with men women have distinguished themselves in the arts of peace and war. . . . [W]hat must be thought of the one who embarks for all in the most precarious of all enterprises, and with a few lieutenants and a score or so of retainers, sets out with a dreary prospect before her, to travel in all kinds of weather, through hundreds of miles of alternating dust and mud, to run a dreadful gauntlet of uncompromising sheriffs, and to fight her way back to the place of starting, richer in purse than she was before? Is not her heroism sublime? Does she not call for our best wishes, and for our most fervent prayers for her success? Such a woman is Madam Agnes Lake. . . . [At the death of Bill Lake] the entire management of the concern devolved upon her, although but a woman, her administration has ever since been so successful that she now has one of the best circuses in the country.[32]

Throughout the rest of the season, Agnes Lake received praise not just for the acts her show provided but for her ability to manage a show, despite her sex. Agnes was not the poster woman for "woman's rights in the ordinary acceptation of that term," argued the *Saline County Journal*, but when Bill Lake was murdered "she rose superior to her desolation, and with a heroism that commands our admiration, addressed . . . the responsible duties of her strange position."[33] The *Nebraska City News* proclaimed that Agnes's management was superb and that she conducted herself "in a business like and lady like manner."[34] The *Laramie Daily Sentinel (Colo.)* stroked Agnes's ego, defended her company, and pronounced Agnes "a lady of refinement and culture." Affirming their belief in women's second-class citizenship, however, the editors wrote: "To her the undertaking was novel and arduous, but with a determination that would honor the sterner sex, she has proved woman's adaptability to control and manage any occupation that circumstances may make imperative for her to undertake — with a heroic resolve to free the circus from many of its traditional vices — she has succeeded in making it a respectable and at the same time legitimate business."[35]

By October 1871, advertisements for Agnes Lake's Hippo-Olympiad reflected the modified conceptions of female circus performers. To remove any doubt as to who was running the show, the first line of the ads boldly pronounced "UNDER A WOMAN'S MANAGEMENT." Notices in the October 19, 1871, issue of the *Terra Haute Daily Gazette* proudly boasted "SIX FEMALE ARTISTS" among the forty featured performers.

The idea of promoting the female performers' strength and agility, mixed with their natural womanliness, was not a novel marketing concept to Agnes Lake. Nearly two decades before, while she traveled with Spalding & Rogers, Agnes's image was routinely featured in one of the major advertising illustrations. Agnes was depicted ascending her slack wire outside the Big Top before the main event, pushing a wheelbarrow with an occupant, as the program promised. The wheelbarrow's occupant was a representation of "Lady Liberty" holding an American flag, surrounded by Spalding & Rogers's logo. Agnes Lake was depicted in a modest costume that was anything but revealing or un-ladylike. What better way to show female modesty and strength than with Agnes Lake, a performer whose athleticism never obscured her femininity?

*   *   *

The year 1871 was a significant one in Agnes Lake's professional life. She conducted a financially successful season with her name at the helm and traveled by railroad nearly the entire season to some of the farthest-flung towns in the United States. Her corps of talent was superb and rendered continual praise from the press. The novelty of the balloon ascension generated greater audiences.

The 1871 season was a significant moment in Agnes Lake's personal life as well. On July 31, 1871, Madame Lake's Hippo-Olympiad arrived by train in Abilene, Kansas, and prepared the circus lot on the west side of town. The town was buzzing with activity: thousands of bellowing longhorn cattle crowded into pens along the railroad tracks awaiting shipment to the East while their chaperones, as many as 5,000 cowboys, spent their time and money in the saloons and bordellos south of the tracks. In April the town's newly elected mayor, Joseph G. McCoy, who had introduced Abilene to the cattle trade in 1867, hired James Butler "Wild Bill" Hickok as the new town marshal to assist the local police force in keeping order.[36] Initially, Hickok was reluctant to accept his new rank as marshal, but he surmised that at least it was steady employment: his salary was $150 per month, plus 25 percent of all fines imposed in court. In addition, Abilene had no shortage of gambling establishments to feed Hickok's liquor and gambling vices. He was acutely aware, however, that his reputation preceded him and might bring him extra trouble, even death.[37]

When Agnes Lake sought out the local marshal, who was responsible for collecting the license fees for public entertainments and arranging security, she encountered the legendary gunfighter, whose name and exploits were well-known. Despite the fact that Hickok was eleven years Agnes's junior, several accounts agree that there was a mutual attraction. Hickok was undoubtedly a handsome man, and Agnes could not fail to have been affected by his presence. Physical descriptions of the man have varied little. Hickok stood over six feet tall. Descriptions of the hue of his hair have varied from blond to auburn, and it fell over his broad shoulders. The intensity of his eyes fluctuates between icy blue and deep pools of gray.

Some versions have overly romanticized their first meeting and claimed that Agnes fell desperately in love with Hickok on the spot. Nevertheless, their meeting left a marked impression on them both.

Agnes's circus performed as scheduled, and Hickok probably watched the show. By the next day Agnes Lake had left Abilene and the handsome city marshal behind. Even with the steep exhibition charges Agnes faced throughout the season, she continued with her itinerary and arrived in Topeka later that day. Her arrival and registry at the luxurious Tefft House, on the corner of Seventh and Kansas avenues, was noted in the newspapers.[38]

The Hippo-Olympiad continued to St. Louis, where Agnes's troupe performed for a week simultaneously with the Great St. Louis Fair in October. The troupe's season finally concluded in Cincinnati on October 28. Agnes returned to her farm in Kentucky and reflected on the season. Agnes's thoughts likely reverted back to the handsome man she had met in Abilene three months earlier. Articles, dime novels, and outrageous tales had been printed about Wild Bill for several years, and she could not help but want to decipher the man behind the myth.

*   *   *

By the time Agnes encountered him, James Butler "Wild Bill" Hickok was already a legend. Hickok was born May 27, 1837, in the small village of Homer (later Troy Grove), Illinois, the son of Polly and William Alonzo Hickok. James, along with his two brothers and two sisters, grew up on the western borders of Illinois, an area still considered part of the frontier.[39]

James left home in June 1856. Over the next fourteen years he worked as a general laborer, as a teamster for Jones & Cartwright and the U.S. Army, and as a courier for General George A. Custer's 7th Cavalry. He was commissioned as a deputy United States marshal in Kansas sometime between August 1867 and 1870.

In April 1871, Hickok was appointed marshal of Abilene, then the principal cattle town in Kansas, where he first met Agnes Lake. They kept in touch. The pair reunited in Cheyenne, Wyoming Territory, in 1876 and married on March 5 of that year. Attracted by the gold rush to the Black Hills, in late June Wild Bill traveled

Fig. 26. James Butler "Wild Bill" Hickok, frontier lawman and legendary hero, met Agnes Lake when her circus played in Abilene, Kansas, on July 31, 1871. Courtesy Denver Public Library, Western History Collection, George G. Rockwood, Z-8870.

to Deadwood, Dakota Territory, a decision that ultimately decided his fate.

Considering the myriad tomes available, especially those by Joseph G. Rosa, the leading authority on Wild Bill, a biography of Hickok does not require repetition here. However, Hickok's relationship with Agnes Lake has become veiled because of a lack of reliable evidence and requires further scrutiny. Their relationship is further obscured by the sensationalized accounts that have continually coupled Martha Jane "Calamity Jane" Canary and Wild Bill Hickok. Calamity Jane's and Wild Bill's "relationship" will be examined in chapter 14.

Over the past 140 years, thousands of published magazine articles and fictionalized accounts, hundreds of biographies, and dozens of films have tried to profess "the truth" about James Butler Hickok's life. As with Agnes, Hickok's "own thoughts were not recorded,"[40] especially regarding his career, celebrity status, and intimate relationships. What has been printed, therefore, is largely derived from secondary sources and from persons who claimed to have had a close friendship with Wild Bill. While some earlier biographical accounts included memoirs by Hickok's legitimate friends, others were forged with a great deal of conjecture. Unfortunately, anyone can claim to have had a relationship with deceased, public entities such as Agnes and Hickok, so how can the public discern between fact and fiction?

Often, the authors had no personal contact with Agnes or with Hickok's family in Illinois, and they frequently repeated erroneous information. Several accounts mistakenly identified Agnes as "Alice" or "Emma." Frank Jenners Wilstach, who published several pieces on Hickok in the 1920s, wrote an article that appeared in the *New York Times Magazine* in September 1925. He wrote that Hickok was "happily married" to "Mrs. Emma Lake" and that they had married in February 1876.[41] Most accounts contained a little bit of truth muddled with a great deal of literary license, and they often quoted dubious sources.

In the dusty cattle town of Abilene, Kansas, that hot July day in 1871, Agnes Lake encountered a man with two personas—the gunfighter, gambler, and emerging folk hero who "had killed hundreds of men," and the man his family knew to be courteous, soft-spoken, and possessed of a sense of humor.[42] The man his family knew was unknown to the American public, and knowledge of that aspect of his personality would have been dismissed by a society that hungered for characters who embodied fabled status.

The myth of Hickok's prowess facilitated the construction of his image as a national folk hero. After his death in 1876, his siblings, nephews, and nieces were constantly refuting lies, rumors, and accusations that stood to damage Hickok's character.

In his 2005 biography of Buffalo Bill, Louis Warren attributed Hickok's rising celebrity to the American "longing for frontier heroes," such as Davy Crockett, Daniel Boone, and Kit Carson.[43] The devastation of warfare had left Americans desperate for antebellum nostalgia. These men were "popularly imagined" to have conquered nature's forces and mastered the wizardry of technology, and they were "peaceful at heart," despite their ability to inflict great carnage.[44] Warren noted that as a national figure, Hickok was an important element in the cultural transition between the antiquated frontier heroes immortalized in literature — like Hawkeye in James Fenimore Cooper's *The Last of the Mohicans* — and the rising western frontier heroes like Buffalo Bill, who was portrayed as a "white Indian."[45] Hickok's attitude, wardrobe, and alleged exploits on the fierce plains of the West straddled the cusp of American folk hero ideology. Hickok's iconic status thus helped usher in the age of the western plainsman, which evolved into the idolized cowboy that saturated U.S. popular culture well into the twentieth century.

Much like Agnes with her forged ancestry, Hickok was proficient in crafting a "convincing imposture" that allowed him to assume a life story that was "part genuine, part invention."[46] Until his likeness was published in *Harper's*, many Americans probably imagined him dressed in a manner akin to his popular predecessors. The photographs that depict him wearing buckskin garments, grasping a carbine, and having a small armory of knives and pistols secured at his waist "implied connections to untamed nature."[47] Warren intimated, however, that while this specific attire was outdated in many parts of the post–Civil War West, many frontiersmen continued to wear buckskins until the 1880s. To easterners, they were unmistakably reminiscent of Hawkeye's and Davy Crockett's frontier garb — two individuals who had helped generate Wild Bill's popular image in the first place. In the photographs taken a few years before his death, however, Hickok's sartorial choices personified the "gentleman of the West." He wore chic dress shirts, checked pants, and pointed boots. Hickok's ability to "exchange" his frontier attire for finer garments "symbolized the frontiersman's essential civility."[48] His demeanor, attitude, and mannerisms befit the gentleman gambler and did not reflect his previous lifestyle as a western lawman.

Hickok's public image, as crafted by the press, is a historical anomaly. According to Rosa, contemporaneous press reports focused on Hickok's skills as a plainsman or scout and less on his notoriety as a killer.[49] Conversely, the chronicles of Hickok's adventures that were published posthumously "devote little attention to his plains skills [and] concentrate almost entirely upon his peacekeeping or gun-fighting roles."[50]

Wild Bill Hickok's "lady-killer" reputation was as well-known as his "man-killer" status. Agnes probably succumbed to the charms and handsome looks that had conquered many women. The origins of the relationship that led to the marriage of Agnes and James, as she called him, are vague. In her letters to Polly and Celinda Hickok, written in 1876, Agnes provides no details of how she first met James. Their first encounter has been one of the most debated and fictionalized accounts in the multitude of Hickok biographies.

When the routes of Agnes's Hippo-Olympiad were reconstructed from newspapers and the painstaking research of Stuart Thayer, the evidence strongly indicated that their first encounter indeed occurred in Abilene, Kansas, on July 31, 1871, and not in Hays,[51] as others have historically suggested. Richard O'Connor believed Agnes and Hickok had met as early as 1869, but there is no proof to substantiate his claim.[52] In fact, Agnes and Bill Lake's circus did not exhibit in Kansas before 1871. While Hickok may have spent time in Hays in or before July of that year, no evidence placed Agnes west of Salina, Kansas, a town nearly one hundred miles east of Hays, before July 1871.[53]

Despite the lack of primary evidence from both Agnes and James, a multitude of biographers, journalists, and "friends" of the couple have distributed a number of versions that describe the star-crossed lovers' first encounter and the subsequent events that resulted in their marriage in 1876. In his 1883 conglomerate biography of Hickok and other familiar western figures, *Heroes of the Plains*, James William Buel relayed the events that set their romance in motion.

According to Buel, Wild Bill learned that the Abilene city council was going to charge Agnes Lake fifty dollars to exhibit her circus.[54] As city marshal, Hickok attended the meeting and recited this monologue:

> I never made a speech in my life, and I don't want to begin now. . . . You fellows live so far outside of civilization that your hearts have dried up like small potatoes left out in the sun, and as you can't read the papers of course you don't know nothing about what's going on east of the coyote's range.
>
> This circus that's advertised to show and furnish a little amusement for us heathens is owned by a woman, one whose pluck catches my sympathy every time. . . . [This] brave little widow, after burying her husband, had to either sell out or go on the road with the circus and circumstances advised her to carry the show. My opinion is that any woman capable to run a circus is a darn sight bigger curiosity in these parts than the leather heads in this village ever heard of, and when I see so much pluck shown by a woman, I just feel like throwing in and helper [*sic*] her.
>
> Now, if you fellows that run this town knowed how to appreciate a good thing for the place, instead of charging Mrs. Lake a license, you would vote an appropriation to pay her for coming out here to show heathens a first class circus. If I've got any authority in [Abilene], Mrs. Lake isn't going to pay this town a cent of license for showing and if any man attempts to stop this show, then just put it down that he's got

me to fight. That's all I've got to say now, so drive on, and we'll see who pays the fiddler.[55]

The fear of fighting Hickok encouraged the council to rescind the proposed fee. When Agnes Lake arrived in Abilene a few days later, she heard of his "disinterested kindness" and introduced him to the entire troupe, including sixteen-year-old Emma. Buel continued to document Hickok's suave banter with Agnes after their first introduction: "Well now . . . do you know the greatest curiosity about this canvas is yourself[?] I never saw a woman before that could run anything, except with a broom handle, and to find one managing one like this is a bigger sight than California Joe when he was tackled by a panther down in the Wachitas."[56]

Subsequent biographers Elmo Scott Watson, Frank Jenners Wilstach, and Richard O'Connor have also included the preceding passage. Watson believed Buel's narrative, although "florid and sentimentalized," was probably the truth,[57] but Buel likely fabricated Hickok's speech to the city council and his subsequent encounters with Agnes. In addition, any dialogue printed in Hickok biographies, especially between Wild Bill and Agnes, should be considered false at worst; they are examples of the authors' poetic license at best. The dialogue included in this work is contextualized within the greater examination and analysis of their relationship, but it still should not be considered factual.

It is interesting that despite the lack of evidence, there is abundant conjecture and debate about who was pursuing whom in the relationship. Buel, Wilstach, and Shannon and Warren Garst intimate that Hickok fervently pursued Agnes. In fact, Buel "quotes" Hickok's declaration to Agnes, almost immediately after their first meeting: "For if I could hitch up with such a business girl as yourself I'd go in search of a parson tomorrow."[58]

Apparently, Hickok did not think Agnes would agree to the match, but that did not hinder his attempts to flirt with the circus widow. Whereas he might have been impressed with Agnes's "pluck," in reality Hickok was unlikely to forfeit his bachelorhood or his ladies who had "no visible means of support" in favor of a wife. Buel painted an interesting image of Hickok swooning over Agnes, "not only on first sight, but even before [their] meeting; he was caught on the hook of her reputation."[59] According to Wilstach, Hickok fell "violently in love" with Agnes. In turn, Agnes found "Bill" a "strikingly handsome man" and "admitted that he inspired in her feelings of affection and admiration."[60]

Others support the idea that Hickok proposed to Agnes in Abilene. Wilstach's book was first published in 1926 as *Wild Bill Hickok: The Prince of Pistoleers*. Following his death in 1933, Cecil B. DeMille used this and other sources for his 1936 cinematic epic *The Plainsman*, although there is no mention of Agnes Lake in his film. This volume was released after the 1937 film of the same name, also directed by Cecil B. DeMille. The inside covers are decorated with stills from the Hollywood epic.

A few years later, Agnes and Hickok crossed paths again when he was performing with Buffalo Bill Cody and Texas Jack Omohundro. Wilstach printed an "account" of their exchange during their tryst, which took place between Hickok's scenes onstage. Hickok confessed that he had never courted a woman before but that she had consumed his thoughts since their first meeting. He reportedly confessed, "Fact is, I'd be mighty glad to hitch up in harness with you, because I think we'd make a splendid team."[61]

Although she was flattered, Agnes was less sure of her feelings and insisted that her current business situation prevented her from accepting his second marriage proposal. "I don't want to insist, but at the same time you suit me to a dot, and I'd give my eyes to marry you; therefore I'll give you time to consider," he responded gallantly.[62]

Shannon and Warren Garst, whose biography of Wild Bill was published in 1952, initially identified Agnes as the pursuing party. The Garsts' biography does not include citations for their sources, but their bibliography includes the previously mentioned publications by Buel and Wilstach and gives erroneous information about Agnes. The Garsts' biography presents a romanticized explanation of Agnes and Wild Bill's relationship and includes fictitious "dialogue" based on their own historical assumptions. The Garsts claim that Agnes had wanted Hickok to marry her and help manage the circus, but he was not thrilled at the prospect of running her "dead husband's business."[63] When Agnes left town after their initial meeting, however, Hickok's sullen demeanor did not go unnoticed by close acquaintances, who knew Wild Bill was smitten with the circus widow.

The Garsts switched positions, however, when Hickok was traveling and performing with Cody. At this point in their publication, the Garsts wrote that Hickok reflected on his brief encounter with Agnes in Abilene. The Garsts asserted that Hickok admired Agnes "more than any woman he had ever known"[64] and that she made "most other woman seem silly and insipid by comparison."[65] Hickok had been a "fool" to ignore her correspondence, but he remained firm in his belief that as long as Agnes's attention was focused on her circus, their marriage would not have succeeded.[66]

The Garsts then described a surprise meeting between Agnes and Hickok that was arranged by Cody. While the Garsts did not provide a source to document the reunion, Agnes and Emma Lake in fact traveled to New York City in March 1874,[67] apparently to meet with both Hickok and Cody; this event could therefore have been based on that information. Hickok allegedly confessed to Agnes how much she meant to him, how he longed for her to marry him, and how sorry he was that he had let her out of his sight.[68] Agnes chastised Hickok for refusing *her* proposal in Abilene three years earlier. She claimed she "forgot [her] womanly modesty" and was embarrassed that she "literally threw" herself at the handsome marshal.[69] Hickok renewed his wish to marry her, but again she declined on account of her circus, remarking: "My circus is as important to me as your plains are to you."[70]

They parted, both thinking it would be their last reunion. The Garsts commented that Hickok "felt a part of him had died"[71] when he realized Agnes had slipped through his fingers a second time.

While Buel, Wilstach, and the Garsts place Hickok as the pursuer in the relationship, Charles Gross, Charles Sturtevant, William Secrest, and O'Connor consign Agnes Lake as a lovelorn widow desperately trying to shackle Hickok in a "paper collar."[72] Perhaps they sought to justify Hickok's sudden and surprising decision to become "domesticated" in 1876. Hickok was a frontier hero whose legend was centered on his exploits and hence was perceived as unlikely to marry.

If Buel, Wilstach, and the Garsts were correct in depicting Hickok as ardently pursuing Agnes, their acuity could have drastically affected Hickok's masculinity in the eyes of the press because Wild Bill was not supposed to let his tender side be known. He was a man-killer, and his folk hero status was reaching mythical proportions. Instead, to protect Wild Bill's masculinity, an essential element of his facade, Agnes was portrayed as a "damsel in distress" looking for a personal hero in Hickok to rescue her from the desolation of widowhood and her supposed floundering circus. Agnes was just another woman "smitten with Wild Bill's charms." More than one source described her as "quickly enamored" of Hickok and reported that she wanted to marry him straightaway, but he "put her off with excuses."[73]

In 1925 Charles Gross, a friend of Hickok's, and John Beach Edwards, a longtime resident of Abilene, exchanged a series of letters in which they discussed Agnes and Hickok. Gross described Agnes falling "all the way *Clear to the Basement*" when she was introduced to the marshal, adding, "I know she was Keene" for Hickok to marry her practically right there and then.[74] According to Gross's letter dated June 15, 1925, Agnes begged Hickok to marry her and help her manage the Hippo-Olympiad. Gross was privy to this information because "Bill told me all about it."[75] Gross confessed that Hickok had asked him to tell Agnes that he was already married and that his wife was waiting for him in Illinois. Gross conveyed the ruse to Agnes in an attempt to dissuade the persistent circus manager from further pursuing his friend.

Gross's letter to Edwards reiterated Hickok's distaste for civilization in the East and repeated a vulgar remark Hickok had made concerning "something essentially feminine" about Agnes.[76] Gross suspected that while there was no real legal reason for him to refuse Agnes's "proposal," Hickok simply did not want a domesticated existence at that juncture in his life. Gross, however, confessed to being the liaison between Agnes's letters and Hickok; however, those letters have yet to surface. The discovery of the letters, supposedly written between 1871 and 1875, would provide invaluable insight into the mysterious relationship of the two legends.

William Secrest's "Bill Hickok's Girl on the Flying Trapeze," published in *Old West* in 1967, described Hickok as "neither gun- nor girl-shy."[77] During his tenure as marshal of Abilene, a few women vied for his attentions, including Mattie Silks, a local madam;[78] Jessie Hazel, a prostitute; and Susannah Moore, a "mystery girl from the Ozarks."[79] While Secrest admitted not knowing the depth of Hickok's feelings toward Agnes, he was sure she was "infatuated" with him. Secrest is equally perplexed concerning her underlying feelings, but he speculated that her attraction to Hickok oscillated between love and the "desire to have a man to lean on."[80]

Richard O'Connor described Hickok as "exceedingly polite, even gallant toward all women,"[81] which could explain Hickok's actions to the city council before Agnes arrived in Abilene — if that event actually occurred. Although Hickok rebuffed her advances in Abilene, O'Connor portrayed Agnes as a "persistent woman" who was "not too discouraged over Hickok's skittishness" at relinquishing his bachelor lifestyle.[82] "The comely widow," O'Connor remarked, "from all accounts, fell in love with Hickok."[83] O'Connor concurred with the contents of Gross's letter written in June 1925, which was also referenced in William Connelly's 1933 biography, *Wild Bill and His Era*.

Joseph G. Rosa dedicated an unprecedented eight pages to Agnes's life, career, and relationship with James in his 1974 revised edition of *They Called Him Wild Bill*. Gil Robinson — Agnes's son-in-law — summarized her entire life, career, and marriages in a paltry three-page analysis in his book *Old Wagon Show Days*, despite his claims that he was going to devote "some detail" to her life. Rosa's presentation of Agnes was prudent, since so little accurate information was available at the time. In addition, he refrained from portraying Agnes as a desperate, man-hungry widow and from including the fictitious dialogue other accounts had "documented." Rosa examined the most authentic sources available, albeit few in number, and treated Agnes with the historical integrity owed to her station. Rather than citing Buel or Wilstach, Rosa used as many primary sources as possible to discern the truth about Hickok's only legal wife. He examined contemporaneous newspapers, the correspondence between Gross and Edwards, and the 1876 letters exchanged between Agnes Lake and Polly and Celinda Hickok. One of the few secondary sources Rosa analyzed was Gil Robinson's memoirs, at the time considered the most reliable source for information concerning Agnes Lake.

Rosa supported the letter from Gross to Edwards that described Agnes's infatuation with Hickok because Gross was deemed a reliable source of information about Wild Bill. Although he agreed with Gross's "detailed account" of the events described in his letters, Rosa argued that the attraction was mutual and not one-sided, as reported in previous versions.

The truth behind the events in Abilene, in New York City, and later in Cheyenne lies somewhere within the fictionalized narratives. There probably was an immediate mutual attraction, although it was not the great, passionate love romanticists have imagined. Agnes and James had different priorities in 1871, which prevented either of them from accepting the other's "proposal." Agnes was a mother first and foremost in her own mind. Emma's well-being, Agnes's lingering grief over Bill Lake's death, and her focus on the financial vigor of the Hippo-Olympiad all precluded thoughts of a second marriage. She was clearly capable of sustaining an adequate livelihood without the assistance of a man in her life and therefore did not "need" to marry Hickok for financial security.

Similarly, Hickok was enjoying his lawman status and possibly looking forward to a long career as a marshal. He had little need or desire for a wife to chain him in a "paper collar," for the roving life of the circus, or for civilization east of the Mississippi River.[84] Ultimately, their priorities were simply not synchronized, and neither was willing to forfeit their current lifestyle in favor of the other.

CHAPTER ELEVEN

"The Monarch and Mastodon of the Road"

1872–1874

During the winter of 1872, Agnes and Emma Lake practiced and refined their manège routines in the spacious training grounds on their Kentucky farm. Agnes reeled from the financial burdens of managing her own circus, and she decided to dissolve Agnes Lake's Hippo-Olympiad and Mammoth Circus and merge with a few other shows that faced the same pecuniary difficulties. The Great Eastern Menagerie, Museum, Aviary, Circus and Balloon Show[1] (subsequently referred to as the Great Eastern Circus)[2] was the result of ventures previously owned by Agnes Lake, Andrew Haight, George W. DeHaven, and Colonel Clark T. Ames, who had died in 1870.[3]

When the *New York Clipper* printed its annual description of traveling circuses and menageries on March 23, 1872, the Great Eastern Circus had barely been assembled. Robert E.J. Miles, Dan Carpenter,[4] Haight, and DeHaven combined the efforts and modest resources of their four defunct shows and became proprietors of the new enterprise. Agnes Lake was no longer proprietor of her own show but was probably paid a handsome salary, since her name and reputation as a moral proprietress attracted large crowds to the circus. Miles and Carpenter shared the bulk of the new outfit's managerial duties and promised an ambitious program.

In his *Bandwagon* series on the Great Eastern Circus, William Slout deemed the nascent enterprise "one of the most audacious . . . ever attempted by a management."[5] In the beginning of the season the *Clipper* reported that the new circus would consist of "twenty-five dens of animals, four tents, sixty horses, two elephants, a drove of camels and 120 men."[6] The proprietors decided that the season would be conducted almost entirely by rail, and they quickly refurbished twenty-five railroad cars needed to transport the colossal ensemble.

Despite a modest budget, the Great Eastern Circus boasted competent managers and renowned performers. Andrew Haight (1831–86) had first partnered with DeHaven in 1865 and had worked as an advance agent and proprietor for a number of shows, including the Empire City Circus he helped organize with P. Bowles Wooten in 1871. Despite a successful season, Haight, Wooten, and DeHaven disagreed over the show's course and mutually dissolved their partnership.[7] Haight and DeHaven kept the bulk of the circus property and merged with Agnes's circus.[8] George DeHaven (1837–1902) had been financially attached to circuses since he was twenty-one and had worked with both Miles and Haight in previous circus endeavors. DeHaven's Imperial Circus is credited with initiating the free balloon ascension as a pre-show entertainment ritual.[9]

The roster featured a troupe of seasoned veterans who showcased their trademark talents. "Madame Lake" and Miss Emma Lake headlined the equestrian corps under the direction of W. B. "Barney" Carroll (1816–89). Known for his "one- and two-horse" leaping, Carroll is credited with accomplishing the daring feat of carrying his "infant son" on his head while riding bareback around the ring.[10] Madame Cordelia, who had been trained by Bill Lake, "La Petite Anna," and George M. Kelley, the world champion who "leaped over twenty-eight horses placed neck to neck,"[11] rounded out the exemplary equestrian unit.

Nearly a dozen clowns, acrobats, and tumblers were employed

as well. Among them, the Miaco Brothers (Thomas and William), Burnell Runnells (1826–1908), and Sam Stickney (1845–1921) were culled from previous shows and touring groups.[12] Professor Francis S. Koppe (or Kopp) led the band during the processional and the post-show concerts. Herr Elijah Lengel performed remarkable feats as a lion tamer, a trade that signed his death warrant eight years later. Navigating the balloon ascension was Professor Reno (or Renno), who had worked in Haight's Empire City Circus the previous season. Finally, taking center stage to direct the show was the veteran ringmaster James Esler (or Essler).[13]

In 1872 the *Clipper* counted thirty-one shows that embarked on the new season. Despite tough competition from some of the biggest and best-known shows managed by P. T. Barnum, "Old John" Robinson, and Isaac Van Amburgh, the Great Eastern Circus — with an experienced managerial team and popular performers in tow — commenced its inaugural season at the National Theatre in Cincinnati on April 1, 1872. Rare surviving newspaper clippings highlight the route followed by Agnes and her colleagues throughout the season. They journeyed by railroad to more than seventy cities across six states, from Minnesota to Ohio, in the spring and summer. Because the circus traveled by railroad, a faster conveyance than the cumbersome wagons used in previous seasons, the troupe performed up to three shows daily — usually at 10 A.M., 2 P.M., and 7 P.M. — during the one- or two-day stands.

In May, the troupe reached Chicago. It had been only seven months since the notorious fire, and Agnes, Emma, and their colleagues were greeted by weary citizens desperate for a brief escape. Charred skeletal remains of buildings stood on scorched streets, and the immense devastation was testimony to the suffering of Chicago's citizens. The *Clipper* commented that the Great Eastern Circus was "very heavily billed" and that over 10,000 notices had been dispersed in Chicago alone.[14] The notices had the intended effect, since the audience was estimated at between 6,000–7,500 patrons for just the first day of the week-long engagement.[15] Next, the troupe visited St. Louis for a week-long run in July. In the first week of August the circus turned south, eager to escape the north before the autumn brought gusting winds and snow. Traveling on the New Orleans & Jackson and the Mississippi Central railroads, the Great Eastern Circus rolled through over fifty cities from the Carolinas to Louisiana.[16] The cities the Great Eastern Circus visited during April, November, and most of December are undocumented, making the season appear shorter than it actually was.

Before the troupe performed in Logansport, Indiana, on August 8, 1872, the *Miami County Sentinel* published an ad in which the Great Eastern Circus boasted that it had "470 men and horses, 1,050 animals, [and] 26 crimson and gold cages."[17] The circus now needed seventy railroad cars to transport it from town to town. The grand procession that preceded the daily show was a mile long. Local newspapers urged citizens to "see the mounted Cavaliers" and "observe the rich banners, paraphernalia, flags, and plumes" that heralded the festivities.[18] No longer showcasing the knights of chivalry or the ladies fair from "two hundred years ago," the Great Eastern Circus now flashed its "Goddesses in Oriental Costumes"[19] and borrowed from the newest fads influenced by Europe's colonization in the Far East. As the British Empire expanded its borders, westerners were increasingly adopting Eastern design motifs and fusing them with traditional Western elements. Circuses, as well as other forms of entertainment, were quick to follow these trends and may have helped spread their popularity throughout small-town America.

A single ticket admitted a patron to the circus's many pavilions, spread out over a few acres that contained the main event, the menagerie, and the museum. "Twenty-Six Gold and Crimson Dens Filled with the rarest specimens of Wild Animals and Birds! And a Startling and Extravagant Display of Wonders, Natural, Scientific and Instructive," read ads that whet the appetites of thousands of curious patrons.[20] Inside the Big Top, through the subtle haze of gas-generated lighting, the performers' colorful costumes and the gold and silver banners created a fantastic world of dazzling color. In a nearby tent, the museum included General Littlefinger, "a fat woman," Professor Owens the magician, a "tank of Alaskan seals," and "Signor Ghio," the "Swiss-bird imitator" and novelty singer, among other curiosities.[21]

By the time the circus reached Pittsburgh a few weeks later, the size of the show had increased again. The exhibition had expanded to fill six pavilions. Besides the menagerie, museum, and aviary, a "Roman hiypodrome" and an "Egyptian caravan" had been added. In Pittsburgh and nearby Allegheny City, now known as the North Side, the *Clipper* noted that patronage was strong. One of the highlights was the trapeze act by the Miaco brothers.[22]

At the end of August, Agnes, Emma, and the Great Eastern Circus traveled to Washington, D.C., for a two-day engagement. By this time the Great Eastern Circus had expanded to include "750 men and women" and "1,050 animals,"[23] an enormous number that undoubtedly counted the hundreds of supporting staff—including costumers, hostlers, and managers—among the gargantuan roster claims. Local newspapers noted that "Old John" Robinson's circus was scheduled to be in the nation's capital ten days after the Great Eastern Circus's visit. Competition between the two shows created such a frenzy of advertising that "fences, sides of houses and bill boards are at a decided premium" as the city excitedly awaited the arrival of the two troupes.[24] Publicity surrounding the circus was a combination of paid advertisements and posters. Press releases and reviews of the attractions and performances, and "leaked information" intended to foster goodwill, were probably written by the advance agents.

Praise and critical acclaim continued for Agnes, Emma, and the entire company of performers. While preparing for scheduled performances in Georgia in September, the proprietors of the Great Eastern Circus made arrangements "with the principal railroad lines" that ran into Albany, Georgia, "to bring people at half fare to witness" the marvelous spectacle of the circus.[25] Circus ads that appeared in the *Albany News* reported that the lions, tigers, and panthers from the menagerie would be loose in the streets during the procession.[26] In Mobile it was revealed that elephants and camels were loose in the streets, but not the lions, tigers, and panthers.[27]

While the troupe was in New Orleans during November, the *Clipper* remarked that the "mammoth ring tent [was] fairly jammed with well pleased audiences," to the point where even standing room was not available.[28] In Hawkinsville, Georgia, circus posters proudly recognized the "10 lady riders," including Agnes and Emma Lake, out of twelve total equestrians.[29] In St. Louis one reporter declared that Emma Lake, besides possessing a "very winning face," was an "exceedingly graceful and dashing equestrienne."[30]

The inaugural season of the Great Eastern Circus officially ended on December 13, 1872, in Selma, Alabama. William Slout remarked that although it was an "infant organization," the troupe was praised for its "surprisingly strong" ring performances and was "easily competitive with Barnum's and [Adam] Forepaugh's" shows.[31] The circus earned high praise indeed when the Clinton, Iowa, *Age* declared that its performance came "nearer [to] fitting the bill advertised than circuses usually do."[32] When the show officially closed for the winter hiatus, the performers were released from their contracts and they scattered — they sought respite from the hectic months of traveling and yet endeavored to be engaged for the approaching season. The *Clipper* was inundated with personal notices as performers advertised their availability for the imminent season. The proprietors — Miles, Carpenter, Haight, and DeHaven — made arrangements to ship the wagons, chariots, and animals back to Cincinnati, where they were housed at the winter quarters.[33] The troupe had traveled over 9,500 miles, nearly all by railroad, and the season's profits were estimated at between $100,000 and $424,000 (approximately $1.65 million to $7 million in 2005) — a large margin indeed for the introductory season.[34]

Agnes and Emma went back to Sunnyside to await the call of the 1873 circus season. Agnes once again took stock of her life. She was forty-six years old, had been performing for a quarter of a century, and had traveled tens of thousands of miles across the country and across an ocean. She had earned fame as a slack wire walker, headlined as the legendary Mazeppa, sustained her legions of fans through her outstanding manège acts, and was highly respected as a moral proprietress in a field where morality was often questioned.

Her body was tired from many years in the saddle, her mind was weary from the demands of managing a business, and her spirit was doleful because of personal loss. She decided that her next circus season would be her last as a performer.

*   *   *

Their winter rest ended all too quickly, and Agnes and Emma were summoned to commence another circus season in March. They packed their cashmere costumes, riding habits, and personal accoutrements into their heavy circus trunks and readied their horses for another season on the road. Agnes and Emma returned to perform with the Great Eastern Circus. In one of Agnes's many obituaries, it was suggested that Agnes and Emma performed together in a choreographed exhibition of "fine riding." In fact, the two women performed simultaneously in two rings, side by side, in one of the first known two-ring exhibitions.[35]

Twenty-two companies headed out on the road for the 1873–74 season, a 30 percent decrease from the previous year.[36] While the number of outfits declined, the competition for patronage remained fierce among the largest shows — P. T. Barnum's, Adam Forepaugh's, and the Great Eastern Circus. The Great Eastern Circus started its second season on March 1, 1873, in Selma, Alabama, where it had finished only a few months earlier. The circus had undergone both cosmetic and personnel changes. "Roman Hippodrome and Egyptian Caravan" was added to the name, extending the company's official moniker to over thirty syllables. The Great Eastern Circus was heralded as the "Avalanche of Amusements" and the "Goliath of Shows" because, as one newspaper noted:

> Its augmentation the past winter makes it four times larger than last year and then it was confessed the Monarch Mastodon of the Road. Over a million dollars [$16.8 million in 2005] have been expended to make this the most stupendous and great World Expositions ever attempted, and TWELVE IMMENSE PAVILLIONS, covering over four acres of ground, and measuring 168,000 YARDS OF CANVAS, are re-

quired to exhibit the forty-one dens of Living Wild Beasts, Breathing Sea Monsters, Plumaged Birds, Flesh-eating Reptiles, and the Colossal Dual Circus Exhibitions, making it A GRAND COMBINATION OF 12 SHOWS IN ONE![37]

Traveling by rail once again, the circus encompassed "100 cars, six passenger coaches, [and] fourteen engines"[38] and used three entrances to facilitate crowd control at each city's circus lot. Nearly 300 people and 190 horses were employed at the beginning of the season, but that number swelled to "over 2,000 men and horses" within a few weeks.[39]

The street parade was "brilliant," gushed the *Clipper*, and thousands of people lined the parade route to hear and see the grand procession that now stretched over two miles. During the parade, three units of musicians played for the crowds. First, music deriving from that "absurd novelty, the steam piano" (the calliope), was "delicious," recalled some spectators.[40] Elsewhere, however, the calliope found little appreciation, as its music was sometimes described as "shrieks from hell."[41] After a performance by the Cooper & Bailey Circus in Adelaide, Australia in 1878, one man wrote to the management asking them to remove that "infernal machine." If they complied, he wrote, "the villagers will think more highly of you and patronize you more largely in the future."[42] According to Slout, the Great Eastern Circus was the only circus to incorporate this musical wonder into its program; in fact, it was the only enterprise since 1860 to use the calliope.[43]

Next, the crowd was treated to the twenty-five-piece orchestra, conducted that season by Professor W. D. Storey. Finally, the martial band marched by, reminiscent of "the days of '76"[44] — an attempt by management to amplify the patriotic spirit that enveloped the nation as it prepared for the centennial celebration. Following the bands in the promenade was a return to chivalry with "a gorgeous chariot," along with "twenty ladies on horseback in procession with an equal number of knights and pages."[45]

The museum expanded its extensive collection of "living curiosities" and for the 1873–74 season included the "wonderful wild men of Borneo, the four-legged child, the beautiful Circassian belle, [and] the illusions of the great Collier."[46] The sideshow adjoining the museum was under the direction of Pat Harris and Windy Sullivan. The roster included "a Punch and Judy" and an "Albino boy."[47] The menagerie, housed in four tents, was an astounding display of exotic and indigenous animals, including the elephant Conqueror, camels, alpacas, porcupines, ocelots, lions, fifty white cockatoos, twenty-one snakes, and thirty-nine varieties of monkeys.[48]

Circus historian George Chindahl noted that menageries first appeared in U.S. cities prior to the Revolution and catered to those who frowned upon the circus's alleged "lascivious behavior."[49] In the early years, a showman would arrive with only "one or a few" imported animals and display them in venues not easily accessible to those unwilling to pay the viewing fee.[50] The compositions of the earliest menageries were "determined by serendipity,"[51] since cargo ships returning from Africa and Asia usually collected animals haphazardly and shipped them in addition to their standard cargo.

After the Civil War, menageries became an integral part of circus performances because they generated additional revenue and introduced the "animal tamer" routines that subjected many circus performers to perilous encounters with wild animals. The importation of animals was no longer a casual occurrence, since business relationships were established between specialized animal dealers in Europe and showmen in the United States.

The *Camden (N.J.) Democrat* commented that the menagerie offered "a most interesting and valuable lesson" in zoology and ornithology.[52] In August 1873, the Scranton, Pennsylvania, paper reported that the "specimens [were] in good order" and comprised an "excellent variety."[53] In Chambersburg, Pennsylvania, a few weeks later, the *Valley Spirit* stated that the menagerie "affords lessons of useful instruction to students of natural history."[54] The Great Eastern Circus repeatedly earned praise and simultaneously quashed some skeptics' concerns that its menagerie was a poorly populated, jumbled fusion of wild beasts. The *New York Clipper* described the animal assembly as "extensive and rare."[55] Further legit-

imizing the menagerie as a learning experience, the *Carlisle (Pa.)
Herald* declared: "The menagerie and aviary naturally present many
attractions to the moral classes and to the student of natural history.
Here are collected, in a splendid zoological institute, the choicest
specimens of the jungle, forest and plain while the ornithological
department embraces the rarest gems of the tropics."[56]

By the 1870s, menageries were so popular that the majority of
circus advertisements featured nothing *but* the menagerie. Forty
documented Great Eastern Circus advertisements in the authors'
collection, dated between 1872 and 1874, were examined. In the
entire collection, only one advertisement prominently featured human talent, while the remaining thirty-nine did not mention it at all.
Rather, the notices are a visual buffet of wild animals — zebras, cattle, snakes, a pair of armadillos — promoting the extensive zoological collection that accompanied the circus. Small samplings of advertisements featured a human working with the animals; however,
no performer's name was given since the management chose to
keep the focus on the menagerie. Often, the only names that did
appear on circus ads were those of the advance agents, who often
wrote the advertisements and notices that appeared in newspapers.

*   *   *

"Miss Emma Lake" and Marie Elise headlined the Great Eastern's
equestrian corps, along with Ferdinand Tourniaire and members of
the Carroll riding family. Charles Lee Fowler and Al Miaco remained
as clowns and were joined by Ben Maginley and Sam McFlinn (or
McFlynn). Fifteen gymnasts, including Charles Spencer, Adolph Barbado, A. P. Durand, and William Painter (William Bracken) — the
latter two of whom had previously doubled in a "brothers" routine —
joined the troupe.[57] George W. Zebold, "champion ticket seller,"
astonished crowds with his lighting-fast speed in distributing the
correct currency and tickets. Johnny Batcheller, tumbler, gymnast,
and "champion leaper," joined the troupe in Montgomery, Alabama, in January 1874.[58] A few months earlier, in November 1873,
the Great Eastern Circus had hired the popular tumbling and comic

clown Billy Burke, whose daughter, Billie, is remembered for her role as Glinda in MGM's *The Wizard of OZ*.[59]

Agnes Lake was on the roster, but she had retired her legendary *Mazeppa* act after nearly a decade of performing in the title role. Long before, she had retired her wire acts — the routines that had introduced her to circus audiences nearly a generation earlier. In her final performance season, Agnes focused on her signature manège acts and readied her debut in a new circus exhibition. Agnes was double-billed as "Mlle. Eugenie De Lonne" and daringly entered the cages of the Great Eastern Circus's felines. Agnes crafted her pseudonym as homage to a friend and former colleague, Eugenia de Lorme, the widow of Clark T. Ames.

Eugenia de Lorme was a lion tamer who had been employed by the Robinson & Lake show from 1859 to 1862. When the Lake and Robinson partnership ended, de Lorme continued to perform with "Old John" Robinson's circuses and then with her husband's shows. Agnes and Eugenia were reunited when Agnes Lake's Mammoth Circus and Ames's Menagerie "commenced a brief season" at the corner of Laurel Street and Central Avenue in Cincinnati in October 1871.[60]

The day before Bill Lake was murdered in Missouri, Eugenia was performing in Sunbury, Pennsylvania, about fifty miles north of Harrisburg, when she was attacked by one of her "trained" lions. Although severely injured, she miraculously survived the mauling. When her husband, Clark Ames, was killed by drunken towners the following year, similar to Bill Lake's murder, Eugenia drew strength and inspiration from Agnes's behavior as a circus widow.[61] Eugenia, like Agnes, managed her late husband's recent entertainment venture — the Crescent City Museum in New Orleans. The equipment for her husband's circus and menagerie, however, remained in storage in Nashville, and Eugenia eventually sold it all. In 1872 she retired from the circus, married a towner, H. K. Robinson, and moved to Memphis.[62]

Agnes, as Eugenie, performed a daring act — "entering the dens of the kings of the forest, and holding them subservient to the magic wand of her influence and the wonderful electricity of her will" — in "two massive performing dens" painted in vibrant emerald, crimson, and gold tones.[63] The *New York Clipper* explained: "[M]lle. Eugenie De Lonne (Madame Agnes Lake) daily takes out unchained, on a grand tableaux car, lions, a Bengal tiger, a jaguar or man-eater, a panther and leopard. She is assisted by H. Saunders, the English expert."[64]

"H. Saunders, the English expert" is possibly John Saunders, the "English rider and leaper," whom Agnes had worked with previously. It was not uncommon for circus performers to change tasks if they became injured or retired from their trademark feats. Many skilled equestrians, including Bill Lake, became clowns or ringmasters after suffering severe leg or back injuries. Many knew no other way of life than living and traveling as a circus performer, and they clung to the itinerant lifestyle as long as they could.

Agnes steeled her nerves as the cages of crimson, gold, and green were wheeled into the ring. Probably armed with the common accessories of the day — a thin chair, a whip, and a starter pistol — Agnes stepped into the cage. Calmly, she commanded the felines through familiar acts such as dancing in formation, leaping through flaming hoops, and hopping over one another, and she rewarded them with tasty treats. In his memoirs first published in 1921, George Conklin, a nineteenth-century wild animal trainer, disclosed that many trainers gave commands in a foreign language to enhance their prowess among the audience.[65] Agnes, who had been claiming French ancestry for years, almost certainly followed this trend. Some animal trainers included birds, dogs, and pachyderms in their routines, but evidence suggests that Agnes worked solely with the large cats.

Circus historian Stuart Thayer noted that in the early years of wild animal acts, more emphasis was placed on the performer entering the cages than on the events that occurred within the enclosure.[66] Unfortunately, few documents reveal a detailed account of Agnes's feats with the lions, tigers, jaguars, and leopards of the Great Eastern Circus. Existing newspapers, personal memoirs of Agnes's contemporaries, and secondary sources help us reconstruct

Agnes's final months of performance. Janet M. Davis has argued that "the image of a 'gentle' woman handling beasts was arousing."[67] How could the public's curiosity (and libido) not be provoked when assaulted by circus advertisements flooded with images of scantily clad women amid great, ferocious felines?

The earliest female circus performers in the cages were usually assistants to the male trainers. Others, like Eugenie de Lorme and, later, Mabel Stark in the twentieth century, used the opportunity to develop their own signature circus acts as animal "tamers." Male trainers were distinctly revered as "models of manly stoicism" and traditionally wore khaki or formal wear, giving them a practical, yet distinguished, authority.[68] Women, on the other hand, were noted as "more physically interactive with their beasts."[69] One stock illustration shared by many circuses portrayed a woman surrounded by snarling lions and tigers, fighting her way through the crowd of felines, armed with only a whip in hand.

The circus meticulously "cultivated the erotic image of women animal trainers" and depicted them wearing glittering formal wear or other fluffy, impractical garb.[70] In reality, many women donned "protective paramilitary clothing"[71] that offered some, albeit little, protection against sharp claws and teeth. The press reported on the copiously spangled costumes, like those featured in the advertisements and lithographs. Those costumes, however, were probably reserved for the parades, when the lions or tigers were secured to the top of the wagons and the performer was in little danger of being attacked. If the press had reported on the unsexy, drab clothing female trainers *did* wear during performances, it would have undermined the danger and sensuality the advertisements promised.

George Conklin started to train animals after his first season on the road, prior to the Civil War. We can surmise that Agnes's experiences were parallel, since both performers subscribed to the old-school principles of animal training. In his memoirs, Conklin remarked that infinite patience was the key to winning the animals' trust.[72] In this respect, Agnes Lake would have had no problem training many of the animals. Although her experience in animal training heretofore had been overwhelmingly equine in nature, she

Fig. 27. This advertisement was circulated by several circuses that had animal taming acts. The subject, a woman wearing a shortened dress and armed with only a whip, displays the unspoken sensuality female animal tamers supposedly embodied. From the collection of Linda A. Fisher.

was acutely aware of how to train animals. It took many months for Agnes to successfully train her horses to obey her vocal commands and silent cues to bow and prance in the ring while simultaneously ignoring circus audiences. One of her horses was blind, increasing the difficultly of training it, and others were trained for months for the intricate *Mazeppa* act. Agnes was infinitely patient — one would have to be to survive in an unpredictable industry like the circus.

Conklin recalled studying the animals by hanging around their cages, talking to them, and stroking them to dissipate their fear of him.[73] Agnes must have acted similarly; she had ample opportunities to become acquainted with the moods, behaviors, and characteristics of the cats that had traveled for over two years with the Great Eastern Circus. Agnes was trained under the watchful eye of Elijah Lengel and learned the delicate intricacies of training the animals with rewards of meat, fish, or sugar, not by striking or clubbing them.

Understanding the moods of individual big cats was crucial for the trainer's safety. Nearly all the animals with which Agnes and other trainers worked had been born in the wild and often exhibited unpredictable behavior. Even after some successful domestic breeding attempts, the animals were never tame like a "big rough dog," as Conklin stated,[74] and accidents were common. Twentieth-century animal trainers Mabel Stark and Clyde Beatty inadvertently startled the animals, which pounced on them, biting into their sinew and nearly severing their limbs. As recently as 2003, Roy Horn, half of the famous duo Siegfried & Roy, was injured during a performance. No reports have surfaced of Agnes being severely injured or mauled during performances or training sessions, although she may have suffered superficial cuts and scrapes.

*   *   *

The first few weeks of the second season on the road were rocky for the Great Eastern Circus. In Louisville the company faced its first crisis; stormy weather not only prevented many would-be patrons from attending the evening performance but also wreaked havoc on those who braved the weather. A blast of wind ripped through the canvas and snapped the center pole in half, sending the spliced ropes whipping through the air. The mammoth canvas crashed to the ground and buried "the vast array of seats, along with their struggling occupants." In addition, the lights were immediately extinguished and the canvas caught fire, leading the reporter to write that "the scene that ensued was beyond description."[75] Adults and children screamed in pain and frantically clawed at one another to escape the inferno, while the caged animals howled and shook their cages in fear.

The *New York Clipper* commented that "too much praise cannot be awarded [to the circus crew] for the heroic manner in which they worked to extricate the sufferers; and had it not been for their prompt action the number killed would have been terrible." At press time the *Clipper* reported that there were no known estimates of human or animal casualties. Andrew Haight, the general manager that season, announced that the company would remain in town and donate the proceeds of subsequent shows to ease the citizens' suffering. While the town boasted a new Exposition Building for performing exhibitions, Haight revealed that the troupe was forced to set up in its canvas tents because James E. Cooper forbade the town to permit another circus to exhibit in the new building after he deposited a $6,000 bond ensuring that his company, Cooper's Circus, would be the first in the new space. Cooper went so far as to serve the Great Eastern Circus and other rival companies with an injunction that prevented them from occupying the Exposition Building.[76]

The tents and pavilions, illuminated by a variety of gas lighting and flame-burning lamps, were known fire hazards. Yet one other piece of circus paraphernalia was surprisingly just as deadly a hazard — the orchestra. In August, during a performance in Lancaster, Pennsylvania, the tent caught fire from a spark originating from a calliope — "that outrageous and unearthly steam pie-anner," as one "ragged urchin" called it.[77] The fire burned a seven-foot hole in the canvas. The editors of Lancaster's *Daily Express* reported the use of the circus lemonade to smother the flames, noting that the acidic liquid "served admirably well."[78] Once the fire had been extinguished, the show resumed. The audience anxiously watched the performers commence their acts. The acrid smell of burned canvas hung in the air, and the equestrians kept a tight rein on their nervous mounts, resulting in mixed reviews from the audience and critics. The Great Eastern Circus earned $2,000–$3,000 that night but left "nothing in exchange but the recollections of a heated tent, tame equestrianism, [and] stale and vulgar jokes,"[79] complained one editor. In addition, the editors alleged that several patrons had been relieved of their pocketbooks.

The dismal reviews from local newspapers were not what Agnes and her colleagues had hoped for, especially after a circus catastrophe had been averted. A third reported fire that season occurred on January 10, 1874, while the troupe was performing in New Orleans. Taking precautions, the management announced that "even smoking in and around the canvas is not permitted." Later that evening, however, the canvas again caught fire, and the day's remaining performances were cancelled. The *Daily Picayune* reported suspicions of arson, since the investigation indicated that the cause of the fire was "the ignition of a quantity of coal oil, supposed to have been committed by some malicious person."[80] The damage was not extensive, however, and the show resumed the following morning.[81]

Fires were not the only risk that jeopardized the circus's schedule. Since the entire troupe traveled by rail, they had to contend with a new set of travel delays with the railroad. While en route to Indianapolis in April, an unidentified "serious blockade" on the tracks postponed the circus for over eight hours. The ensemble eventually arrived to perform the evening show, but only a few hundred citizens had stayed to attend.[82] The following August, while traveling through Pennsylvania's coal country, the circus was delayed at the Mahanoy Tunnel outside Shamokin because they had to remove the wheels from the menagerie cages to pass through the tunnel safely. The troupe arrived and commenced the parade instead of the first show, and hundreds of citizens observed. The *Clipper* reported that "forty-two collieries [coal mines] were idle," since nearly all of Mahanoy had gone to the show.[83] The editors of the *Shamokin Herald,* however, were disappointed by the procession and the steam piano.[84]

Even with the railroad delays, Agnes, Emma, and other veteran performers harbored no desire to return to the "good old days" of the overland shows. Wagons rarely provided adequate shelter in sweltering heat, freezing cold, or during heavy thunderstorms. Railroad cars provided sufficient shelter during even the worst weather conditions, although the cars were often crowded to capacity.

In addition to safety hazards and unexpected traveling delays, the circus's success often depended on the reviews of an unpredictable press. One newspaper editor in New Jersey found writing about circuses tedious and declared that anyone who could "write freshly on a circus show" was a genius.[85] Throughout July 1873, Agnes and the Great Eastern Circus suffered from lackluster reviews and bored editors.

In Paterson, New Jersey, the *Daily Press* suggested the heat was to blame for a condensed troupe. The Great Eastern Circus was expected to "astonish everybody by its prodigiousness [but] must have suffered terribly" because of the "fervent heat."[86] The entire show could have fit into one or two tents rather than the advertised dozen, the media complained. There is no explanation as to why the show was noticeably smaller at that time, although illness, injury, and transportation problems surely played a role. Payroll troubles and tension between management and performers could also account for a reduced roster. A few days later, it was observed that the menagerie was not very extensive. In Trenton, a three-hour delay, compounded by a parade that was shorter than expected and in which the steam piano was muted, resulted in another dreary review. The editor was unimpressed by the parade and did not bother attending the performance.[87]

Elsewhere in New Jersey, especially in Elizabeth, Camden, and Newark, Agnes and the company received positive endorsements anticipating their arrival and left glowing reviews in their wake. The Great Eastern Circus exhibited in Newark during the centennial celebration in July. Local media eagerly waited "the most stupendous exposition of the wonderful ever created."[88] Agnes was situated between two leopards and a tiger, in a heavily spangled costume, during the parade in New Brunswick. In Elizabeth, the *Daily Monitor* wrote that it was superfluous to raise the public's awareness "to the immensity of this largest of modern entertainments," since it was unrivaled in popularity, and added that the circus's corps of talent "is not approached."[89]

Frustrated by the perplexing combination of praise and criticism they received in New Jersey, members of the troupe continued to Pennsylvania, where they were welcomed by large and enthusiastic audiences. The Great Eastern Circus received its highest praise from a Phoenixville newspaper, the *Independent Phoenix*, in August 1873. The menagerie was four times larger than that of most shows, while the arenic attractions are "thrice as great," the newspaper reported:

> [T]his is the mastodon of the period all who have seen it confess. As a giant towers above his fellows, so it overtops and places in the shade all other exhibitions of this age of its popular class. To enumerate the manifold attractions of this Goliath of shows would require more space than we can allow, hence we refer the reader to the small bills and mammoth many-colored posters adorning the walls around the town.[90]

In Reading, the tents were "crowded almost to suffocation," and the company did a "tremendous business."[91] In Harrisburg in the waning days of summer, the *Daily Patriot* noted that nearly 11,000 people had witnessed the circus in its two performances in a single day.[92]

In a rare editorial, the Great Eastern Circus's use of dual rings was noted by two newspapers. In Washington, D.C., the editor of the *Evening Star* endorsed the use of simultaneous performances in two rings, calling it a "novel feature" and a "great improvement on the single ring exhibition."[93] Harrisburg's *Daily Patriot*, however, was not impressed by this "novelty" utilized by the Great Eastern Circus: "The dual ring performance was a novelty, but we cannot say that we admire it. When as good artists as are connected with the Great Eastern favor an audience with such an elegant display of proficiency in their different roles, we think it detracts from the excellence of the performance to have two sets of artists at one time entertaining an audience."[94]

Both Agnes and Emma were exalted in the local media after performing in Carlisle, Pennsylvania, on August 30. They are "*equestriennes* extraordinary," announced the *Herald*; their skills were equaled by their fellow cast mates, including "*la petite* Annie, Adolph Barrabo (or Barbado), and Master Willie."[95] In Washington, D.C., the horses under the guidance of Agnes Lake and the equestrian director, Barney Carroll, "were the prominent features" of the exhibition, noted the *Clipper*.[96] In September the *Richmond Daily Dispatch* remarked that "the performing horses are well trained and well under the control of their female exhibitors."[97] The crowd collectively held its breath "when the daring lion-tamer," Eugenie DeLonne (Agnes), entered the cage "and took the lions through their tricks."[98]

While the troupe was in Baltimore, Emma received a special gift that was mentioned extensively in newspapers in both Baltimore and Washington, D.C. Buffalo Bill Cody had sent Emma a bridle and martingale (a specialized piece of tack used to control head carriage during manège) made from black horsehair woven by American Indians. According to Gil Robinson, both Emma's and Buffalo Bill's names were carved on the silver buckles.[99] The decorative tassels, however, were supposedly "made of hair taken from Indian scalps by Buffalo Bill" himself. She used the tack in that evening's performances.[100]

During his Wild West shows, Buffalo Bill had incorporated "Indian modes of combat" into his repertoire to achieve greater authenticity in his role as a white Indian. But as Louis Warren noted, the "literary and artistic notions of Indian fighting were not easily made real without creating controversy."[101] Cody often displayed the scalp of Yellow Hair, a Cheyenne subchief he had slain in 1876 — the purported "first scalp for Custer"[102] — as part of his exhibition. Most Americans regarded the practice of scalping enemies as a barbaric, "savage gesture beneath civilized society, and beneath professional soldiers, who mostly abhorred the practice."[103] One can only surmise Buffalo Bill's intentions in sending Emma such a controversial gift.

The circumstances surrounding Emma's gift are unclear. There are no accounts of Agnes and Emma having met Cody, although beginning in August 1873, Hickok was performing with Cody and John Baker "Texas Jack" Omohundro. It is reasonable to assume either that Agnes and Hickok had met sometime in the two years since Abilene or that Hickok was so infatuated with Agnes and with Emma's talents that he talked persistently about them to Cody and prompted him to gift Emma with the unique tack.

In late 1873, Cody's troupe appeared in Fred G. Maeder's adapted narrative, *The Scouts of the Plains*. Traveling by train, they appeared in one- or two-night stands in thirteen states. Cody and Texas Jack hoped Hickok's addition to the ensemble would draw greater audiences, but they quickly realized that he was struggling to learn his lines and maintain his focus. Eventually, the plot was edited so Hickok would sit down with Cody and Texas Jack against a trompe l'oeil prairie, the men would pass a bottle of whiskey, and each man would "spout a blood-curdling yarn."[104]

Hickok left "Buffalo Bill's Combination" in March 1874 because he loathed the "sham heroics" portrayed in Maeder's narrative.[105] As a token of their friendship and possibly as a bribe to leave the show, Cody and Texas Jack each gave Hickok five hundred dollars cash, as well as a pair of immaculate .44 caliber Smith & Wesson revolvers.[106] Hickok boarded a train to New York City, but his activities there are obscure.[107]

The audience and local media were greatly impressed by the Great Eastern Circus in Richmond and had only one complaint, one with which modern audiences are sure to identify — the "loud-mouthed vendors." Up and down the bleachers throughout the evening, vendors bellowed at the patrons and peddled lemonade, candy, and concert tickets for the post-circus entertainment. The *Daily Dispatch* wrote that the vendors "constantly [annoyed] people in the midst of the exhibitions. Everybody voted them a great nuisance."[108]

The second season of the Great Eastern Circus came to a close on February 4, 1874, following a two-day exhibition in Memphis. Agnes's circus career had ended after she had traveled thousands of miles and performed with dozens of companies alongside hundreds of colleagues. After nearly thirty years, Agnes left the hippodromes and canvas tents and said goodbye to her circus family. Although not related by blood or marriage, Agnes's circus family had a common livelihood, and they shared the successes and failures that marked each season on the road. Agnes had spent more than half her life with her circus family traveling across the country, first in wagons and steamboats and later by rail. She had performed in front of millions of people and on two continents. Her life was drastically different from the lives of her surviving siblings, her brother Joseph in St. Louis and her sister Elizabeth in Cincinnati. Agnes packed away her once-glittering costumes, now covered with a faint layer of sawdust, along with her props and tack, and prepared to transport her horses back to her farm in Kentucky.

*   *   *

Agnes Lake's acumen as a businesswoman was not confined to circus operations. She recognized the potential of other business ventures and invested in one in particular that she hoped would sustain her throughout her retirement: the blossoming field of lithography.

Lithography, invented in 1798 by Alois Senefelder, is a unique printing process in which the image to be rendered is carved on an ink-receptive surface, such as a smooth stone or a metal plate, and the blank area that receives the image is ink-repellent. The two surfaces are joined, pressure is applied, and a slightly raised image is left when the two halves are separated. In the first half of the nineteenth century, Cincinnati became one of the nation's leading cities in the printing industry—an accolade attributed to the influx of hundreds of German residents who had a working knowledge of the trade before they immigrated to the New World.[109] Between 1825 and 1860, there were over eighty engraving firms in Cincinnati, mostly wood engravers, but several individuals and partnerships diversified with copperplate engraving and lithography.[110]

In his essay "Early Printing and Publishing in Cincinnati," Noel Martin argued that Victorians felt liberated by lithography, since the process "freed the artists from the constraints of [the] letterpress" by making it easier to render images.[111] Victorian artisans flooded advertisements in newspapers and magazines with pictures rather than words alone.[112] Specially designed lithographic crayons and pencils, pens and brushes with liquid tusche, copperplates, and wood engravings facilitated the emerging trade and translated the artist's imagination and creativity into a final design.

Cincinnati, because of its prime location on the Ohio River, was not only an emerging business center but a major entertainment hub as well. For several decades, many circus troupes had established their winter quarters in the surrounding environs while others, including Agnes Lake, the Robinson family, and Spencer Q. Stokes, called Cincinnati home. The Queen City's countless theaters provided world-class entertainment for citizens. Agnes's brother Joseph, for example, attended over seventy theatrical productions between November 1847 and February 1849. Many of those performances were held in Cincinnati's bustling theaters, but traveling music and dance troupes often performed in churches, private homes, and society buildings such as the Masonic Hall. Since the theatrical community boasted strong audiences, many printing firms specialized in producing theatrical and circus posters.

A few years before her retirement, Agnes invested some of the profits from her Hippo-Olympiad in a Cincinnati lithography firm that specialized in printing circus posters. While the company's identity remains another mystery in Agnes's life, research identified two companies — with strong ties to both Cincinnati and the circus — as likely options: the United States Playing Card Company and the Strobridge Lithography Company.[113] Several fires, however, incinerated the majority of Strobridge's business records, and the earliest date on the surviving holdings is 1877. In addition, the business records for the USPCC have not been located, making it difficult to determine where Agnes Lake invested her money. Her obituaries reported that she unfortunately lost much of her money during the Panic of 1873 — in the middle of her last performance season with the Great Eastern Circus.

The Panic of 1873 put thousands of workers' financial futures in jeopardy. In Agnes's case, horses were expensive to care for, and at age forty-eight she could not manage the eighteen-acre farm alone. She was no longer performing, and Agnes doubted that Emma's circus salary would be enough to maintain the farm and a handful of horses while they traveled nine months of the year with the circus. In need of money, Agnes may have asked her brother Joseph Mersman for a short-term loan. Although he had degenerative health problems, the forty-nine year-old Joseph had formed a new partnership with Charles F. Orthwein in 1870. The firm, Orthwein & Mersman, invested in corn and grain and sold it to a number of St. Louis breweries, including Anheuser-Busch. Joseph was extremely fond of Agnes and had helped her financially in the past.[114] In addition, Agnes resolved to sell some of her most prized possessions, including her favorite performing steeds, to stabilize her finances. Two weeks after her final performance season ended, Agnes placed notices in local newspapers and the *Clipper*:

Mme. Agnes Lake offers for sale her gray Arabian stallion D'Jalma, a fine horse (imported in 1867. Lost one eye in coming from Europe) — $500; a long-maned trick mare (Esmiralda) formerly belonging to Col Ames, 8 yrs old; $500, which has been trained to do twelve tricks . . . a Mazeppa costume (cashmere, white merino and red satin — cap and boots), including a jeweled sword and dagger, $50 . . . one white spangled train, 5 lbs of spangles on it, basque trimmed with silver bullion eight inches deep, $50 never worn . . . two dresses suitable for a principal rider; one blue tarlatan, trimmed with silver llama, white satin hip waist trimmed with black bugles and silver bullion, white spangled full waist, $20. The other a white tarlatan, trimmed with silver llama and gold-colored ribbon, purple silk velvet hip waist, trimmed with spangles, and white spangled full waist, $20 — never worn . . . and two wigs. One dark beautiful brown wig, natural curly hair, new $18; blonde wig natural curly, $20.[115]

Agnes had unofficially retired from performing in the circus, and selling her performance accoutrements announced her decision to the public. Many of her obituaries claimed she stopped performing in 1880, but Agnes's name (or aliases) does not appear on any rosters after the 1873 season. The legendary Mazeppa costumes she had worn before thousands of audiences were sold to other performers carrying on the tradition of Mazeppa in the circus — a tradition Agnes had helped initiate.

Throughout her long career, Agnes had endeavored to attach herself to respectable entertainment exhibitions. She shrewdly hired performers who maintained a similar level of moral conduct and kept "lot lice" away from her circus. Even though Agnes knew her own circus career was coming to a close, her daughter Emma was only nineteen and on the precipice of fame. Agnes needed to ensure that Emma's professional and personal reputation would remain intact now that they had to rely on the circus management to keep uncouth performers and characters at bay. Agnes stayed close to her daughter's side as Emma's "witchery on horseback" secured her a contract with "Old John" Robinson's circus. From the unique vantage point of mother, mentor, and chaperone, Agnes witnessed Emma's entrance into circus history as she challenged and perhaps even eclipsed her mother's fame.

CHAPTER TWELVE

Passing the Reins
1874–1877

The year 1874 began with major transitions, both personal and professional, for Agnes Lake. She retired from her successful thirty-year circus career, sold many of her personal mementos, and briefly rested at her Kentucky farm before dashing off to New York City. Agnes and Emma Lake were guests at the posh St. Nicholas Hotel for a week in March,[1] during which time she met up with Wild Bill Hickok, who had recently left Buffalo Bill Cody's theatrical troupe after performances in Rochester. No doubt having read newspaper accounts of Hickok's engagements with Cody, Agnes traced his movements to New York City and hastened there to rendezvous with Wild Bill, whom she may not have seen in over two years.

According to the *New York Clipper*, Agnes and Emma Lake traveled from Kentucky to meet both Cody and Hickok, but Cody remained in Rochester. No reports have been located of the meeting between Hickok and Agnes. The physical and emotional attraction between the couple was reignited, but little had changed in their personal lives to warrant a marriage proposal. Emma was still single and Agnes would not leave her until she was married, but Hickok desperately needed the solace he could find in his beloved western plains. It is believed that at this point in their relationship their correspondence was renewed. However, it would be another two years before the star-crossed lovers met again.

In February, Agnes received some long overdue satisfaction. Jacob Killian, the man who murdered Bill Lake, finally went to trial and was convicted of murder—five years after he committed the atrocity. Once again, the incident saturated newspapers across the country, and communities from Missouri to New York were outraged at the wanton acts that resulted in the murder of a popular circus performer. Once again, Agnes Lake replayed the last moments of her husband's life in her mind. Although time had softened the impact of those events, the grief for a loved one lost through violence is never easily abated.

No reports indicate that Agnes witnessed the trial in person, although she would certainly have been aware of the details of the court proceedings. Residents from Neosho and Granby crowded into the courtroom. Myriad newspapers across the country—from the *St. Louis Globe-Democrat* to the *New York Sun*—provided brief summaries of Lake's murder, Killian's flight from justice across Missouri, and accounts of the trial. Citizens of Neosho were angry that Killian had lived "scot free" for five years before justice was finally served.

Many of the prosecution's scheduled witnesses were employees of the Lakes' circus, but they had scattered across the country since the crime and were difficult to locate. Court documents from the trial have not been located. The testimony gleaned from eyewitness accounts and newspaper details, however, solidly implicated Killian as the murderer, although the defense "fought hard for the prisoner."[2] Neighbors of Killian testified that it was really Lake who had provoked the encounter and threatened to shoot Killian. Others swore that Killian was "a law-abiding citizen," despite the fact that his ocular deformity—the primary identifying physical characteristic of Lake's murderer—was the consequence of him having been caught "in the act of robbery" several years earlier.[3]

A guilty verdict was returned, but his punishment amounted to a paltry reprimand—a mere three years and seven months in prison. Never mind that Killian had announced his intention to murder Lake "if he could get a pistol" and that Bill Lake was murdered only a few minutes later. Never mind that Killian fled the scene and was chased by a posse of forty men for over a month before he was captured on the other side of Missouri. Never mind that Agnes was left a widow and Emma without a father. A great light of the circus had been extinguished when Bill Lake was murdered, and there was undoubtedly outrage from his friends and former colleagues when the verdict and sentencing were announced. Killian apparently "burst into tears" and pleaded to the sheriff, "I would far sooner they had stretched my neck."[4]

Killian served his prison sentence but was killed by A. S. Norton in Short Creek, Kansas, shortly after his release. In May 1878, the *Cincinnati Enquirer* reported that a jury in Columbus, Kansas, had acquitted Norton in Killian's murder and that the result "was anticipated by nearly every one."[5] Gil Robinson's memoirs substantiated this information and also identified Norton not only as Killian's murderer but also as the man apparently responsible for Killian's facial misshapenness.[6]

Agnes's marriage to Bill Lake in 1846 and Killian's conviction in 1874 served as bookends to her circus performance career. She had seen Lake's murder avenged and was finally ready to move on with the rest of her life.

*   *   *

While Agnes's career was ending, her involvement in Emma's career continued. Emma Lake's professional career skyrocketed after she and Agnes "seceded" from the Great Eastern Circus.[7] Emma signed a contract with "John Robinson's Ten Big Shows." On May 2, 1874, an illustration of Emma Lake appeared on the front page of the *New York Clipper*.[8] The illustration showed a poised young woman dressed in a stylish riding habit and top hat, with a firm grasp on her steed's reins. This image thrust Emma Lake into the national spotlight and to the forefront of late-nineteenth-century female equestrianism. She was named the country's "Premiere Equestrienne." The *New York Clipper* raved about the young Emma Lake:

Fig. 28. Emma Lake was prominently featured on the front page of the May 2, 1874, edition of the *New York Clipper*. Shortly thereafter she was called "America's premier equestrian." Courtesy American Antiquarian Society.

There is, perhaps, no lady in the equestrian profession who has won distinction and fame more rapidly than the subject of illustration in our present issue. Notwithstanding the very few years she has been before the public, she has succeeded by skill, grace and daring in winning for herself the reputation of being one of the most accomplished equestriennes of the *haut ecole* that have appeared before the American public. Miss Emma Lake was born in Cincinnati, O., Feb. 22, 1856, and, at a very early age, was introduced to the ring by her father, the late William Lake of managerial fame; but not until after his demise, and under the skillful training

and direction of her mother, Mme. Agnes, did she evince
that wonderful skill and intrepidity which have since won
for her a position so high in her profession. Under this
tuition Miss Lake has developed a style of dash and abandon
most unequaled. In her [manège] act she evokes enthusiastic admiration from every beholder. She displays, [with]
much skill, the different gaits, posturings and leaps of
her thoroughbreds "Bonnie Scotland" and "Duke Alexis,"
which were trained and taught by herself alone, to aid her in
her beautiful and classic acts. Miss Emma commenced an
engagement of one year on April 1 with John Robinson's
Menagerie and Circus.[9]

In the nineteenth century the horse was indisputably the king of
circus performances, while its rider, the écuýere, "was the queen of
the ring."[10] Decades earlier, the English circus impresario Philip
Astley had standardized the dimensions of the circus ring to approximately forty feet in diameter, "primarily to accommodate vaulting
and other acrobatic acts on the horse."[11]

Agnes, Emma, and several of their contemporaries gained fame
through a variety of popular equine exhibitions known as *haute école*,
"high school," and manège.[12] The specific equine education that
subsequently developed from intense circus training was known as
manège — the art of horsemanship — composed of specific commands that render deliberate movements and paces.

Dressage was introduced in the first decade of the nineteenth
century. Although considered the "ultimate in schooled riding,"[13]
its popularity waned until Louise Tourniaire, a French equestrian,
rejuvenated the art form around 1850 while she toured with James
M. June & Company's American and European Amphitheatre.[14]
Tourniaire's talent restored the haute école vogue, and her bareback feats in the ring propelled female equestrians "to the forefront
of riding pursuits."[15] Thus, she paved the way for Agnes, Emma, and
Agnes's other daughter, Alice Lake Wilson, who earned praise for
her equine abilities at a young age.

Emma Lake achieved fame for her skills as a haute école rider.

In classical displays of haute école, the "emphasis should be on the horse."[16] In a circus milieu, the rider is to give the impression that specific paces are "difficult to achieve" while acting in a "dramatic, even frenzied manner,"[17] making the audience believe the horse's tasks are harder to accomplish than they appear.

Emma Lake also incorporated "certain acrobatic feats" into her programs to flaunt her skills as a proficient manège rider and trainer. She demonstrated her horse's ability to rear, dance, and waltz. Other "equestrian eccentricities" included the Spanish walk and trot, in which the horse's forelegs and hind legs crossed and lengthened in an exaggerated gait as the animal slowly moved sideways.[18] Emma furthermore coaxed her steed to jump using its rear legs for support and to perform a pirouette "in which the animal settled back into a sitting position, raised its forelegs, and whirled to change direction for a few paces."[19] In addition, Thayer described a series of calculated paces that suggested the horse possessed a highly developed musical aptitude: "There followed a march step. By raising and lowering its forelegs in a slashing manner, the horse seemed to be keeping time to the music in four or three or two beats, though of course the band was keeping time with the steps."[20]

The finale was a tremendously popular spectacle. Emma, gracefully poised on her mount, commanded her horse to bow down on one flexed leg and kneel in front of the audience. Thayer remarked that "in all likelihood, the cheers were loud and long" because of the popularity of the feat.[21] Emma's equine recital was designed with an "extravagance of movements," so she could "enchant" and "titillate" the audiences.[22]

*   *   *

Agnes Lake accompanied her now-famous daughter Emma throughout the 1874–75 season as they toured with "THE VERY BEST CIRCUS IN THE WORLD,"[23] which included an enormous museum and menagerie. "Old John" Robinson had retired in 1871, but the show retained his name and likeness at the helm. Three of his sons managed the outfit. John F. Robinson, Jr., was the general manager. "The Governor," as he was known, had been "trained as a bareback rider, tum-

Fig. 29. Photograph of Emma Lake at the height of her career, circa 1875, dressed in European-inspired attire for manège performances. Courtesy The York County Heritage Trust, PA.

bler and leaper," but his increasing weight "necessitated withdrawal from performing."[24] Gil Robinson debuted as a tumbling infant in his father's show but ultimately focused on his managerial abilities instead. Gil acted as assistant manager and treasurer, and his younger brother, James Robinson, served as "master of canvas and general supervisor."[25] Agnes and Emma were reunited with familiar faces, including Frederick Bailey, the general agent, and John Wilson, Alice Lake's widower, who served as the equestrian director.

Agnes and Emma must have been astounded at the size of the Robinsons' "10 Big Shows," which nearly dwarfed the Great Eastern Circus. The "unsurpassed" street parade was heralded by Professor M. C. Sexton's Wizard Band of Cornetists.[26] The colossal enterprise owned three steamboats and two barges. When the show traveled by rail, the management chartered "sixty box stock-cars, four passenger coaches and two Pullman palace sleeping cars."[27] The new season commenced in Agnes and Emma's hometown, Cincinnati, on April 4, 1874, with a week-long engagement.[28]

Within only a few weeks, the *Clipper* reported an average attendance of about 7,000 patrons per show. The equestrian corps was already earning praise: "[Emma] Lake, Minnie Marks, [George] M. Kelley and Robert Stickney show to superb advantage."[29] In Pittsburgh, Emma's manège was "witnessed with admiration," and the entire equestrian unit was deemed "worthy [of] the enthusiastic and flattering reception accorded them."[30]

That season, the John Robinson circus traveled through at least ten states, from Ohio to Louisiana and east to North Carolina and Virginia. Good reviews poured in from every city they visited, and the company enjoyed "splendid business, afternoon and evening."[31] In the winter, the company headed deep into the South, and the season ended on January 27, 1875, in Montgomery, Alabama. Agnes and Emma once again returned to their farm in Kentucky.

After a brief winter sojourn, Emma extended her contract with Robinson's show, and Agnes once again accompanied her daughter as the season commenced in Ohio in April 1875. The mammoth troupe trekked across at least six states, from Ohio to Georgia, between April 1875 and January 1876.

Emma Lake's abilities began to eclipse the other ladies in the equestrian corps. In June, during a week-long exhibition in Cincinnati, the *Clipper* ranked Emma "equally as high"[32] as Robert Stickney (the Apollo Belvidere of the Arena)[33] — the premier male equestrian not only in the Robinson show but among all of his contemporaries.

After witnessing a season of Emma Lake's talent in the ring, the Robinson brothers awarded her prominent billing. During the tour of Indiana in July, Emma's name appeared more frequently and with greater prominence than those of most of her female colleagues. The *Kokomo Democrat* printed an advertisement that mentioned only six performers by name — Emma Lake was the sole female performer who received billing in the newspaper. The *Democrat* editors declared Emma "the most graceful, charming and daring young Horsewoman in the profession."[34] In Valparaiso, an advertisement for the circus boasted "fifteen Lady Riders,"[35] although Emma Lake was clearly the featured female performer. Emma's name was in a font that dwarfed the names of her female and most of her male colleagues as well. In Warsaw, Emma was one of six featured performers and again the only woman.[36]

Heading south in the winter, Robinson's "Ten Big Shows" reached Memphis. The local *Daily Appeal* printed an exceptionally flattering endorsement of Emma Lake: "The peerless queen of the arenic circle, who stands to-day in all the world without a rival will . . . appear under Old John Robinson's big tents at every exhibition during the three days stay of the big show in the city."[37] The morning after the first show, the paper declared that the entire company was "like liquor, [it] improves with age, and now offers the public a menagerie and circus of unsurpassed excellence, variety and novelty."[38]

While traveling and performing with the Robinson circus, Emma Lake and Gil Robinson developed a close relationship. They had known each other since childhood, when their families had been partners, but Gil was a decade older than Emma and had paid little attention to her at that time.

In his memoirs, *Old Wagon Show Days*, several images of Gil stare back from the pages. Gil recalled that during the 1870s, when the

Fig. 30. On November 16, 1875, Emma Lake married Gil Robinson, the second son of legendary circus owner "Old John" Robinson. They divorced in 1883 but remarried in 1893. Courtesy The York County Heritage Trust, PA.

Robinson show traveled through the South, "we all looked like we belonged to Jessie James's outlaws, [since] almost everyone had a pair of six shooters around [their] waist."[39] Gil described his rakish appearance as he minded the circus's entrance: a "blue flannel shirt, big diamond pin stuck in a black necktie, boots that came up to my waist, and a big slouch hat, and I looked like I had not been shaved for months."[40] In one image, Gil stands lazily against his rifle, sporting a thick mustache, with his hat cocked at a jaunty angle.[41] This is a far different impression than he creates in figure 30. In this photograph, thought to be taken near the time of his and Emma's wedding, Gil appears fashionably groomed and shaved. He is wearing a suit, complete with a black necktie and a large diamond pin.[42] With his wardrobe and the attitude of a rogue, young Emma Lake was easily dazzled by Gil, who fancied himself a ladies man. Like her mother and sister before her, Emma loved the circus life and looked no further than her own touring company for love and companionship. The circus was a self-contained, nomadic family. Besides, marrying a towner was out of the question as long as Emma desired and achieved greater celebrity.

Gil's memoirs fail to provide any insight into their relationship; in fact, Emma is barely mentioned. As her mother's protégé, Emma Lake's disposition was probably similar to Agnes's: demure, polite, hardworking, and confident. Gil, who was self-centered and arrogant—apparent then and in later years—wooed Emma with his boisterous personality, regaling her with tales of his adventures with his father's circus.

On November 16, 1875, Emma Lake and Gil Robinson were married at the Peabody Hotel in Memphis. The original Peabody Hotel was constructed in 1869 and boasted "seventy-five rooms with private baths, a ballroom, saloon, and lobby."[43] The hotel was considered the epitome of southern hospitality and wealth in the Delta country during the late nineteenth century.

The *Memphis Daily Appeal* reported the wedding two days later and extended good tidings to the couple: "May life be to them an endless dream of unalloyed bliss."[44] The *New York Clipper* also reported the nuptials.[45] Three days after their wedding, the *Daily Ap-*

peal was happy to report that even though Emma Lake was a newly-wed, she would continue performing with the Robinson circus: "We are glad to know this, for [Emma] is an artist of acknowledged grace and talent. . . . [H]er fearless feats upon the courser Bonnie Scotland, evidence both skill and courage."[46]

The season for the John Robinson circus came to a close on January 1, 1876, in Macon, Georgia. The show was extensively advertised and received high praise for its performances. The company returned to its winter quarters in Cincinnati, and Emma and Gil took up residence in Agnes's old family home at 10 West Ninth Street.

In February, Emma placed an advertisement in the *New York Clipper* offering three of her horses for sale.[47] Emma said she was selling them because she had "no use for them."[48] In reality, she was three months pregnant. Emma was probably selling her horses at the request of Gil, who yearned for her to retire from the circus so she could wholly embrace her wifely duties and maternal obligations. Emma, however, had no intention of settling down.

The new circus season started in April, and "John Robinson's 10 Big Shows" opened at Exposition Hall in Cincinnati.[49] Gil remained the show's treasurer. Emma, billed under her maiden name "Lake," performed her signature manège act throughout April, even though she was about five months pregnant.

*   *   *

Agnes left the company in January so Emma could acclimate herself to being a married circus performer who relied on her husband and not on her mother. Departing from Chicago, Agnes traveled west to San Francisco,[50] where a number of her former circus colleagues had established year-round shows in theaters and dance halls along the bustling California coast. On her return journey a few weeks later, Agnes visited an old circus friend, Minnie Wells, who lived in Cheyenne, Wyoming Territory.

Minnie Wells was a former female lion tamer who had worked for a variety of circuses, including Haight's Empire City Circus in 1871.[51] In early 1876, Minnie was on hiatus from circus life and living in Cheyenne with Sylvester Lane "Wes" Moyer, who she married in June 1877.[52] Little is known about Minnie and Wes, although they are not relatives of Agnes, as early Wild Bill Hickok biographers originally believed.

"At this strangely fortuitous moment,"[53] both Agnes and Wild Bill were in Cheyenne in early 1876. There are as many versions of Agnes and Wild Bill's marriage as there are of their courtship. According to Richard O'Connor, Hickok was perhaps lonely. With his star growing dim and "far less confident of the future," he was "now in a mood to be domesticated."[54] O'Connor doubted Agnes's travel plans to California and instead suggested that having been informed by Wells and Moyer of Hickok's presence in Cheyenne, Agnes traveled there too, since Cheyenne was "was not [normally] that kind of place a lady would choose to sojourn" in the middle of winter.[55] This statement buttresses O'Connor's earlier argument that Agnes vigorously pursued James, even though he had done his best to deter her affections.

The details of their rendezvous in Cheyenne, unfortunately, "are concealed behind the mid-Victorian sense of delicacy and discretion in such matters."[56] In any case, most sources agree that Hickok confided in an unidentified friend his loving feelings toward Agnes when his friend excitedly told him Agnes was in town, a guest at Wells and Moyer's home. Hickok was eager to see her after two years, and without delay he made his way to the dwelling where he again "pressed his claim" to marry her. Minnie and Wes saw that "there was a tender regard between the couple" and adjourned from Agnes and James's company;[57] the affection that had taken years to grow was obvious to them both.

According to Shannon and Warren Garst, when Agnes and James reunited in Cheyenne, she apparently said, "You win, Bill. I'll give up the circus. I want to marry you — and our life together will be on your own terms, here in the West."

"I'll devote my life to making you happy," James promised happily.[58]

The Garsts' idealized dialogue created a sentimentalized couple's tryst. They intertwined fact and fiction to generate more drama with a couple whose real lives were dramatic enough.

Regardless of the events, Agnes and James became engaged immediately and were married on March 5, 1876. Their abbreviated courtship led many to suspect that Agnes was not taking any chances on a "skittish suitor." The modest ceremony, conducted by Reverend W. F. Warren, took place in the home of Minnie Wells and Wes Moyer. The host couple also served as official witnesses, with a handful of friends and neighbors in attendance. The photograph of James seated (figure 31) is thought to have been taken on their wedding day. The gentleman standing behind Hickok is Wes Moyer. Hickok's preparation for his wedding is obvious. He appears freshly bathed and groomed, his jacket is clean and tidy, and a crisp white collar peeks out from behind a dark tie and vest.

Although the marriage certificate was completed after the ceremony, the photographs of Agnes and James were attached a few months later. On the marriage license, Hickok's age is listed as forty-five and Agnes's as forty-two. Perhaps this was a gallant gesture of Hickok's to disguise their age difference. He wanted to appear older, while Agnes habitually abridged her true age. In reality, Agnes was just a few months shy of her fiftieth birthday, and James was thirty-eight.

Reverend Warren's marginal note in the church register, "Don't think the[y] meant it," has perplexed scholars and generated intense speculation over the reasons behind the marriage. One accepted notion is that although no traditional romance motivated the couple, there was a deep mutual affection. Suggestions that Agnes married James so he could help her manage her circus company are not plausible because she had liquidated her circus assets and subsequently never acted as a proprietress, although she was fully capable of running and managing her own show. Agnes was well aware of James's abhorrence of acting and would not have asked him to join her in such a venture. And even if she were to manage another show after their marriage, she would not have relied on someone who not only disliked the business but who also lacked the necessary management skills.

Fig. 31. James "Wild Bill" Hickok (seated) and his best man, Sylvester "Wes" Moyer, probably on Wild Bill and Agnes Lake's wedding day, March 5, 1876. Courtesy Wyoming State Archives, Department of State Parks and Cultural Resources, Cheyenne.

News of the wedding spread quickly. Despite the publicized nuptials, some people doubted Hickok's marriage to Agnes Lake for decades. In 1913, when William Connelley was gathering research for his biography of Hickok, he wrote that John Beach Edwards visited him in Topeka and declared that Hickok "was never married to the widow Lake — [he] never married anyone." Edwards also claimed that "Calamity Jane was at Abilene and . . . she and Bill lived together."[59] Twenty years later, when Connelley's *Wild Bill and His Era: The Life and Adventures of James Butler Hickok* was published, doubt and disbelief still lingered. In 1923, John C. Lockwood conversed with Connelley about his own reminiscences of Hickok in Abilene. Lockwood remembered that Hickok frequently socialized with "dance house" ladies, and he, too, "scouted the idea that 'Bill' was ever married."[60]

Nevertheless, on Tuesday, March 7, the *Cheyenne Daily Leader* printed this simple announcement:

MARRIED. —— By the Rev. W. F. Warren, March 5th, 1876, at the residence of S. L. Moyer, Cheyenne, Wyoming Territory, Mrs. Agnes Lake Thatcher, of Cincinnati, Ohio, to James Butler Hickok, WILD BILL, of this city.[61]

The next day, the editors of the *Cheyenne Daily Sun* published their own mirth-laden announcement: " 'Wild Bill,' of Western fame, has conquered numerous Indians, outlaws, bears and buffaloes, but a charming widow has stolen the magic wand. The scepter has departed, and he is as meek and gentle as a lamb. In other words, he has [shuffled] off the coils of bachelorhood."[62]

The *Omaha Daily Bee* congratulated Agnes on capturing the "Wild West's" most eligible bachelor:

Mrs. Lake came to Cheyenne ostensibly for recreation, but really to take advantage of the privileges which leap year gives the ladies. Hickok has always been considered as wild and woolly and hard to curry, but the proprietress of the best circus on the continent wanted a husband of renown, and she laid siege to the not over susceptible heart of the man who had killed his dozens of both whites and Indians. The contest was "short, sharp and decisive," and "Wild Bill" went down in the struggle clasping his opponent in both of his brawny arms, and now sweet little cupids hover over their pathway and sugar, cream and honey for a delicious paste through which [they] honeymoon. Success and happiness attend them, and while on the road of life they may have every joy vouchsafed to mortals, and we feel confidant that Mr. Hickok will see to it that they are never lacking for small Bills.[63]

The suggestion that Agnes traveled to Cheyenne to take advantage of leap year refers to an urban legend that the day gave ladies social acceptance to propose to their beaux.[64] Perhaps Agnes did propose to Hickok on February 29, but it is more likely that romantic editors in myriad cities amended their articles and marriage announcements to correspond with the 1876 leap day.

The evening following the wedding, Agnes and James Hickok traveled by rail to St. Louis to meet Agnes's brother Joseph and his large family. By 1876, Joseph was prospering with his new partnership, Orthwein & Mersman,[65] and six of his eight children were probably living at home: Clara, Arthur, Emma, Otto, Alice, and Ella. After a few days' respite, Agnes and James went on to Cincinnati, where Agnes's daughter, Emma Lake Robinson, awaited the birth of her first child.

Agnes had been gone for almost two months, and this was possibly the first she learned of Emma's pregnancy. Because Emma's husband, Gil, would be away on circus business for many months, Agnes decided to stay in Cincinnati for the final stages of Emma's pregnancy and the delivery of her grandchild. As a result of this unexpected family obligation for Agnes, James returned to the West alone. After only a two-week honeymoon in Cincinnati, Agnes watched James board a train to St. Louis. The couple embraced, unaware that their arms had intertwined for the last time. Agnes's final glimpse of her husband was as he turned to smile at her one

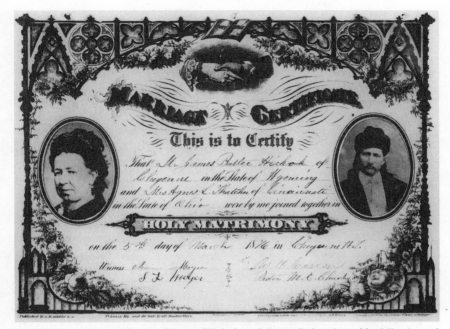

Fig. 32. Marriage certificate of James Hickok and Agnes Lake, signed by Minnie and Wes Moyer and other officiants, March 5, 1876. In lieu of a formal wedding portrait, Agnes inserted photos of herself and James onto the elaborately decorated document, probably while James was en route to Deadwood. Lake/Hickok Wedding Certificate, PG 500, courtesy Connecticut State Library/State Archives, Hartford.

last time. With little apprehension Agnes waved goodbye, expecting to see him in a few weeks.

The *Omaha Daily Bee* reported that "domestic life did not suit such a rover as 'Wild Bill' "[66] and that Agnes and James had permanently separated just weeks after their nuptials. In *Heroes of the Plains*, James Buel recanted the malicious report he had published in his 1880 *Life and Marvelous Adventures of Wild Bill*, purporting that a "final separation had occurred" between the two before Hickok's arrival in Deadwood. In 1883, Buel claimed that "no man ever loved a woman more ardently than Bill did his wife; she was in his very soul; her spirit was his ruling mentor and all his ambition was centered in her happiness."[67] Rumors of the newlyweds' separation explained the absence of Hickok's bride when he returned to Chey-

enne and fueled reports that he arrived in Deadwood with his supposed consort, Calamity Jane.

Before his departure, Agnes and James discussed their future:
she wanted a modest ranch on which she could raise and train
horses. Hickok undoubtedly desired an existence away from "civilization" where he could live in virtual obscurity. Although it had been
several years since Hickok had ceased his official duties as a lawman,
the bull's-eye on his back remained, and his paranoia of being targeted in reprisal no doubt influenced his aspirations to live a quiet
existence on the untamed frontier. Determined to earn a grubstake
so he could finance their new life together, Hickok explored various
opportunities when he returned to St. Louis.[68] Hickok now wanted
"a more stable existence, to put down roots, and to settle" down with
his wife.[69] Joseph G. Rosa surmised that by society's standards, Hickok
may have "faced the grim fact that he was pretty much a failure" as a
man. Without a variety of employment skills or opportunities available
to him, Hickok viewed the recent gold discoveries as a means to retire
with Agnes with tangible assets and to "engage in less dangerous
pursuits," such as gambling.[70]

During his nearly two-month stopover in St. Louis, he advertised
his services as a guide to those hoping to strike it rich in the Black
Hills, where reports of gold discoveries were widely circulated. Hickok's nephew, Howard L. Hickok, wrote, "[H]e resolved to go into
the Hills and win a stake more commensurate with a higher standard of living. He had old fashioned ideas of honor and living on his
wife's money was contrary to his ideas of honor and decency."[71]
However, numerous reports described Hickok's penchant for gambling at every available opportunity while in Deadwood, but he did
not make a fortune from the cards.[72]

Throughout the nineteenth century, America's westward expansion received episodic jolts from discoveries of precious min-
erals. Just as the development of California was boosted by the 1849
Gold Rush, interest in Dakota Territory soared when similar riches
were found in the Black Hills.

In November 1875, gold was discovered north of Custer in the

neighboring areas of Spruce Gulch, Whitewood Creek, and Deadwood Gulch. News of the alluvial gold spread quickly, but the impending winter delayed the feverish rush that deluged the Black
Hills in the spring of 1876. Prospectors found the canyons and
gulches surrounded by a tangled labyrinth of dead trees, testimony
to a forest fire that had burned some years before, which influenced
the name of the settlement. The crude mining hamlet of Deadwood
was established in early 1876, and buildings fashioned from rough-
hewn planks were hastily constructed. There was one main avenue
of activity flanked by saloons and the stage office and surrounded by
the mining camps that dotted the landscape. Throughout the day-
time hours, the street was "packed with jostling men, horses, mules,
oxen, and every conceivable manner of conveyance."[73]

Deadwood was a wretched hive of filth and muck, and the town
harbored a cesspool of humanity: crooks, thieves, and murderers —
the scourges of society. But not all who flocked to Deadwood were
outlaws; many came to dig and prosper and then to return home as
quickly as possible. The earliest miners enacted a rudimentary system of guidelines that established fees, outlined claims, and provided some measure of authority in the illegal village.[74]

The new gold rush beckoned to both young and old prospectors. Some were too young to have participated in California's Gold
Rush, and others sought financial security in the wake of the Panic
of 1873 and the lingering economic effects of Reconstruction. For
only twenty-five dollars, a fortune hunter could purchase a ticket
that would transport him by train from St. Louis to Cheyenne, with
stops in Omaha and Denver. With seemingly little to lose, James
Hickok became one of those fortune hunters.

In June, Hickok reached Omaha, Nebraska, where he wrote a
letter to Agnes from the Metropolitan Hotel:

Omaha, Neb. June 2nd 1876.
Doll one word from Omaha[.] I was very sick all last night
but am feeling very well and happy now[.] I god Bless and
Protect my Agnes is my Prair[.] would I not like to Put my

big hands on your Sholdiers and kiss you rite now[.] Love to emma one Thousand Kises to my wife Agnes[.]

>From your ever loving
Husband
J B Hickok
Wild Bill
By By[75]

Between March and June, Hickok had traveled between St. Louis and Cheyenne, trying to organize a mining party. Finally, he secured a place with a wagon train laden with needed supplies, including prostitutes, bound for the Black Hills. He left Wyoming Territory approximately June 27 and headed for Deadwood with a small company that included "Colorado Charley" Utter, his brother Steve Utter, and White-Eye Anderson.[76] They stopped at Fort Laramie, where an additional thirty wagons and another infamous character of the West—Martha "Calamity Jane" Canary—joined the convoy. She was nursing a hangover when the soldiers, eager to be rid of her, handed her over to the wagon train.[77] The details of the wagon train's overland trek are buried within the "confusion, fiction, and imagination to be found in the printed versions of Wild Bill's last two months of life."[78]

Hickok, the Utters, and the rest of their companions arrived in Deadwood around July 12. During his brief time in Deadwood, Hickok did his best to be a respectable citizen and to live an innocuous existence. He, in turn, was generally left undisturbed to search for a claim, as he alleged in his letters to Agnes, or—as others reminisced—to indulge in his gambling vice.[79] In 1922, the editor of Deadwood's *Telegram* declared, "Wild Bill sought to accumulate gold by manipulating the picture cards rather than by digging in the earth for it."[80]

Shortly after he arrived, Hickok's friends noticed a change in his demeanor. He was restless and depressed and frequently vocalized premonitions of his mortality. On more than one occasion, Hickok reportedly told companions, including Charley Utter and California Joe: "I feel that my days are numbered; my sun is sinking fast; I know I shall be killed here, something tells me I shall never leave these hills alive; somebody is going to kill me. But I don't know who it is or why he is going to do it. I have killed many men in my day, but I never killed a man yet but what it was kill or get killed with me."[81]

Published accounts of his mortal portents were printed in the *Cheyenne Daily Leader* three weeks after his murder. Accounts of him voicing his fears are probably true, as are the reports that his friends dismissed his dismal attitude and paranoia. Tragically, Hickok's fears were realized twenty-one days after he arrived in Deadwood.

In the early afternoon of August 2, 1876, Hickok entered Nuttall and Mann's No. 10 saloon, dressed in "his favorite outfit: a Prince Albert frock coat with all the trimmings."[82] He joined a poker game already in progress that included Carl Mann, Charles Rich, and Captain William R. Massie. Rich refused to bow to Hickok's paranoia and relinquish his position against the wall, so Hickok reluctantly occupied a seat that left him in a vulnerable position. He trained his eyes on the front door, of which he had an unobstructed view, and was conscious of the rear exit a few paces behind him.

A few hours later, Jack McCall, another recent arrival to Deadwood, entered the No. 10 and silently stalked his way down the bar, edging ever closer to his target. When he was finally behind Hickok, he quickly drew his pistol, positioned it at the back of Wild Bill's head, and reportedly shouted, "Damn you, take that!"[83]

The bullet entered at the base of Hickok's skull and exited through his right cheek, jettisoning a "portion of the cerebellum" and probably a few teeth when it exited.[84] Hickok's head jerked forward, and for a few moments his body remained rigid before he "toppled back from the stool to the floor" and spilled his cards, what has subsequently been named "Aces and Eights — the Dead Man's Hand."[85]

McCall dashed outside and fired his pistol at those who attempted to thwart his flight. He fired in vain, however: although he had loaded each chamber of his pistol that morning, the only round that fired properly had sailed through Hickok's head. McCall was captured in a local butcher shop and remained in custody until his trial commenced.

The next day, dressed in his black broadcloth suit, his wounds closed, and his glossy hair combed and parted over his brawny shoulders, Hickok was laid in a coffin constructed of rough pine lumber and buried in Ingleside Cemetery on the edge of town.[86] Sometime later, Colorado Charley replaced the crude grave marker with a proper headstone on which was carved:

Wild Bill — J.B. Hickock. Killed by the assassin Jack McCall in Deadwood Black Hills, August 2nd 1876. Pard we will meet again in the Happy Hunting ground to part no more. Good Bye — Colorado Charley. C H. Utter.[87]

As Hickok was being buried in Ingleside on August 3, McCall's trial began at McDaniel's Theatre, designated as the courtroom. Despite overwhelming evidence of premeditated murder, McCall was acquitted and hastily left town. A few weeks later McCall was captured and sent to Yankton for a second trial; he was found guilty on December 6, 1876. Since Deadwood was an illegal settlement, his first trial was null and void; thus, he was not subject to constitutional protection that prevented double jeopardy. He was sentenced to death and was hanged on March 1, 1877. Agnes did not attend the trial or the execution, but Lorenzo Butler Hickok, James's brother, traveled from Illinois and reportedly glared at McCall throughout the second trial.[88]

As often happens in areas of rapid growth, the needs of the living outweighed the needs of the dead. To accommodate the ever-increasing population, the occupants of Deadwood's Ingleside Cemetery were removed to the new Masonic cemetery, Mount Moriah. In June 1879, Colorado Charley purchased a new lot and personally arranged to exhume and rebury his "pard" Hickok. On August 3, 1879, three years to the day since Hickok had been buried, his remains were exhumed and reburied in the new cemetery.

A small service was conducted at Hickok's new gravesite, and a new headstone was placed. The story of Hickok's death was already assuming mythic proportions, and his burial site was becoming a destination for souvenir hunters. Over the years, a number of headstones and statues were placed to memorialize Hickok's resting place, but they were hacked to pieces.[89] Currently, the grave is enclosed by a wrought-iron fence, and a bronze replica of J. B. Riordan's 1891 bust of Hickok crowns a stone pillar.

*   *   *

Meanwhile, in Cincinnati, more than a month after Agnes received his Omaha letter, she received a second letter from her husband. We believe this was the last authentic letter Hickok wrote to his bride:

> Dead Wood Black Hills, Dacota July, 17th 1876.
> MY OWN DARLING WIFE AGNES.
> I have but a few moments left before this letter Starts[.] I never was as well in my life[;] but you would laughf to see me now[.] just got in from Prospecting[.] Will go away again to morrow[.] will write In the morning, but god nowse when It will start[.] my friend will take this to Cheyenne if he lives[.] I dont expect to hear from you[,] but it is all the same[;] I no my agnes and only live to love hur[.] never mind Pet we will have a home yet then we will be so happy[.] I am almost shure I will do well hear[.] the man is huring me[.] Good by Dear wife love to Emma
> J B Hickok
> Wild Bill[90]

While Hickok was en route to Cheyenne and Deadwood, Agnes made the necessary arrangements to relocate. In July, she sold the Sunnyside farm in Kentucky.[91] The quiet farm a few miles south of Cincinnati had once served as an escape for Agnes and Emma following the murder of Bill Lake and had worked well as their off-season residence, but neither had resided there in quite some time. The money from the sale would help Agnes and James establish a new homestead together out West. Throughout the spring and summer, Agnes and Emma prepared for the arrival of the baby. Gil resumed his administrative duties with the Robinson circus.

Agnes also began corresponding with Hickok's mother, Polly, and sister, Celinda, who resided in Illinois. The five letters written between April 26 and November 19, 1876, are the only known documentary evidence of Agnes Lake by her own hand. Each letter is signed "Your loveing Daughter (or Sister), Agnes Hickok." The whereabouts and contents of the reply letters from Polly and Celinda — referenced in the letters Agnes wrote — are unknown. Agnes told her new in-laws that she had been in love with James since about 1873, but her maternal obligations to Emma prevented her from marrying him before March 1876. Her own happiness, she wrote, was secondary to Emma's well-being, and she had waited until Emma was married before she considered accepting James's proposal.

In her first letter, dated April 26, Agnes wrote, "Loveing James as I doo beeing a Woman of tender fealings I don't see why we will not git along to gether; I shal doo all in my power to git along."[92] She asked for James's exact birth date so she could enter it on their marriage certificate. Perhaps Agnes did not know how much younger than she he really was; she wrote, "he plays and Larkes with me so mutch" about his age that she wanted the truth from Polly Hickok. Agnes, in turn, fibbed about her own age and claimed she had been born in 1832. Agnes's use of 1832 as her birth year mirrored the fictionalized information in her numerous biographies already in public distribution.

Agnes wrote to Polly and Celinda twice in June and promised to remit James's recent letter, dated June 2, the one from Omaha. The original letter was never returned to Agnes and was sold as Lot 15 of the "Important James B. 'Wild Bill' Hickok Letters, Photography and Documents from the Estate of Celinda Hickok" by Greg Martin Auctions in June 2003. The June 2 letter, estimated at between $40,000 and $60,000 in value, was regarded as a "historic gem . . . the crown of any Western Americana collection."[93] The single-page note written on the hotel's stationery sold on June 16, 2003, for an astonishing $190,400 — nearly five times its original estimate.

According to Agnes's June 30 letter to her "Sister Cenlinda,"[94] James had been delayed in St. Louis until the end of May. She was clearly worried about him and his lack of letters. Agnes assumed he

Fig. 33. Portrait of Agnes Lake, about the time of her marriage to James Hickok. Courtesy The York County Heritage Trust, PA.

was sicker than he described and feared his pride would not permit him to elaborate on his infirmity.

Agnes received another letter from James on August 9, one week after his death. It is probably the letter James wrote on July 17, from "Dead Wood Black Hills, Dacota," after he returned from a long day of prospecting. The original letter is currently missing. It is doubtful that Agnes forwarded this letter to the Hickok family, since it was not discovered as part of Celinda's estate.

In 1883, Buel claimed Agnes gave him the original letter after he visited her in Cincinnati. She also gave him Hickok's "diary," which, according to him, Hickok had hoped Buel would publish posthumously.[95] He argued that Agnes gave him the letters and diary "with her full permission in order to construct a more truthful biography of her deceased husband." In addition, Buel alleged in 1880 that Agnes had invited him to her hotel when she was in St. Louis that year, but he does not elaborate on their conversation. As a result, however, Buel published his claims (although he recanted most of them three years later) that the couple had separated and that it was "her fault."[96] Besides the fact that there is no evidence to buttress Buel's claim that Wild Bill even kept a diary, it is unlikely that Agnes would have surrendered her husband's personal effects to a journalist or to anyone else outside her family.

The Greg Martin Auctions catalog claimed the United States Playing Card Company (USPCC) had displayed the letter in its museum in 1947, but the exhibited letter was in fact a photograph of the July 17 letter taken in the 1920s. When Rosa published his Hickok biography in 1964, he discredited Buel's claims. He argued that the letter was reprinted in multiple newspapers after Hickok's death, by Agnes's authority, and the fact that Buel included it in his manuscript does not mean he had the original.[97] In 1980, William Secrest claimed the Adams Museum and House in Deadwood had the original letter. It has been confirmed, however, that Deadwood has a photographic copy of the original.[98]

In all likelihood, Agnes kept the last letter from her husband, and it ended up in Gil Robinson's possession after Agnes's death. Gil's position as a director at the USPCC explains why the company's museum had it on display in the 1940s or at least had it in the 1920s to photograph it. Current research has yet to uncover the original.

Agnes was still ignorant of James's assassination when the July 17, 1876, letter reached her, since she wrote to Polly and Celinda that she expected him to send for her at any time. In the August 9 letter to her mother- and sister-in-law, Agnes acknowledged that while James hated acting, she herself was a good actress. She described her Mazeppa performances in Prussia before the king and added that she "Can git five thousand Dollers a year" (about $94,000 today) from her manège appearances.[99] But Agnes explained that James "did not Marrie me to work. he only wants me to please him and not the Public."[100] Although she had retired from circus performing, Agnes was willing to return to the sawdust rings if required to do so. Nervous about relying on Hickok's ability to locate a lucrative gold lode and his penchant for gambling, Agnes was prepared to return to the ring to generate steady earnings to buy their ranch out West.

It is not known how Agnes eventually learned of James's murder. Like the rest of the country, she probably read the headlines splashed across the front pages of Cincinnati newspapers, but perhaps someone she knew informed her. Over the next few days, Agnes's emotional fortitude was tested; she had to place her grief on hold as she helped Emma through childbirth. On August 15, 1876, just days after learning that Hickok had been killed, Agnes became a grandmother. Emma Lake Robinson gave birth to a daughter, whom she baptized Agnes Emma Robinson but called "Daisy" to distinguish her from her famous grandmother.

Agnes did not write to Polly and Celinda again until November 12, 1876. Her grief, along with taking care of Emma and Daisy, consumed her time, and Agnes wrote on the "first leasure moment . . . that I have had for about 3 months."[101] According to the letter, Emma had had a difficult delivery and a slow recovery, and Daisy was a fussy and cross baby. Gil was still traveling with the Robinson circus, and Agnes does not mention his presence in any of her letters.

The November 12 letter is significant because Agnes does not mention an alleged August 1 letter in which James eerily spoke of his impending demise. This letter was first "quoted" by the self-titled "Poet Scout" Captain Jack Crawford and was seamlessly woven into his poem "Wild Bill's Grave," which appeared in the August 4, 1877, edition of the *Virginia (Nev.) Evening Chronicle*. A four-line stanza preceded the "letter":

And now let me show you the good that was in him —
The letters he wrote to his Agnes — his wife.
Why, a look or a smile, one kind word could win him,
Hear part of this letter — the last of this life:

"AGNES DARLING: If such should be we never meet again, while firing my last shot I will gently breathe the name of my wife — Agnes — and with a kind wish even for my enemies, I will make the plunge and try to swim to the other shore."[102]

This letter has been reprinted in several Hickok biographies since its initial appearance, but its current whereabouts — if authentic — are unknown. Buel's *Heroes of the Plains* printed a version of the letter, along with Crawford's poem, but Buel "gave no hint that he had ever seen the original letter."[103] Frank Jenners Wilstach also reprinted the letter in his first biography of Hickok, *Wild Bill Hickok, the Prince of Pistoleers,* published in 1926.

Since only Crawford claimed to have seen the original — in fact, he boasted that Agnes gifted it to him — it is plausible that the letter was fabricated as a literary ploy to romanticize the tragedy of Hickok's death. Among those who questioned the letter's authenticity was Elmo Scott Watson, who speculated that much of the letter was "an example of Captain Jack's poetic license."[104]

This letter, along with the original marriage certificate and other Hickok artifacts, was believed to have been donated to the USPCC museum by Gil Robinson shortly before his death in 1928. However, since the museum is currently closed, verification of its collections is difficult. Despite his notoriety as a killer, Hickok's words betray a tenderness and deep affection for the woman he left behind only weeks after their marriage: "I [know] my Agnes and only live to love hur."[105] Although the short letters were meant to update Agnes on his whereabouts and progress in the Black Hills, the language Hickok employed is similar to that of a journal entry.

Comparatively, the conveniently dated "August 1, 1876," letter embodies a unique phraseology akin to the era's ubiquitous dime novels. Victorian ideals dictated a specific way husbands and wives corresponded with one another, but Hickok was not the epitome of a Victorian husband and thus was less likely to subscribe to strict Victorian codes. Compared with the other letters we know Hickok penned to Agnes, the language in this brief note is strikingly different. In those letters, Hickok is frank in his details and uses erratic capitalization and non-standardized spellings. While Hickok applied contemporary epithets such as "darling wife" and "Pet" when he addressed Agnes in the July 17 letter, the idioms in the "August 1" letter seem more feminine and romanticized than masculine. Speculation over the letter's authenticity will remain until its whereabouts are discovered or more substantial proof is provided.

While Emma was recovering from childbirth, Agnes expressed her desire to visit Polly and Celinda in Illinois, but no evidence suggests that she actually did so. Agnes pushed through her grief over James, just as she had when Bill Lake died, and she was determined to continue the plans she and James had developed. Agnes appeared to move forward with her intention to retire out West, in the rugged land James had loved so much. Specifically, Agnes hoped to go to the Black Hills and remain near his grave. Her grief at the loss of James reverberated through her November 12, 1876, letter, the last known correspondence to Polly and Celinda. She lamented, "[I]t is impossible for [a] human beeing to Love eny better then what I did him[.] I can see him Day and night before me: the longer he is Dead the worse I feal. . . . [N]ow I have more time for Retropecsian [and] I grieve all the time."[106]

Agnes's grief must have been magnified by the uncanny similarities between the deaths of Bill Lake and James Hickok; they were too eerie for her to ignore. Lake and Hickok were both murdered in the month of August and were shot at point-blank range by belligerent assailants. Hickok was shot from behind, and his murderer remained faceless to him. Lake, however, saw his killer's face as he fired the fatal bullet. Killian was angry because Lake had thrown him out of the concert when he refused to pay for a ticket, and McCall claimed his actions were retribution for slain kin, although he later admitted that he killed Hickok because of a row over cards. In both cases, death was virtually instantaneous.

Killian and McCall had similar physical characteristics: Killian's right eye had been shot out, and McCall was described as cross-eyed. Both men were about twenty-five years old, had a mass of chestnut-colored hair, and were slim. Both attackers ran from the scene and were pursued for weeks before finally being apprehended and held for lawful trials.

During the trials, defense witnesses testified on behalf of the murderers' personal attributes. Killian was described as a "law abiding citizen," and McCall was said to be "quite peaceable,"[107] while both Lake and Hickok were demonized during their respective trials. While Killian served his sentence but was later murdered, McCall received capital punishment. Agnes was absent from both murder trials and did not attend McCall's execution. In both marriages, Agnes and her respective husbands were on the verge of purchasing land in which to begin new phases of their lives together. Lake and Hickok each had two funerals. Lake's funerals in Granby and Cincinnati were grand spectacles with dozens of mourners. Hickok's funerals were more intimate, with only close friends in attendance. Overall, it is eerily coincidental, and certainly tragic, that lighting struck twice in Agnes's marriage bed.

The following summer, 1877, Agnes traveled to Cheyenne and spent several months training horses, probably on the Moyers' ranch on Upper Horse Creek, since there is no evidence that she purchased her own land. She considered ranching and consulted Minnie and Wes Moyer about possibilities. In June, her presence was noted in the *Daily Sun*:

> MADAME HICKOK. The Queen of the Circus Ring . . . a lady who for many years shone as the queen of the profession of the sock and buskin, the stars, the spangles, and the sawdust.

Almost daily she is to be seen riding gracefully on horseback on our thoroughfares, and the inquiry is made by the non-show-going people, "Who is that?" It is seen at once by the practiced horseman that she thoroughly understands equestrianism.[108]

By late August, Agnes knew she would return East to be closer to her daughter, but she wanted to visit James's grave before she left. On September 3, 1877, Agnes, accompanied by "Buckskin Charley" Dalton, his wife, and "Texas George" Carson, arrived in Deadwood. She went to James's gravesite, still at Ingleside, and sat beside the wooden marker for several hours, privately grieving. She made arrangements for a headstone and a secure enclosure to deter souvenir hunters and grave robbers.[109]

Agnes considered the logistical problems of bringing James's body back East so it would be closer to the people who loved him. Hickok's other survivors, especially his mother and sister Celinda, resided in Illinois, far away from Agnes. In Cincinnati, Agnes owned a large plot in Spring Grove Cemetery, but the marker was engraved "Thatcher" and included Agnes's first husband, Bill Lake. Hickok had not wanted to play second fiddle to Lake when he was alive, and Agnes knew he would be displeased at spending eternity next to him. Neither option seemed better than leaving James in the frontier he had loved. Hickok's friends, including Charley Utter, urged Agnes not to remove the body from its resting place, and there he remains, far from the graves of his wife and family.

When Agnes returned to Cheyenne at the end of September, she obtained a third marriage license. "Texas George" Carson, her twenty-eight-year-old escort to Deadwood, was the groom. Wes and Minnie Moyer again served as witnesses. The marriage was recorded in the Laramie County Marriage Books. Cheyenne's two leading newspapers, the *Daily Leader* and the *Daily Sun*, printed nearly identical announcements on the same day:

Married. Carson-Hickok. In this city, Sept. 27th, by Judge Chas. F. Miller, Mrs. Agnes Lake Hickok to Mr. Geo. Carson.

The bride is the widow of "Wild Bill," the scout and Mr.
Carson is a frontiersman, widely and favorably known.[110]

If scholars and western enthusiasts were perplexed at her marriage to Wild Bill, Agnes's marriage to the elusive "Texas George"
is even more confounding. Perhaps Agnes was overwhelmed with
grief at the loss of her second husband, especially after visiting his
grave. She may have seen James's likeness in Carson and married
him to fill an empty void in her heart. Carson has since faded into
obscurity. Nothing is known about his past or his life after his surprising marriage to Agnes. Like so many elements of Agnes's story,
Carson's fate remains a mystery.

CHAPTER THIRTEEN

Agnes's Season Closes

"Good Night, Goodbye"

1877–1907

A gnes's later years were devoted to her daughter and grand-daughter. She cared for her granddaughter Daisy while Emma performed for half a dozen companies between 1876 and 1892.[1] On June 24, 1878, Emma gave birth to a second daughter, whom she named Emma, but the child died eleven days later as a result of "weakness." The infant was buried alongside Bill Lake in Spring Grove Cemetery.

Gil constantly implored Emma to retire, but she refused. The ensuing tension in her marriage prompted her to explore circus companies not owned by the Robinson family. In 1879 she joined P. T. Barnum's "New and Greatest Show on Earth." The legendary showman P. T. Barnum billed Emma as "America's premier eques-trienne" when she toured with his company from 1879 to 1881. At the time, his circus encompassed more than three hundred people and fifty-one railway cars. Emma Lake was crowned "America's Side Saddle Queen" and shared prominent billing with the other five female equestrians in Barnum's show, including Linda Jeal and

Madame Elise Dockrill.[2] Emma stood out as the only rider on the roster who did not perform a bareback routine. Linda Jeal, a flamboyant equestrienne known as "the Queen of the Flaming Zone,"[3] produced an amazing hurdle and barrier act that concluded with her horse leaping through flaming hoops. Agnes, Emma, and Linda Jeal developed a close friendship that lasted a number of years.[4]

Emma Lake's performances were routinely featured in both circus advertisements and reviews in local newspapers. Her feats were hailed as "graceful" and commanded admiration from circus patrons. In Worcester, Massachusetts, the *Evening Gazette* extolled Emma's routine as a "study for every lady who ever sits a side-saddle."[5] Barnum quickly capitalized on her skills, and Emma's performances were highlighted with unique graphics in the newspapers (variations of figure 34).

Now in her twenties, Emma was not only an accomplished performer but also an excellent trainer. Like Agnes, Emma only rode horses she had raised and trained herself. Thus, she was familiar with each equine's personality and could control it accordingly, but that did not always assure accident-free performances. While she was touring in Kentucky early in the 1879 season, Emma Lake's horse, Brilliant, seriously injured circus veteran John Jay Nathans. One of Brilliant's popular stunts was to rear straight up and walk around the ring while Emma leaned backward. On April 14 something startled Brilliant, and he attempted to bolt from the ring. Nathans hastened to assist Emma. Nathans held up his hands to grab the reins, but he was struck in the chest by Brilliant's forelegs and knocked to the ground. Amazingly, Nathans sustained only a broken collar bone and two fractured ribs.[6]

In August 1880, P. T. Barnum's show reached Cheyenne, Wyoming Territory. The *Cheyenne Daily Leader* boasted the arrival of Wild Bill's widow, who accompanied her daughter, Barnum's "daring equestrienne."[7] The newspaper reported that Agnes was Emma's "constant companion" but made no mention of Gil Robinson's or "Texas George" Carson's (the man Agnes married in 1877) presence with the group. Until her death, Agnes was often referred to as "Hickok's Widow" or "Mrs. Hickok." Agnes and Emma visited Min-

Fig. 34. This courier for P. T. Barnum's circus billed Emma Lake as "America's Side-Saddle Queen" in 1879. Courtesy Somers Historical Society, Somers, New York.

nie and Wes Moyer but discovered the couple had separated since Agnes had last seen them three years before.[8]

By 1882, Emma and Gil's marriage was tumultuous. Emma was tired of Gil's alleged philandering, while Gil relentlessly urged Emma to retire so she could focus on being a wife and mother. Emma basked in the limelight of Barnum's show, while Gil worked for his brothers on a limited salary from his family's company, the John Robinson circus. Gil struggled with the fact that Emma was the proverbial breadwinner in their household, and the tension between the pair "finally led to a coolness" that facilitated jealousy.[9] Emma and Gil divorced in February 1883. The judge awarded Emma two hundred dollars alimony plus the cost of the suit and legally restored her maiden name.[10]

Agnes, Emma, and six-year-old Daisy sought to escape the familiar haunts of Cincinnati, where the Robinson family dominated the social, economic, and circus arenas. The Lake women moved to Jersey City, New Jersey, and resided with their friend Linda Jeal, who owned an equestrian training facility.

In 1887 a minor media fracas erupted between Emma Lake and Annie Oakley. While she was performing in Buffalo Bill Cody's show in New York City, Annie Oakley boasted that she was the only equestrienne to attempt a "brand-new stunt." The stunt involved untying a handkerchief secured to her horse's pastern "as she rode sidesaddle at full speed" around the arena.[11] The Ladies Riding Club of New York was so impressed that Annie was awarded a gold medal for her extraordinary equestrian skills.[12] When Emma Lake heard of Annie Oakley's boasts, she wrote to the editors of the *New York Clipper* and stated that she had been performing the same feat at Linda Jeal's West End Training Academy in Jersey City for the previous two months on a horse "fifteen hands high."[13] Almost immediately, Cody hired Emma for his Wild West Exhibition. Was it the added publicity between Annie Oakley and Emma Lake that urged Cody into action? Or was it truly based on Emma's skills as a rider? The reason is unclear but the result is certain because Emma, Agnes, and ten-year-old Daisy joined "Buffalo Bill's Wild West" as it headed to the American Exhibition in London.

Fig. 35. Challenges between circus performers were a popular method to garner media attention and boost attendance. This poster, circa 1878–81, for W. C. Coup's Equescurriculum billed a manège competition between the "Rival Emmas" — Emma Lake and Emma Stokes, daughter of Spencer Q. Stokes, Agnes and Bill Lake's former employer. Courtesy Hertzberg Circus Collection, Witte Museum, San Antonio, Texas.

Fig. 36. Agnes Lake, Emma Lake, and Agnes "Daisy" Robinson sailed to England with Buffalo Bill Cody in 1887. Agnes, with a white scarf on her head, stands to the reader's right, with Daisy to her right and Emma behind her. Courtesy Library of Congress, Collection 604073, LC-USZ62-48354.

The ship transporting the Wild West Exhibition, the *State of Nebraska*, embarked at New York City on March 31, 1887, with more than 200 personnel (performers and supporting staff), 180 horses, and a humble menagerie composed of buffalo, elk, "Texas steers," donkeys, and deer. The passengers and crew gathered on deck, and a photograph (see figure 36) immortalized the historic event. The Wild West show arrived in England on April 16, 1887, and docked in Gravesend, about twenty-five miles east of London.

Buffalo Bill Cody's show in England coincided with Queen Victoria's jubilee, and his presence generated a feverish sensation throughout London. The show's venue at Earl's Court, about a mile south of Kensington Palace, was quickly inundated with hordes of curious visitors. The Grand Duke Michael of Russia, Lady Randolph

Churchill, and former Prime Minister William E. Gladstone and his wife, Catherine,[14] along with numerous London residents, called on Cody within a few days of his arrival. Hundreds of people flocked to the site and observed as the vacant field, about a third of a mile in circumference, was transformed into the wild prairies of America. Four days before the show's official debut, Albert, Prince of Wales (later Edward VII), his wife, Princess Alexandra, and their daughters, Louise, Victoria, and Maude, arrived for a private performance.[15]

Referred to as "one of the western girls,"[16] Emma directed her horse to prance and rear on its hind legs. She also performed "fancy riding stunts" and "some fine dressage to music from the Cowboy Band."[17] Buffalo Bill's Wild West also included horse races, Annie Oakley's sharp shooting, and choreographed attacks on both a pioneer cabin and the Deadwood stagecoach by a conglomerate "tribe" of American Indians. Emma was also featured in one of Cody's heroic exploits:

> The emigrant trail slowly makes its way across the arena, pulled by mules and bullocks led by old John Nelson. The wagons halt by a pool, campfires are started and a meal is prepared. Before the pioneers bed down for the night, there is a little entertainment. Emma Hickok — "America's Queen of the side-saddle" — displays her talents on her dancing horse. The cowboys and western girls join forces and dance the Virginia reel on horseback to the accompaniment of their accordions and banjos, plus the ever-present Cowboy Band.[18]

Agnes and Daisy were probably some of the "pioneers" during the quaint montage. Emma's role in the performances appears limited, and her likeness is not often reflected in the surviving ephemera. Was this an obvious snub by Buffalo Bill? Why would he bring "America's Side-Saddle Queen" across the ocean only to subsequently ignore her (and Wild Bill's widow) in the local media? A simple and practical explanation is that since Emma was hired shortly before the company departed, the lithographic firms probably lacked adequate time to add her to the advertisements. The absence of Emma Lake Hickok's presence in surviving ephemera is more likely attributed to this oversight by printing firms than to a willful or conscious attempt to exclude her from the media frenzy.

The private preview for Prince Albert was rewarded with excellent reviews, and Queen Victoria commanded her own royal performance on May 11. Afterward, the queen wrote in her diary, "[A] young girl, who through the 'haute école,' certainly sat the most marvellous plunges beautifully, sitting erect, [and] being completely master of her horse."[19] That young girl, of course, was Emma Lake. During her time with Cody, though, she was billed as Emma Hickok.

Queen Victoria ordered a second recital for her honored guests — including many crowned heads of Europe — on June 20, just days before her official jubilee celebrations commenced. The fact that Queen Victoria commanded two private performances did not go unnoticed by her subjects, who had barely seen their queen in the quarter century since her husband, Prince Albert, had died. As Louis Warren remarked: "There was something more than envy in these demonstrations. Unrest in the London theatrical world echoed a wider public dissatisfaction with the queen's continuing insistence on private showings of the few entertainments she did attend, and exclusive, private viewings of public exhibits, including the American Exhibition, which was closed to the public during her visit."[20]

During the second performance, Buffalo Bill safely steered the Deadwood stagecoach and his imperial passengers — the kings of Denmark, Greece, Belgium, and Saxony, as well as the future Edward VII — through the "attack."[21]

Many of the Wild West Exhibition performers — including Annie Oakley, Lillian Smith, and Red Shirt, a member of the Sioux tribe — were presented to Queen Victoria.[22] The *New York Clipper* stated that Emma "was honored by the royal command to appear at Windsor."[23] The *Jersey City Mirror* reported, "Mrs. Robinson . . . rode before the Queen, who was so delighted with her performance that she sent her a bouquet of flowers."[24] As late as 1925, Gil Robinson reportedly retained a "pressed bunch of roses" Emma had received from Queen Victoria.[25]

After the American Exhibition closed its London venue in October, the troupe traveled to industrial cities in the north, including Manchester and Birmingham. Agnes, Emma, and little Daisy returned to America in May 1888 aboard the vessel *Persian Monarch*.[26] The three did not join Cody's exhibition when it commenced a European tour in subsequent years. Instead, they settled into their New Jersey home. Throughout the winters of 1888 and 1889, Emma toured with Sturgis & Donovan's Gran Circo Estrellas Del Nortis. Agnes and Daisy accompanied Emma and the other principal performers, including Robert Stickney, Linda Jeal and her sister Elena, on the six-month season throughout the West Indies, Central America, and Venezuela.[27]

*   *   *

In August 1888, "Old John" Robinson died at his home in Cincinnati. Hundreds of mourners gathered outside his residence and awaited their turn to pass the coffin bearing the remains of one of the greatest nineteenth-century showmen.[28] Only a few dozen, however, were allowed to cross the threshold to pay their respects. Unlike the elaborate funeral cortege for Bill Lake that included over forty wagons and carriages, the patriarch of the Robinson dynasty had requested a small, private funeral. "Old John" was laid to rest in a simple yet elegant coffin inside the Robinson mausoleum at Spring Grove Cemetery, beside his wife, Elizabeth, and two of his children, Katie and James.[29] Robinson's will directed that Gil receive some real estate property, but his fiscal inheritance would be placed in a trust from which he would receive semiannual installments. In addition, Robinson specified that neither Gil's fiscal nor his real estate inheritance would "be liable in any manner whatsoever to any claims, demands, legal processes, or enforcements made by or through, or in behalf" of, Emma Lake. Twelve-year-old Daisy Robinson received no inheritance from her paternal grandfather.[30]

Five years later, in 1893, a "romantic twist of fate" swiftly changed the course of Emma's and Daisy's lives. The Lake women were living

Fig. 37. Agnes "Daisy" Robinson and her mother, Emma Lake, with a lion cub and family dog, undated photograph. From the collection of Agnes Cromack.

in New Jersey and one day, according to some newspaper reports, Gil Robinson appeared at their home. Agnes and Emma had fallen on hard financial times. Even though Joseph Mersman had left a small but gainful bequest to his sister Agnes when he died in 1892, their cash flow had ebbed. An unidentified newspaper wistfully described Emma as having "known fortune's decay[,] and life's battle had become a struggle that promised few laurels in the end."[31] Gil, on the other hand, had become a millionaire since his father's death, and knowing of Emma's misfortunes, he left Cincinnati to pay her a visit.[32] He "presented himself to the surprised woman" and declared that he had come to "fix things so that in the future they [Emma and Daisy] should never know want."[33]

Seventeen-year-old Daisy recited to Gil her mother's "ceaseless hours of sorrow . . . the hopes cast down, the whispers of the love of the past and the recited joys long dead and gone."[34] Although Gil kept his thoughts private, "he, too, had spent sleepless nights thinking of his young girl love, she with the [brunette] hair so long the pet of the arena."[35] Even though Emma and Gil had rarely interacted with one another since their divorce a decade earlier, Gil's closest friends knew "that his love for the pretty girl of his boyhood days had lost but little of its fervor."[36] Even his gruff father, "Old John," had remarked before his death, "[Gil] loves that girl yet."[37]

Like Agnes, Emma's love life was cast in a variety of sentimentalized tales. A newspaper clipping retells the story in a romanticized milieu: "A little over a year ago he came East from his home in Cincinnati to see his daughter. While visiting her he met her mother, and the sight of her aroused all the love of his youth. 'Let's try married life over again, Emma' said he. The lady was agreeable . . . and now they are as happy as a pair of turtledoves."[38]

To nearly everyone's surprise, Emma and Gil remarried on May 14, 1893,[39] in a little church in Jersey City, with only a few family members and close friends in attendance. Over the next few years, Gil Robinson embarked on a few worldwide tours, but neither Emma nor Daisy accompanied him. Gil purchased some wild animals during his expeditions in Africa and Asia and likely purchased the prized pair of Arabian stallions Emma rode when she returned to perform with the Robinson's circus in subsequent seasons.[40]

As is the case with their first marriage, little is known about Emma and Gil Robinson's second marriage, which lasted eighteen years until Emma's death. At the time of the 1900 census, their household included Agnes Lake, who lived to see the birth of her great-granddaughter, also named Emma. Emma and Gil, along with Agnes, moved several times to fashionable addresses in New York City, Long Island, and Jersey City before they settled in Somers Point, New Jersey, in 1907. Various New Jersey and New York City directories from 1883 to 1903 listed the matriarch as "Agnes Lake, widow of William," and made no reference to either Hickok or Carson. In 1906, Emma and Gil attended the funeral of James A. Bailey at his home in Mount Vernon, New York,[41] but Agnes was too frail to attend. In many of Bailey's obituaries, the Lake's circus was credited as the cradle of Bailey's success in the circus business.

While Gil enjoyed touring across the globe, Emma remained in New Jersey caring for the elderly Agnes. By 1901, Agnes, once a robust and "handsome woman," appeared frail in the photograph that captured four generations of Lake and Robinson women (see figure 38). The young woman holding the baby is Agnes "Daisy" Robinson. Daisy married Francis Reed, the grandson of legendary showman Dan Rice, in 1894, at age eighteen. The 1900 federal census documents Daisy at home with her parents and Agnes in Jersey City. She claims to have been married and lists the circus as her occupation.[42] Daisy Robinson Reed continued the family tradition — she trained as an equestrienne and joined Hargreaves' Circus — but her circus career was short-lived, since only a few newspapers document her involvement. The fate of her marriage to Francis Reed and her succinct employment with Hargreaves' Circus remains unknown. Daisy Robinson Reed died in 1950 at her home in Somers Point, New Jersey. Her body was transported to Cincinnati and was laid to rest in Spring Grove Cemetery, in the Thatcher plot.

By 1907, Agnes's health had begun to deteriorate. Despite her declining health, she remained in "charge of the linen and darning" in the home she shared with Emma and Gil.[43] Agnes was allegedly still darning stockings in the days just before her death. In addition, Agnes reportedly went to as many circus performances as possible when various companies pitched their tents nearby. She would bemoan that the quality of the troupes, especially the clowns — in her opinion the apex of the circus — had been replaced in favor of a greater quantity of mediocre performers adorned in glitter.

On August 21, 1907, just three days before her eightieth birthday, Agnes Lake died at her home in New Jersey. Her death certificate listed her death as a result of old age, so Agnes may have died in

Fig. 38. Four generations posed for a photograph in 1901: from left to right, Emma Lake Robinson, Agnes "Daisy" Robinson Reed, Emma Reed (later McCue) (1901–78), and Agnes Lake. From the collection of Agnes Cromack.

her sleep. The outpouring of grief among the circus community was astonishing. Her obituaries were printed in newspapers from New York to the Black Hills. She was referred to as the "Circus Queen" and "Wild Bill's Widow." The obituaries contained some inaccurate statements that originated from Agnes herself.

> born in Doehm, Alsace . . . her parents' name being Messman. Her parents came to this country shortly after her birth and settled in Cincinnati when she was about 16 years old.   *New York Times*, August 23, 1907

> The career of . . . Mrs. Agnes Lake . . . was one of the most remarkable in the history of the circus in America.
> *Indianapolis News*, August 24, 1907

After lying in a public vault for nearly two months, Agnes's body traveled one last time, from Jersey City to Cincinnati, for burial beside her first husband.[44]

*   *   *

Emma's later years were devoted to caring for her elderly mother and to giving occasional performances, since she had no desire to retire permanently. In 1908, however, Emma fell during a performance, and the injury plagued her during the final years of her life.[45] In March 1911, Emma Lake was admitted to the New Jersey State Hospital (now Greystone Park Psychiatric Hospital) in Morris Plains for "exhaustion."

Forty-nine days later, on May 11, Emma Lake Robinson died at age fifty-five. Her death certificate listed "paretic dementia" — a condition attributed to syphilis — as the cause of death. This could have been the tertiary stage of syphilis, during which the bacteria, if left untreated, attack the neurological system and render the victim in a near psychotic state. This final stage of syphilis often afflicts the victim nearly two decades after the initial infection. If the origin of Emma's malady was indeed syphilis, a diagnosis that can only be speculated, it is reasonable to hypothesize that Gil Robinson transmitted the disease to Emma when they remarried in 1893. It is unlikely that Emma suffered from syphilis before Daisy was born, since her daughter did not appear to be afflicted with the characteristic physical traits of congenital syphilis such as notched teeth, facial deformities, or deafness.[46]

Emma Lake's body was returned to Cincinnati, and she was buried in Spring Grove Cemetery alongside her family. Her obituary was reprinted in several newspapers, but even though her circus celebrity nearly eclipsed her mother's, her obituaries were less widely circulated. The *New York Clipper* praised Emma's ambition and opined that "with [her] boundless enthusiasm . . . she outdistanced all rivals."[47]

After Emma's death, Gil Robinson continued his travels around the globe, lived in New Jersey for a number of years, and documented his family's circus accolades. In 1925 his memoirs, *Old Wagon*

Fig. 39. Enormous wreaths adorn Agnes's grave after her burial beside her first husband, Bill Lake, in October 1907. For unknown reasons, only William's name is engraved on the granite obelisk; the other family names are listed only in the cemetery records. From the collection of Agnes Cromack.

Show Days, were published. Gil summarized Agnes's life and added to the legends associated with his famous mother-in-law. Although his account contains many inaccuracies, it was Agnes's solitary biographical resource until this volume. The information regarding Agnes, now mostly considered erroneous, has been repeated in countless biographies and articles and has suffocated the facts of Agnes's actual life.

A few years before his death, Gil started a second manuscript about the history of John Robinson's circus, although he died before completing the text. The 200-plus page unpublished manuscript contains biographical accounts of several circus notables, including the Lakes.

Unfortunately, once again Gil diminished the Lake family's accomplishments and influence in the annals of American circus history. The biographical sketches of Agnes, Emma, and Bill Lake encompass only a few lines or at most two paragraphs, whereas some of their contemporaries' biographies are several pages long. In addition, Robinson revised the partnership between his father and Bill Lake. *Old Wagon Show Days* clearly identified Bill Lake as the partner of "Old John" Robinson from 1859 to 1863;[48] but in the unpublished manuscript, Gil listed Lake as Robinson's "assistant manager."[49]

Gil's efforts to minimize the lives of Agnes and Bill Lake, and especially that of his wife, Emma, are perplexing and disappointing. As one of the few people who knew the Lakes for decades, he squandered the opportunity to document the amazing lives of his mother-in-law and his wife, two women whose individual fame eclipsed so many of their contemporaries. Gil was quick to declare kinship with Wild Bill Hickok, however, and he even claimed he was in Abilene in 1871 when Agnes and Hickok first met. That statement is false; the Robinson circus was traveling in Iowa, at least five hundred miles from Abilene,[50] and in 1871 there would have been no reason for Gil to travel with Agnes Lake's Hippo-Olympiad. Furthermore, Robinson and Hickok were hardly close confidants—especially since they probably met only once, when Agnes and Hickok spent a mere two weeks in Cincinnati during their honeymoon in March 1876 at Gil and Emma's residence. Gil's blatant self-promotion camouflaged many facts and, sadly, has shrouded the true stories of Agnes and Emma.

Gil Robinson died August 17, 1928, at age eighty-three at his home in Cincinnati. He was buried in the Robinson mausoleum in Spring Grove Cemetery, alongside his siblings and parents.

*   *   *

In lieu of her personal writings, one can gain significant insight into Agnes Lake's personality through her business dealings. She was acutely aware that her character, and the character of her employees, reflected the moral fiber of her shows, and vice versa. She consistently maintained a zero-tolerance policy regarding the gamblers and vagabonds who often attached themselves to traveling shows. Agnes's business transactions, known mostly through newspaper reports and circus advertisements, profile a woman unafraid to operate her show and assert feminine authority in a patriarchal society. Agnes conducted herself in accordance with female social conventions, earned respect from her male colleagues and the public, and managed her show with minimal outside assistance.

Agnes was keenly aware that photographs captured a person's specific image and attitude. As a result, she always appeared appropriately dressed and posed, carefully controlling and preserving her public image. Despite her career path, she never gave anyone reason to doubt her morals or feminine virtue.

Agnes also possessed a strong work ethic. When faced with running the circus alone and assuming all its economic burdens, she condensed the troupe rather than liquidate its assets. Agnes forged ahead, doing whatever she could to generate income, just as her father had spent hundreds of nights rolling cigars to pay the family's debts in Germany.

Agnes was adventurous. She willingly went to Europe to perform before royalty in an era when crossing the Atlantic Ocean was a precarious journey fraught with danger. The excursion proved beneficial: her performances boosted her reputation and popularity in America.

Agnes was fiercely dedicated to her craft. At the beginning of her circus career, she spent a year rehearsing her slack-wire routine in which she pushed an occupant in a wheelbarrow to the summit of the Big Top canvas, more than a hundred feet above the ground. Later, Agnes dedicated an entire year to adapting the traditional stage play *Mazeppa* for her one-ring circus. It took additional months to train her horses for the intense manège acts before they were ready to perform in a crowded and noisy arena.

Wherever she traveled, she encountered people who had a pre-conceived notion of a circus performer's life. That perception oscillated between the dregs of humanity and romantic adventurers. Agnes was determined to fight the stereotype, and she crafted a biography in a context similar to Hickok's — she added enough "local and contemporary elements to create a convincing imposture, assuming a life story that was part genuine, [and] part invention."[51] Agnes, like many immigrants, participated in a collective amnesia that veiled her true heritage. Throughout a period of anti-immigration sentiment and demonstrations, immigrants sought to disguise their origins and blend into America rather than be targets of hatred during a time of political and social unrest.[52]

At the zenith of Agnes's circus career, the American public adored nearly everything with a French influence — clothing, food, literature, and entertainment. Agnes adopted a French ancestry and thus made herself a commodity the public's voracious appetite would consume. She was an entertainment chameleon, constantly changing and shifting her "appearance" to blend in with the conception of a circus performer's presumed life.

Twentieth-century journalists, western and circus enthusiasts, and historians have, through little fault of their own, perpetuated Agnes's lies. She used a variety of surnames, and extensive research on any of those identities has abruptly ceased when the trail went cold. Many of her legal records, land deeds, and census enumerations are recorded under the name "Thatcher," but that was a name she rarely used publicly.

Agnes Lake, like many of her contemporaries employed by entertainment enterprises such as the theater and circus, invented her own life's story. She omitted aspects of her life that might be unpopular with audiences and assumed a fabricated identity. Audiences expected an unconventional biography from those who lived outside society's norms. A circus performer was expected to have lived an exotic life filled with wondrous adventures and was also expected to be from an equally exotic, or at least a foreign, country. Shrewdly, Agnes tailored herself to fit society's expectations. However, because she was simply playing the game like her contemporaries, she unknowingly made it difficult for a factual examination of her life to be made after she died.

CHAPTER FOURTEEN

The Usurpation of
Mrs. Wild Bill Hickok

"Agnes, We Hardly Knew Ye"

T he railroad opened the West to more than just land for curious folks from the East. Circuses and other traveling entertainers employed the railroad to expand their seasonal itineraries. Companies utilized the railroad to transport all manner of goods — firearms and ammunition, mining and agricultural equipment, and general merchandise — to the far reaches of U.S. civilization. In addition, many of Hickok's contemporaries — such as Calamity Jane, Buffalo Bill, and William F. "Doc" Carver — recognized that the railroad could be a valuable tool to help spread their notoriety beyond local audiences. Those seeking to increase publicity about themselves tended to migrate to the larger cities along the Union Pacific track because of the continual flow of tourists, writers, and professional journalists who disembarked from the trains in these locales, hoping to meet the living folk heroes they read about in *Harper's New Monthly Magazine* or *Beadle's Dime Novels*.

Over a hundred years later, these figures have retained their iconic status as symbols of the American West. Cultural nostalgia beckons their resurrection, and their likenesses appear in films, television dramas, and romance novels. The pervasive nature of nineteenth-century popular literature immortalized these people in the collective American memory. Their legends, first penned in omnipresent pamphlets and sensationalized novels, were intended to exaggerate the lives and adventures of a handful of frontiersmen and women, but the fictionalized narratives are commonly (and dangerously) interpreted and accepted as truth. Despite their contributions to American society and culture, those men and women, whose personas were ignored or shunned by dime novels and yellow journalists, have faded into oblivion.

Dime novels in particular helped build the legends of a few adventurous figures. "Not coincidentally," Louis S. Warren, Buffalo Bill's biographer, remarked, "every single one of these figures appeared in dime novels . . . [and] went on to careers . . . in show business before 1880."[1] However, only a few, such as Buffalo Bill and Doc Carver, parlayed their dime novel appearances and late-nineteenth-century celebrity status into a lifelong relationship with show business. In fact, both men had touring companies that exhibited stage acts and equine novelties well into the first half of the twentieth century.

To date, no known dime novels of Agnes Lake — or any other circus notables — have been uncovered, a fact that has had a significant impact on her subsequent omission from the collective American memory in general and from the story of Wild Bill Hickok in particular. Dime novel authors not only diminished Agnes's role as Mrs. Hickok, but they actively perpetuated the yarns spun around her eventual usurper, Calamity Jane — even though the latter professed a platonic friendship with Wild Bill in her 1896 autobiography, *Life and Adventures of Calamity Jane, by Herself.* The extent of their relationship was magnified in some of Calamity Jane's obituaries, which publicized that she and Wild Bill had lived together in Deadwood and were affianced at the time of his murder.[2] Later purveyors of popular culture, especially Hollywood motion picture producers, latched onto these stories and removed Agnes from the scene altogether. The combination of this diminution of Agnes's public image and the murkiness of her true identity — caused in

part by her own deliberate alterations of her biographical information — makes it almost understandable that the hundreds of published biographies and biographical sketches of Wild Bill Hickok
have paid scant attention to her.

Typically, any mention of Agnes in the numerous biographies of
Wild Bill has been limited to a few sentences, possibly as much as a
paragraph, and some scholars have actually doubted her existence.
The most extensive treatment of Agnes to date has been in Joseph G.
Rosa's definitive biography of Wild Bill, published in 1964, which
dedicated an unprecedented eight pages to Agnes's life, career, and
relationship with the legend. His examination of Agnes exceeded
that of her own son-in-law, Gil Robinson, who summarized her life,
career, and marriages in a paltry three-page analysis in his memoirs.[3]

As examined in earlier chapters, Agnes's historical treatment is
often reduced to portraying her as a damsel in distress: she is looking for a hero to rescue her and her floundering circus from bankruptcy and oblivion. In previous publications, several authors simply repeated information already in circulation and did not attempt
to conduct new research on the woman Wild Bill married. Despite
the lack of additional research, however, each publication incorporated a new — and faulty — character analysis of Agnes Lake. Besides
a damsel in distress, she was often depicted as a materialistic shrew
or a circus performer unaware that she was past her prime, one who
tried to disguise her aged body under layers of makeup and moth-
eaten costumes. Many publications fabricated elaborate conversa-
tions between Agnes and Wild Bill to explain what their "research"
had failed to yield.

This image of a simpering and manipulative Agnes did not fit
well with Wild Bill Hickok's legend, and the role of his companion,
lover, and even wife was soon filled by the persona of a brave adven-
turess, embodied by Calamity Jane. Richard O'Connor's 1959 biography of Hickok suggested that rumors of a romantic relationship
between Calamity Jane and Wild Bill began shortly after his death in
1876. Dime novelists in Deadwood undoubtedly salivated at the idea
of coupling these famous personalities in matching buckskins, even
though Calamity Jane's fame was mostly regional until her fictional

portrayals in the "Deadwood Dick" serials. To the dime novelists, the newly widowed Agnes Lake, far away in Ohio, was a distant memory, and they wasted little time in placing Calamity Jane at Wild Bill's side as he lay dying. O'Connor even included fictitious dialogue from an undocumented dime novel. As Calamity Jane cradled Hickok's head in her lap after Jack McCall had fired the fatal bullet, she pleaded, "Don't go away from me, Bill, I love you."

"My heart has been yours from the first,"[4] Hickok replied.

Thanks to the ubiquitous dime novels, his last words were allegedly intended for Calamity Jane, and they continue to linger in fictional infamy and enhance his legend. Agnes, hundreds of miles away in Cincinnati, could do little when she heard tales about Calamity Jane and Wild Bill's supposed relationship. Agnes probably realized that exchanging barbs with his alleged mistress would prove nothing; the man she loved would still be dead, and any altercation between the two women would only fuel the dime novelists' imaginations.

The legends festered in fictional pamphlets and serials. When Calamity Jane died in 1903, she was buried next to Wild Bill in Mount Moriah Cemetery—but how was that decision made? Some believe Calamity Jane announced that her last wish was to be buried next to the "only man she ever loved." Others suggest inebriated celebrants, toasting the memory of Calamity Jane at a Deadwood saloon, thought it would be a good joke on Wild Bill. Still others credit the Society of Black Hills Pioneers, which hoped to bolster a growing tourism industry by placing the imagined couple next to each other for eternity.[5] Certainly, the proximity of the two graves suggests a close relationship in life, but in fact their physical closeness belies any romantic affiliation.

Equally guilty of removing the historical memory of Agnes Lake are the portrayals of Wild Bill Hickok and Calamity Jane on the silver screen. To date, the only known on-screen depiction of Agnes Lake has been in the television program *The Great Adventure*, a series that featured dramatized biographies of historical figures. In the 1964 episode, "Wild Bill Hickok——the Legend and the Man," Sheree North portrayed the circus queen, and Lloyd Bridges depicted her second ill-fated husband. Unfortunately, no copy of this episode has been located, so an examination of Agnes Lake on film cannot be conducted.

In contrast, there have been numerous celluloid pairings of Wild Bill and Calamity Jane, beginning with a film produced by the Black Hills Feature Film Company of Chadron, Nebraska, in 1915 titled *In the Days of '75 and '76*. Wild Bill and Calamity Jane, portrayed by A. L. Johnson and Freeda Hartzell Romine, respectively, were shown scouting together and were married in the film. The relationship was depicted as a union of equals, clad in nearly identical buckskins and sombreros and each holding a rifle.[6]

Nearly a decade later, William S. Hart, a popular actor known for his cowboy portrayals, wrote and starred in the silent film *Wild Bill Hickok* (Paramount, 1923).[7] Cecil B. DeMille's *The Plainsman* (Paramount, 1936) also perpetuated the fictitious romance between Wild Bill Hickok and Calamity Jane and has been perhaps more influential than any other popular cinematic contribution. DeMille (1881–1959) was an enormously talented director, and because of his visionary masterpieces on the silver screen, every subsequent Wild Bill Hickok "biography" film has been directly influenced by DeMille's 1936 motion picture. Interestingly, the movie was originally intended to be a biopic of Buffalo Bill Cody. The resulting screenplay, however, was inspired by the film version of *The Last Frontier* (Metropolitan-PDC, 1926), based on the 1921 novel by Courtney Ryley Cooper, and by Frank J. Wilstach's *The Prince of Pistoleers,* which was republished in 1937 and re-titled *The Plainsman* to highlight its relationship to the film.

DeMille initially seemed interested in creating a truthful depiction of the lives and adventures of Wild Bill Hickok and Buffalo Bill Cody, and his crew began to research their subjects. The screenplay's "bibliography" included many published works on Wild Bill — including those by William Connelley, whom the Hickok family endorsed; Frank Wilstach, whom the family detested; and the silent script from Hart's film in 1923.[8] DeMille and his crew quickly discovered that only a few primary accounts were available to document Wild Bill's life and career, and DeMille wielded a great deal of creative license in the trajectory of the screenplay.[9] The director, however, overlooked one essential source of Wild Bill's history—the Hickok family, which still possessed much of Wild Bill's personal correspondence.

Colleagues remembered that even after weeks of intense research and "combing all the libraries . . . for every fact and figure bearing on his theme," DeMille would "just as methodically set about throwing out that data" that did not enable his personal conception of the film.[10] The result was a film that was cinematically entertaining but "historically cockeyed," since the characters and events were strung together "with ruthless disregard of time and space and biographical fact."[11] DeMille "decided to weave history and fiction into a rousing, idealized Western adventure pitting gun runners and Indians against Wild Bill Hickok and Buffalo Bill Cody, with a romance between Wild Bill and Calamity Jane added for spice."[12] Agnes is not mentioned in the film.

Thirty years later, in 1966, David Lowell Rich directed Don Murray and Abby Dalton in a remake of *The Plainsman* (Universal Pictures). As recently as 1995, Walter Hill's quasi-biographic film, *Wild Bill* (United Artists), starring Jeff Bridges and Ellen Barkin, continued to deny the existence of Agnes Lake.

These early filmmakers, particularly DeMille, continued the tradition forged in the dime novels of a passionate, even tawdry, love affair between Wild Bill and Calamity Jane. This precedent has endured throughout cinematic history, despite its reliance on historical inaccuracies and anachronisms—and much to the consternation of the families and friends of Agnes Lake and Wild Bill. William S. Hart's 1923 portrayal of the legendary lawman, although popular with audiences, was not well received by the Hickok family. Howard L. Hickok, Wild Bill's nephew who was the son of his brother Horace, was disgusted by the film's implication that Wild Bill and Calamity Jane were married, which reinforced the legends the Hickok family had been trying to debunk since Wild Bill's death nearly forty years earlier.[13]

Howard Hickok's reaction to DeMille's film was equally negative. When he learned of the film's subject matter, he wrote to DeMille to express the family's displeasure at the film's central themes. Howard Hickok's letter to DeMille, dated August 26, 1936, charged the director with assassinating his uncle's character, just as Hart had done in his 1923 film. In addition, Howard blasted DeMille for his decision to include the supposed romance between his uncle and Calamity Jane. "You couple his name with a known and recognized underworld character," he wrote angrily. Howard was upset that his wonderful "Aunt Agnes" was once again ejected from Wild Bill's life in favor of "the worst woman in his generation."[14] Over a month later, Howard received a response from DeMille. DeMille denounced Howard's allegations of fabricating stories, professing that he intended to "produce a very carefully prepared motion picture of the events of the period between 1865 and 1876."[15]

Further, he refused to accept responsibility for the characters' portrayals. DeMille claimed they were based on the fictional characterizations forged, and later immortalized, in Ned Buntline's plays and Beadle's dime novels. Buntline and Beadle, he argued, exaggerated the personas of Buffalo Bill Cody and Wild Bill Hickok "to a point of legendary accomplishment that the public now believe to be fact."[16]

The film wove together various and often unrelated events that occurred over the period of a dozen years and even imbued some of the characters' controversial actions (such as Wild Bill killing cavalry soldiers) with patriotic fervor. DeMille also defended the supposed relationship of Calamity Jane and Wild Bill and claimed that his movie did no more than suggest a "romantic acquaintance." By definition, acquaintance implies a casual familiarity, but certain scenes in the film extend beyond this definition. For example, Gary Cooper's Wild Bill Hickok carries a photograph of the couple in his pocket watch, which is frequently mentioned and opened for the audience to view. Jean Arthur's Calamity Jane continually fawns over Wild Bill. Even though he squirms at her needless fondling, she finds every opportunity to touch him. She also frequently asks if he loves her, to which he always shrugs off her question and changes the subject. But at the moment of Wild Bill's almost certain death, he declares his love for her.

Agnes's granddaughter, Daisy Robinson Reed, also wrote to DeMille and expressed her displeasure with his fabricated historical epic. Daisy remarked, "There was enough romance in Wild Bill's meeting of Mrs. Lake and his interest in her which culminated in their marriage without making up a fictitious romance with another party."[17] She received the same verbatim letter Howard Hickok received, which outlined DeMille's goals for the film, and he reiterated his use of Calamity Jane as the love interest only because of her recognizable name.

Another angry party, Bertha Rath Meyers, indicated that she had had a lifelong friendship with Mrs. Lake, although she incorrectly identified her as "Alice." In her letter to DeMille dated April 29, 1936, Meyers forwarded a copy of a photograph of Mrs. Lake so that a "true conception" of Wild Bill's romantic life could be portrayed instead of "the flamboyant misconceptions that have been fostered heretofore."[18] Although a copy of the photograph was not found among the letters, from Meyers's description it is believed to have been another copy of figure 33, a photo in which Agnes is wearing a dark hat. DeMille's secretary, Gladys Rosson, replied to Meyers and reminded her that the screenplay did not include Wild Bill's wife because the film focused on his life when he was a scout and a plainsman.[19]

Rosson's declaration to Bertha Meyers contradicts her boss's statements. If DeMille intended to direct a film that focused solely on Wild Bill's adventures as a scout and plainsman before he married Agnes Lake, her removal from the screenplay is justified. But the fact that he kept Calamity Jane as the love interest is a clear misrepresentation of history—especially since the two did not meet until just a few weeks before his death, long after he served as a scout. DeMille knowingly removed Agnes from the plot and in the process set a dangerous precedent for future Wild Bill Hickok films.

Beneath the larger-than-life depictions of these silver screen legends lie the real Wild Bill Hickok and Calamity Jane, whose exact relationship is still debated. Wild Bill's biographers, including Wilstach and Rosa, adamantly deny that anything more than a platonic acquaintance—and certainly not a romantic relationship—existed between the two. That view is supported by contemporaneous accounts, such as the one of White-Eye Anderson, a member of the Hickok-Utter wagon train en route to Deadwood in July 1876. Anderson was "adamant" that after Calamity Jane joined the convoy at Fort Laramie, Wild Bill barely spoke to her "except to allow her access to his five-gallon keg of whiskey." In fact, he added, "all the women called him 'Mr. Hickok' for he let it be known that he was only interested in his wife."[20] William Secrest substantiated Anderson's reminiscences and remarked that some of the men said "Hickok seemed to think of his wife often and intended to send for her as soon as he had made a stake."[21] Ellis T. "Doc" Peirce, who was in Deadwood when the wagon train arrived, emphatically stated, "[B]y no means was Calamity Jane a paramour of Bill's. He was a married man and seemed to think much of his wife, and I never saw him associating with lewd women."[22]

With the exception of James McLaird's 2005 biography, an opposing interpretation of their relationship has been presented by many Calamity Jane biographers. These authors have ardently proclaimed that the dime novel pair were involved in a love story akin to *Romeo and Juliet*, with Agnes Lake and Jack McCall representing the dram of poison and "happy dagger" that took Wild Bill from Calamity Jane.

Another damaging piece of historical "evidence" that facilitates the dismissal of Agnes from Wild Bill's life in favor of Calamity Jane was furnished by Montana native Jean McCormick. On May 6, 1941, McCormick was a guest on the popular CBS radio program *We, the People*, on which she revealed a bundle of documents — including a diary and letters purportedly written by Calamity Jane, who McCormick proclaimed was her mother. The diary's fifteen entries are dated between 1877 and 1902 and were written on the yellowed pages of a vintage photograph album. The album also contains twelve entries written on loose pages dated between 1879 and 1903.[23] The accounts were written in the style of letters, addressed "Dear Janey" or a similar endearment. McCormick alleged that she was the offspring of Wild Bill Hickok and Calamity Jane, born September 25, 1873, in Montana, but that she was adopted by sea captain James O'Neil and his family and remained ignorant of her biological ancestry until O'Neil's death in 1912.

One of the most remarkable documents included in the bundle was the purported marriage certificate of Calamity Jane and Wild Bill. According to the diary and letters, Calamity Jane and Wild Bill fell in love in 1870 after she saved his life by warning him of an ambush. Shortly thereafter, while en route to Abilene where Wild Bill would assume his duties as marshal, they crossed paths with a pair of parsons, the Reverends W. F. Warren and W. K. Sipes, and were married. The remarkable—indeed, almost stunning—coincidence that Hickok was allegedly married twice by Reverend W. F. Warren has been noted by several scholars. The certificate reads:

Sept. 1, 1870

ENROUTE TO ABILENE, KANSAS

I, W. F. Warren, Pastor not having available a proper marriage Certificate find it necessary to use as a substitute this Page from the Holy Bible and unite in Holy Matrimony —Jane Cannary, age 18. J. B. Hickok—31.

Witnesses

Carl Cosgrove Abilene, Kansas

Rev. W. K. Sipes Sarasville, Ohio

Tom P. Connel Hays City Kansas[24]

The diary purports that Wild Bill and Calamity Jane's marriage dissolved when he abandoned her on the roadside in the midst of her labor pains to resume his bachelor lifestyle, subsequently forgetting about her until he rekindled his romance with Agnes Lake in Cheyenne. At that point, he sought out Calamity Jane to divorce her so he would be free to marry Agnes. Calamity Jane's feelings toward Agnes are recorded in McCormick's diary, including those she harbored during Wild Bill's subsequent arrival in Deadwood without Agnes—which is known to have generated rumors that he had abandoned his bride (it is certainly more plausible that Agnes stayed behind to help Emma through her pregnancy). After meeting her lost love again, says "Jane" in the album, "We met one day, and we both found we still loved each other better than ever. . . . [W]e both lived a life of lies. He was meant for me, not Agnes Lake, or he would have stayed with her instead of coming back to me."[25] Similar statements in the diary suggest that Calamity Jane harbored resentment toward Agnes Lake because Wild Bill, whom she still deeply loved, needed to divorce Calamity before he could marry the circus doyenne.

McCormick's diary and letters were immediately accepted and endorsed by the radio program, and the following month she was invited to join the "Wild Bill Frontier" celebrations in Abilene, Kansas. She was even welcomed with "tears and kisses" by some members of the Hickok family.[26] Also in 1941, the Yellowstone County, Montana, Department of Public Welfare accepted the diary as proof of McCormick's birth date, in lieu of a genuine birth certificate, and awarded her financial assistance.[27] This "endorsement" of the diary's "facts" provided legitimacy to subsequent scholarship.

Carl Anderson, a historian who lived near Fort Collins, Colorado, examined McCormick's "family treasures" and also endorsed the items and convinced others of their authenticity. Vivien Skinner a source close to *We, the People*, noted that McCormick brought "reams and reams of writing," and she judged McCormick's character as unable to contrive such forgeries.[28]

After her initial disclosure of the items in 1941, McCormick's claims and tales changed slightly with each subsequent interview, prompting widespread suspicion. Specifically, as additional information about Calamity Jane's life came to light — provided by new research or reminisces by acquaintances — the diary miraculously reflected those changes on "recently discovered" loose pages. Furthermore, the diary seemed to have an uncanny ability to supply direct responses to any inquiry, and it conveniently explained away historical discrepancies and inconsistencies. Tests were suggested to confirm the album's age, but then an entry was discovered in which "Calamity" wrote: "I sometimes find it impossible to carry the old album to write in so you will find now & then extra pages."[29]

Consequently, since the "discovery" of these documents, several scholars have categorically disproved the authenticity of the contents of the diary and letters. McLaird claimed that the "tenor of McCormick's Calamity differs dramatically from that in Martha's 1896 autobiography and in the historical record"[30] and does not refer to events in which she participated after 1896. The diary's language implied that Calamity Jane was more literate than historians had previously believed. When compared with one another, the "simple language of [her] autobiography" conflicts drastically with the illustrative language in the diary and letters. McLaird reminds us that Calamity Jane was probably illiterate, especially since no authenticated piece of her handwriting has ever been produced. The diary also neglects to mention two other children she possibly gave birth to in 1884 and 1887, respectively, as well as at least three other men Calamity Jane called husband (Bill Steers, George Cosgrove, and Robert Dorsett) besides Clinton Burke.[31] Deadwood business leaders were never convinced of McCormick's parentage, and she dropped her plans to operate a dining establishment with an attached museum composed of her supposed parents' items and memorabilia.

Despite the debunking of the diary and letters for historical inaccuracy, interest in the items has not been quelled. Since their inclusion into the historical record and legend of Calamity Jane, the items have initiated dozens of ostensibly scholastic articles and biographies, influenced popular historical novels, and inspired poetry and musical compositions.

Glenn Clairmonte published several pieces that heavily relied on the diary's "truths." In her article "The Double Nature of Wild Bill Hickok," published in the *Denver Westerners Monthly Roundup* in August 1960, she relied on the diary's contents to create an imaginary timeline that contradicted existing information about specific and well-known events in both Wild Bill's and Calamity Jane's lives. Clairmonte's article also presented McCormick's claims of Wild Bill and Calamity Jane's alleged marriage and relayed the diary's version of their tragic romance. Based on this information, Clairmonte concluded that Wild Bill believed his marriage to Agnes would be "the crowning accomplishment in his life of adventure" and "the Open Sesame to grandeur."[32] Agnes, she remarked, believed the marriage would be similarly auspicious for her. In addition, some of Clairmonte's conclusions are surprising. She described Wild Bill as a prudish man who was terrified of sexual activity with women, who married Agnes Lake only for materialistic gains, and who participated in a homosexual relationship with his "pard" Colorado Charley.[33]

Stella Foote purchased the diary and letters from Jean McCormick sometime after 1950 for an undisclosed sum and spent thirty years studying their contents. She displayed the items in her Billings, Montana, Wonderland Museum and published select passages. In her biographical account of Calamity Jane, *A History of Calamity Jane, Our Nation's First Liberated Woman* (1995), Foote promoted using the diary as authentic source material, ignored the inconsistencies and inaccuracies, and suggested that "proponents of McCormick's claims will ignore the evidence proving [the] diary and letters forgeries."[34]

Much debate remains surrounding McCormick's motives in disclosing, and perhaps writing, the diary and letters. McLaird remarked that "fame and personal identity" were probably the largest factors. By revealing the diary and "finding" lost entries, McCormick maintained control over the items and made it possible for her to be paid for appearances.[35] Both McLaird and Joseph G. Rosa surmised that McCormick was an orphan who chose the pair as her fantasy parents, and she forged the diary, hoping to escape from obscurity.[36] Whatever McCormick's motives were in disclosing the diary, the documents resulted in enduring confusion, not only in the historical record and legacies of Wild Bill Hickok and Calamity Jane but subsequently in those of Agnes Lake.[37]

Chronological and personality inaccuracies aside, the diary introduced new facets, including motherhood and feminine vulnerability, into Calamity Jane's persona hitherto associated with traditional masculine attributes — cussing, smoking, and shooting.[38] Perhaps it is the allure of this insight that has made some scholars reluctant to denounce the documents as fakes. In 2004, McCormick's items were sold at the Cody Old West Show & Auction in Cody, Wyoming, for over $60,000.[39] The authors hope the buyer realizes that they are forgeries and treats them accordingly. If they are to be published, we further hope the items are published as examples of historical fraud — not as truth.

Nyle Miller, former secretary of the Kansas State Historical Society, once remarked, "People who have lived with the myths and legends of the past for most of their lives are not interested in learning the truth when it runs contrary to what they believe."[40] The truth about Agnes Lake as Wild Bill's wife and lover challenges many popular myths of Calamity Jane, and some might even identify Agnes as "the other woman," since she is relatively unknown. Some might find it difficult to surrender the legendary mythical romance of Wild Bill and Calamity Jane for a wife nobody has heard of or believes truly existed.

Kent Ladd Steckmesser argued that there is "something cold and abstract" about the truth, while romance and legends "are warm and colorful."[41] James McLaird added that removing the legends from historical figures can be unpopular and warned that the "romanticized versions" of Calamity Jane and Wild Bill "inevitably led to scurrilous attacks on their reputations."[42] In the process, they have further erased Agnes Lake from Wild Bill's life. But do the American people love and admire George Washington any less when they realize the fable of the cherry tree is false or that his dentures were not made of wood?

Embracing Agnes Lake as a new facet of the Wild Bill legend does not detract from his mythical status or injure his historical record. Wild West enthusiasts should not balk at the idea of Agnes Lake. Their love story, as Daisy wrote to DeMille in November 1936, was full of enough adventure and romance without the need to add a third party, and it did not warrant her grandmother's deletion from Wild Bill's biographies. Just as the forged diary supplied by Jean McCormick added motherhood to the legend of Calamity Jane, Agnes Lake adds a gentler, more domestic side to the man often thought of as a gunfighter.

Epilogue
Cincinnati, Ohio

The picturesque hillsides of Spring Grove Cemetery are strewn with nineteenth-century tombstones. Gothic chapels and family mausoleums are surrounded by headstones engraved with boldly carved surnames and endearing epitaphs. Grotesque angels and macabre carvings crown several headstones, and modern wreaths and silk flowers dot the landscape. Many granite headstones have withstood decades of harsh winters and hot summers, while others made of sandstone have eroded beyond identification. Flowering trees add to the beauty each spring and provide shade during the summer months. In winter, the air is crisp and cold. Melting snow and ice mix with small pebbles on the pathways and crunch under visitors' feet on a guided tour. The ponds are covered with a thin sheet of ice. The local waterfowl take refuge in the fractures on the surface that allow access to the cold water below.

One towering granite obelisk engraved "Thatcher" marks a plot near a pathway. Other obelisks stand in close proximity, a testament to vintage funerary art. There, the woman once crowned the "Queen of the Arena," who most often called herself Agnes Lake and sometimes Agnes Hickok, sleeps eternally. She lies beside her first husband, Bill Lake, her daughter, Emma, and her granddaughter, Daisy, but her name does not appear on the monument above her body. In fact, no one could find her by reading the markers, so her rest is undisturbed. The woman who attracted crowds in life now plays to an empty house in Cincinnati, while her second husband — who preferred the frontier's open spaces and abhorred his time on the stage — endures busloads of tourists in Deadwood.

*   *   *

Years of careful examination and extensive research in newspapers, memoirs, immigration records, and miles of microfilm have culminated in this volume. The goals were to dispel the most erroneous reports of Agnes's life, to interpret the clues she left behind as accurately as possible, and to celebrate the life of a woman who defied cultural expectations. Despite personal challenges and tragedies, she lived her life the way she wanted to live it. Researching Agnes Lake was no easy task when the subject artfully dodged the truth in her own lifetime, invented a counterfeit ancestry, and left only a few known pages of documentary evidence. Anyone attempting to research her life using only the clues she provided would find nothing but her homespun yarns. Perhaps that is why so little of Agnes exists in the many Hickok biographies and circus histories.

In addition, Agnes fell victim to the many drawbacks that beset members of her sex in American history. Women who left little evidence of their lives are subjected to fictionalized narratives or are easily dismissed in the annals of history. There were many attempts to study Agnes Lake, as both a circus performer and as Wild Bill's only known legal wife, before this volume. Joseph G. Rosa recognized the intrigue of Agnes's life story while examining Wild Bill for his 1964 publication and advocated a "book-length study" on this "remarkable person."[1] Scholars who previously attempted to examine her life, however, quickly faced a brick wall. The key to unlocking Agnes's past was not the legends she spun herself but, surprisingly, her brother's diary, which was unknown until recently when a burgeoning historian accidentally stumbled upon it while looking for personal narratives about the 1849 cholera outbreak in St. Louis.

While millions of German immigrants remained in ethnic communities and celebrated their European culture long after they settled in America, Agnes disguised her origins. Agnes avoided the traditional role that limited most German women to "Kinder, Kirche, und Küche" (children, church, and kitchen). She challenged her family's personal and cultural expectations and joined the circus to live an unconventional and often unpredictable existence. She found within herself the natural skill and inherent talent to become one of the nineteenth century's most celebrated circus performers.

Death visited her often — she lost at least two infants, her teenage daughter Alice, and two of her husbands in similar circumstances — but she did not dissolve into reclusive widowhood. Instead, she transcended her grief and continued to live her life on her terms.

This book is by no means the end of Agnes's story. Rather, it is the authors' hope that a new dialogue on Agnes is engaged. There may be countless untold stories, letters, and photographs still undiscovered that will enhance our understanding of this historical anomaly.

David Carlyon called nineteenth-century showman Dan Rice "the most famous person you have never heard of," and a similar appellation describes Agnes Lake. Few mid-nineteenth-century women stand out in such sharp relief against the broad backdrop of U.S. history. Unlike her contemporaries such as Susan B. Anthony, Carrie Nation, and Elizabeth Cady Stanton, who championed national causes such as temperance and women's suffrage, Agnes unwittingly facilitated the women's rights movement simply through the choices she made. Because of the way she operated her show and treated her employees, she became a respected businesswoman and performer both within the circus community and across the nation. She earned even more national attention when she lassoed one of the West's most eligible bachelors and garnered international fame when she performed in Berlin before royalty.

Rarely was an entire family of circus performers — Bill, Agnes, Alice, and Emma Lake — described as "peerless" performers of the sawdust arena. Their individual and combined talents spanned nearly seven decades, but hitherto, their talents have been largely unknown to modern audiences. Without the Lakes' and countless others' contributions, modern circuses might look and feel drastically different.

Agnes played a unique role in the ever-changing world of circuses. Her performances of *Mazeppa* bridged the gap between traditional stage productions and the circus arena. Later, again demonstrating her acuity for popular trends, she exhibited a free-balloon ascension and was one of the few female animal trainers in nineteenth-century circuses. She was the first female proprietor to own and operate a tent show in America, and she also headed one of the first companies to use the railroad as its main conveyance throughout a season. Both she and Emma participated in the revitalization of the haut école. Agnes was furthermore a member of the troupe that initiated the two-ring circus, a drastic change from the centuries-old use of a solo ring.

Circuses continue to revise their acts and diversify their corps of talents. Once, however, the Lakes were there — shining stars in the circus world. Significantly, both Agnes and Emma achieved a level of celebrity rarely attained by women in the nineteenth century. Stuart Thayer once wrote that "the real measure of a woman rider was when she had her own place in the program."[2] Agnes Lake had more than her "own place in the program"; she evolved into a nineteenth-century icon and was crowned "the Queen of the Circus."

Circus Companies and Route Sheets for Agnes Lake, 1846–1874

1846

Great Western Circus
Dennison Stone, Eaton Stone, and
Thomas McCollum, proprietors; Spencer
Q. Stokes, principal agent. Agnes Lake is
not yet in the roster; she is learning the
tightrope and equestrian acts. William
Lake, dog acts.

Apr 23–May 2	Cincinnati, Ohio
May 4–9	Louisville, Ky.
May 11+	Cincinnati, Ohio
May 15–23	Pittsburgh, Pa.
Jun 4	Steubenville, Pa.
Jun 6	Wheeling, Va.
Jun 30–Jul 4	Cincinnati, Ohio
Jul 16–18	Louisville, Ky.
Aug 7–15	Saint Louis, Mo.
Aug	Galena, Ill.
Aug 25–Sep 5	Saint Louis, Mo.
Sep 17	Memphis, Tenn.
Oct 14–17	Natchez, Miss.
Oct 20–Jan 10	New Orleans, La.

1847

Rockwell & Co. New York Circus
Henry Rockwell, proprietor. Agnes Lake
is not yet a featured performer; William
Lake, trained dogs.

Apr 26–28	Indianapolis, Ind.
Apr 29	Franklin, Ind.
Apr 30	Edinburgh, Ind.
May 10–12	Louisville, Ky.
May 17	Perryville, Ky.
May 18	Danville, Ky.
May 19	Harrodsburg, Ky.
May 20	Lawrenceburg, Ky.
May 21	Frankfort, Ky.
May 22	Versailles, Ky.
May 24–25	Lexington, Ky.

Jun 12	West Union, Ohio	Aug 4	Mansfield, Ohio
Jun 14	Portsmouth, Ohio	Aug 5	Gallon, Ohio
Jun 15	Lucasville, Ohio	Aug 6	Bucyrus, Ohio
Jun 16	Piketon, Ohio	Aug 7	Marion, Ohio
Jun 17	Jackson, Ohio	Aug 9	Delaware, Ohio
Jun 18	Richmond, Ohio	Aug 10	Marysville, Ohio
Jun 19	Chillicothe, Ohio	Aug 11	Middleburg, Ohio
Jun 21	Bainbridge, Ohio	Aug 12	Mechanicsburg, Ohio
Jun 22	Greenfield, Ohio	Aug 13	Urbana, Ohio
Jun 23	Washington, Ohio	Aug 14	Springfield, Ohio
Jun 24	Williamsport, Ohio	Aug 16	Dayton, Ohio
Jun 25	Circleville, Ohio	Aug 17	Troy, Ohio
Jun 26	Lancaster, Ohio	Aug 18	Piqua, Ohio
Jun 28	Somerset, Ohio	Aug 19	Greenville, Ohio
Jun 29	Baltimore, Ohio	Aug 20	Lewisburg, Ohio
Jun 30	Lithopolis, Ohio	Aug 21	Eaton, Ohio
Jul 1	Lockbourne, Ohio	Aug 23	Richmond, Ind.
Jul 2–3	Columbus, Ohio	Sep 6	Covington, Ind.
Jul 5	Newark, Ohio	Sep 7	Attica, Ind.
Jul 7–8	Zanesville, Ohio	Sep 8	Fayette, Ind.
Jul 9	Norwich, Ohio	Sep 9	Delphi, Ind.
Jul 10	Cambridge, Ohio	Sep 10	Logansport, Ind.
Jul 12	Coshocton, Ohio	Sep 20–22	Chicago, Ill.
Jul 13	Newcomerstown, Ohio	Sep 24	Waukegan, Ill.
Jul 14	New Philadelphia,	Sep 25	Kenosha, Wis.
	Ohio	Sep 27	Racine, Wis.
Jul 15	Waynesburg, Ohio	Sep 28–29	Milwaukee, Wis.
Jul 17	Carrollton, Ohio	Oct 5	Elgin, Ill.
Jul 19	East Springfield, Ohio	Oct 6	Saint Charles, Ill.
Jul 20	Steubenville, Ohio	Oct 7	Aurora, Ill.
Jul 21	Wellsville, Ohio	Oct 8	Naperville, Ill.
Jul 22	New Lisbon, Ohio	Oct 10	Joliet, Ill.
Jul 23	Hanover, Ohio	Oct 12	Ottawa, Ill.
Jul 24	Salem, Ohio	Oct 13	Peru, Ill.
Jul 26	Canfield, Ohio	Oct 14	Hennepin, Ill.
Jul 27	Warren, Ohio	Oct 15	Lacon, Ill.
Jul 28	Newton Falls, Ohio	Oct 16	Peoria, Ill.
Jul 29	Ravenna, Ohio	Oct 18	Farmington, Ill.
Jul 30	Akron, Ohio	Oct 19	Canton, Ill.
Jul 31	Medina, Ohio	Oct 20	Lewiston, Ill.
Aug 2	Wooster, Ohio	Oct 21	Havana, Ill.
Aug 3	Ashland, Ohio	Oct 22	Petersburg, Ill.

Oct 23	Springfield, Ill.
Oct 27	Beardstown, Ill.
Oct 28	Rushville, Ill.
Oct 29	Mount Sterling, Ill.
Oct 30	Columbus, Ill.
Nov 1	Quincy, Ill.
Nov 2	Hannibal, Ill.
Nov 3	Barry, Ill.
Nov 4	Pittsfield, Ill.
Nov 5	Winchester, Ill.
Nov 6	Whitehall, Ill.
Nov 8	Carrolton, Ill.

1848

Rockwell & Co. Circus
Henry Rockwell, proprietor. Spencer Q. Stokes, manager. Agnes Lake, rope (slack wire); William Lake, clown.

Apr 16	Madison, Ind.
Apr 24	Maysville, Ky.
May 6+	Pittsburgh, Pa.
May 18	Marietta, Ohio
Jun 4	Cincinnati, Ohio
Jun 12–13	Louisville, Ky.
Jun 24	Evansville, Ind.
Jul 3–4	Memphis, Tenn.
Jul 10	Ohio City, Mo.
Jul 17–18	Saint Louis, Mo.
Jul 25	Warsaw, Ill.
Jul 29	Hannibal, Mo.
Aug 23	Columbia, Mo.
Sep 4	Liberty, Mo.
Oct 6–7	Springfield, Mo.
Oct 21–23	Van Buren, Ark.
Oct 24–25	Fort Smith, Ark.
Nov 4–7	Little Rock, Ark.
Nov 27–29	Vicksburg, Miss.
Dec 1–2	Natchez, Miss.
Dec 6–7	Baton Rouge, La.
Jan 4+ (1849)	New Orleans, La.

1849

South-Western Circus
Spencer Q. Stokes, proprietor. Agnes Lake, tightrope, William Lake, clown.

Apr 16	Covington, Ky.
Apr 19	Fulton, Ky.
Apr 22	Cincinnati, Ohio
Jun 1–2	Cincinnati, Ohio
Jun 12	Louisville, Ky.
Jun 13	Jefferson, Ind.
Jun 14–15	New Albany, Ind.
Jun 28–29	Evansville, Ind.
Jun 30	Henderson, Ky.
Jul 2	Mount Vernon, Ind.
Jul 3	Uniontown, Ky.
Jul 4	Shawneetown, Ill.
Jul ?	Ohio City, Mo.
Jul 13–14	Saint Louis, Mo.
Jul 23	Burlington, Iowa
Jul 26	Albany, Wis.
Jul 27	Bellevue, Iowa
Jul 28	Dubuque, Iowa
Jul 30	Potosi, Wis.
Jul 31	Cassville, Wis.
Aug 1	Prairie du Chien, Wis.
Aug 2	Guttenberg, Iowa
Aug 4	Galena, Ill.
Aug 6	Savanna, Ill.
Aug 9	Davenport, Iowa
Aug 13	Oquawka, Ill.
Aug 17	Warsaw, Ill.
Aug 18	Tully, Ill.
Aug 20	Quincy, Ill.
Aug 21	Hannibal, Mo.
Aug 22	Louisiana, Mo.
Aug 24	Saint Louis, Mo.
Sep	Unknown
Oct 1–9	Saint Louis, Mo.
Oct 10	Chester, Mo.
Oct 11	Wittenberg, Mo.

Oct 12	Cape Girardeau, Mo.
Oct 13	Commerce, Mo.
Oct 15	Cairo, Ill.
Nov	Unknown
Dec 10–28	New Orleans, La.

1850

American Circus

Samuel B. Burgess, proprietor and manager. Agnes Lake, slack wire; William Lake, clown.

Apr 18	Lafayette, Ind.
Apr 26–27	Terra Haute, Ind.
May 3	New Harmony, Ind.
May 6	Evansville, Ind.
May 13–14	Louisville, Ky.
Jun 2	Marietta, Ohio
Jun 4	Parkersburg, Va. (now W.Va.)
Jun 10	Maysville, Ky.
Jun 15	Fulton, Ohio
Jun 17	Covington, Ky.
Jun 18–19	Cincinnati, Ohio
Jun 25	West Port, Ky.
Jun 26	Utica, Ind.
Jun 27	Jeffersonville, Ind.
Jun 28–29	Louisville, Ky.
Jul 3	Newburgh, Ind.
Jul 4	Evansville, Ind.
Jul 17	Cape Girardeau, Mo.
Jul 22–27	Saint Louis, Mo.
Aug 5	Savannah, Mo.
Aug 6	Saint Joseph, Mo.
Aug 8	Weston, Mo.
Aug 23	Jefferson City, Mo.
Sep 5	Peoria, Ill.
Sep 15	Peoria, Ill.
Sep 17	Cape Girardeau, Mo.
Sep 23	Naples, Ill.
Sep 24	Jacksonville, Ill.

Sep 25–26	Springfield, Ill.
Sep 27	Petersburg, Ill.
Sep 28	Va., Ill.
Oct 4	Louisiana, Mo.

**Ceased operation

Model Circus

John M. LeThorn, manager. Agnes Lake, slack wire and rider; William Lake, clown.

Dec 1–7	New Orleans, La.
Jan 1–22	New Orleans, La.
Jan 23	Algeria, La.

1851

Spalding, Rogers, & Van Orden's People's Circus

Gilbert R. Spalding, Charles J. Rogers, and Wessel T.B. Van Orden, proprietors. Dennison Stone, manager. Agnes Lake, slack wire and rider; William Lake, clown.

Apr 16–19	Cincinnati, Ohio
May 2	Gallipolis, Ohio
May 14	McConnellsville, Ohio
May 15	Beverly, Ohio
May 16	Lowell, Ohio
May 17	Marietta, Ohio
May 21	Wellsburg, Ohio
May 22	Steubenville, Ohio
May 26–31	Pittsburgh, Pa.
Jun 23–24	Louisville, Ky.
Jun 25	Jeffersonville, Ky.
Jun 27–28	Cincinnati, Ohio
Jul 2	Middletown, Ohio
Jul 16	Wabash, Ind.
Jul 17	Logansport, Ind.
Jul 18	Peru, Ind.
Jul 19	Lagro, Ind.
Jul 28	Ohio City, Ohio
Jul 29–30	Cleveland, Ohio

Aug 1	Akron, Ohio
Aug 2	Ravenna, Ohio
Aug 11	Lisbon, Ohio
Aug 12	Hanover, Ohio
Aug 15	Bolivar, Ohio
Aug 16	North Philadelphia, Ohio
Aug 18	Newcomerstown, Ohio
Aug 22	Newark, Ohio
Aug 25	Athens, Ohio
Aug 26	Nelsonville, Ohio
Aug 27	Logan, Ohio
Aug 28	Lancaster, Ohio
Aug 29	Winchester, Ohio
Aug 30	Bloomfield, Ohio
Sep 1–2	Columbus, Ohio
Sep 3	Circleville, Ohio
Sep 4	Chillicothe, Ohio
Sep 11	Vevay, Ind.
Sep 20	Evansville, Ind.
Sep 30–Oct 11	Saint Louis, Mo.
Oct 13	Alton, Ill.
Oct 20	Keokuk, Iowa
Oct 21	Warsaw, Ill.
Oct 23	Quincy, Ill.
Oct 28	Hannibal, Mo.
Nov 11–13	Vicksburg, Miss.
Nov 17–19	Natchez, Miss.
Nov 27–28	New Orleans, La.
Nov 29	Carrolton, La.
Nov 30	Lafayette, La.
Dec 1–2	Algiers, La.

1852

Floating Palace (The company began the season as Spalding, Rogers, & Van Orden's American and European Amphitheatre and often played in more than one city per day).
Gilbert R. Spalding and Charles J. Rogers, proprietors; Wessel T.B. Van Orden, manager. Agnes Lake, slack rope; William Lake, clown.

Mar 13–15	New Orleans, La.
Mar 18–19	Baton Rouge, La.
Mar 23–24	Natchez, Miss.
Mar 26–27	Vicksburg, Miss.
Apr 8	Memphis, Tenn.
Apr 12–16	Nashville, Tenn.
Apr 17	Clarksville, Tenn.
Apr 27	Louisville, Ky.
Apr 29–May 8	Cincinnati, Ohio
May 29	Cincinnati, Ohio
***on *Floating Palace*	
Jun 1–4	Pittsburgh, Pa.
Jun 5–6	Steubenville, Ohio
Jun 7	Wellsberg, Va.
Jun 21	Elizabeth, Va.
Jun 22	Starfish, Va.
Jun 22	New Martinsville, Va.
Jun 23	Sistersville, Va.
Jun 23	Grandview, Ohio
Jun 24	Saint Marys, Va.
Jun 24	Newport, Ohio
Jun 25	Marietta, Ohio
Jun 26	Harmar, Ohio
Jun 28–Jul 1	Cincinnati, Ohio
Jul 2	Fulton, Ohio
Jul 5–6	Cincinnati, Ohio
Jul 7	Newport, Ky.
Jul 8	Covington, Ky.
Jul 9–10	Cincinnati, Ohio
Jul 22–24	Louisville, Ky.
Jul 26	Portland, Ind.
Jul 27	New Albany, Ind.
Aug 4	Evansville, Ind.
Aug 5	Henderson, Ky.
Aug 14	Commerce, Mo.
Aug 14	Cape Girardeau, Mo.
Aug 17–19	Saint Louis, Mo.
Aug 20	Saverton, Mo.
Aug 20	Hannibal, Mo.

Aug 21	Marion, Ill.	Dec 29	Washington, Ala.
Aug 21	Quincy, Ill.	Dec 30–Jan 1	Montgomery, Ala.
Aug 23	Keokuk, Iowa		
Aug 24	Warsaw, Ill.		
Aug 24	Alexandria, Mo.		**1853**
Aug 25	Gregory Landing, Mo.		
Aug 25	Tully, Mo.		Spalding & Rogers's Circus on the
Aug 25	LaGrange, Mo.		*Floating Palace*
Aug 26	Cincinnati, Mo.		Gilbert R. Spalding and Charles J. Rogers,
Aug 26	Scott's Landing, Mo.		proprietors. Agnes Lake, slack wire;
Aug 26	Louisiana, Mo.		William Lake, clown.
Aug 27	Clarksville, Mo.	Jan 1	Montgomery, Ala.
Aug 28	Johnson's Landing,	Jan 3	Wetumpka, Ala.
	Mo.	Jan 19–26	Mobile, Ala.
Aug 28	Grafton, Ill.	Mar 2	Fort Adams, Miss.
Aug 30–31	Saint Louis, Mo.	Mar 3	Vidalia, Miss.
Sep 1	Milan, Ill.	Mar 4–5	Natchez, Miss.
Sep 1	Grafton, Ill.	Mar	Vicksburg, Miss.
Sep 2	Alton, Ill.	Apr 4	Palmyra, Tenn.
Sep 3	Brooklyn, Ill.	Apr 5	Clarksville, Tenn.
Sep 3	Illinoistown, Ill.	Apr 6–9	Nashville, Tenn.
Sep 6	Saint Mary, Mo.	Apr 18	Mount Carmel, Ill.
Sep 6	Chester, Ill.	Apr 19	Vincennes, Ind.
Sep 7	Liberty, Mo.	Apr 20	Russellville, Ill.
Sep 7	Williams, Mo.	Apr 21	Hutsonville, Ill.
Sep 7	Wittenberg, Mo.	Apr 22	Darwin, Ill.
Sep 8	Willard's	Apr 23	Terra Haute, Ind.
Sep 8	Thebes, Ill.	Apr 27	Independence, Ind.
Sep 13–16	Memphis, Tenn.	Apr 28	Attica, Ind.
Sep 27–29	Vicksburg, Miss.	Apr 30	Terra Haute, Ind.
Oct 4–6	Natchez, Miss.		****Agnes and Bill Lake leave the *Floating*
Oct 11–12	Baton Rouge, La.		*Palace* and join Spalding & Rogers's
Oct 16–26	New Orleans, La.		overland troupe, the North American
Dec 6–8	New Orleans, La.		Circus.
Dec 16–18	Mobile, Ala.	May 3	Germantown, Ohio
Dec 20	Claiborne, Ala.	May 4	Eaton, Ohio
Dec 21	Peach Tree, Ala.	May 5	Hamilton, Ohio
Dec 22	Portland, Ala.	May 6	Mount Pleasant, Ohio
Dec 23	Cahaba, Ala.	May 7	Covington, Ky.
Dec 24–25	Selma, Ala.	May 9–14	Cincinnati, Ohio
Dec 27	Benton, Ala.	May 16	Morrow, Ohio
Dec 28	Vernon, Ala.	May 19	Middletown, Ohio

May 21	Columbus, Ohio	Apr 26	New Milford, Conn.
May 27	Cambridge, Ohio	Apr 27	Danbury, Conn.
May 28	Winchester, Ohio	Apr 28	Norwalk, Conn.
Jun 11	Fremont, Ohio	Apr 29	Stamford, Conn.
Jun 15	Blissfield, Ohio	May 1	Bridgeport, Conn.
Jun 16	Adrian, Mich.	May 5	Waterbury, Conn.
Jun 17	Tecumseh, Mich.	May 9–10	Hartford, Conn.
Jun 25	Kalamazoo, Mich.	May 25	Groton, Conn.
Jun 27	Battle Creek, Mich.	May 29–30	Providence, R.I.
Jun 28	Marshall, Mich.	May 31	Woonsocket, R.I.
Jun 29	Albion, Mich.	Jun 1	Pawtucket, R.I.
Jun 30	Jackson, Mich.	Jun 2	Bristol, R.I.
Jul 1	Dexter, Mich.	Jun 3	Fall River, Mass.
Jul 2	Ann Arbor, Mich.	Jun 5	New Bedford, Mass.
Jul 4–6	Detroit, Mich.	Jun 6	Wareham, Mass,
Jul 21	Galt, Ont.	Jun 7	Plymouth, Mass.
Jul 22	Guelph, Ont.	Jun 8	Taunton, Mass.
Aug 16–17	Kingston, Ont.	Jun 9	North Bridgewater,
Aug 19	Brockville, Ont.		Mass.
Aug 20	Prescott, Ont.	Jun 10	Quincy, Mass.
Aug 30–Sep 3	Montreal, Quebec	Jun 12	Roxbury, Mass.
Sep 19	Littleton, N.H.	Jun 13–16	Boston, Mass.
Sep 27	Walpole, N.H.	Jun 17	Charlestown, Mass.
Sep 28	Keene, N.H.	Jun 19	South Boston, Mass.
Sep 29	Peterboro, N.H.	Jun 20	East Boston, Mass.
Sep 30	Hillsboro, N.H.	Jun 21	Lawrence, Mass.
Oct	Lowell, Mass.	Jun 22	Haverhill, Mass.
Oct 4–5	Manchester, N.H.	Jun 23	Newburyport, Mass.
Oct 7	Salem, Mass.	Jun 24	Exeter, N.H.
Oct 15	Milford, Mass.	Jun 26	Portsmouth, N.H.
Oct 17	Worcester, Mass.	Jun 27	Great Falls, Maine
Oct 20–21	Springfield, Mass.	Jun 28	Biddeford, Maine
Oct 26	Bristol, Conn.	Jun 29	Portland, Maine
Oct 27	Naugatuck, Conn.	Jun 30	Brunswick, Maine
Oct 28	Woodbury, Conn.	Jul 3	Gardner, Maine
		Jul 4	Augusta, Maine
		Jul 5	Britton's Mills
1854		Jul 13	Unity, Maine
		Jul 14	Newport, Maine
Spalding & Rogers's Two Circuses		Jul 15	Dexter, Maine
Gilbert R. Spalding and Charles J. Rogers,		Jul 17	East Corinth, Maine
proprietors. Agnes Lake, slack wire and		Jul 18	Old Town, Maine
rider; Bill Lake, clown.			

Jul 19	Bangor, Maine	Sep 23	Trenton, N.J.
Jul 20	Belfast, Maine	Sep 25	Mount Holly, N.J.
Jul 27	Yarmouth, Maine	Sep 26	Camden, N.J.
Jul 28	Portland, Maine	Sep 27	Glassboro, N.J.
Jul 29	Springvale, Maine	Sep 28	Penn's Grove, N.J.
Jul 31	Manchester, N.H.	Sep 29	Wilmington, Del.
Aug 1	Nashua, N.H.	Oct 2	Havre de Grace, Md.
Aug 2	Lowell, Mass.	Oct 3–6	Baltimore, Md.
Aug 5	Fitchburg, Mass.	Oct 9	Frederick, Md.
Aug 7	Winchendon, Mass.	Oct 10	Boonsboro, Md.
Aug 8	South Orange, Mass.	Oct 11	Hagerstown, Md.
Aug 9	Greenfield, Mass.	Oct 16	Alexandria, Va.
Aug 10	Northampton, Mass.	Oct 17	Georgetown, D.C.
Aug 11	Springfield, Mass.	Oct 18–19	Washington, D.C.
Aug 14	Great Barrington, Mass.	Oct 24–26	Petersburg, Va.
Aug 15	Pittsfield, Mass.	Oct 27–28	Lynchburg, Va.
Aug 16	North Adams, Mass.	Oct 31–Nov 3	Richmond, Va.
Aug 17	Hoosick Falls, N.Y.	Nov 13	Weldon, N.C.
Aug 18	Troy, N.Y.	Nov 14	Warrenton, N.C.
Aug 19	Cahoes, N.Y.	Nov 15	Henderson, N.C.
Aug 21	Saratoga, N.Y.	Nov 16	Franklinton, N.C.
Aug 22	Schenectady, N.Y.	Nov 17–18	Raleigh, N.C.
Aug 23	Albany, N.Y.	Nov 20	Goldsboro, N.C.
Aug 24	Coxsackie, N.Y.	Nov 21	Warsaw, N.C.
Aug 25	Hudson, N.Y.	Nov 22–25	Wilmington, N.C.
Aug 26	Catskill, N.Y.	Nov 27	Fair Bluff, N.C.
Aug 28	Saugerties, N.Y.	Dec 4–9	Augusta, Ga.
Aug 29	Kingston, N.Y.	Dec 11–22	Charleston, S.C.
Aug 30	Poughkeepsie, N.Y.	Dec 25–30	Savannah, Ga.
Aug 31	Newburgh, N.Y.		
Sep 1	Cold Spring, N.Y.		
Sep 2	Sing Sing, N.Y.		**1855**
Sep 4	Yonkers, N.Y.		
Sep 5	Harlem, N.Y.	Spalding & Rogers's Two Circuses United	
Sep 6	Williamsburgh, N.Y.	Gilbert R. Spalding and Charles J. Rogers,	
Sep 8–9	Brooklyn, N.Y.	proprietors. Agnes Lake, tightrope, slack	
Sep 11–15	New York City, N.Y.	wire, and rider; Bill Lake, clown.	
Sep 18	Jersey City, N.J.	Jan 1–4	Macon, Ga.
Sep 19	Paterson, N.J.	Jan 5–8	Columbus, Ga.
Sep 20	Newark, N.J.	Jan	Montgomery, Ala.
Sep 21	Rahway, N.J.	Feb	Unknown
Sep 22	New Brunswick, N.J.	Mar 6	Cartersville, Ga.

Mar 7	Kingston, Ga.	Jul 19	Lockport, N.Y.
Mar 10	Adairsville, Ga.	Jul 21	Brockport, N.Y.
Mar 19	Nashville, Tenn.	Jul 23	Rochester, N.Y.
Mar 27–31	Saint Louis, Mo.	Jul 25	Canandaigua, N.Y.
Apr 7	Alton, Ill.	Jul 28	Havana, N.Y.
Apr 9	Peoria, Ill.	Jul 30	Ithaca, N.Y.
Apr 11–14	Chicago, Ill.	Jul 31	Moravia, N.Y.
Apr 19–21	Louisville, Ky.	Aug 15	Hamilton, N.Y.
Apr 23–28	Cincinnati, Ohio	Aug 16	Sherburn, N.Y.
May 2	Bridgewater, Pa.	Aug 17	Norwich, N.Y.
May 3	Alleghany, Pa.	Aug 18	Greene, N.Y.
May 5	Birmingham, Pa.	Aug 20	Binghamton, N.Y.
May 7–12	Pittsburgh, Pa.	Aug 21	Oswego, N.Y.
May 16	Saint Clairsville, Ohio	Aug 22	Athens, N.Y.
May 31	Ashland, Ohio	Aug 23	Elmira, N.Y.
Jun 2	Galion, Ohio	Aug 24	Troy, Pa.
Jun 4	Marion, Ohio	Aug 25	Towanda, Pa.
Jun 5	Delaware, Ohio	Aug 27	Tunkhannock, Pa.
Jun 6	Columbus, Ohio	Aug 28	Wilkes-Barre, Pa.
Jun 9	Lancaster, Ohio	Aug 29	White Haven, Pa.
Jun 11	Circleville, Ohio	Sep 13	Altoona, Pa.
Jun 12	Chillicothe, Ohio	Sep 14	Hollidaysburg, Pa.
Jun 13	Greenfield, Ohio	Sep 15	Huntingdon, Pa.
Jun 14	Hillsboro, Ohio	Sep 17	Lewiston, Pa.
Jun 15	Wilmington, Ohio	Sep 19	Bloomfield, Pa.
Jun 16	Morrow, Ohio	Sep 20	Carlisle, Pa.
Jun 18	Hamilton, Ohio	Sep 21	York, Pa.
Jun 19	Middletown, Ohio	Sep 22	Columbia, Pa.
Jun 20	Dayton, Ohio	Sep 25	Middletown, Pa.
Jun 21	Springfield, Ohio	Sep 26–27	Harrisburg, Pa.
Jun 22	Urbana, Ohio	Sep 28	Lebanon, Pa.
Jun 23	Bellefontaine, Ohio	Sep 29	Womelsdorf, Pa.
Jul 3–5	Cleveland, Ohio	Oct 1	Schuylkill Haven, Pa.
Jul 7	Ashtabula, Ohio	Oct 2	Hamburg, Pa.
Jul 9	Erie, Pa.	Oct 3	Kutztown, Pa.
Jul 10	Northeast, Pa.	Oct 4	Reading, Pa.
Jul 11	Westfield, N.Y.	Oct 5	Pottstown, Pa.
Jul 12	Jamestown, N.Y.	Oct 6	Norristown, Pa.
Jul 13	Fredonia, N.Y.	Oct 8	West Chester, Pa.
Jul 14	Silver Creek, N.Y.	Oct 9	Wilmington, Del.
Jul 16–17	Buffalo, N.Y.	Oct 10	Chester, Pa.
Jul 18	Niagara Falls, N.Y.	Oct 11	Manayunk, Pa.

Oct 12	Bristol, Pa.	Jun 16	Almont, Mich.
Oct 13	Lambertville, Pa.	Jun 17	LaPeer, Mich.
Oct 15	Easton, Pa.	Jun 18	Goodrich, Mich.
Oct 16	Allentown, Pa.	Jun 19	Flint, Mich.
Oct 17	Cherryville, Pa.	Jun 20	Saginaw, Mich.
Oct 19	Belvidere, N.J.	Jun 21	Pine Run, Mich.
Oct 20	Stroudsburg, Pa.	Jun 23	Fentonville, Mich.
Oct 24	Troy, Pa.	Jun 24	Corunna, Mich.
Oct 25	Towanda, Pa.	Jun 25	DeWitt, Mich.
		Jun 26	Lansing, Mich.

1856

Spalding & Rogers's Two Circuses
Gilbert R. Spalding and Charles J. Rogers,
proprietors. Agnes Lake, slack wire and
rider; William Lake, clown.

Jun 27	Mason, Mich.
Jun 28	Williamstown, Mich.
Jun 30	Howell, Mich.
Jul 1	Milford, Mich.
Jul 2	Pontiac, Mich.
Jul 3–4	Detroit, Mich.
Jul 5	Ypsilanti, Mich.

May 2	Binghamton, N.Y.	Jul 7	Saline, Mich.
May 3	Oswego, N.Y.	Jul 8	Ann Arbor, Mich.
May 6	Corning, N.Y.	Jul 9	Chelsea, Mich.
May 7	Bath, N.Y.	Jul 10	Jackson, Mich.
May 8	Hornellsville, N.Y.	Jul 11	Eaton Rapids, Mich.
May 13	Batavia, N.Y.	Jul 18–19	Grand Rapids, Mich.
May 14–15	Rochester, N.Y.	Jul 21	Hastings, Mich.
May 16	Brockport, N.Y.	Jul 22	Prairie View, Mich.
May 17	Albion, N.Y.	Jul 25	Paw Paw, Mich.
May 20	Lockport, N.Y.	Jul 26	Dowagiac, Mich.
May 21–22	Buffalo, N.Y.	Jul 28	Niles, Mich.
May 23	Niagara Falls, N.Y.	Jul 29	South Bend, Ind.
May 24	Saint Catherines, Ont.	Jul 30	Elkhart, Ind.
May 26	Caledonia, Ont.	Jul 31	Goshen, Ind.
May 27	Simcoe, Ont.	Aug 1	Ligonier, Ind.
May 28	Brantford, Ont.	Aug 6	Coldwater, Mich.
May 29	Dundas, Ont.	Aug 7	Hillsdale, Mich.
May 30	Hamilton, Ont.	Aug 8	Addison, Mich.
May 31	Guelph, Ont.	Aug 9	Adrian, Mich.
Jun 2	Galt, Ont.	Aug 11	Monroe, Mich.
Jun 3	Paris, Ont.	Aug 12	Toledo, Ohio
Jun 6	London, Ont.	Aug 13	Maumee, Ohio
Jun 10	Chatham, Ont.	Aug 14	Delta, Ohio
Jun 13	Mount Clemens, Mich.	Aug 15	Napoleon, Ohio
Jun 14	Utica, Mich.	Aug 16	Defiance, Ohio

Aug 18	Auburn, Ind.	(began overland tour)	
Aug 19	Fort Wayne, Ind.	Oct 30	Germantown, Tenn.
Aug 20	Bluffton, Ind.	Oct 31	Somerville, Tenn.
Aug 21	Huntington, Ind.	Nov 1	LaGrange, Tenn.
Aug 22	Wabash, Ind.	Nov 18	Marietta, Ga.
Aug 23	Peru, Ind.	Nov 19–20	Atlanta, Ga.
Aug 25	Logansport, Ind.	Nov 21	Griffin, Ga.
Aug 26	Delphi, Ind.	Nov 22	Forsythe, Ga.
Aug 27	Lafayette, Ind.	Nov 24–25	Macon, Ga.
Aug 30	Indianapolis, Ind.	Nov 26	Fort Valley, Ga.
Sep 8	Marion, Ind.	Nov 27–29	Columbus, Ga.
Sep 9	Hartford, Ind.	Dec 1–4	Montgomery, Ala.
Sep 10	Portland, Ind.	Dec 5	Wetumpka, Ala.
Sep 11	Winchester, Ind.	Dec 6	Prattville, Ala.
Sep 12	Greenville, Ind.	Dec 8	Autaugaville, Ga.
Sep 13	Richmond, Ind.	Dec 9	Lowndesboro, Ala.
Sep 15	Brookville, Ind.	Dec 15	Mobile, Ala.
Sep 16	Connersville, Ind.	Dec 27–Feb 27	New Orleans, La.
Sep 17	Cambridge, Ind.		
Sep 18	Shelbyville, Ind.		
Sep 19	Ravenna, Ind.		

1857

Spalding & Rogers's Three Circuses
Combined (overland troupe)
Gilbert R. Spalding and Charles J. Rogers,
proprietors. Agnes Lake, tightrope and
rider; William Lake, clown.

Sep 20	Greensburg, Ind.		
Sep 22	Columbus, Ind.		
Sep 23	Edinburgh, Ind.		
Sep 24	Franklin, Ind.		
Sep 25	Martinsville, Ind.		
Sep 26	Mooresville, Ind.		
Sep 29	Greencastle, Ind.	Apr 20	Vincennes, Ind.
Sep 30	Crawfordsville, Ind.	Apr 23	Lawrenceville, Ind.
Oct 1	Covington, Ind.	Apr 29	Belleville, Ill.
Oct 2	Danville, Ind.	May 1	Alton, Ill.
Oct 3	Newport, Ind.	May 2	Jerseyville, Ill.
Oct 4	Rockville, Ind.	May 4	Carrollton, Ill.
Oct 7	Clinton, Ind.	May 5	Whitehall, Ill.
Oct 8	Paris, Ill.	May 7	Jacksonville, Ill.
Oct 9	Charleston, Ill.	May 8	Beardstown, Ill.
Oct 10	Paradise, Ill.	May 16	Lewiston, Ill.
Oct 14	Terra Haute, Ind.	May 18	Canton, Ill.
Oct 17	Vincennes, Ind.	May 19	Farmington, Ill.
(boarded *Floating Palace* at Cairo, Ill.,		May 21	Monmouth, Ill.
Oct 19)		May 22	Oquawka, Ill.
Oct 27–29	Memphis, Tenn.	May 23	Keithsburg, Ill.

May 27	Tipton, Iowa	Aug 10	Millersburg, Ohio
May 28	Lisbon, Iowa	Aug 11	Wooster, Ohio
May 29	Anamosa, Iowa	Aug 12	Massillon, Ohio
May 30	Cedar Rapids, Iowa	Aug 13	Akron, Ohio
Jun 1	Iowa City, Iowa	Aug 14–15	Cleveland, Ohio
Jun 2	Washington, Iowa	Aug 17	Painesville, Ohio
Jun 3	Lancaster, Iowa	Aug 18	Chagrin Falls, Ohio
Jun 4	Fairfield, Iowa	Aug 19	Ravenna, Ohio
Jun 5	Mount Pleasant, Iowa	Aug 20	Warren, Ohio
Jun 6	Burlington, Iowa	Aug 21	Youngstown, Ohio
Jun 9	Davenport, Iowa	Aug 22	New Castle, Pa.
Jun 13	Cascade, Iowa	Aug 24	Greenville, Pa.
Jun 15	Dubuque, Iowa	Aug 25	Meadville, Pa.
Jun 16	Galena, Ill.	Aug 26	Franklin, Pa.
Jun 17	Hazel Green, Wis.	Aug 31	Kittaning, Pa.
Jun 18	Platteville, Wis.	Sep 1	Freeport, Pa.
Jun 19	Mineral Point, Wis.	Sep 2	Butler, Pa.
Jun 20	Darlington, Wis.	Sep 3–5	Pittsburgh, Pa.
Jun 24	Rockford, Ill.	Sep 7	McKeesport, Pa.
Jun 25	Belvidere, Ill.	Sep 8	Greensburg, Pa.
Jun 26	Beloit, Wis.	Sep 9	Connellsville, Pa.
Jun 27	Janesville, Wis.	Sep 10	Brownsville, Pa.
Jun 28	Madison, Wis.	Sep 11	Uniontown, Pa.
Jul 6	Green Bay, Wis.	Sep 12	Morgantown, Pa.
Jul 7	Neenah, Wis.	Sep 14	Waynesburg, Pa.
Jul 8	Oshkosh, Wis.	Sep 15	Washington, Pa.
Jul 9	Berlin, Wis.	Sep 16	West Alexander, Pa.
Jul 13	Waukesha, Wis.	Sep 17	Wheeling, Va. (now
Jul 14–15	Milwaukee, Wis.		W.Va.)
Jul 16	Racine, Wis.	Sep 18	Barnesville, Ohio
Jul 17	Kenosha, Wis.	Sep 19	Woodsfield, Ohio
Jul 18	Waukegan, Wis.	Sep 23	Beverly, Ohio
Jul 20–24	Chicago, Ill.	Sep 24	Marietta, Ohio
Jul 27	Toledo, Ohio	Sep 25	Plymouth, Ohio
Jul 29	Fremont, Ohio	Oct 2	Galliopolis, Ohio
Aug 1	Tiffin, Ohio	Oct 10	Hillsboro, Ohio
Aug 3	Findlay, Ohio	Oct 12	Georgetown, Ohio
Aug 4	Upper Sandusky, Ohio	Oct 13	Batavia, Ohio
Aug 5	Bucyrus, Ohio	Oct 14–17	Cincinnati, Ohio
Aug 6	Marion, Ohio	Nov 18	Cairo, Ill.
Aug 7	Mount Gilead, Ohio	(boarded *Floating Palace*)	
Aug 8	Mount Vernon, Ohio	Dec 8–Jan 31	New Orleans, La.

1858

Nixon's Great American Circus and
Kemp's Mammoth English Circus
James M. Nixon and William H. Kemp,
proprietors. Agnes Lake, tightrope and
rider; William Lake, clown.

May 1–3	Indianapolis, Ind.
May 4	Lafayette, Ind.
May 6	Logansport, Ind.
May 11	Toledo, Ohio
May 15	Hillsdale, Mich.
May 18	Adrian, Mich.
May 21–22, 24	Detroit, Mich.
Jun 1	London, Ont.
Jun 9	Galt, Ont.
Jun 10	Brantford, Ont.
Jun 14	Oakville, Ont.
Jun 15	Georgetown, Ont.
Jun 16	Brampton, Ont.
Jun 17–18	Toronto, Ont.
Jul 6	Napanee, Ont.
Jul 7	Bath, Ont.
Jul 9	Gananoque, Ont.
Jul 10	Mallory, Ont.
Jul 12	Brockville, Ont.
Jul 20	Vaudreuil, Quebec
Jul 21	La Prairie, Quebec
Jul 22	Saint Jean, Quebec
Jul 23	Chambley, Quebec
Jul 24	Saint Hyacinthe, Quebec
Jul 27–29	Montreal, Quebec
Jul 30	Sorel, Quebec
Jul 31	Trois Rivieres, Quebec
Aug 1–6	Quebec, Quebec (by railroad)
Aug 12	Lewiston, Maine
Aug 13	Portland, Maine
Aug 14	Biddeford, Maine
Aug 16	Dover, N.H.
Aug 17	New Market, Mass.
Aug 18	Newburyport, Mass.
Aug 19	Haverhill, Mass.
Aug 20	Lawrence, Mass.
Aug 23	Lowell, Mass.
Aug 24	Salem, Mass.
Aug 25	Salem, Mass.
Aug 27	Charlestown, Mass.
Aug 28	Cambridge, Mass.
Aug 30–Sep 1	Boston, Mass.
Sep 2	South Boston, Mass.
Sep 3	Waltham, Mass.
Sep 4	Natick, Mass.
Sep 6	Canon, Mass.
Sep 7	North Bridgewater, Mass.
Sep 8	Taunton, Mass.
Sep 9	New Bedford, Mass.
Sep 10	Newport, R.I.
Sep 11	Fall River, Mass.
Sep 13	Bristol, R.I.
Sep 14–15	Providence, R.I.
Sep 16	Pawtucket, R.I.
Sep 17	Woonsocket, R.I.
Sep 18	Milford, Mass.
Sep 19	Worcester, Mass.
Sep 20	Brookfield, Mass.
Sep 23	Springfield, Mass.
Sep 24	Northampton, Mass.
Sep 25	Westfield, Mass.
Sep 27	Lee, Mass.
Sep 28	Pittsfield, Mass.
Sep 29	North Adams, Mass.
Sep 30	Hoosic Falls, N.Y.
Oct 4	Troy, N.Y.
Oct 5	Albany, N.Y.
Oct 9	Kingston, N.Y.
Oct 11	Poughkeepsie, N.Y.
Oct 14	Sing Sing, N.Y.
Oct 15	Yonkers, N.Y.
Oct 16	Harlem, N.Y.
Oct 18–21	Brooklyn, N.Y.
Nov 27	Partnership dissolved

1859

Robinson & Lake's Great Southern
Menagerie
John Robinson and William Lake,
proprietors. Agnes Lake, tightrope;
William Lake, clown; Alice Lake, rider.

Apr 14	Williamsburgh, Ohio
Apr 15	Batavia, Ohio
Apr 16	Newton, Ohio
Apr 18–20	Cincinnati, Ohio
Apr 21	Newport, Ky.
Apr 22	Covington, Ky.
Apr 23	Florence, Ky.
Apr 25	Crittenden, Ky.
Apr 26	Eagle Bridge
Apr 27	Williamstown, Ky.
Apr 28	Georgetown, Ky.
Apr 29	Lexington, Ky.
Apr 30	Richmond, Ky.
May 2	Lancaster, Ky.
May 3	Hustonville, Ky.
May 4	Liberty, Ky.
May 5	Neateburg, Ky.
May 6	Columbia, Ky.
May 7	Edmonton, Ky.
May 9	Lafayette, Ky.
May 10	Glasgow, Ky.
May 11	Scottsville, Ky.
May 12	Morrow, Ky.
May 13	Franklin, Ky.
May 14	Cross Plains, Tenn.
May 16–18	Memphis, Tenn.
May 19	Lebanon, Tenn.
May 20	Rome, Tenn.
May 21	Dixon Springs, Tenn.
May 23	Carthage, Tenn.
May 24	Alexandria, Tenn.
May 25	Smithville, Tenn.
May 26	Sparta, Tenn.
May 27	Cookeville, Tenn.
May 28	Gainesboro, Tenn.
May 30	Livingston, Tenn.
May 31	Monroe, Tenn.
Jun 2	Albany, Tenn.
Jun 3	McGinnis, Tenn.
Jun 4	Jamestown, Tenn.
Jun 6	Montgomery, Tenn.
Jun 7	Oliver, Tenn.
Jun 8	Clinton, Tenn.
Jun 9–10	Knoxville, Tenn.
Jun 11	Maryville, Tenn.
Jun 13	Madisonville, Tenn.
Jun 14	Philadelphia, Tenn.
Jun 15	Athens, Tenn.
Jun 16	Calhoun, Tenn.
Jun 17	Benton, Tenn.
Jun 18	Cleveland, Tenn.
Jun 20	Ringgold, Ga.
Jun 21	Dalton, Ga.
Jun 22	Gordon Springs, Ga.
Jun 23	Lafayette, Ga.
Jun 24	Summerville, Ga.
Jun 25	Dirt Town, Ga.
Jun 27	Rome, Ga.
Jun 28	Calhoun, Ga.
Jun 29	Kingston, Ga.
Jun 30	Cartersville, Ga.
Jul 1	Acworth, Ga.
Jul 2	Marietta, Ga.
Jul 4	Dallas, Ga.
Jul 5	Villa Rica, Ga.
Jul 6	Campbellton, Ga.
Jul 7–9	Atlanta, Ga.
Jul 11	Lawrence, Ga.
Jul 12	Shake Rag, Ga.
Jul 13	Cummings, Ga.
Jul 14	Greenville, Ga.
Jul 15	Jefferson, Ga.
Jul 16	Athens, Ga.
Jul 18	Danielsville, Ga.
Jul 19	Mrs. Rumsey's
Jul 20	Brickensville, Ga.

Jul 21	Elberton, Ga.	Sep 8	Independence, Va.
Jul 22	Lowndesville, Ga.	Sep 9	Grayson's PO, Va.
Jul 23	Abbeville, Ga.	Sep 10	Hillsville, Va.
Jul 25	Greenwood, S.C.	Sep 12	Wytheville, Va.
Jul 26	Cross Hill, S.C.	Sep 13	Shannon Springs, Va.
Jul 27	Newberry, S.C.	Sep 14	Burke's Garden, Va.
Jul 28	Mayington, S.C.	Sep 15	Jeffersonville, Va.
Jul 29	Monticello, S.C.	Sep 16	Blue Stone, Va.
Jul 30	Winnsboro, S.C.	Sep 17	Princeton, Va.
Aug 1	Chester, S.C.	Sep 19	Ferrysburg, Va.
Aug 2	Unionville, S.C.	Sep 20	Blacksburg, Va.
Aug 3	Cross Anchor, S.C.	Sep 21	Salem, Va.
Aug 4	Clinton, S.C.	Sep 22	White Sulphur Springs,
Aug 5	Laurens, S.C.		Va. (now W.Va.)
Aug 6	Gilland, S.C.	Sep 23	Beauford, Va.
Aug 8	Wilmington, S.C.	Sep 24	Liberty, Va.
Aug 9	Anderson, S.C.	Sep 26	Boyd's Store
Aug 10	Pendleton, S.C.	Sep 27	Rocky Mount, Va.
Aug 11	Wallahalla, S.C.	Sep 28	Brook's Store
Aug 12	Pickens CH, S.C.	Sep 29	Mitchell's Store
Aug 13	Pickensville, S.C.	Sep 20	Pittsylvania Court
Aug 15	Greenville, S.C.		House, Va.
Aug 16	Lyman, S.C.	Oct 1	Danville, Va.
Aug 17	Hendersonville, N.C.	Oct 3	Halifax, Va.
Aug 18	Sheffords, N.C.	Oct 4	Clarksville, Va.
Aug 19	Asheville, N.C.	Oct 5	Boydton, Va.
Aug 20	Alexander, N.C.	Oct 6	Forkville, Va.
Aug 22	Greenville, N.C.	Oct 7	Lawrenceville, Va.
Aug 23	Martin, N.C.	Oct 8	Gaston, N.C.
Aug 24	Rogersville, N.C.	Oct 10	Warrenton, N.C.
Aug 25	Lyon's Store	Oct 11	Brindell, N.C.
Aug 26	Kingsport, N.C.	Oct 12	Enfield, N.C.
Aug 27	Estelleville, Va.	Oct 13	Rocky Mount, N.C.
Aug 29	Pattonsville, Va.	Oct 14	Wilson, N.C.
Aug 30	Stone Creek, Va.	Oct 15	Tarboro, N.C.
Aug 31	Old Court House, Va.	Oct 17	Greenville, N.C.
Sep 1	Lebanon, Va.	Oct 18	Snow Hill, N.C.
Sep 2	Abingdon, Va.	Oct 19	Goldsboro, N.C.
Sep 3	Ballard Smith's, Va.	Oct 20	Mount Olive, N.C.
Sep 5	Marion, Va.	Oct 21	Clinton, N.C.
Sep 6	Mount Arat, Va.	Oct 22	Warsaw, N.C.
Sep 7	Elk Creek PO, Va.	Oct 24	Kenansville, N.C.

Oct 25	Teachey Depot, N.C.	Dec 23	Americus, Ga.
Oct 26	Long Creek, N.C.	Dec 24	Preston, Ga.
Oct 27–29	Wilmington, N.C.	Dec 26	Cuthbert, Ga.
Oct 31	Whiteville, N.C.	Dec 27	Dawson, Ga.
Nov 1	Wiggen's Store	Dec 28	Albany, Ga.
Nov 2	Elizabethtown, N.C.	Dec 29	Newton, Ga.
Nov 3	Maysville, N.C.	Dec 31	Colquitt, Ga.
Nov 4–5	Fayetteville, N.C.		
Nov 7	Lumberton, N.C.		
Nov 8	White House, N.C.		**1860**
Nov 9	Fair Bluff, N.C.		
Nov 10	Marion, N.C.		Robinson & Lake's Great Southern
Nov 11	Colyeuter, S.C.		Menagerie and Circus
Nov 12	Florence, S.C.		John F. Robinson and William Lake,
Nov 14	Darlington, S.C.		proprietors. Agnes Lake, rider; William
Nov 15	Bishopville, S.C.		Lake, clown.
Nov 16	Lynchburg, S.C.		
Nov 17	Sumter, S.C.	Jan 2	Bainbridge, Ga.
Nov 18	Stateburg, S.C	Jan 3	Quincy, Fl.
Nov 19	Camden, S.C.	Jan 4–5	Tallahassee, Fl.
Nov 21–23	Columbia, S.C.	Jan 6	Waukeenah, Fl.
Nov 24	Lexington, S.C.	Jan 7	Monticello, Fl.
Nov 25	Perry, S.C.	Jan 9	Thomasville, Ga.
Nov 26	Edgefield, S.C.	Jan 10	Groversville, Ga.
Nov 28	Graniteville, S.C.	Jan 11	Quitman, Ga.
Nov 29–Dec 1	Augusta, Ga.	Jan 12	Troopville, Ga.
Dec 2	Waynesboro, Ga.	Jan 13	Madison, Fl.
Dec 3	Louisville, Ga.	Jan 14	Belleville, Fl.
Dec 5	Davisboro, Ga.	Jan 16	Jasper, Fl.
Dec 6	Saundersville, Ga.	Jan 17	Warm Springs, Fl.
Dec 7	Brick Store	Jan 18	Alligator, Fl.
Dec 8–9	Milledgeville, Ga.	Jan 19	Providence, Fl.
Dec 10	Clinton, Ga.	Jan 20	Newmansville, Fl.
Dec 12	Macon, Ga.	Jan 21	Gainesville, Fl.
Dec 13	Marion, Ga.	Jan 23	Micanopy, Fl.
Dec 14	Irvington, Ga.	Jan 24	Waldo, Fl.
Dec 15	Cold Spring, Ga.	Jan 25	Starkville, Fl.
Dec 16–17	Hawkinsville, Ga.	Jan 26	Middleburg, Fl.
Dec 19	Perry, Ga.	Jan 27–28	Jacksonville, Fl.
Dec 20	Henderson, Ga.	Jan 30	Callahan, Fl.
Dec 21	Vienna, Ga.	Jan 31	Kingsburg, Fl.
Dec 22	Drayton, Ga.	Feb 1	Saint Marys, Fl.
		Feb 2	Jeffersonville, Fl.

Feb 3	Rainsville, Fl.	Apr 11	Windsor, N.C.
Feb 4	Brunswick, Ga.	Apr 12	Colerain, N.C.
Feb 6–7	Darien, Ga.	Apr 13	Gatesville, N.C.
Feb 8	Riceboro, Ga.	Apr 14	Edenton, N.C.
Feb 9	Hinesville, Ga.	Apr 16	Hertford, N.C.
Feb 10	Bryant Court House,	Apr 17	Elizabeth City, N.C.
	Ga.	Apr 18	South Mills, N.C.
Feb 11–18	Savannah, Ga.	Apr 19	Camden, N.C.
Feb 20	Grahamville, S.C.	Apr 20	Currituck, N.C.
Feb 21	Gillisonville, S.C.	Apr 21	Shingle Landing, N.C.
Feb 22	Salkahatchee Bridge,	Apr 23	Princess Anne Court
	S.C.		House, Va.
Feb 23	Walterboro, S.C.	Apr 24	Great Bridge, Va.
Feb 24	Georgia Station	Apr 25–26	Norfolk, Va.
Feb 25	Summerville, S.C.	Apr 27–28	Portsmouth, Va.
Feb 27–Mar 6	Charleston, S.C.	Apr 30	Suffolk, Va.
Mar 7	King's Tree, S.C.	May 1	Smithfield, Va.
Mar 8	Black Mingo, S.C.	May 2	Surry Court House, Va.
Mar 9–10	Georgetown, S.C.	May 3	Cabin Point, Va.
Mar 12	Conwaysboro, S.C.	May 4–5	Petersburg, Va.
Mar 13	Iron Hill, S.C.	May 6–10	Richmond, Va.
Mar 14	Whiteville, N.C.	May 11	Charles City, Va.
Mar 15	Flemington, N.C.	May 12	Burnt Ordinary
Mar 16	Black Rock, N.C.	May 14	Warwick Court House,
Mar 17, 19	Wilmington, N.C.		Va.
Mar 20	Alexandria, N.C.	May 15	Hampton, Va.
Mar 21	Gold Place, N.C.	May 16	Yorktown, Va.
Mar 22	Jacksonville, N.C.	May 17	Williamsburg, Va.
Mar 23	Richlands, N.C.	May 18	New Kent, Va.
Mar 24	Trenton, N.C.	May 19	King William Court
Mar 26–27	Newbern, N.C.		House, Va.
Mar 28	Swift Creek, N.C.	May 21	King & Queen Court
Mar 29–30	Washington, N.C.		House, Va.
Mar 31	Bath, N.C.	May 22	Centerville, Va.
Apr 2	Swanquarter, N.C.	May 23	Gloucester Court
Apr 3	Middlebrook, N.C.		House, Va.
Apr 4	Fairfield, N.C.	May 24	Mathews Court House,
Apr 5	Nelson's Cradle, N.C.		Va.
Apr 6	Lynchville, N.C.	May 25	Saluda, Va.
Apr 7	Fox Swamp, N.C.	May 26	Tappahannock, Va.
Apr 9	Plymouth, N.C.	May 28	Loretto, Va.
Apr 10	Williamston, N.C.	May 29	Port Royal, Va.

May 30–Jun 1	Fredericksburg, Va.	Jul 19	Traveler's Rest
Jun 2	Louisa Court House,	Jul 20	Cheat Mountain, W.Va.
	Va.	Jul 21	Beverly, Va.
Jun 4	Charlottesville, Va.		(now W.Va.)
Jun 5	Eagleville, Va.	Jul 23	Buckhannon, Va.
Jun 6	Stanartsville, Va.		(now W.Va.)
Jun 7	Madison Court House,	Jul 24	Phillipi, Va.
	Va.		(now W.Va.)
Jun 8	Culpeper, Va.	Jul 25	Pruntytown, Va.
Jun 9	Warrenton, Va.		(now W.Va.)
Jun 11	Salem, Va.	Jul 26	Evansville, Va.
Jun 12	Leesburg, Va.		(now W.Va.)
Jun 13	Drainesville, Va.	Jul 27	Kingwood, Va.
Jun 14–16	Washington, D.C.		(now W.Va.)
Jun 18–19	Georgetown, D.C.	Jul 28	Brandonville, Va.
Jun 20–21	Alexandria, Va.		(now W.Va.)
Jun 22	Fairfax Court House,	Jul 30	Morgantown, W.Va.
	Va.	Jul 31	Fairmont, Va.
Jun 23	Aldies, Va.		(now W.Va.)
Jun 25	Snickersville, Va.	Aug 1	Prentistown, Va.
Jun 26	Charlestown, Va.		(possibly Pruntytown,
	(now W.Va.)		W.Va.)
Jun 27	Harper's Ferry, Va.	Aug 2	Clarksburg, Va.
	(now W.Va.)		(now W.Va.)
Jun 28	Sharpsburg, Md.	Aug 3	Milford, Va.
Jun 29	Clear Springs, Md.		(now W.Va.)
Jun 30	Hancock, Md.	Aug 4	Weston, Va.
Jul 2	Oakland, Va.		(now W.Va.)
Jul 3	Martinsburg, Va.	Aug 6	Glenville, Va.
Jul 4	Winchester, Va.		(now W.Va.)
Jul 5	Front Royal, Va.	Aug 7	Arnoldsburg, Va.
Jul 6	Flint Hill, Va.		(now W.Va.)
Jul 7	Sperryville, Va.	Aug 8	Spencer, Va.
Jul 9	Luray, Va.		(now W.Va.)
Jul 10	New Market, Va.	Aug 9	Ripley, Va. (now W.Va.)
Jul 11	Harrisonburg, Va.	Aug 10	Sissonville, Va.
Jul 12	Port Republic, Va.		(now W.Va.)
Jul 13	Waynesboro, Va.	Aug 11	Charleston, Va.
Jul 14	Staunton, Va.		(now W.Va.)
Jul 16	Cloverdale, Va.	Aug 13	Buffalo, Va.
Jul 17	Warm Springs, Va.		(now W.Va.)
Jul 18	Huntersville, Va.	Aug 14	Point Pleasant, Ohio

Aug 15	Galliopolis, Ohio	Oct 3	Lima, Ohio
Aug 16	Centreville, Ohio	Oct 4	Wapakoneta, Ohio
Aug 17	Jackson, Ohio	Oct 5	Roundhead, Ohio
Aug 18	Piketon, Ohio	Oct 6	Kenton, Ohio
Aug 20	Chillicothe, Ohio	Oct 8	Bellefontaine, Ohio
Aug 21	Bainbridge, Ohio	Oct 9	Dulney, Ohio
Aug 22	Hillsboro, Ohio	Oct 10	Sidney, Ohio
Aug 23	Fayetteville, Ohio	Oct 11	Piqua, Ohio
Aug 24	Williamsburg, Ohio	Oct 12	Tippecanoe, Ohio
Aug 25	Batavia, Ohio	Oct 13	Dayton, Ohio
Aug 27	Milford, Ohio	Oct 15	Germantown, Ohio
Aug 28	Lebanon, Ohio	Oct 16	Eaton, Ohio
Aug 29	Waynesville, Ohio	Oct 17	Euphenia, Ohio
Aug 30	Wilmington, Ohio	Oct 18	Richmond, Ohio
Aug 31	Sylvania, Ohio	Oct 19	East Germantown, Ohio
Sep 1	Washington, Ohio		
Sep 3	Jamestown, Ohio	Oct 20	Liberty, Ohio
Sep 4	Xenia, Ohio	Oct 22	Oxford, Ohio
Sep 5	Fairborn, Ohio	Oct 23	Middletown, Ohio
Sep 6	New Carlisle, Ohio	Oct 24	Hamilton, Ohio
Sep 7	Saint Paris, Ohio	Oct 25	Reading, Ohio
Sep 8	Urbana, Ohio	Oct 26	Newtown, Ohio
Sep 10	Mechanicsburg, Ohio	Dec 5–?	Cincinnati, Ohio
Sep 11	Marysville, Ohio		
Sep 12	Delaware, Ohio		
Sep 13	Cardington, Ohio		

1861

Robinson & Lake's Great Menagerie and Circus

John F. Robinson and William Lake, proprietors. Agnes Lake, rider; William Lake, clown; Alice Lake, rider.

Sep 14	Marion, Ohio		
Sep 15	Upper Sandusky, Ohio		
Sep 17	Bucyrus, Ohio		
Sep 18	Galion, Ohio		
Sep 19	Mansfield, Ohio		
Sep 20	Plymouth, Ohio		
Sep 21	New London, Ohio	Jan 1–4	Cincinnati, Ohio
Sep 22	Norwalk, Ohio	May 11	Newport, Ky.
Sep 24	Sandusky, Ohio	May 22	Indianapolis, Ind.
Sep 25	Bellevue, Ohio	Jun 1	Lafayette, Ind.
Sep 26	Attica, Ohio	Jun 3	Delphi, Ind.
Sep 27	Tiffin, Ohio	Jun 4	Logansport, Ind.
Sep 28	Fremont, Ohio	Jun 5	Peru, Ind.
Sep 29	Fostoria, Ohio	Jun 6	Wabash, Ind.
Oct 1	Findlay, Ohio	Jun 7	Manchester, Ind.
Oct 2	Pendleton, Ohio	Jun 11	Columbia, Ind.

Jun 12	Warsaw, Ind.	Oct 14	Wheaton, Ill.
Jun 22	Jonesville, Ind.	Oct 15	Chicago, Ill.
Jun 24	Hudson, Ind.	Nov 4	Vincennes, Ind.
Jun 25	Adrian, Ohio		
Jun 26	Sylvania, Ohio		
Jun 27–28	Toledo, Ohio		**1862**
Jun 29	Monroe, Mich.		

Robinson & Lake's Great Western Circus
John F. Robinson and William Lake, proprietors. Agnes Lake, rider and slack wire; William Lake, clown; Alice Lake, rider.

Jul 2	Dearborn, Mich.		
Jul 3	Detroit, Mich.		
Jul 5	Pontiac, Mich.		
Jul 19	Grand Rapids, Mich.		
Jul 23	Hastings, Mich.		
Aug 1	Plymouth, Mich.	Apr 23	Cincinnati, Ohio
Aug 2	Ann Arbor, Mich.	Apr 24	Reading, Ohio
Aug 3	Saline, Mich.	Apr 25	Lebanon, Ohio
Aug 9	Marshall, Mich.	Apr 28	Hamilton, Ohio
Aug 10	Battle Creek, Mich.	Apr 29	Springfield / Xenia, Ohio
Aug 12	Galesburg, Mich.		
Aug 17	Niles, Mich.	Apr 30	Dayton, Ohio
Aug 19	South Bend, Ind.	May 3	Delavan, Ohio
Aug 20	Carlisle, Ind.	May 5	Columbus, Ohio
Aug 30	Delaware, Wis.	May 6	Zanesville, Ohio
Sep 9	Princeton, Ill.	May 26	Attica, Ohio
Sep 10	Sheffield, Ill.	May 27	Bucyrus, Ohio
Sep 16	Peoria, Ill.	May 28	Upper Sandusky, Ohio
Sep 18	Canton, Ill.	Jun 3	Toledo, Ohio
Sep 19	Lewistown, Ill.	Jun 6	Detroit, Mich.
Sep 20	Havana, Ill.	Jun 16	London, Mich.
Sep 21	Petersburg, Ill.	Date ?	Brantford, Ont.
Sep 23	Jacksonville, Ill.	Date ?	Hamilton, Ont.
Sep 24	Berlin, Ill.	Date ?	Toronto, Ont.
Sep 25	Springfield, Ill.	Date ?	Belleville, Ont.
Sep 26	Mechanicsburg, Ill.	Date ?	Kingston, Ont.
Sep 27	Decatur, Ill.	Date ?	Montreal, Quebec
Sep 28	Clinton, Ill.	Date ?	Brockville, Ont.
Sep 30	Bloomington, Ill.	Jul 16	LaGrange, Ind.
Oct 1	El Paso, Ill.	Jul 18	Goshen, Ind.
Oct 8	Morris, Ill.	Jul 28	Eaton Rapids, Mich.
Oct 9	Ottawa, Ill.	Jul 29	Leslie, Mich.
Oct 10	Earleville, Ill.	Jul 30	Jackson, Ind.
Oct 11	Newark, Ill.	Aug 15	Angola, Ind.
Oct 12	Bristol, Ill.	Sep 1	Columbus City, Ind.

Sep 2	Warsaw, Ind.
Sep 6	Logansport, Ind.
Sep 10	Lafayette, Ind.
Sep 20	New Madison, Ind.
Sep 22	Richmond, Ind.
Sep 28–Oct 1	Indianapolis, Ind.

1863

Lake & Co.'s Great Western Circus
William Lake, Horace Norton, and Levi J.
North, proprietors. Agnes Lake, rider,
slack wire; William Lake, clown; Alice
Lake, rider; Emma Lake, rider.

May 5–6	Springfield, Ill.
May 16–18	Saint Louis, Mo.
Jun 6	Keokuk, Iowa
Jun 8	Warsaw, Ill.
Jun 9	Carthage, Ill.
Jun 10	Augusta, Ill.
Jun 11	Mattoon, Ill.
Jun 19	Davenport, Iowa
Jul 14	Peoria, Ill.
Jul 25	Canton, Ill.
Aug 28	Terre Haute, Ind.
Sep 25–27	Indianapolis, Ind.
Oct 12–17	Cincinnati, Ohio
Nov 3–28	Nashville, Tenn.
Dec 5	Bowling Green, Ky.
Dec 8	Cairo, Ill.

1864

Lake and Company's Mammoth Circus
William Lake and Horace Norton,
proprietors. Agnes Lake, slack wire and
rider; William Lake, animal trainer; Alice
Lake, rider; Emma Lake, rider.

Apr 18–22	Louisville, Ky.
Apr 25–27	Lexington, Ky.

May 2–7	Cincinnati, Ohio
May 14	Springfield, Ohio
May 25	Ironton, Ohio
Jun 4	Logan, Ohio
Jun 7	Somerset, Ohio
Jun 15	Hanover, Ohio
Jun 16	Wellsville, Ohio
Jun 17	New Lisbon, Ohio
Jun 18	Salem, Ohio
Jun 22	Warren, Ohio
Jun 23	Ravenna, Ohio
Jun 24	Akron, Ohio
Jun 28	Norwalk, Ohio
Jul 4	Toledo, Ohio
Jul 8	Detroit, Mich.
Jul 11	Birmingham, Mich.
Jul 12	Attica, Mich.
Jul 13	Mount Clemens, Mich.
Jul 14	Romeo, Mich.
Jul 15	Almont, Mich.
Jul 16	Lapeer, Mich.
Jul 18	E. Saginaw, Mich.
Jul 20	Pine River, Mich.
Jul 28	Grand Rapids, Mich.
Aug 6	Jackson, Mich.
Aug 10	Coldwater, Mich.
Aug 20	Fort Wayne, Ind.
Aug 29	Findlay, Ohio
Sep 1	Upper Sandusky, Ohio
Sep 26	Allegheny City, Pa.
Sep 27–Oct 1	Pittsburgh, Pa.
Oct 6	Wheeling, W.Va.
Oct 10	Steubenville, Ohio
Oct 24–25	Zanesville, Ohio
Nov 14–Dec 16	Nashville, Tenn. (Howes & Norton's Champion Circus)

1865

Lake's Hippo-Olympiad
William and Agnes Lake, proprietors.

Agnes Lake, rider and slack wire; William Lake, animal trainer; Alice Lake, rider; Master Willie, rider; Emma Lake, rider.

Apr 20	Zanesville, Ohio
Apr 21	Brownsville, Ohio
Apr 22	Newark, Ohio
Apr 25	Mansfield, Ohio
Apr 26	Plymouth, Ohio
May 1	Toledo, Ohio
May 5	Saline, Mich.
May 6	Ann Arbor, Mich.
May 8	Dexter, Mich.
May 26	Warsaw, Ind.
May 27	Manchester, Ind.
May 30	Marion, Ind.
Jun 2–3	Indianapolis, Ind.
Jun 19–24	Louisville, Ky.
Jul 4	Vincennes, Ind.
Jul 17–22	Saint Louis, Mo.
Jul 24	Alton, Ill.
Jul 25	Jerseyville, Ill.
Jul 26	Springfield, Ill.
Jul 27	Bloomington, Ill.
Jul 29	Jacksonville, Ill.
Aug 1–2	Springfield, Ill.
Aug 17	Terre Haute, Ind.
Aug 18	Brazil, Ind.
Aug 19	Greencastle, Ind.
Aug 21	Danville, Ill.
Aug 24	Thorntown, Ind.
Aug 25	Lebanon, Ind.
Aug 26	Zionsville, Ind.
Sep 8	Covington, Ky.
Sep 9	Fulton, Ky.
Sep 11	Newport, Ky.
Oct 11	Gallipolis, Ohio
Dec 13–24	Berlin, Ger. (Agnes stars in *Mazeppa* at the Victoria Theatre)

1866

Lake's Hippo-Olympiad and Mammoth Circus
William and Agnes Lake, proprietors.
Agnes Lake, rider and slack wire; William Lake, animal trainer; Alice Lake, rider; Master Willie, rider; Emma Lake, rider.

May 21	Lancaster, Ohio
May 23	Chillicothe, Ohio
Jun 8–11	Cincinnati, Ohio
Jun 19	Huntington, Ind.
Jun 20	Wabash, Ind.
Jun 21	Peru, Ind.
Jun 22	Logansport, Ind.
Jun 23	Delphi, Ind.
Jun 25	Lafayette, Ind.
Jun 26	Attica, Ind.
Jun 27	Covington, Ind.
Jun 28	Danville, Ill.
Jun 29	Rossville, Ill.
Jun 30	Watseka, Ill.
Jul 2	Onargo, Ill.
Jul 3	Paxton, Ill.
Jul 4	Champaign, Ill.
Jul 5	Tuscola, Ill.
Jul 6	Mattoon, Ill.
Jul 7	Charlestown, Ill.
Jul 10	Paris, Ill.
Jul 11	York, Ill.
Jul 12	Palestine, Ill.
Jul 13	Vincennes, Ind.
Jul 14	Petersburg, Ind.
Jul 16	Princeton, Ind.
Jul 17	Evansville, Ind.
Jul 23	Mount Camel, Ind.
Jul 24	Olney, Ill.
Aug 22–25	Saint Louis, Mo.
Aug 27	East Saint Louis, Ill.
Aug 29	Edwardsville, Ill.
Aug 30	Hanker Hill, Ill.

Aug 31	Carlinville, Ill.
Sep 1	Girard, Ill.
Sep 3	Waverly, Ill.
Sep 4	Manchester (Winchester), Ill.
Sep 5	Jacksonville, Ill.
Sep 28	Kankakee, Ill.
Sep ?	Elkhart, Ind.
Oct 1	Lowell, Ind.
Oct 4	La Porte, Ind.
Oct 24	Columbus, Ind.

1867

Lake's Hippo-Olympiad and Mammoth Circus
William and Agnes Lake, proprietors.
Agnes Lake, rider and slack wire; Emma Lake, rider.

Apr 20	Columbus, Ind.
Apr 22	Seymour, Ind.
May 6	Terre Haute, Ind.
May 9	Danville, Ill.
May 16	Bloomington, Ill.
May 18	Peoria, Ill.
May 20	Princeton, Ill.
May 21	Toulon, Ill.
May 22	Victoria, Ill.
May 23	Galesburg, Ill.
May 25	Monmouth, Ill.
May 27	Prairie City, Ill.
May 28	Macomb, Ill.
May 29	Augusta, Ill.
May 30	Camp Point, Ill.
May 31–Jun 1	Quincy, Ill.
Jun 3	Hannibal, Mo.
Jun 4	Bolivar, Mo.
Jun 5	LaGrange, Mo.
Jun 6	Monticello, Mo.
Jun 11	La Platta, Mo.
Jun 12	Macon City, Mo.

Jun 13	Clarence, Mo.
Jun 17	Mexico, Mo.
Jun 18	Fulton, Mo.
Jun 22	Glasgow, Mo.
Jun 27	Carrolton, Mo.
Jun 28	Richmond, Mo.
Jun 29	Lexington, Mo.
Jul 1	Missouri City, Mo.
Jul 2–4	Kansas City, Mo.
Jul 14	Warrensburg, Mo.
Jul 26	Brookfield, Mo.
Jul 27	Linneus, Mo.
Jul 30	Chillicothe, Mo.
Aug 12	Maysville, Mo.
Aug 15	Stewartsville, Mo.
Aug 30	Saint Joseph, Mo.
Sep 11	Omaha, Neb.
Sep 20	Saint Joseph, Mo.
Sep 23	Atchison, Kans.
Sep 24	Valley Falls, Kans.
Sep 25	Oskaloosa, Kans.
Sep 26	Lawrence, Kans.
Oct 2	Mound City, Kans.
Oct 3	Fort Scott, Kans.
Oct 7	Greenfield, Mo.
Oct 8–9	Springfield, Mo.
Oct 10	Mount Vernon, Mo.
Oct 15	Memphis, Tenn.
Oct 21, 27	Fort Smith, Ark.
Oct 31–Nov 2	Little Rock, Ark.
Nov 28	Henderson, Tex.
Dec 31	Brenham, Tex.

1868

Bill Lake's Hippo-Olympiad and Mammoth Circus
William and Agnes Lake, proprietors.
Agnes Lake, rider; William Lake, animal trainer and ringmaster; Master Willie, rider; Emma Lake, rider.

Jan 3–4	Belleville, Tex.	Sep 7	Olney, Ill.
Jan 6	San Felipe, Tex.	Sep 8	Lawrenceville, Ind.
Jan 8	Houston, Tex.	Sep 9	Vincennes, Ind.
Jan 10–21	Galveston, Tex.	Sep 10	Petersburg, Ind.
Jan 23–25	Houston, Tex.	Sep 11	Jasper, Ind.
Jan 31	Brenham, Tex.	Sep 17–19	Louisville, Ky.
Feb 1	Bryan City, Tex.	Oct 12	Princeton, Ky.
Feb 6	Huntsville, Tex.	Oct 14	Hopkinsville, Ky.
Mar 2–7	Shreveport, La.	Oct 16	Russellville, Ky.
Mar 9	Marshall, Tex.	Oct 26	Murfreesboro, Tenn.
Mar 13	Jefferson, Tex.	Oct 28	Franklin, Tenn.
Mar 18	Linden, Tex.	Oct 29	Columbia, Tenn.
Mar 20	Jefferson, Tex.	Oct 30	Mount Pleasant, Tenn.
Mar 25	Bayou Sara, La.	Oct 31	Lawrence, Tenn.
Apr 10	Jackson, Miss.	Nov 2	Florence, Ala.
Apr 11	Canton, Miss.	Nov 18	Columbus, Miss.
Apr 20	Granada, Miss.	Nov 19	Columbus, Miss.
Apr 30–May 2	Memphis, Tenn.	Dec 18–19	Montgomery Ala.
May 4	Cairo, Ill.		
May 8	Du Quoin, Ill.		
May 9	Centralia, Ill.		

1869

Lake's Hippo-Olympiad and Mammoth Circus
William and Agnes Lake, proprietors.
Agnes Lake, rider; William Lake, animal trainer and ringmaster; Master Willie, rider; Emma Lake, rider.

May 11	Effingham, Ill.		
May 12	Mattoon, Ill.		
May 19–23	Saint Louis, Mo.		
May 24	Saint Charles, Mo.		
Jun 4	Hannibal, Mo.		
Jun 6	LaGrange, Mo.		
Jun 8	Canton, Mo.		
Jun 9	Alexandria, Mo.	Jan 1	Silver Run
Jun 11	Keokuk, Iowa	Jan 2	Crawford, Ga.
Jun 12	Montrose, Iowa	Jan 4	Columbus, Ga.
Jun 13	Fort Madison, Iowa	Jan 5	Hamilton, Ga.
Jun 15	Burlington, Iowa	Jan 6	Talbotton, Ga.
Jul 4	Warsaw, Ill.	Jan 7	Pleasant Hill, Ga.
Jul 13	Quincy, Ill.	Jan 8	Thomaston, Ga.
Jul 15	Carthage, Ill.	Jan 9	Barnesville, Ga.
Jul 16	Blandinsville, Ill.	Jan 11	Indian Springs, Ga.
Jul 17	Macomb, Ill.	Jan 12	Forsythe, Ga.
Jul 18	Prairie City, Ill.	Jan 13	Macon, Ga.
Jul 21	Galesburg, Ill.	Jan 14	Fort Valley, Ga.
Aug 10	Carlinville, Ill.	Jan 15	Montezuma, Ga.
Aug 16	Salem, Ill.	Jan 16	Ellaville, Ga.

Jan 18	Buena Vista, Ga.	Mar 10	Lincolnton, Ga.
Jan 19	Cusseta, Ga.	Mar 11	Danburg, Ga.
Jan 20	Lumpkin, Ga.	Mar 12	Elberton, Ga.
Jan 21	Cuthbert, Ga.	Mar 13	Hartwell, Ga.
Jan 22	Fort Gaines, Ga.	Mar 15	Carnesville, Ga.
Jan 23	Blakely, Ga.	Mar 16	Homer, Ga.
Jan 25	Colquitt, Ga.	Mar 17	Gillsville, Ga.
Jan 26	Bainbridge, Ga.	Mar 18	Gainesville, Ga.
Jan 27	Quincy, Fl.	Mar 19	Jefferson, Ga.
Jan 28	Concord, Fl.	Mar 20	Athens, Ga.
Jan 29	Tallahassee, Fl.	Mar 22	Lexington, Ga.
Feb 1	Monticello, Fl.	Mar 23	Washington, Ga.
Feb 2	Thomasville, Ga.	Mar 24	Woodstock, Ga.
Feb 3	Cairo, Ga.	Mar 25	Union Point, Ga.
Feb 4	Camilla, Ga.	Mar 26	Greensboro, Ga.
Feb 5	Newton, Ga.	Mar 27	Madison, Ga.
Feb 6	Milford, Ga.	Mar 29	Eatonton, Ga.
Feb 8	Morgan, Ga.	Mar 30	Monticello, Ga.
Feb 9	Dawson, Ga.	Mar 31	Jackson, Ga.
Feb 10	Albany, Ga.	Apr 1	Griffin, Ga.
Feb 11	Starkville (now	Apr 2	Zebulon, Ga.
	Leesburg), Ga.	Apr 3	Woodbury, Ga.
Feb 12	Smithville, Ga.	Apr 5	Greenville, Ga.
Feb 13	Americus, Ga.	Apr 6	LaGrange, Ga.
Feb 15	Vienna, Ga.	Apr 7	Hogansville, Ga.
Feb 16	Hawkinsville, Ga.	Apr 8	Franklin, Ga.
Feb 17	Jeffersonville, Ga.	Apr 9	Newnan, Ga.
Feb 18	Irwinton, Ga.	Apr 10	Palmetto, Ga.
Feb 19	Gordon, Ga.	Apr 12	Fayetteville, Ga.
Feb 20	Milledgeville, Ga.	Apr 13	Jonesboro, Ga.
Feb 22	Sparta, Ga.	Apr 14	McDonough, Ga.
Feb 23	Linton, Ga.	Apr 15	Covington, Ga.
Feb 24	Sandersville, Ga.	Apr 16	Monroe, Ga.
Feb 25	Penn's Bridge (now	Apr 17	Lawrenceville, Ga.
	Davisboro), Ga.	Apr 19–20	Atlanta, Ga.
Feb 26	Louisville, Ga.	Apr 21	Campbellton, Ga.
Feb 27	Waynesboro, Ga.	Apr 22	Villa Rica, Ga.
Mar 2	Warrenton, Ga.	Apr 23	Dallas, Ga.
Mar 3	Thomson, Ga.	Apr 24	Van Wert, Ga.
Mar 4	Beulah, Ga.	Apr 26	Cedartown, Ga.
Mar 5–6	Augusta, Ga.	Apr 27	Rome, Ga.
Mar 8	Appling, Ga.	Apr 28	Kingston, Ga.

Apr 29	Cartersville, Ga.	Jun 19	Columbus, Ky.
Apr 30	Acworth, Ga.	Jun 21	Blandville, Ky.
May 1	Marietta, Ga.	Jun 22	Cairo, Ill.
May 3	Alpharetta, Ga.	Jun 23	Charleston, Mo.
May 4	Cumming, Ga.	Jun 24	Morley, Mo.
May 5	Dawsonville, Ga.	Jun 25	Cape Girardeau, Mo.
May 6	Dahlonega, Ga.	Jun 26	Jackson, Mo.
May 7	Cleveland, Ga.	Jun 28	Marble Hill, Mo.
May 8	Dinsmore, Ga.	Jun 29	Beesville, Mo.
May 10	Blairsville, Ga.	Jun 30	Fredericktown, Mo.
May 11	Haysville, Tenn.	Jul 1	Farmington, Mo.
May 12	Murphy, Tenn.	Jul 2	Ironton, Mo.
May 13	Isaac Ricco	Jul 3	Caledonia, Mo.
May 14	Hiawassee, Ga.	Jul 5	Potosi, Mo.
May 15	Morganton, Ga.	Jul 6	Desoto, Mo.
May 17	Ellijay, Ga.	Jul 7	Richmond, Mo.
May 18	Gregory Farm	Jul 8	Saint Clair, Mo.
May 19	Spring Place, Ga.	Jul 9	Franklin, Mo.
May 20	Varnell, Ga.	Jul 10	Kirkwood, Mo.
May 21	Cleveland, Ga.	Jul 12–17	Saint Louis, Mo.
May 22	Harrison, Ga.	Jul 19	Saint Charles, Mo.
May 24	Nashville, Tenn.	Jul 20	Wentzville, Mo.
May 26	Springfield, Tenn.	Jul 21	New Mele, Mo.
May 27	Keysberg, Ky.	Jul 22	Augusta, Mo.
May 28	Trenton, Tenn.	Jul 23	Washington, Mo.
May 29	Clarksville, Tenn.	Jul 24	Herman, Mo.
May 31	Lafayette, Tenn.	Jul 26	High Hill, Mo.
Jun 1	Palmyra, Tenn.	Jul 27	Montgomery City, Mo.
Jun 2	Charlotte, Tenn.	Jul 28	Williamsburg, Mo.
Jun 3	Waverly, Tenn.	Jul 29	Fulton, Mo.
Jun 5	Centreville, Tenn.	Jul 30	New Bloomfield, Mo.
Jun 7	Linden, Tenn.	Jul 31	Jefferson City, Mo.
Jun 8	Decaturville, Tenn.	Aug 2	California, Mo.
Jun 9	Lexington, Tenn.	Aug 3	Tipton, Mo.
Jun 10	Huntington, Tenn.	Aug 4	Osterville, Mo.
Jun 11	Camden, Tenn.	Aug 5	Sedalia, Mo.
Jun 12	Paris, Tenn.	Aug 6	Warrensburg, Mo.
Jun 14	Conyersville (now	Aug 7	Holden, Mo.
	Puryear), Tenn.	Aug 9	Pleasant Hill, Mo.
Jun 15	Murray, Ky.	Aug 10	Independence, Mo.
Jun 16	Benton, Ky.	Aug 11–12	Kansas City, Mo.
Jun 18	Milburn, Ky.	Aug 13	Olathe, Mo.

Aug 14	Paola, Mo.	Oct 2	Cotton Plant, Ark.
Aug 16	Mound City, Mo.	Oct 4	Clarendon, Ark.
Aug 17	Fort Scott, Mo.	Oct 6	Des Arc, Ark.
Aug 18	Nevada, Mo.	Oct 7	West Point, Ark.
Aug 19	Lamar, Mo.	Oct 8	Searcy, Ark.
Aug 20	Carthage, Mo.	Oct 9	Stoney Point, Ark.
Aug 21	Granby, Mo.	Oct 11	Austin, Ark.
Aug 23	Sarcoxie, Mo.	Oct 12	Brownsey, Ark.
Aug 24	Mount Vernon, Mo.	Oct 13–15	Little Rock, Ark.
Aug 25	Greenfield, Mo.	Oct 16	Benton, Ark.
Aug 26	Stockton, Mo.	Oct 18	Rockport, Ark.
Aug 27	Bolivar, Mo.	Oct 19	Princeton, Ark.
Aug 28	Springfield, Mo.	Oct 20	Holly Springs, Ark.
Aug 30	Marshfield, Mo.	Oct 21	Canton, Ark.
Aug 31	Lebanon, Mo.	Oct 22	Seminary, Ark.
Sep 1	Buffalo, Mo.	Oct 23	Magnolia, Ark.
Sep 2	Urbana, Mo.	Oct 25	Falcon, Ark.
Sep 3	Hermitage, Mo.	Oct 26	Lewisville, Ark.
Sep 4	Quincy, Mo.	Oct 27	Spring Hill, Ark.
Sep 6	Warsaw, Mo.	Oct 28	Washington, Ark.
Sep 7	Cole Camp, Mo.	Oct 29	Fulton, Ark.
Sep 8	Versailles, Mo.	Oct 30	Rondo, Ark.
Sep 9	Mount Pleasant, Mo.	Nov 1	Boston, Tex.
Sep 10	Tuscumbia, Mo.	Nov 2	Dekalb, Tex.
Sep 11	Vienna, Mo.	Nov 3	Clarksville, Tex.
Sep 13	Arlington, Mo.	Nov 4	Paris, Tex.
Sep 14	Rolla, Mo.	Nov 5	Honey Grove, Tex.
Sep 15	Saint James, Mo.	Nov 6	Bonham, Tex.
Sep 16	Steelville, Mo.	Nov 8	Pilot Point, Tex.
Sep 17	Cook Station, Mo.	Nov 9	McKinley, Tex.
Sep 18	Salem, Mo.	Nov 10	Farmersville, Tex.
Sep 20	Licking, Mo.	Nov 11	Greenville, Tex.
Sep 21	Houston, Mo.	Nov 12	Cumby, Tex.
Sep 22	Hutton Valley, Mo.	Nov 13	Sulphur Springs, Tex.
Sep 23	West Plains, Mo.	Nov 15	Mount Vernon, Tex.
Sep 24	Salem, Ark.	Nov 16	Mount Pleasant, Tex.
Sep 25	Franklin, Ark.	Nov 17	Daingerfield, Tex.
Sep 27	Evening Shade, Ark.	Nov 18	Hickory Hills, Tex.
Sep 28	Batesville, Ark.	Nov 19	Jefferson, Tex.
Sep 29	Sulphur Rock, Ark.	Nov 20	Marshall, Tex.
Sep 30	Jackson, Ark.	Nov 23–25	Shreveport, La.
Oct 1	Augusta, Ark.	Nov 26	Minden, La.

Nov 27	Homer, La.
Nov 29	Arcadia, La.
Nov 30	Vienna, La.
Dec 1	Vernon, La.
Dec 2	Forkville, La.
Dec 3	Trenton, La.
Dec 4	Monroe, La.
Dec 6	Bastrop, La.
Dec 7	Oak Grove, La.
Dec 8	Bastrop, La.
Dec 9	Ouachita City, La.
Dec 10	Farmerville, La.
Dec 11	Hillsboro, Ark.
Dec 13	El Dorado, Ark.
Dec 14	Camden, Ark.
Dec 15	Hampton, Ark.
Dec 16	Warren, Ark.
Dec 17	Monticello, Ark.
Dec 23	Memphis, Tenn.

1870

Lake's Hippo-Olympiad
Agnes Lake, proprietor and manager.
Agnes Lake, rider; Emma Lake, rider.

Early Jan	Saint Louis, Mo. (making arrangements to exhume William Lake's body)
Jan 12–13	Cincinnati, Ohio (William Lake's funeral and burial in Spring Grove Cemetery)
Feb 21 (auction)	Memphis, Tenn.
Dec 29–31	New Orleans, La.

1871

Madam Lake's Hippo-Olympiad and
Mammoth Circus

Agnes Lake, proprietor. Agnes Lake, rider; Emma Lake, rider.

Jan 1	New Orleans, La.
Jan 2–4	Mobile, Ala.
Jan 9	Montgomery, Ala.
Jan 13	Columbus, Ga.
Jan 16	Augusta, Ga.
Jan 17	Thomson, Ga.
Jan 18	Albany, Ga.
Jan 19	Camilla, Ga.
Jan 20	Quitman, Ga.
Jan 21	Valdosta, Ga.
Jan 23	Quincy, Fl.
Jan 24	Tallahassee, Fl.
Jan 25	Monticello, Fl.
Jan 26	Madison, Fl.
Jan 27	Lake City, Fl.
Jan 28	Jackson, Fl.
Jan 30	Gainesville, Fl.
Jan 31	Fernandina, Fl.
Feb 1	Live Oak, Fl.
Feb 2	Blackshear, Ga.
Feb 4	Augusta, Ga.
Feb 6–7	Charleston, S.C.
Feb 8	Orangeburg, S.C.
Feb 9	Blackville, S.C.
Feb 10	Aiken, S.C.
Feb 11	Augusta, Ga.
Feb 13	Warrenton, Ga.
Feb 14	Sparta, Ga.
Feb 15	Milledgeville, Ga.
Feb 17	Hawkinsville, Ga.
Feb 18	Brunswick, Ga.
Feb 20	Washington, Ga.
Feb 21	Forsyth, Ga.
Feb 22	Athens, Ga.
Feb 24	Atlanta, Ga.
Apr 13	Dayton, Ohio
Apr 17	Toledo, Ohio
Apr 26	Decatur, Ill.
Apr 27	Springfield, Ill.

May 4	Quincy, Ill.	Aug 22	Paola, Kans.
May 13	Nebraska City, Neb.	Aug 23	La Cygne, Kans.
May 14–15	Council Bluffs, Iowa	Aug 24	Pleasanton, Kans.
May 27	Fort Dodge, Iowa	Aug 25	Girard, Kans.
Jun 6	Omaha, Neb.	Aug 26	Seneca, Kans.
Jun 7	Fremont, Neb.	Aug 27	Baxter Springs, Kans.
Jun 8	Columbus, Neb.	Aug 28	Seneca, Kans.
Jun 9	Grand Island, Neb.	Aug 29	Neosho, Mo.
Jun 10	North Platte, Neb.	Aug 30	Springfield, Mo.
Jun 12	Cheyenne, Wyo. Terr.	Aug 31	Mansfield, Mo.
Jun 13–15	Denver, Colo.	Sep 1	Rolla, Mo.
Jun 16	Golden City, Colo.	Sep 9	Kansas City, Mo.
Jun 17	Idaho City, Colo.	Sep 21	Ironton, Mo.
Jun 19	Georgetown, Colo.	Sep 29	Du Quoin, Ill.
Jun 20	Central City, Colo.	Oct 2–7	Saint Louis, Mo.
Jun 22	Border City, Colo.	Oct 19	Terra Haute, Ind.
Jun 23	Burlington, Colo.	Oct 24–28	Cincinnati, Ohio
Jun 24	Greeley, Colo.		
Jun 25	Osden, Colo.		
Jun 26	Laramie, Wyo.		

1872

The Great Eastern Menagerie, Museum, Aviary, Circus and Balloon Show Robert E.J. Miles, Dan Carpenter, Andrew Haight, and George DeHaven, proprietors. Agnes Lake, rider; Emma Lake, rider.

Jun 30–Jul 6	Salt Lake City, Utah		
Jul 7	American Fork, Utah		
Jul 8	Provo, Utah		
Jul 10	Springfield, Utah	Apr 1	Cincinnati, Ohio
Jul 11	Payson, Utah	May 2	Evansville, Ind.
Jul 12	Silver City, Utah	May 3	Princeton, Ind.
Jul 13	Stockton, Utah	May 4	Vincennes, Ind.
Jul 14	Tooele, Utah	May 6	Sullivan, Ind.
Jul 29	Salina, Kans.	May 7	Terre Haute, Ind.
Jul 31	Abilene, Kans.	May ?	Mattoon, Ill.
Aug 1	Topeka, Kans.	May ?	Pana, Ill.
Aug 2	Leavenworth, Kans.	May 8	Decatur, Ill.
Aug 3	Wyandotte, Kans.	May 9	Bloomington, Ill.
Aug 4	Lawrence, Kans.	May 10	Peoria, Ill.
Aug 5	Wamego, Kans.	May 11	Springfield, Ill.
Aug 7	Manhattan, Kans.	May 13	Bloomington, Ill.
Aug 8	Junction City, Kans.	May 14	Joliet, Ill.
Aug 11	Humboldt, Kans.	May 15–21	Chicago, Ill.
Aug 12	Chetopa, Kans.		
Aug 16	Clinton, Kans.		
Aug 19	Fort Scott, Kans.		
Aug 21	Olathe, Kans.		

May 28	Rockford, Ill.	Aug 6	Attica, Ill.
May 29	Freeport, Ill.	Aug 7	Lafayette, Ind.
May 31	Baraboo, Wis.	Aug 8	Delphi, Ind.
Jun 1	Madison, Wis.	Aug 8	Logansport, Ind.
Jun 3	Janesville, Wis.	Aug 9	Peru, Ind.
Jun 4	Fond du Lac, Wis.	Aug 10	Wabash, Ind.
Jun 5	Appleton, Wis.	Aug 12	Huntington, Ind.
Jun 6	Green Bay, Wis.	Aug 13	Fort Wayne, Ind.
Jun 7	Oshkosh, Wis.	Aug 14	Defiance, Ohio
Jun 8	Watertown, Wis.	Aug 15	Toledo, Ohio
Jun 10	Columbus, Wis.	Aug 23	Allegheny, Pa.
Jun 11	Portage City, Wis.	Aug 24	Pittsburgh, Pa.
Jun 12–13	Sparta, Wis.	Aug 26–27	Washington, D.C.
Jun 14	Winona, Minn.	Sep 7	Wilmington, N.C.
Jun 15	Red Wing, Minn.	Sep 9	Marion, S.C.
Jun 16	Hasting, Minn.	Sep 11	Columbia, S.C.
Jun 18	Saint Paul, Minn.	Sep 12	Augusta, Ga.
Jun 19	Stillwater, Minn.	Sep 13	Charleston, S.C.
Jun 28	Dubuque, Iowa	Sep 23	Albany, Ga.
Jun 29	Galena, Ill.	Sep 28	Jacksonville, Ga.
Jul 1	Dixon, Ill.	Sep 30	Hawkinsville, Ga.
Jul 2	Sterline, Ill.	Oct 1	Macon, Ga.
Jul 3	Clinton, Ill.	Oct 7	Newnan, Ga.
Jul 4	Davenport, Iowa	Oct 8	La Grange, Ga.
Jul 5	Rock Island, Ill.	Oct 9	West Point, Ga.
Jul 6	Kanawa, Ill.	Oct 10	Dadeville, Ala.
Jul 8	Galesburg, Ill.	Oct 11	Opelika, Ala.
Jul 9	Macomb, Ill.	Oct 12	Columbus, Ga.
Jul 10	Monmouth, Ill.	Oct 14	Selma, Ala.
Jul 11	Burlington, Ill.	Oct 17	Greenville, Ala.
Jul 12	Fort Madison, Ill.	Oct 24–30	New Orleans, La.
Jul 13	Keokuk, Iowa	Oct 31	Osyka, Miss.
Jul 15	Quincy, Ill.	Nov 1	Summit, Miss.
Jul 16	Palmyra, Ill.	Nov 2	Brookhaven, Miss.
Jul 17	Hannibal, Mo.	Nov 4	Hazelhurst, Miss.
Jul 18	Louisiana, Mo.	Nov 5	Jackson, Miss.
Jul 19	Jacksonville, Mo.	Nov 6	Vicksburg, Miss.
Jul 20	Alton, Mo.	Nov 7	Canton, Miss.
Jul 22–27	Saint Louis, Mo.	Nov 8	Durant, Miss.
Aug 1	Pekin, Ill.	Nov 9	Winona, Miss.
Aug 3	Lincoln, Ill.	Dec 5	Tuscaloosa, Ala.
Aug 5	Danville, Ill.	Dec 12	Marion, Ala.

1873–74

The Great Eastern Menagerie, Museum, Aviary, Circus, Balloon Show, Roman Hippodrome, and Egyptian Caravan Andrew Haight, proprietor. Agnes Lake, rider and animal trainer (as Eugenie DeLonne); Emma Lake, rider.

Mar 10	Louisville, Ky.
Mar 17	Shelbyville, Ky.
Mar 18	Frankfort, Ky.
Mar 19	Mount Sterling, Ky.
Mar 20	Lexington, Ky.
Mar 21	Paris, Ky.
Mar 22	Cynthiana, Ky.
Mar 24	Covington, Ky.
Mar 25–30	Cincinnati, Ohio
Apr 1	Dayton, Ohio
Apr 2	Piqua, Ohio
Apr 3	Sidney, Ohio
Apr 4	Lima, Ohio
Apr 5	Toledo, Ohio
Apr 7	Richmond, Ind.
Apr 8	Connersville, Ind.
Apr 9–10	Indianapolis, Ind.
Apr 10	Terre Haute, Ind.
Apr 11	Vincennes, Ind.
Apr 12	Evansville, Ind.
Apr 14	Belleville, Ind.
Apr 15–20	Saint Louis, Mo.
Apr 28	Peoria, Ill.
May 12	Hillsdale, Mich.
May 13	Jackson, Mich.
May 14	Ypsilanti, Mich.
May 15	Ann Arbor, Mich.
May 16	Marshall, Mich.
May 17	Battle Creek, Mich.
May 19	Kalamazoo, Mich.
May 20	South Bend, Ind.
May 21	Niles, Mich.
May 22	Saint Joseph, Mich.
May 23	Muskegon, Mich.
May 24	Grand Rapids, Mich.
May 26	Lansing, Mich.
May 27	Saginaw, Mich.
May 28–29	Detroit, Mich.
Jun 12–13	Buffalo, N.Y.
Jun 16	Rochester, N.Y.
Jun 17	Dansville, N.Y.
Jun 18	Geneseo, N.Y.
Jun 19	Bath, N.Y.
Jun 20	Corning, N.Y.
Jun 21	Hornesville, N.Y.
Jun 26	Binghamton, N.Y.
Jun 27	Oswego, N.Y.
Jun 28	Susquehanna, Pa.
June 30	Port Jervis, N.Y.
Jul 1	Middletown, N.Y.
Jul 2	Kingston, N.Y.
Jul 3	Newburgh, N.Y.
Jul 4	Paterson, N.J.
Jul 5	Newark, N.J.
Jul 7	Jersey City, N.J.
Jul 8	Hoboken, N.J.
Jul 9	Brooklyn, N.Y.
Jul 10	Williamsburg, N.J.
Jul 14	Elizabeth, N.J.
Jul 15	New Brunswick, N.J.
Jul 16	Williamsburg, N.J.
Jul 17	Camden, N.J.
Jul 18	Trenton, N.J.
Jul 19	Lambertville, N.J.
Jul 21	Phillipsburg, Pa.
Jul 22	Easton, Pa.
Aug 6	Scranton, Pa.
Aug 9	Mahanoy, Pa.
Aug 14	Tamaqua, Pa.
Aug 15	Shamokin, Pa.
Aug 16	Ashland, Pa.
Aug 18	Pottsville, Pa.
Aug 19	Phoenixville, Pa.
Aug 20	Norristown, Pa.

Aug 21	Pottsville, Pa.	Oct 22	Charlotte, N.C.
Aug 22	Wilmington, Del.	Oct 23	Chester, S.C.
Aug 23	Reading, Pa.	Oct 24	Columbia, S.C.
Aug 25	Lancaster, Pa.	Oct 25	Augusta, Ga.
Aug 26	Columbia, Pa.	Oct 29–31	Macon, Ga.
Aug 27	Lebanon, Pa.	Nov 1	Albany, Ga.
Aug 28	Harrisburg, Pa.	Nov 4	Camilla, Ga.
Aug 29	Mechanicsburg, Pa.	Nov 5	Bainbridge, Ga.
Aug 30	Carlisle, Pa.	Nov 6	Thomasville, Ga.
Sep 1	Shippensburg, Pa.	Nov 7	Quitman, Ga.
Sep 2	Chambersburg, Pa.	Nov 8	Valdosta, Ga.
Sep 3	Greencastle, Pa.	Nov 10	Quincy, Fl.
Sep 4	Hagerstown, Md.	Nov 11	Tallahassee, Fl.
Sep 5	Frederick, Md.	Nov 12	Monticello, Fl.
Sep 6	Westminster, Md.	Nov 13	Lake City, Fl.
Sep 8–10	Baltimore, Md.	Nov 14	Jacksonville, Fl.
Sep 11	Annapolis, Md.	Nov 15	Gainesville, Fl.
Sep 12–13	Washington, D.C.	Nov 17–18	Savannah, Ga.
Sep 15	Leesburg, Va.	Nov 19–20	Charleston, S.C.
Sep 16	Alexandria, Va.	Nov 21	Orangeburg, S.C.
Sep 24–25	Richmond, Va.	Nov 22	Camden, S.C.
Sep 27	Norfolk, Va.	Nov 24	Columbia, S.C.
Sep 29	Portsmouth, Va.	Nov 25	Newberry, S.C.
Sep 30	Franklin, Va.	Nov 26	Abbeville, S.C.
Oct 1	Weldon, N.C.	Nov 27	Anderson, S.C.
Oct 2	Henderson, N.C.	Nov 28	Greenville, Ga.
Oct 3	Raleigh, N.C.	Nov 29	Spartanburg, Ga.
Oct 4	Fayetteville, N.C.	Dec 1	Buford, Ga.
Oct 5	Smithfield, N.C.	Dec 2	Atlanta, Ga.
Oct 7	Rocky Mountain, N.C.	Dec 4	La Grange, Ga.
Oct 8	Tarboro, N.C.	Dec 5	West Point, Ga.
Oct 9	Wilson, N.C.	Dec 6	Newnan, Ga.
Oct 10	Goldsboro, N.C.	Dec 8	Senoia, Ga.
Oct 11	Newbern, N.C.	Dec 9	Griffin, Ga.
Oct 13	Kinston, N.C.	Dec 10	Jonesboro, Ga.
Oct 14	Magnolia, N.C.	Dec 11	Barnesville, Ga.
Oct 15	Wilmington, N.C.	Dec 12	Forsyth, Ga.
Oct 16	Whiteville, N.C.	Dec 13	Eatonton, Ga.
Oct 17	Marion, S.C.	Dec 15	Perry, Ga.
Oct 18	Florence, S.C.	Dec 16	Fort Valley, Ga.
Oct 20	Sumter, S.C.	Dec 17	Montezuma, Ala.
Oct 21	Winnsboro, S.C.	Dec 18	Americus, Ga.

Dec 19	Dawson, Ga.	Jan 17	Brookhaven, Miss.
Dec 20	Fort Gaines, Ga.	Jan 19	Crystal Springs, Miss.
Dec 22	Cuthbert, Ga.	Jan 20	Jackson, Miss.
Dec 23	Clayton, Ala.	Jan 21	Canton, Miss.
Dec 24	Eufaula, Ala.	Jan 22	Durant, Miss.
Dec 25	Union Springs, Ala.	Jan 23	Winona, Miss.
Dec 26	Troy, Ala.	Jan 24	Water Valley, Miss.
Dec 27	Columbus, Ga.	Jan 26	Jackson, Tenn.
Dec 29	Dadeville, Ala.	Jan 27	Bolivar, Tenn.
Dec 30	Opelika, Ala.	Jan 28	Holly Springs, Miss.
Jan 1	Montgomery, Ala.	Jan 29	Oxford, Miss.
Jan 2	Selma, Ala.	Jan 30	Grenada, Miss.
Jan 3	Uniontown, Ala.	Jan 31	Batesville, Miss.
Jan 7–8	Mobile, Ala.	Feb 2	Hernando, Miss.
Jan 9–14	New Orleans, La.	Feb 3	Memphis, Tenn.
Jan 15	Osyka, Miss.	Feb 4	Memphis, Tenn.
Jan 16	Summit, Miss.		

Notes

Prologue

1. Personal communication with the Deadwood Visitors Bureau, Deadwood, South Dakota. Data for the year 2002, provided January 8, 2004.

2. Rosa, *They Called Him Wild Bill*, 298.

3. *Black Hills Daily Times* (Deadwood, S.Dak.), 4 September 1877.

4. Ibid., 5 August 1879.

5. Agnes Lake Death Certificate (1907), State Bureau of Vital Statistics and Registration.

6. Halttunen, *Confidence Men and Painted Women*, 31.

7. The Diary of Joseph J. Mersman, 1847–64, Missouri Historical Society, St. Louis. See Mersman, *The Whiskey Merchant's Diary*.

8. Mersman's naturalization documents indicate that he emigrated from the Grand Duchy of Oldenburg, and his diary reveals his Catholic faith as well as the names and ages of his siblings. The connection was made by searching parish registers for a family that fit Mersman's description.

9. Agnes Lake Hickok Letters, Kansas State Historical Society, Topeka (hereafter Agnes Lake Letters, KSHS).

Chapter 1

1. Robinson, *Old Wagon Show Days*, 128.

2. Ostendorf, *Zur Geschicte der Auswanderung*, 164–279.

3. Mersman, *The Whiskey Merchant's Diary*, ed. Linda A. Fisher, is a complete

transcription of the diary Joseph J. Mersman kept from 1847 until 1864 when complications from syphilis rendered him blind. The diary details Mersman's bachelor days in Cincinnati and the St. Louis whiskey and tobacco business that amassed his personal fortune.

4. Kirchenbuch, 1650–1875, Taufen, 1820–39, Katholische Kirche Damme [Amtsgericht Vechta], FHL Microfilm 909912. The parish register documents the use of the farm name by the family of Friedrich Pohlschneider, born Messmann.

5. Eckhard and Schmidt, *Geschichte des Landes Oldenburg*, 677.

6. Schomaker-Langenteilen, *Das Alte Volk*, 19; Hegeler and Schute, *Das Oldenburger Münsterland*, 43, 67, 92, 94.

7. Bernd Mütter and Robert Meyer, "Die Modernisierung der Landwirtschaft zwischen Reichsgründung und Erstem Weltkrieg," in Bade et al., *Damme: Eine Stadt*, 364.

8. Kamphoefner, Marschalck, and Nolte-Schuster, *Von Heuerleuten*, 15–23.

9. Personal communication with Moses Lapp, Lebanon, Pennsylvania, December 25, 2002.

10. Schlumbohm, *Lebensläufe, Familien, Höfe*, 370–76, 532–33.

11. Walker, *Germany and the Emigration*, 42–69.

12. An inventory of the Pohlschneider Farm appears in the Notary Document of Justus Graff, March 10, 1812, Rep. 958, No. 7, Vol. I, 128–31, Staatsarchiv Osnabrück.

13. Helmut Ottenjann, "Zur Geschichte der Bauern- und Heuerlingshäuser," in Bade et al., *Damme: Eine Stadt*, 238, 246–51.

14. Kaiser and Ottenjann, *Museumsführer*, 72-74, 200, 202.

15. Nineteenth-century spelling was not standardized, and parish records were written in Latin. To avoid confusion in this chapter, the most common form of each German name appears for each individual, although actual documents may have a variety of spellings.

16. Kirchenbuch, 1650–1875, Tote, 1830–55, 156, Katholische Kirche Damme, FHL Microfilm 909913. Documentation of the births of Friedrich Messmann and his siblings appears in the Kirchenbuch, 1650–1875, Taufen, 1751–87, 436, 476, 510, 544, 576, 611, Katholische Kirche Damme, FHL Microfilm 909910; Taufen, 1787–1801, 32, 100, FHL Microfilm 909911. At her death, Friedrich Messmann's mother resided at "*Lupke-Ossenbecks Leibzucht* [retirement cottage]," so the Messmanns themselves did not own a farm.

17. Kirchenbuch, 1650–1875, Heiraten, 1723–87, 254, Katholische Kirche Damme, FHL Microfilm 909910.

18. Baptism records Latinize the names as Anna Maria, Catharina Elisabeth, Catharina Maria, and Maria Angela.

19. Kirchenbuch, 1650–1875, Taufen, 1751–87, 580, 615, FHL Microfilm 909910; Taufen, 1787–1801, 62, 124, 182, 267, 341, FHL Microfilm 909911.

20. Lammers, *Commemorative Look at Minster*, 5.

21. Kirchenbuch, 1650–1875, Tote, 1787–1817, 160, Katholische Kirche Damme, FHL Microfilm 0909911.

22. Schlumbohm, *Lebensläufe, Familien, Höfe,* 152–56.

23. Ostendorf, *Zur Geschichte der Auswanderung,* 238.

24. Schlumbohm, *Lebensläufe, Familien, Höfe,* 105, notes that class affected the age of marriage as well.

25. Kirchenbuch, 1650–1875, Heiraten, 1787–1812, 167, 180, 186–87, Katholische Kirche Damme, FHL Microfilm 909911. Elisabeth married Hermann Heinrich Elking, a widower five years older, and they made their home in the Heuerhaus on the Klonnen Farm in Rüschendorf, a hamlet about a mile north of Borringhausen. The youngest daughter, Angela, married Heuermann Johann Heinrich Stricker and joined him on the Neinaben Farm in Rottinghausen, two miles southeast of Borringhausen.

26. Schlumbohm, *Lebensläufe, Familien, Höfe,* 506–509.

27. Ibid., 525. This limited spatial mobility was typical of the landless. Married couples usually lived in the immediate vicinity of their parents or shared their living quarters.

28. Christoph Reinders-Düselder, "Bevölkerungsentwicklung 1650–1850," in Bade et al., *Damme: Eine Stadt,* 295. Mortality statistics peaked in 1812, suggesting a community-wide epidemic.

29. Notary Document of Justus Graff, August 5, 1812, Rep. 958, No. 7, Vol. I, 128–31. The thaler, the official currency in the German states of the Holy Roman Empire beginning in the sixteenth century, was valued at approximately 90 cents U.S.

30. Ibid.

31. Kirchenbuch, 1650–1875, Taufen, 1801–20, 334, 417, 482, 558, FHL Microfilm 909911; Taufen 1820–39, 57, 144, 227, 297, FHL Microfilm 909912.

32. Reinders-Düselder, "Bevölkerungsentwicklung 1650–1850," 298–99; Schlumbohm, *Lebensläufe, Familien, Höfe,* 152–56.

33. The spelling of Elisabeth's name changed for a variety of reasons throughout her life, but for consistency, the authors have chosen to anglicize her name with a "Z," as we have done with her siblings.

34. Kirchenbuch, 1650–1875, Tote, 1811–19, 234, FHL Microfilm 909911; Tote, 1819–1929, 329, FHL Microfilm 909912.

35. Schlumbohm, *Lebensläufe, Familien, Höfe,* 476; Ostendorf, *Zur Geschichte der Auswanderung,* 274.

36. These relationships are clear from studying Damme parish registers, for the records of marriages, births, and deaths often mentioned the residence of the individuals.

37. "All under One Roof in Germany," http://www.heritagequest.com/genealogy/europe/html/barn.html.

38. *Von Baltimore nach Bünde,* 29–32.

39. Ibid., 30.

40. 1828 Census, Best. 76-25, 520, Staatsarchiv Oldenburg.

41. *Auswanderung Bremen, USA*, 8–17, 26–44; Thernstrom, Orlov, and Handlin, *Harvard Encyclopedia of American Ethnic Groups*, 411.

42. Duden, *Report on a Journey*, 43–44.

43. Ibid., xxii.

44. Ibid., 104.

45. "so beautiful, so fertile, and so cheap." Ibid., 185.

46. Ibid., 102.

47. Ibid., 76–77.

48. Ibid., 251.

49. Ibid.

50. Ibid., 44.

51. Quoted in Hartmutt Bickelmann, "The Venture of Travel," in Moltmann, *Germans to America*, 47–48, 129–33.

52. Legal document: *Christopher Luermann and Bernd Stricker v. Friedrich Pohlschneider*, April 19, 1832, Best. 76, 25, Ab. No. 112, 173–75, Staatsarchive Oldenburg; Ostendorf, *Zur Geschicte der Auswanderung*, 256. Friedrich Messmann Pohlschneider had tried to sell the farm and leave Damme as early as 1832, but the sale of the farm fell through and he took the buyer to court, delaying his departure for several months.

53. Kirchenbuch, 1650–1875, Tote, 1830–66, 74, Katholische Kirche Damme, FHL Microfilm 909913.

54. Duden, *Report on a Journey*, 249.

55. Entry for Fredk Meisman [*sic*] and family; Second Quarter 1833, p. 46, lines 30–34, in *Quarterly Abstracts of Passenger Lists of Vessels Arriving in Baltimore, 1820–69*: January 1, 1830–Dec. 31, 1833, NA Microfilm M596, Roll 2, Records of the Central Office; Records of the Immigration and Naturalization Service, Record Group 85, National Archives, Washington, D.C.

56. Ostendorf, *Zur Geschicte der Auswanderung*, 169–70; Roseboon and Weisenburger, *History of Ohio*, 119. People fleeing the city spread the disease to Mercer County, aggravating the hardships in Stallo's settlement.

57. Ostendorf, *Zur Geschicte der Auswanderung*, 171; Ferguson, *Ohio Lands*, 31; Williamson, *History of Western Ohio*, 838; Lammers, *Commemorative Look at Minster*, 11; Hoying, Hoying, and Hoying, *Pilgrims All*, 1–4, 13–17. In 1839 the village was incorporated under the anglicized name "Minster" that it bears today. Originally in Mercer County, Minster is now located in Auglaize County, which was created in 1848.

58. Records of St. Augustine Parish, Minster, Ohio, transcribed by Rita Hoying and David Hoying, Minster, Ohio, 2001. The priest at St. Augustine Catholic Church assessed school tuition for two "Pohlschneider" children, likely the two youngest boys, Joseph and Frank, since girls were not accepted as students.

59. Bek, "Followers of Duden," 14, no. 1, 66, 70 (original emphasis).

60. Ibid., 66.

61. Ibid., nos. 3–4, 439.

62. Bek, "Followers of Duden," 15, no. 3, 524.

63. Shelby County Deed Book L: 287–88. Frederick Messmann made his first Ohio land purchase in 1833 in nearby Shelby County.

64. Thayer, *Annals of the American Circus*, 185, 280.

65. Ibid., 185.

65. Ibid.

66. Ibid., 279–80.

Chapter 2

1. *Cincinnati Daily Republican*, 20 April 1842, 5. According to newspapers, the Dickens party lodged at the Broadway Hotel, although local legend claims Edmund Dexter also provided overnight accommodations for the honored guests.

2. Writers' Program of the WPA, *Guide to Cincinnati*, 59.

3. Rorabaugh, *The Alcoholic Republic*, 115–16.

4. Cist, *Cincinnati in 1841*, 93–95.

5. *Oliver Twist* (1837–39) and *Nicholas Nickleby* (1838–39) were among his best-sellers at the time.

6. Dickens, *American Notes*, 207. All citations refer to the Penguin Classics edition, *American Notes for General Circulation*, ed. John S. Whitley and Arnold Goldman (London, reprint 1985), in the bibliography.

7. *Nashville Daily Press*, 22 November 1864.

8. Writers' Program of the WPA, *Guide to Cincinnati*, 58.

9. Ibid., 57–58.

10. Ibid., 58.

11. The exact number onboard was unknown, so a precise count of casualties is impossible. Klein, *Ohio River Collection*, 182–85, 265; Writers' Program of the WPA, *Guide to Cincinnati*, 58–59.

12. Dickens, *American Notes*, 202.

13. A description of Franz Christian Nulsen's (Anthony's father) vocation as a wholesale tobacco dealer in Europe is found in Johann Joseph Nuelsens Tagebuch, 1833–39, Missouri Historical Society, St. Louis. See also Stevens, *St. Louis, the Fourth City*, 3, 238–41.

14. Geise-Messman marriage, May 23, 1843, in Holy Trinity Catholic Church Marriage Record, unpaginated, arranged by date, Historical Archives of the Chancery, Cincinnati, Ohio. While Henry was the impetus behind changing the family name once more, the 1840 Federal Census lists Henry as "Messmann," while the city directory that same year includes him as "Mersman." Henry's marriage license in 1842 records his surname as "Mersman" (Hamilton County Marriage Book 14:75, William Howard Taft Center, Cincinnati, Ohio), as does the 1842 city direc-

tory. However, an 1843 church record lists Agnes's surname as "Messmann." See also Cash file for Joseph Messmann, Final Patent 11, 487, August 14, 1839, Land Case Files, Patents Issued under the Act of June 22, 1838, Government Land Office, Lima, Ohio, Record Group 49, Bureau of Land Management, National Archives, Washington, D.C.

15. Ostendorf, *Zur Geschichte der Auswanderung*, 256, 258, 273, 274; Mersman, *The Whiskey Merchant's Diary*, February 18, 1849, 182. Among those who followed were Agnes's paternal uncle, Johann Heinrich Messmann; paternal aunt, Catharina Angela, and her husband, Heinrich Decker; and cousins from the Elking, Stricker, Decker, and Messmann families.

16. A full biographical index describing their many friends and business acquaintances appears in Mersman, *The Whiskey Merchant's Diary*, 313–47.

17. *Cincinnati Enquirer*, 31 December 1848; Wimberg, *Over-the-Rhine*, 8; Mersman, *The Whiskey Merchant's Diary*, April 17, 1848, 66.

18. *Troy (N.Y.) Daily Budget*, 2 September 1834; see also Thayer, *Annals of the American Circus*, 239.

19. Thayer, *Annals of the American Circus*, 239; Thayer, *Traveling Showmen*, 15.

20. Thayer, *Annals of the American Circus*, 279. Some circus historians suggest that "Lake" was his mother's maiden name.

21. Slout, *Olympians of the Sawdust Circle*, 164. According to William Slout, "Madame Cordelia" was trained by Bill Lake and assumed the surname for herself, hoping his famous name would increase her recognition. Bill was also instrumental in training Agnes Lake and their children.

22. Thayer, *Annals of the American Circus*, 275, 312, 320–21; Robinson, *Old Wagon Show Days*, 129; Parkinson and Fox, *The Circus Moves by Rail*, 331. Lake is listed on the rosters of these troupes: Fogg & Stickney (1840–41), John Mateer (1843–44), Rich & Rowe (1844), Great Western Circus (1846), and Stone & McCollum (1846).

23. *St. Louis Republican*, 18 November 1847.

24. *Cincinnati Daily Commercial*, 25 March 1846.

25. Ibid., 1–23 April 1846.

26. Thayer, *Annals of the American Circus*, 321.

27. Robinson, *Old Wagon Show Days*, 128–29.

28. Ibid., 128.

29. Parkinson and Fox, *The Circus Moves by Rail*, 338; Slout, *Olympians of the Sawdust Circle*, 164. The Robinson & Eldred Circus was owned and operated in 1845–46 by "Old John" Robinson and Gilbert Eldred. No evidence suggests that Bill Lake was employed by their company at this time.

30. Thayer, *Annals of the American Circus*, 309–10. According to Thayer, the Robinson & Eldred Circus (and all variations thereof) never exhibited north of the Mason-Dixon Line and performed only in Georgia, North Carolina, South Carolina, and Virginia.

31. Ibid., 312.

32. Ibid., 319–20.

33. Ibid., 308.

34. Ibid., 312.

35. Ibid., 320.

36. Thayer, *Annals of the American Circus,* 213, 320. Duriastus Rich and Joseph Andrew Rowe (1819–87) were proprietors of the Rich & Rowe Circus in 1844. Both Rowe and Lake had worked for John Mateer in 1843 and early 1844, so it is likely that the pair met during that time.

37. Ibid., 192; New York *Morning Telegraph,* 30 December 1906.

38. Marriage Licenses issued by Jefferson Parish, William Lake Thatcher and Mary Agnes Mersmann, May 1, 1846, VCP 670M, p. 279. Jefferson Parish contained the town of Lafayette, which was incorporated into New Orleans in the early 1850s and is not to be confused with the town of Lafayette about 130 miles west of New Orleans.

39. Thayer, *Traveling Showmen,* 7–8.

40. *Williams' Cincinnati Directory 1850–51,* 151.

41. Thayer, *Annals of the American Circus,* 319–20.

42. Ibid., 321.

43. Ibid., 320.

Chapter 3

1. Chindahl, *History of the Circus,* 7–8, 54; Fox, *Performing Horses,* 36; Vail, "This Way to the Big Top!" LaVahn G. Hoh and William H. Rough stated that Washington was so impressed with John Ricketts's circus that he "ultimately sold his favorite white charger, Old Jack, to Ricketts for $150, for display at his circus." Hoh and Rough, *Step Right Up,* 54.

2. *Louisville Morning Courier,* 4 April 1848. Rockwell & Company and Spalding's Monster Circus both boasted over "200 men and horses" in their troupes in copious newspaper advertisements.

3. Chindahl, *History of the Circus,* 1–2. Chindahl noted that "a tropical animal was a great curiosity. . . . [A] 'Lyon of Barbary' was exhibited in America in the year 1716, a camel in 1721, a polar bear in 1733 and a leopard in 1768" (p. 2). After the American Revolution, menageries advertised "birds, reptiles, snakes, and quadrupeds . . . orangutan[s], a sloth, a baboon, a tiger, a buffalo, a crocodile, and various other creatures" (p. 2). Chindahl remarked that menageries catered "particularly to those who frowned upon the circus."

4. Thayer, *Traveling Showmen,* 5–6.

5. Ibid., 7.

6. Ibid., 1–3. According to Thayer, the leading circus in the United States at the time was Price & Simpson. The proprietors, Stephen Price, a lawyer, and Ed-

mond Simpson, an actor, purchased James West's circus company in 1822 in a vain attempt to decrease competition.

7. Ibid., 1.

8. Robinson, *Old Wagon Show Days*, 114–15.

9. Thayer, *Traveling Showmen*, 14–16.

10. Ibid., 16; McKennon, *Circus Lingo*, 63.

11. McKennon, *Circus Lingo*, 52.

12. Ibid., 26, 34, 81.

13. Thayer, *Traveling Showmen*, 23–24.

14. Ibid., 50.

15. Ibid., 50–51.

16. *Louisville Morning Courier*, 8 May 1847.

17. *Illinois Journal* (Springfield), 16 September 1847.

18. *Missouri Republican* (St. Louis), 9 November 1847; Thayer, *Annals of the American Circus*, 308; *St. Louis Republican*, 23 December 1847.

19. *St. Louis Reveille*, 20 January 1848.

20. *Missouri Republican* (St. Louis), 15 November 1847–22 January 1848; Thayer, *Annals of the American Circus*, 458–60.

21. Mersman, *The Whiskey Merchant's Diary*, January 28, 1848, 39–40.

22. Ibid.

23. *Cincinnati Daily Commercial*, 2 February 1848; Mersman, *The Whiskey Merchant's Diary*, February 2, 1848, 41; February 27, 1848, 46–47.

24. *Cincinnati Daily Commercial*, 25 March 1848; Mersman, *The Whiskey Merchant's Diary*, March 25, 1848, 60.

25. Mersman, *The Whiskey Merchant's Diary*, March 25, 1848, 60.

26. *Cincinnati Daily Commercial*, 25 March 1848.

27. Thayer, *The Performers*, 104.

28. Ibid.

29. Mersman, *The Whiskey Merchant's Diary*, April 23, 1848, 68.

30. Ibid., June 6, 1848, 98.

31. *Cincinnati Enquirer*, 30 October 1848. The land troupe of Rockwell & Company returned to Cincinnati at the end of October.

32. *Arkansas Intelligencer* (Van Buren), 7 October 1848.

33. *Vicksburg Daily Whig*, 25 November 1848 (original emphasis).

34. For an in-depth discussion of the effects of cholera in nineteenth-century America, see Rosenburg, *The Cholera Years*.

35. Fisher, "Summer of Terror," 200. On May 17, 1849, a devastating fire started on the steamboat *White Cloud*, which was filled with immigrants. The fire spread to the St. Louis levee, destroying fifteen city blocks in the business district. In the following weeks, anti-immigrant street violence filled the evenings, targeting the Irish and frightening everyone.

36. Rosenberg, *The Cholera Years*, 101.

37. *Cincinnati Daily Commercial*, 6 January 1849.

38. Fisher, "Summer of Terror."

39. Ibid., 204.

40. Mersman, *The Whiskey Merchant's Diary*, July 14, 1849, 201.

41. Ibid., June 25, 1849, 194–95; Fisher, "Summer of Terror," 202.

42. Mersman, *The Whiskey Merchant's Diary*, June 10, 1849, 193.

43. Ibid., July 14, 1849, 201; Thayer, *Traveling Showmen*, 18–19. For an in-depth discussion of circus economics, see Thayer, *Traveling Showmen*, 9–21.

44. Mersman, *The Whiskey Merchant's Diary*, July 14, 1849, 201.

45. Ibid., February 18, 1849, 182–83; June 19, 1849, 194–95; July 9, 1851, 257–58; July 28, 1853, 270. Mersman wrote his will four different times throughout the span of his diary.

46. Hankins and Silverman, *Instruments*, 49.

47. Carlyon, *Dan Rice*, 206–14.

48. Thayer, *Annals of the American Circus*, 468–69. The show also had three runs in St. Louis (July 13, August 24, and October 1–9) and one in Cincinnati (June 1–2).

49. Bruesch, "Disasters and Epidemics of a River Town," 296–98.

50. Slout, *Olympians of the Sawdust Circle*, 35–36, 238, 258. Victor Piquet (d. 1849), a contortionist, died in New Orleans.

51. Thayer, *Annals of the American Circus*, 356.

52. *Daily Courier* (Lafayette, Ind.), 16 April 1850.

53. *Evansville (Ind.) Daily Journal*, 3 May 1850; *Missouri Republican* (St. Louis), 24 July 1850.

54. Mersman, *The Whiskey Merchant's Diary*, June 16, 1850, 234–35.

55. Ibid., June 15, 1850, 234.

56. Personal communication from Stuart Thayer, June 5, 2005.

57. USC 1850, M432, Roll 417, p. 121, lines 10–12.

58. *Cincinnati Enquirer*, 20 June 1850.

59. Mersman, *The Whiskey Merchant's Diary*, September 22, 1850, 245–46; October 20, 1850, 247.

60. Ibid., September 22, 1850, 245–46.

61. Research has not confirmed Winn's identity.

62. Mersman, *The Whiskey Merchant's Diary*, October 20, 1850, 247; November 10, 1850, 247–48; November 24, 1850, 248–50; December 8, 1850, 250; December 29, 1850, 251–52. The limited information available comes from Mersman's diary.

63. Thayer, *Annals of the American Circus*, 333.

64. Ibid., 300, 314; *Missouri Republican* (St. Louis), 4 February 1880. Gilbert Spalding foreclosed on Samuel H. Nichols's Great Western Circus and renamed it the North American Circus prior to its opening in Albany, New York, in March 1844.

65. Slout, *Olympians of the Sawdust Circle*, 258–59.

66. *State Capital Fact* (Columbus, Ohio), 29 August 1851.

67. *Nashville Union*, 7 November 1863.

68. Ibid.

69. Ibid.

70. *American Union* (Steubenville, Ohio), 21 May 1851. Whereas the Drummond light was used primarily for outdoor areas, gaslights illuminated the interior of the tent.

71. *Louisville Morning Courier*, 25 June 1851.

72. *The Morgan Herald* (McConnelsville, Ohio), 9 May 1851.

73. *Ohio State Journal* (Columbus), 2 September 1851; *Memphis Daily Eagle*, 20 November 1850.

Chapter 4

1. Thayer, *Annals of the American Circus*, 359. The first American show to use a steamboat for transportation was Pepin & Barnet's circus in 1822.

2. *Ibid.*, 360.

3. Leavitt-May, "Entertainments Aboard," 24.

4. Way, *Way's Packet Directory*, #4231, 350.

5. Ibid., #2946, 242; Chindahl, *History of the Circus*, 56–57. It was replaced by the *James Raymond*, a 274-ton side-wheeler that was built in Cincinnati in 1853 and was also the setting of "dramatic and minstrel performances."

6. Thayer, *Annals of the American Circus*, 360.

7. *Cincinnati Enquirer*, 29 April 1852.

8. *Democratic Banner* (Henderson, Ky.), 22 July 1853; *Nashville Union,* 10 April 1852; see also Thayer, *Annals of the American Circus*, 360. Spalding spent at least $45,000 on construction of the *Floating Palace*, although some publicity claimed the theater's cost was $100,000.

9. *Pittsburgh Chronicle*, 3 June 1852; *Covington (Ky.) Journal*, 3 July 1852.

10. *Cincinnati Enquirer*, 29 May 1852; Thayer, *Traveling Showmen*, 52.

11. *Pittsburgh Chronicle*, 31 May, 1 June 1852.

12. Ibid., 2 June 1852.

13. Ibid., 4 June 1852.

14. Ibid., 3 June 1852.

15. *Missouri Republican* (St. Louis), 12 August 1852.

16. *Cincinnati Enquirer*, 4 July 1852.

17. *Missouri Republican* (St. Louis), 7 August 1852.

18. *Evansville (Ind.) Daily Journal*, 3 August 1852.

19. *Steubenville (Ohio) American Union*, 9 June 1852.

20. Identities of the performers are from Slout, *Olympians of the Sawdust Circle*, 170–71, 289, 304.

21. Thayer, *Annals of the American Circus*, 361.

22. Ibid., 479.

23. *Cincinnati Enquirer*, 1 July 1852.

24. Ibid.

25. Thayer, *Annals of the American Circus*, 479–81.

26. Slout, *Clowns and Cannons*, 85.

27. *Daily Zanesville (Ohio) Courier*, 19 May 1853; *Battle Creek (Mich.) Journal*, 17 June 1853.

28. Thayer, *Annals of the American Circus*, 332.

29. Amidon, "Stalking the Apollonicon," 16.

30. *Lynchburg Daily Virginian*, 25 October 1854; *Tri-Weekly Standard* (Bridgeport, Conn.), 19 April 1854.

31. *Richmond Daily Dispatch*, 4 November 1854.

32. *Daily Sun* (Columbus, Ga.), 19 and 29 November 1856.

33. *Logansport (Ind.) Journal*, 23 August 1856.

34. *Daily Sun* (Columbus, Ga.), 26 November 1856.

35. Ibid.

36. *Logansport (Ind.) Journal*, 24 April 1858.

37. At the time of her death in December 1867, Alice was newly married to John Wilson, so she must have been at least seventeen years old, making her birth date circa 1850.

38. *Mahoning County (Ohio) Register*, 27 August 1857.

39. Draper, "Willie O'Dale," 22–24. The father, O. Dale, a rider, became blind and was hospitalized in Cincinnati for months before he died in 1866. The child should not be confused with the offspring of William T. O'Dell (or Odell), an equestrian director who died in Philadelphia in 1866 of complications from a compound fracture caused by falling from a horse.

40. *Cincinnati Enquirer*, 5 May 1852.

41. *Democratic Herald* (Butler, Pa.), 2 September 1857.

42. *Hancock Courier* (Findley, Ohio), 25 July 1857; *Democratic Union* (Upper Sandusky, Ohio), 20 August 1857; *Monmouth (Ill.) Review*, 15 May 1857.

43. *Mahoning County (Ohio) Register*, 27 August 1857.

44. *Chicago Daily Democrat*, 11 July 1857.

45. Thayer, *Annals of the American Circus*, 411.

46. *Anamosa (Iowa) Gazette*, 26 May 1857.

47. Thayer, *Annals of the American Circus*, 358, 409–10; Slout, *Olympians of the Sawdust Circle*, 158, 231.

48. Thayer, *Traveling Showmen*, 93–94.

49. Ibid.

50. *Waynesburg (Pa.) Messenger*, 16 September 1857.

51. Thayer, *Traveling Showmen*, 83–93.

52. The *Wheeling (Va.) Intelligencer*, 17 September 1857, noted that a dozen

persons' pockets had been relieved of their contents at the Spalding & Rogers circus.

53. *Waukegan (Ill.) Weekly Gazette*, 18 July 1857.

54. Thayer, *Traveling Showmen*, 88–89.

55. Ibid., 76, 89.

56. *Daily Herald* (Newburyport, Mass.), 13 August 1858.

57. Equestrians on the roster included the Australian James Melville (1835–92), the German Frederick Rentz (1838–72), and the American Omar Richardson (1835–59).

58. *Logansport (Ind.) Journal*, 24 April 1858.

59. *Lynn (Mass.) News*, 30 March 1858.

60. *The Bay State* (Lynn, Mass.), 29 July 1858. A boatswain's pipe, a high-pitched whistle that summoned the crew's attention, likely inspired the choice of this pseudonym.

61. *Lynn (Mass.) News*, 17 August 1858.

62. [Translated from Latin] "The voice of the people, the voice of God."

63. BDSDS, 1858, American Antiquarian Society.

64. *Lynn (Mass.) News*, 24 August 1858. The *Lynn News* was "a family newspaper, devoted to politics, literature, science, art, temperance, agricultures, general intelligence, &c."

65. *New York Herald*, 5 and 21 November 1858.

66. *New York Times*, 23 October 1858.

67. *Salem (Mass.) Gazette*, 24 August 1858.

68. *New York Herald*, 16 November 1858.

Chapter 5

1. Thayer, *Annals of the American Circus*, 387–422. Proprietors of the defunct circuses included Spalding & Rogers; Edmund and Jeremiah Mabie; Dan Rice; Lewis B. Lent; Sands, Nathans & Company; Rivers & Derious; Joe Pentland; Henry C. Lee; Levi J. North; Hiram Orton & Pardon Older; Van Amburgh & Company; George F. Bailey & Company; Harry Buckley; Yankee Robinson; Nixon & Company; Antonio & Wilder; John Sears; Milo Kimbal; Harry Whitby; Davis & Crosby; Dan Gardner; John Wilson; J. W. Tanner; Louisa Wells; Frank Hyatt; Rogers & Archer; and Reynolds.

2. While the Dun Company created extensive records concerning the creditworthiness of Agnes Lake's brothers, Henry and Joseph Mersman, and her brother-in-law, Arnd Kattenhorn, there are none for William Lake Thatcher.

3. Thayer, *Traveling Showmen*, 12–13.

4. Slout, *Olympians of the Sawdust Circle*, 256–57.

5. Ibid., 90. Between 1845 and 1855 the Robinson & Eldred Circus had six

different names: National Circus (1845), Great National Circus (1848), New York Circus (1849–50), Great Southern Circus (1851, 1853, 1855), Southern Circus (1852), and Combined Circus, Menagerie, and Hippodrome (1854). In 1846 and 1847, however, Robinson and Eldred operated separate shows as individual proprietors. Thayer, *Annals of the American Circus*, 309–10, 442–44, 489–93.

6. Thayer, *Annals of the American Circus*, 338–39. The site of Robinson's birth is disputed, but his Southern sympathies are not.

7. Conover, *John Robinson*, 20–21; Hubbard, *Great Days*, 131; Robinson, *Old Wagon Show Days*, 45.

8. Thayer, *Annals of the American Circus*, 393; *St. Louis Globe-Democrat*, 25 February 1888.

9. Robinson, *Old Wagon Show Days*, 23.

10. Ibid., 45; Thayer, *Annals of the American Circus*, 393. According to Gil Robinson, Eldred boasted that within five years his fame and fortune would eclipse that of John Robinson; however, the opposite happened: the Robinson name was attached to dozens of shows until the early twentieth century, while Eldred's future circus ventures failed and he died penniless in Spain.

11. John Robinson Circus Company Records, 1856–1963, Mss 849, Cincinnati Museum Center.

12. *Ottawa (Kans.) Republican*, 28 September, 5 October 1861.

13. Robinson & Lake's Great Circus & Menagerie, 1860, Circus World Scrapbook, Baraboo, Wisconsin.

14. *Cincinnati Enquirer*, 19 April 1859 (original emphasis).

15. Ibid.

16. *(Macon) Georgia Citizen*, 9 December 1859.

17. *Daily Chronicle & Sentinel* (Augusta, Ga.), 2 December 1859.

18. *Charleston Daily Courier*, 1 March 1860.

19. *New York Clipper*, 19 December 1924.

20. *Bloomington (Ill.) Daily Pantagraph*, 30 September 1861. This was part of the standard circus advertisement run in newspapers promoting the show's arrival.

21. Robinson, *Old Wagon Show Days*, 39.

22. *Delphi (Ind.) Journal*, 29 May 1861; *Hastings (Mich.) Republican Banner*, 17 July 1861; *Weekly Sentinel* (Jacksonville, Mo.), 16 September 1861; *Weekly Pantagraph* (Bloomington, Ill.), 25 September 1861; *Ottawa (Kans.) Republican*, 28 September, 5 October 1861.

23. Kunhardt, Kunhardt, and Kunhardt, *P. T. Barnum*, 272; Slout, *Olympians of the Sawdust Circle*, 14.

24. *Daily Toledo (Ohio) Blade*, 19 June 1861; *Niles (Mich.) Republican*, 17 August 1861; *Bloomington (Ind.) Daily Pantagraph*, 20 September 1861.

25. Robinson, *Old Wagon Show Days*, 102.

26. Slout, *Olympians of the Sawdust Circle*, 165, 257.

Chapter 6

1. Slout, *Clowns and Cannons*, 131; Parkinson, *Directory of American Circuses*, 171. John Robinson distanced himself from his own reputation by changing his company's name to the "Great Union Combination" in 1863 and 1865.

2. Thayer, "America's Own Horseman," 24–25; Slout, *Clowns and Cannons*, 131; *Nashville Union*, 3 November 1864.

3. Parkinson, *Directory of American Circuses*, 29; Slout, *Olympians of the Sawdust Circle*, 6. Three Antonio brothers — Guglielmo (1820–1902), Philip Augustus (d. 1895), and Lorenzo (1826–?) — all acrobats, owned a circus that toured from 1860 to 1862.

4. Durham, *Nashville: The Occupied City*, 3.

5. Ibid., 63–66.

6. Ibid., 66, 88.

7. Durham, *Reluctant Partners*, 207; see also *Nashville Dispatch*, 27 November 1864.

8. *Nashville Dispatch*, 27 November 1864.

9. *(Springfield) Illinois Journal*, 5 May 1863.

10. Ibid., 9 May 1863.

11. *Indianapolis Daily Journal*, 26 September 1863.

12. *Canton (Ohio) Weekly Register*, 20 July 1863.

13. *Nashville Daily Press*, 4 November 1863; *Nashville Union*, 3 November 1863. Stevens organized advertising for the circus in Nashville and continued to be involved with the show after its premiere.

14. *Nashville Daily Press*, 11 November 1863.

15. *Nashville Union*, 21 November 1863.

16. Ibid., 20 November 1863.

17. *Nashville Dispatch*, 26 November 1863.

18. *Nashville Daily Press*, 18 November 1863.

19. Ibid., 19 November 1863.

20. *Nashville Dispatch*, 22 November 1863.

21. Ibid., 17 and 19 November 1863; *Nashville Union*, 17 November 1863.

22. *Nashville Dispatch*, 29 November 1863. All participating soldiers were arrested and punished.

23. Ibid., 27 November 1863.

24. Hankins and Silverman, *Instruments*, 72–85. The cat piano was first written about by Athanasius Kircher in his *Musurgia universalis* in 1650. According to Hankins and Silverman, the piano was created "to raise the spirits of an Italian prince burdened by the cares of his position" (p. 73).

25. Slout, *Olympians of the Sawdust Circle*, 222.

26. Slout, *Clowns and Cannons*, 155.

27. *Louisville Daily Democrat*, 19 April 1864; *Cincinnati Enquirer*, 7 May 1864.

28. http://www.brycchancarey.com/sancho; http://www.loc.gov/loc/lcib/0

001/royall.html. The black mule, Sancho, was likely named for Ignatius Sancho (1729–80), an African who lived in London. *Paul Pry*, a newspaper published in 1831–36 by Anne Newport Royall, was dedicated to exposing political evil and religious fraud.

29. *Cincinnati Enquirer*, 7 May 1864.

30. Ibid., 2 May 1864.

31. Ibid., 4 May 1864.

32. *Daily Zanesville (Ohio) Courier*, 19 October 1864.

33. Ibid., 24 October 1864. The Lakes left about ninety horses behind.

34. *Nashville Dispatch*, 15 November 1864.

35. *Nashville Daily Press*, 21 November 1864.

36. Durham, *Reluctant Partners*, 277.

37. *Nashville Union*, 16 and 24 November 1864.

38. *Nashville Dispatch*, 9 December 1864.

39. *Nashville Union*, 24 November 1864. "Hippo" comes from the Greek root for "horse."

40. Thayer, *Traveling Showmen*, 12.

41. *Nashville Dispatch*, 11 and 19 November 1864.

42. *Nashville Daily Press*, 27 November 1863. Descriptions of the countryman act appear in Glenroy, *Ins and Outs*, 11.

43. *Nashville Dispatch*, 22 November 1864.

44. *Nashville Union*, 3 December 1864.

45. Ibid., 26 and 27 November 1864.

46. Davis, *Battlefields of the Civil War*, 293.

47. *Nashville Union*, 14 and 20 December 1864.

48. *Nashville Dispatch*, 4 December 1864.

49. *Nashville Union*, 2 December 1864.

50. Johnson and Buel, *Battles and Leaders of the Civil War*, 4:473.

51. *Nashville Daily Press*, 9 December 1864.

52. "The Circus in the War," Cincinnati Special to the *New York Sun*, undated clipping from the files of Stuart Thayer.

53. *Nashville Daily Press*, 8 December 1864.

54. "The Circus in the War."

55. Glenroy, *Ins and Outs*, 137–38.

56. *Nashville Daily Press*, 14 December 1864.

57. Slout, *Clowns and Cannons*, 179.

58. *Nashville Dispatch*, 19 December 1864.

59. MacDonald, *Great Battles of the Civil War*, 168–75.

60. Mersman, *The Whiskey Merchant's Diary*, April 24, 1864, 282–83.

61. DUN Ohio, 78:181. Henry's excessive alcohol intake was noted in the records kept by the Dun Company and may have contributed to him dissolving his partnership with Anthony Nulsen in 1861. It also may have played a role in his death.

Chapter 7

1. Two sources provided the basis for the tale of Ivan Mazeppa (1664–1709): *The History of Charles XII of Sweden* by Voltaire and *Histoire des Kosaques* by Charles-Louis Lesure.

2. The spelling in some early manuscripts is Casimer or Casimir. The nineteenth-century spelling of Tartar or Tartary in newspaper advertisements and book titles is considered ethnic slang today.

3. Coleman, *Mazeppa, Polish and American*, 58–65.

4. Sentilles, *Performing Menken*, 91–114.

5. See chapter 4, note 24.

6. *Cincinnati Daily Commercial*, 13 December 1861.

7. Sentilles, *Performing Menken*, 152–53. Sentilles claimed the length of the contract was a critical issue for Menken in choosing not to transport animals for short runs. In contrast, Agnes Lake always traveled with her horses, regardless of the length of the performance run.

8. Ibid.

9. *New York Clipper*, 1 November 1862; Robinson, *Old Wagon Show Days*, 87. Gil Robinson's memoir also alleges that John Robinson provided the "wild steed." Robinson's account names the wrong theater and makes him the center of the action, undermining his credibility for the rest of the story.

10. *Cincinnati Daily Commercial*, 21 October 1862.

11. Sentilles, *Performing Menken*, 167–69.

12. *New York Clipper*, 10 August 1867. Adah I. Montclain hired William R. Derr as her manager and traveled with the horse Don Juan.

13. *Nashville Daily Union*, 10 November 1863.

14. *Daily Zanesville (Ohio) Courier*, 17 March 1866. "Minnehaha" was a horse trained by Robert E.J. Miles.

15. *Nashville Daily Union*, 24 November 1863.

16. Coleman, *Mazeppa, Polish and American*, 68.

17. Sentilles, *Performing Menken*, 241–42.

18. Disher, *Fairs, Circuses, Music Halls*, 29.

19. *New York Clipper*, 27 May 1865.

20. Alexander Dumas and Algernon Charles Swinburne were among Menken's lovers. The details of Menken's life and loves are most accurately described in Sentilles, *Performing Menken*.

21. Ibid., 275. Adah Isaacs Menken's exact birth date remains uncertain, but it was approximately 1835.

22. Slout, *Olympians of the Sawdust Circle*, 281.

23. *Daily Zanesville (Ohio) Courier*, 5 April 1865.

24. *Oxford English Dictionary*, 7:241, 10:782.

25. *New York Clipper*, 16 March 1867.

26. Ibid., 13 January 1866.

27. *Deutsche National-Zeitung* (Berlin), 13 December 1865.

28. The phrase "from New York" was used to enhance Agnes's American biography, just as she claimed to be French, since few people in Berlin had likely heard of Cincinnati.

29. Prince Karl, born Friedrich Karl Alexander, Prince of Prussia (1801–83), was the third son of King Friedrich Wilhelm III of Prussia (1770–1840).

30. This translation of the German was made by Reinhard Hennig.

31. *Deutsche National-Zeitung* (Berlin), 15 December 1865.

32. *Daily Zanesville (Ohio) Courier*, 19 and 25 April 1866. Two "German trick horses" received billing during the 1866 season: D'Yalma (also spelled D'Jalma) and Zadd. Apollo first appeared in advertisements in 1867.

33. The identity of "Laura" has not been determined, but her placement in the roster suggests she is a member of Agnes's family. William Slout's *Olympians of the Sawdust Circle* includes an entry for a Laura Lake, but only for Lake's Hippo-Olympiad in 1867. However, this may be an example of padding the roster, since the indenture papers in 1866 reveal Laura as the child's middle name. Perhaps another young girl adopted Lake as her surname after Bill Lake tutored her in circus equestrianism.

34. *New York Clipper*, 31 March 1866. The roster also includes C[lark] Gibbs, John Lowlow, Monste [Brothers], [William] Sparks, [Frank] Lee, H[arry] Bernard, Collins and Sig. Castelio [William Costello].

35. *Danville (Ill.) Plaindealer*, 2 May 1867.

36. Personal communication from Stuart Thayer, November 2003. See the appendix for detailed route sheets.

37. Hamilton County Recorder's Documents, Miscellaneous Records Book #1, pp. 64–65, Microfilm, Cincinnati Historical Society.

38. *Missouri Republican* (St. Louis), 4 February 1880.

39. Emma Lake Robinson Death Certificate, May 11, 1911. State Bureau of Vital Statistics and Registration, New Jersey.

40. *Mahoning County (Ohio) Register*, 27 August 1857.

41. Agnes Lake Hickok to Polly and Celinda Hickok, April 26, 1876, Agnes Lake Letters, KSHS.

42. Robinson, *Circus Lady*, 119–20.

43. Kunhardt, Kunhardt, and Kunhardt, *P. T. Barnum*, 48.

44. Ibid., 20–21.

Chapter 8

1. *Illinois Journal* (Springfield), 4 August 1865.

2. *New York Clipper*, 12 May, 29 December 1866; Slout, *Olympians of the Sawdust Circle*, 256.

3. *New York Clipper,* 19 January 1867.

4. Ibid., 14 December 1869.

5. *Bainbridge (Ga.) Argus,* 16 January 1869.

6. *New York Clipper,* 25 March 1865.

7. Ibid., 8 June 1867.

8. Ibid., 25 March 1865.

9. McCaddon Collection of the Barnum and Bailey Circus, Box 17. Used by permission of Princeton University, Firestone Library (hereafter referred to as McCaddon Collection).

10. Robinson, *Old Wagon Show Days,* 222.

11. *Mobile (Ala.) Daily Advertiser & Register,* 22 December 1867.

12. Slout, *Olympians of the Sawdust Circle,* 331. Wilson's real name was John R. McDonough.

13. Grant's Pass, now part of the Intracoastal Waterway, is located at the southwest entrance to Mobile Bay.

14. *New York Clipper,* 17 January 1868.

15. Slout, *Olympians of the Sawdust Circle,* 164.

16. *Keokuk (Iowa) Daily Gate City,* 7 June 1868; *Vincennes (Ind.) Weekly Western Sun,* 5 September 1868.

17. *Louisville Daily Democrat,* 18 September 1868.

18. *Vincennes (Ind.) Weekly Western Sun,* 5 September 1868. This part of the advertisement ran in almost every subsequent ad for the Lake circus throughout 1868 and 1869.

19. The 1868 and 1869 route sheets were compiled based on information from Stuart Thayer.

20. *Montgomery (Ala.) Daily Advertiser,* 14 December 1868. Subsequent newspaper editors and advertisements printed the name of her horse, Apollo, as "Appello," "Appollo," and "Alleppo."

21. *Daily Sun* (Columbus, Ga.), 5 January 1869.

22. Ibid., 3 and 5 January 1869; *Columbus (Ga.) Daily Enquirer,* 24–31 December 1868.

23. Slout, *Olympians of the Sawdust Circle,* 11, 199.

24. *Daily Sun* (Columbus, Ga.), 5 January 1869.

25. *Cartersville (Ga.) Express,* 15, 22, 28 April 1869.

26. *Weekly Tribune* (Jefferson City, Mo.), 28 July 1869.

27. *Central Georgian* (Sandersville, Ga.), 3 March 1869.

28. Ibid.

29. *Daily Sun* (Columbus, Ga.), 5 January 1869.

30. *Bainbridge (Ga.) Argus,* 23 January 1869.

31. *Daily Chronicle & Sentinel* (Augusta, Ga.), 26 February, 2–5 March 1869.

32. *Burlington (Iowa) Daily Hawkeye,* 6 June 1868.

33. *Edwards' Directory*, 412. C. L. Hoblitzelle and George Cousland had a saddlery and harness shop at 414 North Fourth Street.

34. *Missouri Republican* (St. Louis), 20 May 1869.

35. McCaddon Collection, Box 35.

36. *Cheyenne Daily Sun*, 29 June 1877.

37. *Weekly Ledger* (Pleasant Hill, Mo.), 6 August 1869.

38. *Marietta (Ga.) Daily Journal*, 23 April 1869.

39. *Spring River Fountain* (Mt. Vernon, Mo.), 26 August 1869.

40. For the sake of clarity, the most consistent spelling of his surname is used.

41. Articles about Lake's murder were reprinted in many newspapers, including the *Spring River Fountain* (Mt. Vernon, Mo.), 26 August 1869; *Springfield (Mo.) Leader*, 26 August 1869; *Sedalia (Mo.) Weekly Bazoo*, 31 August 1869; and the *New York Clipper*, 4 September 1869.

42. *Spring River Fountain* (Mt. Vernon, Mo.), 26 August 1869; *Springfield (Mo.) Leader*, 26 August 1869; *Sedalia (Mo.) Weekly Bazoo*, 31 August 1869; *New York Clipper*, 4 September 1869.

43. *Sedalia (Mo.) Weekly Bazoo*, 31 August 1869. "A Mr. Thompson" is not identified — he was likely a citizen of Granby and a witness to the initial encounter between Killian and Bill Lake.

44. Ibid.

45. *New York Clipper*, 4 September 1869.

46. *New York Sun*, 27 February 1874.

47. Avery and Shoemaker, *Messages and Proclamations*, 4:513–14.

48. *Daily Atchison (Kans.) Patriot*, 4 September 1869. The newspaper reprinted an article from the *Springfield (Mo.) Leader*, which reported that Killian "put in most of his time last summer in interupting [*sic*] and insulting Democratic meetings."

49. *New York Clipper*, 4 September 1869. On September 4, 1869, the *Daily Atchison (Kans.) Patriot* described the game of cards in which Killian's eye was nearly shot out. The bullet entered the outer corner of Killian's right eye and traveled into the back of his neck, where it lodged. His right eyeball became sunken, and he suffered vision loss.

50. McCaddon Collection, Box 17.

51. Ibid.

Chapter 9

1. *Carthage (Mo.) Weekly Banner*, 2 September 1869.

2. Robinson, *Old Wagon Show Days*, 129.

3. *Morgan County Weekly Banner* (Versailles, Mo.), 28 August, 4 September 1869.

4. "Black Friday" (or the Fisk-Gould Scandal) occurred on September 24,

1869. Speculators James Fisk and Jay Gould led a group of financiers and caused a major financial panic when they tried to corner the gold market.

5. *Jefferson (Tex.) Radical*, 2 November 1869.

6. *Carthage (Mo.) Weekly Banner*, 2 September 1869.

7. Ibid.

8. *Sedalia (Mo.) Democrat*, 2 September 1869.

9. Robinson, *Old Wagon Show Days*, 130.

10. *Missouri Republican* (St. Louis), 21 January 1870.

11. *Cincinnati Daily Commercial*, 12 January 1870.

12. Ibid., 14 January 1870.

13. *Memphis Daily Appeal*, 19–20 February 1870.

14. Thomas P. Parkinson Collection, 1825–1939 [1955–95], Center for American History, University of Texas at Austin.

15. McCaddon Collection, Box 35.

16. Ibid.

17. Campbell County (Newport, Ky.) Deed Book, 8, p. 354.

18. *Newark (N.J.) Evening Star*, 7 October 1915.

19. *Billboard*, 7 December 1901, 16.

20. Hamilton County (Cincinnati, Ohio), Probate Court, Guardianship Docket, Vol. 4, p. 493.

21. USC 1870, M593, Roll 453, p. 274, lines 2–6; Slout, *Olympians of the Sawdust Circle*, 176, 218.

22. *Times-Picayune* (New Orleans), 31 December 1870.

23. *Southern Recorder* (Milledgeville, Ga.), 15 February 1871.

24. Slout, *Olympians of the Sawdust Circle*, 206.

25. *New York Clipper*, 14 January 1871.

26. Ibid., 11 March 1871.

27. Ibid., 4 March 1871; Slout, *Olympians of the Sawdust Circle*, 156. Agnes's roster also included George Mankin, a heavy balancer; John Davenport and Lew Ginger, who headlined as clowns; and George Richards, who juggled cannonballs. Additionally, the family of gymnasts known as the Kincade (or Kingcade) Brothers — Edward, George, James, and Frederick — also toured with her troupe. According to Slout, the brothers toured with Van Amburgh in 1871, but they might have changed employers halfway through the season.

28. Slout, *Olympians of the Sawdust Circle*, 267.

29. Possibly Orrin M. Hollis, the brother-in-law of John Davenport, Sr., a veteran clown in Agnes's troupe.

30. *Daily Nonpareil* (Council Bluffs, Iowa), 9 May 1871.

31. Slout, "En Route to the Great Eastern," 50, no. 3, 32.

32. Parkinson, "Circus Balloon Ascensions."

33. Scamehorn, *Balloons to Jets*, 6–8.

34. Parkinson, "Circus Balloon Ascensions."

35. Ibid.; *Chicago Tribune*, 26 February 1961.
36. *Nebraska City News*, 6 May 1871.
37. Ibid.
38. *Daily Quincy (Ill.) Herald*, 5 May 1871.
39. *The Nationalist* (Manhattan, Kans.), 4 August 1871.
40. *Daily Nonpareil* (Council Bluffs, Iowa), 16 May 1871.
41. *Saline County (Kans.) Journal*, 3 August 1871.
42. *New York Clipper*, 6 May 1871.
43. Ibid., 21 May 1871; *Nebraska City News*, 20 May 1871.
44. *New York Clipper*, 21 May 1871.

Chapter 10

1. Davis, *The Circus Age*, 19.
2. Dahlinger, "Development of the Railroad Circus," 27, no. 6, 7.
3. Ibid., 8.
4. Ibid., 7.
5. Ibid, 8.
6. Davis, *The Circus Age*, 51.
7. Dahlinger, "Development of the Railroad Circus," 28, no. 1, 17.
8. Ibid., 27, no. 6, 9.
9. Ibid.
10. Davis, *The Circus Age*, 22. See also pp. 11–12, 19–25, 77–79.
11. Ibid., 28, no. 1, 16.
12. *New York Clipper*, 27 May 1871.
13. *Junction City (Kans.) Union*, 12 August 1871.
14. *Fort Dodge (Iowa) Times*, 1 June 1871.
15. *Nebraska City (Neb.) News*, 6 May 1871.
16. *Neosho (Mo.) Times*, 24 August 1871.
17. Ibid., 29 August 1871.
18. *Cheyenne Daily Leader*, 16 June 1871.
19. *New York Clipper*, 27 May 1871.
20. *Colorado Miner* (Georgetown, Colo.), 19 and 22 June 1871.
21. *Cheyenne Daily Leader*, 24 July 1871.
22. Ibid.
23. *Saline County (Kans.) Journal*, 3 August 1871.
24. Ibid.
25. Ibid., 26 July 1871.
26. *Laramie Daily Sentinel* (Colorado), 23 June 1871.
27. *Salt Lake Desert News*, 1 July 1871.
28. Ibid.
29. *Salt Lake Tribune*, 4 July 1871.

30. Davis, *The Circus Age*, 83.

31. Dr. Mary Edwards Walker (1832–1919) was the first female recipient of the Medal of Honor (awarded in 1865), in recognition of her work as a surgeon during the Civil War.

32. *Topeka Daily Commercial*, 1 August 1871.

33. *Saline County (Kans.) Journal*, 27 July 1871.

34. *Nebraska City (Neb.) News*, 6 May 1871.

35. *Laramie Daily Sentinel* (Colorado), 23 June 1871.

36. Rosa, *They Called Him Wild Bill*, 180, 205.

37. Ibid., 181.

38. King, *Circus World of Willie Sells*, 157, 159; *Topeka State Journal*, 9 October 1876. The Tefft House was designed and built as a luxurious oasis by Dr. Erasmus Tefft in 1859, when Topeka was barely settled. In 1881 Allen Sells of the Sells Brothers' Circus purchased, renamed, and refurbished the hotel. It was eventually razed in 1926.

39. Rosa, *Man and Myth*, 15. The Hickok family had deep roots in America, dating back to Puritan New England, where the family had emigrated in the mid-seventeenth century.

40. Ibid., 31.

41. Wilstach, "Time Widens."

42. Rosa, *Man and Myth*, 3, 31.

43. Warren, *Buffalo Bill's America*, 63.

44. Ibid.

45. Ibid.

46. Ibid., 65.

47. Ibid., 73.

48. Ibid.

49. Rosa, *Man and Myth*, 77.

50. Ibid.

51. Originally called Hays City, the town is now known simply as Hays and will be referred to as such in subsequent references for clarity.

52. O'Connor, *Wild Bill Hickok*, 173.

53. See the appendix.

54. Many sources have historically suggested Hays City as the town in which Agnes Lake and Wild Bill first met, but since no evidence has placed Agnes in Hays City, the city of Abilene is given in this book whenever a location is suggested.

55. Buel, *Heroes of the Plains*, 151–52.

56. Watson, "Forgotten Frontier Romance"; Buel, *Heroes of the Plains*, 152.

57. Watson, "Forgotten Frontier Romance"; Wilstach, *The Plainsman*, 183.

58. Watson, "Forgotten Frontier Romance"; Buel, *Heroes of the Plains*, 152.

59. Watson, "Forgotten Frontier Romance"; Buel, *Heroes of the Plains*, 152.

60. Wilstach, *The Plainsman*, 247.

61. Ibid., 250.

62. Ibid.

63. Garst and Garst, *Wild Bill Hickok*, 154, 163.

64. Ibid., 163.

65. Ibid.

66. Ibid.

67. *New York Clipper*, 28 February, 7 March 1874.

68. Garst and Garst, *Wild Bill Hickok*, 163.

69. Ibid.

70. Ibid., 164.

71. Ibid.

72. Charles Gross to J. B. Edwards, June 15, 1925, J. B. Edwards Collection, 1872–1935, Kansas State Historical Society (hereafter cited as Edwards Collection); Rosa, *They Called Him Wild Bill*, 236-37. Edwards's memoirs were first published in the newspapers in 1896 and later in a book, *Early Days in Abilene*, in 1940.

73. Sturtevant, *White Tops*, 15; Gard, *The Chisholm Trail*, 176.

74. Gross to Edwards, June 15, 1925, Edwards Collection; Rosa, *They Called Him Wild Bill*, 236–37.

75. Gross to Edwards, June 15, 1925, Edwards Collection; Rosa, *They Called Him Wild Bill*, 236–37.

76. Gross to Edwards, June 15, 1925, Edwards Collection; Rosa, *They Called Him Wild Bill*, 237.

77. Secrest, "Bill Hickok's Girl," 30.

78. Ibid.

79. O'Connor, *Wild Bill Hickok*, 172; Rosa, *They Called Him Wild Bill*, 191.

80. Secrest, "Bill Hickok's Girl," 30.

81. O'Connor, *Wild Bill Hickok*, 170.

82. Ibid., 174.

83. Ibid., 173.

84. Gross to Edwards, June 15, 1925, Edwards Collection; Rosa, *They Called Him Wild Bill*, 236–37.

Chapter 11

1. Slout, "En Route with the Great Eastern," 50, no. 2, 28.

2. This is not to be confused with the Great Eastern Circus founded in 1881 by John H. Gray and Charles H.C. Wheeler.

3. Ames died in 1870. His estate held an auction in November in Cincinnati and sold a "performing den of lions," the elephants Bismarck and Pet, and the remaining occupants of the menagerie to Andrew Haight's circus.

4. Slout, "En Route to the Great Eastern," 50, no. 5, 18. According to Slout, Dan Carpenter "soon disappeared from the management rosters," and his whereabouts after the first season are unknown.

5. Ibid., no. 2, 28.

6. *New York Clipper*, 23 March 1872.

7. Ibid.; Slout, *Olympians of the Sawdust Circle*, 119.

8. Jacob Haight, Andrew's brother, was hired as the show's treasurer.

9. *New York Clipper*, 23 March, 29 June 1872; Slout, *Olympians of the Sawdust Circle*, 75–76, 87–88, 269; Slout, "En Route with the Great Eastern," 50, no. 3, 32. William W. Durand (1837–86) (general agent), A. R. Scott (advertising agent), and "W. Scott" and Charles Whitney (program agents) were additional managerial staff.

10. *New York Clipper*, 23 March 1872; Slout, *Olympians of the Sawdust Circle*, 44–45.

11. *New York Clipper*, 23 March 1872; Slout, *Olympians of the Sawdust Circle*, 112, 153–54 (quote on 154), 298, 319. Fred Sylvester (1835–87), Adolph "Chili" Gonzales (1850–1901), and Thomas V. Watson were additional equestrian performers.

12. *New York Clipper*, 23 March 1872; Slout, *Olympians of the Sawdust Circle*, 6, 102, 205–206, 262, 290, 308, 328, 338. Jerome Tuttle, Jean Zacco, Charles Lee Fowler, Billy Andrews (1840–95), John Wilcock, and Al Miaco were additional tumblers.

13. *New York Clipper*, 23 March 1872; Slout, *Olympians of the Sawdust Circle*, 92, 160, 173, 245.

14. *New York Clipper*, 18 May 1872.

15. Slout, "En Route with the Great Eastern," 50, no. 5, 19.

16. *New York Clipper*, 23 November 1872.

17. *Miami County Sentinel* (Logansport, Ind.), 1 August 1872.

18. Ibid., 25 July 1872.

19. Ibid.

20. *Albany (Ga.) News*, 20 September 1872.

21. Ibid.

22. *New York Clipper*, 7 September 1872.

23. *Washington (D.C.) Star*, 19 and 24 August 1872.

24. *New York Clipper*, 31 August 1872.

25. *Albany (Ga.) News*, 20 September 1872.

26. Ibid.

27. *Mobile (Ala.) Daily Register*, 8 January 1874.

28. *New York Clipper*, 9 November 1872.

29. *Hawkinsville (Ga.) Dispatch*, 19 September 1872.

30. *St. Louis Democrat*, 26 July 1872; Slout, "En Route with the Great Eastern," 50, no. 5, 22.

31. Slout, "En Route with the Great Eastern," 50, no. 5, 18–19.

32. Ibid, 20.

33. *New York Clipper*, 7 December 1872.

34. Slout, "En Route with the Great Eastern," 50, no. 5, 25.

35. *Indianapolis Daily News*, 24 August 1907.

36. *New York Clipper*, 26 April 1873.

37. *Daily Morning Democrat* (Grand Rapids, Mich.), 11 May 1873.

38. *Battle Creek (Mich.) Daily Journal*, 9 May 1873.

39. Ibid.

40. "Delicious" quote in *Broome Republican* (Binghamton, N.Y.), 18 June 1873; steam piano quote in *Camden (N.J.) Democrat*, 12 July 1873.

41. Conover, "The Calliope," 4.

42. Ibid.

43. Slout, "En Route with the Great Eastern," 50, no. 5, 18.

44. *Niles (Mich.) Democrat*, 17 May 1873.

45. *New York Clipper*, 19 April 1873.

46. *Broome Republican* (Binghamton, N.Y.), 18 June 1873.

47. *New York Clipper*, 10 May 1873.

48. Ibid., 19 April 1873; *The Mirror* (Leesburg, Va.), 10 September 1873. Other animals in the menagerie included zebras, moose, kangaroos, bears, tigers, hyenas, and antelope.

49. Chindahl, *History of the Circus*, 197.

50. Ibid.

51. Harriet Ritvo, "The Order of Nature," in Hoage and Deiss, *New World, New Animals*, 44; Richard W. Flint, "American Showmen," in Hoage and Deiss, *New World, New Animals*, 97.

52. *Camden (N.J.) Democrat*, 12 July 1873.

53. *Scranton (Pa.) Daily Times*, 6 August 1873.

54. *Valley Spirit* (Chambersburg, Pa.), 2 September 1873.

55. *New York Clipper*, 21 June 1873.

56. *Carlisle (Pa.) Herald*, 21 August 1873.

57. *New York Clipper*, 26 April 1873. According to the *Clipper*, George M. Kelley, the champion vaulter, had retired from show business and opened a restaurant in Binghamton, New York.

58. Slout, *Olympians of the Sawdust Circle*, 21–22; *New York Clipper*, 17 January 1874.

59. *New York Clipper*, 29 November 1873.

60. *Cincinnati Daily Gazette*, 25 October 1871.

61. Slout, *Olympians of the Sawdust Circle*, 5. According to Slout, Clark T. Ames was "shot in the groin and killed" by "drunken rowdies trying to force their way into a matinee" during the performance in Dawson, Georgia.

62. *Cheyenne (Wyo.) Daily Sun*, 29 June 1877.

63. Conklin, *Ways of the Circus*, 55.

64. Thayer, *The Performers*, 129.

65. Ibid., 130.

66. Ibid., 132.

67. Davis, *The Circus Age*, 101.

68. Ibid., 160–61.

69. Ibid., 101, 160–61.

70. Ibid., 160–61.

71. Ibid., 102.

72. Conklin, *Ways of the Circus*, 47.

73. Ibid.

74. Ibid., 46.

75. *New York Clipper*, 22 March 1873.

76. Ibid.; McCaddon Collection, Box 17.

77. *Daily Express* (Lancaster, Pa.), 26 August 1873.

78. Ibid.

79. Ibid.

80. *Daily Picayune* (New Orleans), 14 January 1874.

81. *New York Clipper*, 24 January 1874.

82. *Evening News* (Indianapolis), 9 April 1873.

83. *New York Clipper*, 9 August 1873.

84. *Shamokin Herald*, 21 August 1873.

85. *Daily True American* (Trenton, N.J.), 19 July 1873.

86. *Paterson (N.J.) Daily Press*, 5 July 1873.

87. *Daily Star Gazette* (Trenton, N.J.), 19 July 1873.

88. *Newark (N.J.) Daily Journal*, 5 July 1873.

89. *Elizabeth (N.J.) Daily Monitor*, 10 July 1873.

90. *Independent Phoenix* (Phoenixville, Pa.), 23 August 1873.

91. *Reading (Pa.) Times Dispatch*, 25 August 1873.

92. *Daily Patriot* (Harrisburg, Pa.), 29 August 1873.

93. *Evening Star* (Washington, D.C.), 13 September 1873.

94. *Daily Patriot* (Harrisburg, Pa.), 29 August 1873.

95. *Carlisle (Pa.) Herald*, 21 August 1873.

96. *New York Clipper*, 20 September 1873.

97. *Richmond Daily Dispatch*, 25 September 1873.

98. Ibid.

99. John Robinson Circus Company Records, 1856–1963, Mss 849, Cincinnati Museum Center; *The Observer* (Jersey City, N.J.), 23 August 1907.

100. *Evening Star* (Washington, D.C.), 13 September 1873.

101. Warren, *Buffalo Bill's America*, 186.

102. Ibid.

103. Ibid.

104. Rosa, *They Called Him Wild Bill*, 253.

105. Rosa and May, *Buffalo Bill*, 51.

106. Ibid.; Warren, *Buffalo Bill's America*, 185; Yost, *Buffalo Bill*, 74.

107. Rosa, *They Called Him Wild Bill*, 260.

108. *Richmond Daily Dispatch*, 25 September 1873.

109. Noel Martin, "Early Printing and Publishing in Cincinnati," in Cornell, *Art as Image*, 19.

110. Virginius C. Hall, appendix A, "Cincinnati Engravers, 1825–1860," in Cornell, *Art as Image*, 191–95.

111. Martin, "Early Printing and Publishing in Cincinnati," 21.

112. Ibid.

113. Ronald Decker, "Promotional Playing Cards: From Sultans to Salesmen, 1300–1900," in Cornell, *Art as Image*, 117–18; www.usplayingcard.com/history.html.

114. See Mersman, *The Whiskey Merchant*, for a detailed examination of Joseph Mersman's entrepreneurship in St. Louis.

115. *New York Clipper*, 14 February 1874.

Chapter 12

1. *New York Clipper*, 7 March 1874.

2. *New York Sun*, 27 February 1874.

3. *Galveston (Tex.) News*, 22 January 1907.

4. *New York Sun*, 27 February 1874.

5. *Cincinnati Enquirer*, 4 May 1878.

6. Robinson, *Old Wagon Show Days*, 127; *Galveston (Tex.) News*, 22 January 1907; *Indianapolis Daily News*, 23 August 1907.

7. *New York Clipper*, 7 March 1874.

8. Ibid., 2 May 1874.

9. Ibid.

10. Nelson, *The Écuýere*, 35.

11. Ibid., 21.

12. Thayer, *The Performers*, 110.

13. Stuart Thayer, e-mail message to Bowers, January 2, 2007.

14. Thayer, *Annals of the American Circus*, 471–72.

15. Thayer, *The Performers*, 111.

16. Nelson, *The Écuýere*, 29.

17. Ibid.

18. Ibid., 29–30.

19. Thayer, *The Performers*, 109–10.

20. Ibid.

21. Ibid.

22. Nelson, *The Écuýere*, 29–31.

23. *Pittsburgh Daily Gazette*, 20 April 1874.

24. Slout, *Olympians of the Sawdust Circle*, 257.

25. *New York Clipper*, 14 March 1874. Other members of the administrative staff included James Quinton (assistant treasurer), Augustus Rosston, Samuel H. Joseph, Spencer Forbes (chief billposter), and Jeff Posey (master of horses).

26. Ibid., 18 April 1874; *Louisville Courier-Journal*, 22 May 1874.

27. *New York Clipper*, 18 April 1874.

28. Ibid., 4 April 1874.

29. Ibid., 18 April 1874. The *Clipper* mistakenly typed "Alice Lake" instead of Emma Lake.

30. *Pittsburgh Daily Gazette*, 23 April 1874.

31. *New York Clipper*, 15 August 1874.

32. Ibid., 26 June 1875.

33. Slout, *Olympians of the Sawdust Circle*, 289.

34. *Kokomo (Ind.) Democrat*, 8 July 1875.

35. *Porter County Vidette* (Valparaiso, Ind.), 22 July 1875.

36. *Weekly Northern Indianaian* (Warsaw, Ind.), 22 July 1875.

37. *Memphis Daily Appeal*, 14 November 1875.

38. Ibid., 17 November 1875.

39. Robinson, *Old Wagon Show Days*, 113.

40. Ibid.

41. Images and photographs are not paginated in his memoirs, but this particular image appears just after page 116.

42. York County Heritage Trust, Pennsylvania.

43. http://www.peabodymemphis.com. Hotel rooms cost $3–$4 a day with meals; there were additional charges for fire or gas lighting.

44. *Memphis Daily Appeal*, 18 November 1875.

45. *New York Clipper*, 27 November 1875.

46. *Memphis Daily Appeal*, 19 November 1875.

47. *New York Clipper*, 26 February 1876.

48. Ibid.

49. Ibid., 15 April 1876. The paper reported featured acts and performers on 22 April 1876.

50. *Cheyenne Daily Sun*, 29 June 1877.

51. Slout, *Olympians of the Sawdust Circle*, 321. She was also possibly known as "M'lle Minnetta," the iron-jawed lady.

52. Minnie Wilkinson Wells and Sylvester Lane Moyer Marriage Certificate, State of Colorado, Marriage Record Report, Book 65, p. 239, Division of Vital Statistics, Department of Health, Marriages 1900–39, Roll 67. The actual date of the couple's marriage is unknown; their marriage record states June 16, while their subsequent divorce papers list June 20.

53. O'Connor, *Wild Bill Hickok*, 233.

54. Ibid.

55. Ibid.

56. Ibid.

57. Wilstach, *The Plainsman*, 251.

58. Garst and Garst, *Wild Bill Hickok*, 168.

59. William Connelley Collection, Box 4, Letterbook 1, Western History Collection, Denver Public Library.

60. Ibid.

61. *Cheyenne Daily Leader*, 7 March 1876.

62. *Cheyenne Daily Sun*, 8 March 1876; Rosa, *They Called Him Wild Bill*, 238.

63. *Omaha (Neb.) Daily Bee*, 31 March 1876; Rosa, *They Called Him Wild Bill*, 238.

64. Pickering, *Superstitions*, 280–81.

65. Mersman, *The Whiskey Merchant's Diary*, 291–92.

66. *Omaha (Neb.) Daily Bee*, 16 August 1876; Rosa, *They Called Him Wild Bill*, 281.

67. Buel, *Heroes of the Plains*, 187.

68. Agnes Lake Hickok to Polly and Celinda Hickok, April 26, 1876, Agnes Lake Letters, KSHS.

69. Rosa, *They Called Him Wild Bill*, 280–81.

70. Ibid.

71. Howard Hickok quoted in ibid., 281.

72. Ibid., 290.

73. Rosa, *They Called Him Wild Bill*, 279–80.

74. *Deadwood: The Myth, Legend, and Reality*, DVD, directed by Wayne Paananen (Historical Footprints, 2005).

75. The transcription is from the Greg Martin Auctions catalog published prior to the sale of documents from the Estate of Celinda Hickok in 2003. Punctuation has been added for clarity, but original spelling has been retained.

76. Rosa, *They Called Him Wild Bill*, 286.

77. McLaird, *Calamity Jane*, 54, 57.

78. Rosa, *They Called Him Wild Bill*, 285.

79. Rosa, *Man and Myth*, 192.

80. *Deadwood (S.Dak.) Telegram*, 13 November 1922; Wilstach, *The Plainsman*, 273–74.

81. *Cheyenne Daily Leader*, 26 August 1876; Rosa, *They Called Him Wild Bill*, 290, 295. Specifically, he said to Charley Utter, "Charley, I feel this is going to be my last camp, and I won't leave it alive" (Rosa, p. 295).

82. Rosa, *They Called Him Wild Bill*, 297.

83. Ibid., 298.

84. Ibid., 299; *Chicago Inter-Ocean*, 17 August, 1876.

85. Rosa, *They Called Him Wild Bill*, 298.

86. Ibid., 300.

87. Ibid., 301.

88. For more on the trials of Jack McCall, see ibid., 314–17, 323–29; Turner, "The Shooting of Wild Bill"; Rosa, *Jack McCall, Assassin*; Rosa, *Man and Myth*, 199–201.

89. Rosa, *They Called Him Wild Bill*, 306.

90. Ibid., 242–43; Buel, *Heroes of the Plains*, 188.

91. Sale of property from Mary Agnes Hickok to B. R. Vandergrift, July 17, 1876, Campbell County (Ky.) Deed Book 19, p. 462.

92. Agnes Lake Hickok to Polly and Celinda Hickok, April 26, 1876, Agnes Lake Letters, KSHS.

93. "Important James B. 'Wild Bill' Hickok Letters, Photography and Documents from the Estate of Celinda Hickok." San Francisco, Greg Martin Auctions, Lot 15, 2003, unpaginated.

94. Agnes misspelled her sister-in-law's name in this letter.

95. Buel, *Heroes of the Plains*, 2–4; quote on p. 3.

96. Ibid.

97. Rosa, *They Called Him Wild Bill*, 288–89n.

98. Joseph G. Rosa, e-mail message to Bowers, March 26, 2007.

99. Agnes Lake Hickok to Polly and Celinda Hickok, August 9, 1876, Agnes Lake Letters, KSHS.

100. Ibid.

101. Agnes Lake Hickok to Polly and Celinda Hickok, November 12, 1876, Agnes Lake Letters, KSHS; Rosa, *They Called Him Wild Bill*, 308.

102. *Virginia (Nev.) Evening Chronicle*, 4 August 1877; Buel, *Heroes of the Plains*, 210–11; Rosa, *They Called Him Wild Bill*, 295–96.

103. Rosa, *Man and Myth*, 257 n.13.

104. Watson, "Forgotten Frontier Romance," *Weston County Gazette* (Upton, Wyo.), 29 August 1929.

105. Rosa, *Man and Myth*, 192.

106. Agnes Lake Hickok to Polly and Celinda Hickok, November 12, 1876, Agnes Lake Letters, KSHS; Rosa, *They Called Him Wild Bill*, 308.

107. Rosa, *Man and Myth*, 200.

108. *Cheyenne Daily Sun*, 29 June 1877. The article also reported on some of Agnes's career highlights, her trip to California the previous year, and Hickok's July 17 letter.

109. *Black Hills (S.Dak.) Daily Times*, 4 September 1877; Turner, *Deadwood City*, 219–21.

110. *Cheyenne Daily Leader*, 28 September 1877; *Cheyenne Daily Sun*, 28 September 1877.

Chapter 13

1. After Emma's tenure with Robinson's (1874–78) and Barnum's (1879–80) circuses ended, she traveled with Barnum, Bailey & Hutchinson's show (1881), John Robinson's (1882), William O'Dale Stevens's Australian Circus (1883), Sheldon Hopkins Barrett's New United Monster Rail Road Show (1884–85), Barnum

(1886), Buffalo Bill's Wild West Show (1887), Sturgis & Donovan's Gran Circo Estrellas Del Nortis (1888–89), and John Robinson's (1891–92).

2. Katie Stokes (daughter of Spencer Q. Stokes), Lizzie Marcellus, a "Miss Holloway," "Miss Smithson," and "Miss Ashly" (or possibly Ashby or Ashley) were also routinely featured equestriennes.

3. Slout, *Olympians of the Sawdust Circle*, 146; *Republican Standard* (New Bedford, Mass.), 16 May 1879.

4. Slout, *Olympians of the Sawdust Circle*, 81–82.

5. *Worcester (Mass.) Evening Gazette*, 15 May 1879.

6. Bernard, "Circusiana."

7. *Cheyenne Daily Leader*, 3 August 1880.

8. *Wyoming Tribune* (Cheyenne), 4 April 1896; State of Colorado, Division of Vital Statistics, Divorce Record Report, Divorces through 1939, Reel 12, Denver Public Library. The Moyers' divorce records show the date of their divorce as May 20, 1884, which means Minnie remarried while still legally wed to Wes.

9. Unidentified newspaper clipping, Private Collection of Agnes Cromack, Florida.

10. *New York Clipper*, 3 February 1883.

11. Ibid., 12 March 1887; Kasper, *Annie Oakley*, 64.

12. Kasper, *Annie Oakley*, 64.

13. *New York Clipper*, 12 March 1887; *Gopsill's 1883 Directory*, 358. Linda Jeal's West End Training Academy was located at 23 Lewis Avenue, near St. Paul's Avenue in Jersey City.

14. Yost, *Buffalo Bill*, 188.

15. Ibid., 189; Warren, *Buffalo Bill's America*, 284, 321; Rosa and May, *Buffalo Bill*, 119.

16. Gallop, *Buffalo Bill's British Wild West*, 84.

17. Ibid., 100.

18. Ibid., 144.

19. Rosa and May, *Buffalo Bill*, 119.

20. Ibid., 116–77; 125; Warren, *Buffalo Bill's America*, 321–24.

21. Warren, *Buffalo Bill's America*, 198. The kings were Christian IX of Denmark (r. 1863–1906), George I of Greece (r. 1863–1913), Leopold II of Belgium (r. 1865–1909), and Albert I of Saxony (r. 1873–1902).

22. *London Times*, 12 May 1887.

23. *New York Clipper*, 20 May 1911.

24. *Jersey City (N.J.) Mirror*, 31 August 1907; Rosa, *They Called Him Wild Bill*, 241.

25. Robinson, *Old Wagon Show Days*, 132.

26. *Passenger Lists of Vessels Arriving at New York*, 1820–97, M237, Roll 520, p. 1, lines 16–18.

27. *New York Clipper*, 19 January 1889.

28. *Cincinnati Enquirer*, 7 August 1888; Private Collection of Agnes Cromack.

29. Slout, *Olympians of the Sawdust Circle*, 254, 256, 258; http://www.springgrove .org/sg/genealogy/stats/31998.tif.pdf; http://www.springgrove.org/sg/genealog y/stats/34495.tif.pdf; http://www.springgrove.org/sg/genealogy/ stats/30529.tif .pdf.

30. *Commercial Gazette* (Cincinnati), undated clipping, Private Collection of Agnes Cromack. While some of Robinson's male grandchildren were listed as beneficiaries, Daisy Robinson would not receive any money from her grandfather unless Gil died before he received the full amount held in trust in his name.

31. Private Collection of Agnes Cromack.

32. Ibid.

33. Ibid.

34. Ibid.

35. Ibid.

36. Ibid.

37. Ibid.

38. *New York Advertiser*, undated clipping, Private Collection of Agnes Cromack.

39. Private Collection of Agnes Cromack.

40. Ibid.

41. McCaddon Collection, Box 32; *New York World*, 15 April 1906.

42. USC 1900, T623 979, p. 122, line 26.

43. *Indianapolis Daily News*, 24 August 1907.

44. The reason for the delay in her burial is not known.

45. *New York Clipper*, 20 May 1911; *Billboard*, 20 May 1911, 24.

46. Mersman, *The Whiskey Merchant's Diary*, 287–88.

47. *New York Clipper*, 20 May 1911.

48. Robinson, *Old Wagon Show Days*, 127.

49. John Robinson Circus Company Records, 1856–1963, Mss 849, Cincinnati Museum Center.

50. Stuart Thayer, e-mail message to Bowers, January 15 and 16, 2007.

51. Warren, *Buffalo Bill's America*, 65.

52. Fisher, "Summer of Terror."

Chapter 14

1. Warren, *Buffalo Bill's America*, 76.

2. *Deadwood Daily Pioneer-Times*, 8 August 1903; McLaird, *Calamity Jane*, 217.

3. Rosa refrained from including any fictitious dialogue and examined the most authentic sources available (albeit few in number): contemporaneous newspapers, the correspondence between Charles Gross and J. B. Edwards, and the 1876 letters exchanged between Agnes and Polly and Celinda Hickok. Most important, Rosa did not portray Agnes unfairly.

4. O'Connor, *Wild Bill Hickok*, 262.

5. McLaird, *Calamity Jane*, 215.

6. McLaird included a photograph of the pair in costume in his biography (ibid.).

7. Unfortunately, inquiries to both the William S. Hart Ranch and Museum in Newhall, California, and several film archives from California to New York failed to yield a copy of the screenplay or the film.

8. Additionally, DeMille used Edmund Pearson's dime novels, Frank Leslie's newspapers between 1874 and 1875, Estelline Bennett's *Old Deadwood Days*, and Wilbert Edwin Eisele's *The Real Wild Bill Hickok*. Cecil B. DeMille, *The Plainsman*: List of Books Used in Research, Cecil B. DeMille Collection, L. Tom Perry Special Collections, Harold B. Lee Library, Brigham Young University, Provo, Utah (hereafter referred to as the DeMille Collection).

9. Birchard, *DeMille's Hollywood*, 295.

10. Cary, *Hollywood Posse*, 222.

11. Photocopy of *Wyoming Stockman-Farmer* (Cheyenne), undated clipping from March 1937, Private Collection of the authors.

12. Birchard, *DeMille's Hollywood*, 294–95.

13. Howard L. Hickok to Cecil B. DeMille, August 26, 1936, DeMille Collection.

14. Ibid.

15. Cecil B. DeMille to Howard L. Hickok, September 28, 1936, DeMille Collection.

16. Ibid.

17. Agnes Robinson Reed to Cecil B. DeMille, November 13, 1936, DeMille Collection.

18. Bertha Rath Meyers to Cecil B. DeMille, April 29, 1936, DeMille Collection.

19. Gladys Rosson to Bertha Rath Meyers, May 28, 1936, DeMille Collection.

20. Anderson quoted in Rosa, *They Called Him Wild Bill*, 287.

21. Secrest, "Bill Hickok's Girl," 68.

22. Peirce quoted in Wilstach, *The Plainsman*, 256.

23. McLaird, *Calamity Jane*, 238–39.

24. Rosa, *They Called Him Wild Bill*, 230. This document has appeared in several versions, and the date sometimes fluctuates.

25. Ibid., 232; Wright, "The Real Calamity Jane."

26. McLaird, *Calamity Jane*, 240–41; Cynthia Rosinski, e-mail message to Bowers, April 13, 2007. The Hickok family members who welcomed McCormick were distant cousins of Wild Bill.

27. McLaird, *Calamity Jane*, 250.

28. Ibid., 242.

29. Ibid., 248.

30. Ibid., 244.

31. Ibid.

32. Clairmonte, "Double Nature," 21–22.

33. Ibid., 22–23. Clairmonte intimated that Calamity realized Hickok's "main affections turned toward the men who admired him," especially "to the curly-haired Colorado Charley," who, when Hickok was murdered, "held a big funeral as a widow might have done."

34. Quoted in McLaird, *Calamity Jane*, 251.

35. Ibid., 250.

36. Ibid.; Rosa, *Man and Myth*, 11.

37. McLaird, *Calamity Jane*, 250.

38. Ibid., 252; McLaird, "Myth and Reality," 30; Sollid, *Calamity Jane*, xvii.

39. "The Stella Foote Collection of Western Memorabilia: Treasures of the West," Cody, Wyoming, Brian Lebel's 15th Cody Old West Show & Auction, Lot 263, 2004.

40. Quoted in Drago, "Debunking Outlaws," 3.

41. Quoted in McLaird, *Calamity Jane*, 269.

42. McLaird, "Myth and Reality," 31.

Epilogue

1. Rosa, *They Called Him Wild Bill*, 234.

2. Thayer, *The Performers*, 32.

Bibliography

Library of Congress (LOC), Washington, D.C.

American Memory Homepage (*http://memory.loc.gov/ammem*) Culture and Folk
  Life (Dance) Collection, Video Directory
Prints and Photographs Collection

National Archives (NA), Washington, D.C.
Microfilm Publications

RG 29, Records of the Bureau of the Census
  M704, 1840 Census (USC 1840), Roll 399
  M432, 1850 Census (USC 1850), Roll 417
  M653, 1860 Census (USC 1860), Roll 976
  M593, 1870 Census (USC 1870), Roll 453
  T9, 1880 Census (USC 1880), Rolls 237, 722, 1025, 1329
  T623, 1900 Census (USC 1900), Rolls 894, 1339
  T624, 1910 Census (USC 1910), Rolls 975, 979
RG 36, Records of the United States Customs Service, 1820–ca. 1891
  M237, *Passenger Lists of Vessels Arriving at New York, 1820–97*, Roll 520
  M255, *Passenger Lists of Vessels Arriving at Baltimore, 1820–91*, Roll 3
  M596, *Quarterly Abstracts of Passenger Lists of Vessels Arriving at Baltimore, 1820–69*,
    Rolls 2, 4

Textual Records

RG 49, Bureau of Land Management
    Government Land Office, Lima, Ohio, Land Case Files

Unpublished Primary Records

California
    San Diego Probate Court
        Probate Records
Colorado
    Denver Public Library, Division of Vital Statistics
        Department of Health, Marriages 1900–39, Roll 67
        Divorce Record Report, Divorces through 1939, Reel 12
    Denver Public Library, Western History Collection
        William Connelley Collection
Connecticut
    Connecticut State Library (Hartford)
        Photographs
Florida
    Private Collection of Agnes Cromack
Germany
    Staatsarchiv Oldenburg
        Census Reports
        Court Records
        Tax Records
    Staatsarchiv Osnabrück
        Notary Documents of Justus Graff
Illinois
    Illinois State University, Milner Library (Normal)
        Circus Collection
    Private Collection of Bernice Seaverns Berth
Indiana
    Private Collection of Leif E. Nulsen
Kansas
    Kansas State Historical Society (Topeka)
        J. B. Edwards Collection, 1872–1935
        Agnes Lake Hickok Letters
        Photograph Collection
    Topeka and Shawnee County Public Library (Topeka)
        Special Collections

Kentucky
   Campbell County Courthouse (Newport)
      Deed Records
   Filson Club Historical Society (Louisville)
      Vertical Files
   Jim Beam Distillery (Clermont)
      Interview with Jerry Dalton, Master Distiller
   Kenton County Courthouse (Covington)
      Deed Records
      Marriage Records
   Kenton County Courthouse (Independence)
      Deed Records
      Marriage Records
   Kentucky Department for Libraries and Archives (Frankfort)
      Deed Records
      Marriage Records
Louisiana
   Jefferson Parish Archives (Jefferson)
      Marriage Records
Massachusetts
   American Antiquarian Society (Worcester)
      Handbill Collection
   Harvard University, Houghton Library
      Theatre Collection
Missouri
   City of St. Louis Court Archives
      Circuit Court Records
   City of St. Louis Department of Health
      Birth Records
   Missouri Historical Society (St. Louis)
      Business Letterheads Collection
      Joseph J. Mersman Diary, 1847–64
      Joseph Nuelsen's Tagebuch, 1833–39
      Theater Programs Collection
   Private collection of William E. Giraldin
   St. Louis Civil Courts Building
      Circuit Court Record Books
   St. Louis City Hall
      Deed Records
      Marriage Records
      Real Estate Tax Records

New Jersey
    Atlantic County Courthouse (Mays Landing)
        Deed Records
    State Bureau of Vital Statistics and Registration (Trenton)
        Birth Records
        Death Records
        Marriage Records
    Princeton University, Firestone Library
        McCaddon Collection of the Barnum & Bailey Circus
New York
    The New-York Historical Society (New York)
        Print Collection
    Somers Historical Society (Somers)
        Broadside Collection
        Photograph Collection
Ohio
    Archives, St. Augustine Parish (Minster)
        Transcriptions by Rita and David Hoying
    Auglaize County Courthouse (Wapakoneta)
        Deed Records
        Probate Records
    Cincinnati Museum Center, Cincinnati Historical Society Library
        John Robinson Circus Company Records, 1856–1963
    Hamilton County Courthouse (Cincinnati)
        Court Records
        Deed Records
    Hamilton County Government, William Howard Taft Center (Cincinnati)
        Marriage Records
        Probate Records
        Register of Ministers' Licenses
        Wills
    Historical Archives of the Chancery, Roman Catholic Archdiocese of Cincinnati
        Baptism Records
        Death Records
        Marriage Records
    Mercer County Courthouse (Celina)
        Deed Records
    Miami County Courthouse (Troy)
        Deed Records
    Montgomery County Courthouse (Dayton)
        Deed Records
    Pfening Archives (Columbus)

Photographs
The Public Library of Cincinnati and Hamilton County (Cincinnati)
Photographs
Shelby County Courthouse (Sidney)
Deed Records
Spring Grove Cemetery (Cincinnati)
Interment Records
Walnut Hills Cemetery (Cincinnati)
Interment Records
Pennsylvania
York County Heritage Trust (York)
James W. Shettle Collection of Photographs
Texas
Hertzberg Circus Collection (San Antonio)
University of Texas (Austin), Center for American History
Thomas P. Parkinson Collection
Utah
Brigham Young University (Provo), Harold B. Lee Library
Cecil B. DeMille Collection, within the L. Tom Perry Special Collections
Family History Library (Salt Lake City)
Katholische Kirche, Damme (AG Vechta), Germany
Kirchenbuch, 1650–1875, Microfilms 909909–909913
Katholische Kirche, Nörten (Kr. Northeim), Germany
Kirchenbuch, 1645–1886, Microfilms 1258473–1258475
Holy Ghost Evangelical Protestant Church, St. Louis, Missouri
Church Records, 1833–1961, Microfilms 1433231–1433236 and 1503026–1503029
Wisconsin
Circus World Museum and Library (Baraboo)
Manuscripts
Posters
Wyoming
Buffalo Bill Cody Historical Center (Cody)
Manuscripts
Laramie County Clerk's Office (Cheyenne)
Marriage Records
Wyoming State Archives (Cheyenne)
Photograph Collection, James Butler Hickok Biographical File

Books, Articles, and Auction Catalogs

Amidon, C. H. "Stalking the Apollonicon." *Billboard* 20, no. 2 (March–April 1976): 15–18.

Atkins, Bernadette Loeffel. *Widow's Weeds and Weeping Veils: Mourning Rituals in 19th Century America*. Gettysburg, Pa.: B. L. Atkins, 2002.

Auf Auswandererseglern: Berichte von Zwischendecks und ajütenpassagieren, no. 5. Bremerhaven, Ger.: Führer des Deutschen Schiffahrtsmuseums, 1976.

Auswanderung Bremen, USA: die Ausstellung Auswanderung Bremen-USA entstand in Zusammenarbeit zwishcen die Staatsarchiv Bremen und die Deutsches Schiffartsmuseum Bremerhaven, no. 4. Bremerhaven, Ger: Führer des Deutschen Schiffahrtsmuseums, 1976.

Avery, Grace G., and Floyd C. Shoemaker, eds. *The Messages and Proclamations of the Governors of Missouri*, vol. 4. Columbia: State Historical Society of Missouri, 1924.

Bade, Klaus J., Jürgen Kessel, Hannelore Oberpenning, and Anton Schindling. *Damme: Eine Stadt in ihrer Geshichte*. Sigmaringen, Ger.: Jan Thorbecke Verlag GmbH, 1993.

Bartlett, Vernon. *The Past of Pastimes*. London: Chatto & Windus, 1969.

Beadle. *Beadle's Dime Ballroom Companion and Guide to Dancing*. New York: Beadle, 1868.

Beaver, Patrick. *Victorian Parlor Games*. Nashville: Nelson, 1974.

———. *Victorian Parlour Games for Today*. London: Davies, 1974.

Bek, William G. "The Followers of Duden." *Missouri Historical Review* 14, no. 1 (October 1919): 29–73; 14, no. 2 (January 1920): 217–32; 14, nos. 3–4 (April–July 1920): 436–58; 15, no. 3 (April 1921): 519–44; 15, no. 4 (July 1921): 660–99; 16, no. 1 (October 1921): 119–45; 16, no. 2 (January 1922): 289–307; 16, no. 3 (April 1922): 343–83; 16, no. 4 (July 1922): 523–50; 17, no. 1 (October 1922): 28–56; 17, no. 3 (April 1923): 331–47; 17, no. 4 (July 1923): 479–504; 18, no. 1 (October 1923): 36–54; 18, no. 2 (January 1924): 212–49; 18, no. 3 (April 1924): 415–37; 18, no. 4 (July 1924): 562–84; 19, no. 1 (October 1924): 114–29; 19, no. 2 (January 1925): 338–52.

Bennett, Estelline. *Old Deadwood Days*. New York: J. H. Sears, 1928.

Bernard, Charles. "Circusiana." *Hobbies* (August 1935): 22.

Birchard, Robert S. *Cecil B. DeMille's Hollywood*. Foreword by Kevin Thomas. Lexington: University Press of Kentucky, 2004.

Brown, T. Allston. *History of the American Stage: Containing Biographical Sketches of Nearly Every Member of the Profession That Has Appeared on the American Stage, from 1733 to 1870*. New York: Blom, 1969.

———. *Amphitheatres and Circuses: A History from Their Earliest Date to 1861, with Sketches of Some of the Principal Performers*. San Bernardino: Borgo, 1994.

Bruesch, S. R., M.D. "The Disasters and Epidemics of a River Town: Memphis, Tennessee, 1819–1879." *Bulletin of the Medical Library Association* 40, no. 3 (July 1952): 288–305.

Buel, James William. *Heroes of the Plains, or, Lives and Wonderful Adventures of Wild Bill, Buffalo Bill, Kit Carson, Capt. Payne, "White Beaver," Capt. Jack, Texas Jack, California Joe, and Other Celebrated Indian Fighters, Scouts, Hunters and Guides.* St. Louis: Historical Publishing, 1883.

Carlyon, David. *Dan Rice: The Most Famous Man You've Never Heard Of.* New York: Public Affairs, 2001.

Carson, Gerald. *The Social History of Bourbon: An Unhurried Account of Our Star-Spangled American Drink.* New York: Dodd, Mead, 1963.

Cary, Diana Serra. *The Hollywood Posse: The Story of a Gallant Band of Horsemen Who Made Movie History.* Norman: University of Oklahoma Press, 1996.

Chindahl, George Leonard. *A History of the Circus in America.* Caldwell, Idaho: Caxton, 1959.

Cist, Charles. *Cincinnati in 1841: Its Early Annals and Future Prospects.* Cincinnati: Morgan, 1841.

———. *The Cincinnati Directory for 1842.* Cincinnati: Morgan, 1842.

———. *The Cincinnati Directory for 1843.* Cincinnati: Brooks, 1843.

———. Sketches *and Statistics of Cincinnati in 1851.* Cincinnati: Moore, 1851.

Clairmonte, Glenn. "The Double Nature of Wild Bill Hickok." *Denver Westerners Monthly Roundup* 16, no. 8 (August 1960): 14–23.

Clark, C. M., ed. *Clark's Guide-Books of the States Cities, and Picturesque Water-ways and Railroad Routes of the United States.* No. 1 of the Third Series, *The Picturesque Ohio.* Cincinnati: Cranston & Stowe, 1888.

Coleman, Marion Moore. *Mazeppa, Polish and American: A Translation of Slowacki's Mazeppa, Together with a Brief Survey of Mazeppa in the United States.* Chesire, Conn.: Cherry Hill Books, 1966.

Conklin, George. *The Ways of the Circus: Being the Memories and Adventures of George Conklin, Tamer of Lions.* Barcelona, Spain: Athena Books, 2004 [original publ. New York: Harper, 1921].

Conover, Richard E. "The Calliope, Its Origin and Appreciation." *Billboard* 2 (February 1954): 3–4.

———. *Give 'Em a John Robinson: A Documentary on the Old John Robinson Circus.* Xenia, Ohio: Richard E. Conover, 1965.

Cornell, Alice M., ed. *Art as Image: Prints and Promotion in Cincinnati, Ohio.* Athens: Ohio University Press in association with University of Cincinnati Digital Press, 2001.

Coup, William Cameron. *Sawdust and Spangles: Stories and Secrets of the Circus.* Chicago: H. S. Stone, 1901.

Dahlinger, Fred, Jr. "The Development of the Railroad Circus." *Bandwagon* 27, no. 6 (November–December 1983): 6–11; 28, no. 1 (January–February 1984): 16–27; 28, no. 2 (March–April 1984): 28–36; 28, no. 3 (May–June 1984): 29–36.

Dahlinger, Fred, Jr., and Stuart Thayer. *Badger State Showmen: A History of Wisconsin's Circus Heritage.* Madison, Wis.: Grote, 1998.

Davis, Janet M. *The Circus Age: Culture and Society under the American Big Top*. Chapel Hill: University of North Carolina Press, 2002.

Davis, William C. *The Battlefields of the Civil War: The Bloody Conflict of North against South Told through the Stories of Its Great Battles*. Norman: University of Oklahoma Press, 1996.

Day, Charles H. *Ink from a Circus Press Agent: An Anthology of Circus History from the Pen of Charles H. Day*. San Bernardino: Borgo, 1995.

DeBow, J. D. B. *The Seventh Census of the United States, 1850*. Washington, D.C.: Armstrong, 1853.

Dickens, Charles. *American Notes for General Circulation*. Ed. John S. Whitley and Arnold Goldman. London: Penguin English Library, 1975; reprint, London: Penguin Classics, 1985 [original publ. London: Chapman and Hall, 1842]. Page references are to the 1985 edition.

Disher, M. Willson. *Fairs, Circuses, and Music Halls*. London: William Collins & Sons, 1942.

Drago, Harry Sinclair. "Debunking Outlaws and Some Noted Lawmen." *Quarterly of the National Association and Center for Outlaw and Lawman History* 17, no. 4 (Winter 1982–83): 3–4.

Draper, John Daniel. "Willie O'Dale and Willie O'Dell." *Bandwagon* 48, no. 1 (January–February 2004): 22–25.

Duden, Gottfried. *Report on a Journey to the Western States of North America and a Stay of Several Years along the Missouri (during the Years 1824, '25, '26, 1827)*. Ed. and trans. James W. Goodrich, George H. Kellner, Elsa Nagel, Adolf E. Schroeder, and W. M. Senner. Columbia: State Historical Society of Missouri and University of Missouri Press, 1980.

Durham, Walter T. *Nashville: The Occupied City: The First Seventeen Months, February 16, 1862, to June 30, 1863*. Nashville: Tennessee Historical Society, 1985.

———. *Reluctant Partners: Nashville and the Union, July 1, 1863, to June 30, 1865*. Nashville: Tennessee Historical Society, 1987.

Dykstra, Robert. "Wild Bill Hickok in Abilene." *Journal of the Central Mississippi Valley American Studies Association* 2, no. 2 (April 1961): 20–48.

Eckhard, Albrecht, and Heinrich Schmidt, eds. *Geschichte des Landes Oldenburg: Ein Handbuch*. Oldenburg, Ger.: Heinz Holzberg Verlag, 1987.

Edwards' Eleventh Annual Directory in the City of St. Louis for 1869. St. Louis: Charless Publishing and Manufacturing, 1869.

Eisele, Wilbert Edwin. *The Real Wild Bill Hickok: Famous Scout and Knight Chivalric of the Plains — A True Story of Pioneer Life in the Far West*. Denver: W. H. Andre, 1931.

Ferguson, Thomas E. *Ohio Lands: A Short History*. Columbus: Ohio Auditor of State, 1991.

Fisher, Linda A. "A Summer of Terror: The Cholera Epidemic of 1849." *Missouri Historical Review* 99, no. 3 (April 2005): 189–211.

Fox, Charles, et al. *The Explosion of the Moselle*. Cincinnati: Flash, 1838.

Fox, Charles Philip. *A Pictorial History of Performing Horses.* New York: Bramhall, 1959.

Fox, Charles Philip, and Tom Parkinson. *Billers, Banners, and Bombast: The Story of Circus Advertising.* Boulder, Colo.: Pruett, 1985.

———. *The Circus in America.* Santa Monica: Hennessey & Ingalls, 2002.

Gallop, Alan. *Buffalo Bill's British Wild West.* Gloucestershire, Eng.: Sutton, 2001.

Gard, Wayne. *The Chisholm Trail.* Norman: University of Oklahoma Press, 1954.

Garst, Shannon, and Warren Garst. *Wild Bill Hickok.* New York: Julian Messner, 1952.

Glenroy, John H. *Ins and Outs of Circus Life, or Forty-Two Years Travel of John H. Glenroy, Bareback Rider, through United States, Canada, South America and Cuba.* Boston: M. M. Wing, 1885.

Gopsill's Jersey City and Hoboken Directory for the Year Ending April 30, 1883. Washington, D.C.: William H. Boyd, 1883.

Green, Harvey. *The Light of the Home: An Intimate View of the Lives of Women in Victorian America.* Fayetteville: University of Arkansas Press, 2003.

Hall, James. *The West: Its Commerce and Navigation.* Cincinnati: H. W. Derby, 1848.

Halttunen, Karen. *Confidence Men and Painted Women: A Study of Middle-Class Culture in America, 1830–1870.* New Haven: Yale University Press, 1982.

Hankins, Thomas L., and Robert J. Silverman. *Instruments and the Imagination.* Princeton: Princeton University Press, 1995.

Hegeler, Hans Gerd, and Ursula Maria Schute. *Das Oldenburger Münsterland.* Oldenburg, Ger.: Heinz Holzberg Verlag, 1985.

Herman, Eleanor. *Sex with Kings: Five Hundred Years of Adultery, Power, Rivalry, and Revenge.* New York: Perennial, 2004.

Hijiya, James A. "American Gravestones and Attitudes toward Death: A Brief History." *Proceedings of the American Philosophical Society* 127, no. 5 (October 14, 1983): 339–63.

Hoage, R. J., and William A. Deiss, eds. *New World, New Animals: From Menagerie to Zoological Park in the Nineteenth Century.* Foreword by Michael H. Robinson. Baltimore: Johns Hopkins University Press, 1996.

Hoh, LaVahn G., and William H. Rough. *Step Right Up! The Adventure of Circus in America.* White Hall, Va.: Betterway, 1990.

Holt, Glen E. The Shaping of St. Louis, 1763–1860, 2 vols. PhD Dissertation, University of Chicago, 1975.

Hoying, Louis A., Rita M. Hoying, and David A. Hoying. *Pilgrims All: A History of Saint Augustine Parish, Minster, Ohio, 1832–1982.* Minster: St. Augustine Parish, 1982.

Hubbard, Freeman. *Great Days of the Circus.* New York: American Heritage, 1962.

"Important James B. 'Wild Bill' Hickok Letters, Photography and Documents from the Estate of Celinda Hickok." San Francisco: Greg Martin Auctions, Lot 15, 2003.

Joblin, Maurice. *Cincinnati Past and Present: Its Industrial History as Exhibited in the Life-Labors of Its Leading Men*. Cincinnati: Elm Street Printing, 1872.

John, Richard R. *Spreading the News: The American Postal System from Franklin to Morse*. Cambridge: Harvard University Press, 1995.

Johnson, Robert Underwood, and Clarence Clough Buel. *Battles and Leaders of the Civil War*, vol. 4. New introduction (1959) by Roy F. Nichols. New York: Thomas Yoseloff, 1959; reprint Edison, N.J.: Castle, 1982.

Johnson, William. *The Rose-Tinted Menagerie*. London: Heretic Books, 1990.

Jones and Robinson. *Robinson & Jones' Cincinnati Directory for 1846*. Cincinnati: Robinson & Jones, 1846.

Kaiser, Hermann, and Helmut Ottenjann. *Museumsführer: Museumsdorf Cloppenburg*. Cloppenburg, Neth.: Niedersächsisches Freilichtmuseum, 1998.

Kamphoefner, Walter D., Peter Marschalck, and Birgit Nolte-Schuster. *Von Heuerleuten und Farmern*. Bramsche, Ger.: Landschaftsverband Osnabrücker Land e.V., 1999.

Kasper, Shirl. *Annie Oakley*. Norman: University of Oklahoma Press, 1992.

King, Orin C. "The Circus World of Willie Sells, with Accounts of Circus Performances in Topeka, 1858–1908." *Shawnee County Historical Society*. Topeka: Shawnee County Historical Society, 1983.

Klein, Benjamin F., ed. *The Ohio River Collection: The Ohio River Handbook and Picture Album*, rev. ed. Cincinnati: Young & Klein, 1969.

Kunhardt, Phillip B., Jr., Phillip B. Kunhardt III, and Peter W. Kunhardt. *P. T. Barnum: America's Greatest Showman*. New York: Alfred A. Knopf, 1995.

Lachs, Johannes. *Schiffe aus Bremen. Bilder und Modelle im Focke Museum*. Bremen, Ger.: Hauschild, 1994.

Lammers, Robert J., ed. *Remembering . . . A Commemorative Look at Minster, Ohio, 1832–1982*. Minster: Midmark, 1982.

Leavitt-May, Penelope. "Entertainments Aboard G. R. Spalding's Circus Showboat, The Floating Palace." *Billboard* 24, no. 6 (November–December 1979): 19–24.

Lijsen, H. J. *Classical Circus Equitation: Liberty, High School, Quadrilles and Vaulting*. Trans. Anthony Hippisley Coxe and Sylvia Stanier. London: J. A. Allen, 1993.

Lindsay, Hugh. *History of the Life, Travels, and Incidents of Col. Hugh Lindsay*. Philadelphia: n.p., 1859.

Londré, Felicia Hardison, and Daniel J. Watermeier. *American Theater: The United States, Canada, and Mexico: From Pre-Columbian Times to the Present*. New York: Continuum, 1999.

MacDonald, John. *Great Battles of the Civil War*. Kent, U.K.: Grange Books, Michael Joseph, 1988; reprint London: Marshall, 1998.

McCusker, John J. *How Much Is That in Real Money? A Historical Commodity Price Index for Use as a Deflator of Money Values in the Economy of the United States*. Worcester, Mass.: American Antiquarian Society, 2001.

McKennon, Joe. *Circus Lingo*. Sarasota, Fla.: Carnival Publishers of Sarasota, 1980.

McLaird, James D. "Calamity Jane and Wild Bill: Myth and Reality." *Journal of the West* 37, no. 2 (April 1998): 23–32.

———. *Calamity Jane: The Woman and the Legend*. Norman: University of Oklahoma Press, 2005.

Mersman, Joseph J. *The Whiskey Merchant's Diary: An Urban Life in the Emerging Midwest*, ed. Linda A. Fisher. Athens: Ohio University Press, 2007.

Merten, John W. "Stone by Stone along a Hundred Years with the House of Strobridge." *Bulletin of the Historical and Philosophical Society of Ohio* 8, no. 1 (January 1950): 4–48.

Moltmann, Günter, ed. *Germans to America: 300 Years of Immigration, 1683 to 1983*. Stuttgart: Institute for Foreign Cultural Relations, 1982.

Nelson, Hilda. *The Écuyère of the Nineteenth Century in the Circus*. Cleveland Heights, Ohio: Xenophon, 2001.

O'Connor, Richard. *Wild Bill Hickok*. New York: Konecky & Konecky, 1959.

Odell, George Clinton Densmore. *Annals of the New York Stage*, 15 vols. New York: AMS Press, 1970.

Ostendorf, Johannes. *Zur Geschichte der Auswanderung aus dem alten Amt Damme (Oldb.), insbesondere nach Nordamerika, in den Jahren 1830–1880*. Oldenburger Jahrbuch, vols. 46–47. Oldenburg, Ger.: Hermann Luebbing, 1942–43.

Parker, Watson. *Gold in the Black Hills*. Pierre: South Dakota State Historical Society, 2000.

Parkinson, Robert L. "Circus Balloon Ascensions." *Bandwagon* 5, no. 2 (March–April 1961): 3–6.

———. *Directory of American Circuses, 1793–2000*. Baraboo, Wis.: Circus World Museum, 2002.

Parkinson, Tom, and Charles Philip Fox. *The Circus Moves by Rail*. Boulder, Colo.: Pruett, 1978.

Pickering, David. *Cassell's Dictionary of Superstitions*. New York: Sterling, 1995.

Quimby, Mildred. *Quimby's Harbor Guide*. St. Louis: Waterways Journal, 1984.

Riske, Milt. "Wild Bill's Women." *Real West* 23, no. 168 (March 1980): 22–24.

Robinson, Gilbert N. *Old Wagon Show Days*. Cincinnati: Brockwell, 1925.

Robinson, Josephine De Mott. *The Circus Lady*. New York: Thomas Y. Crowell, 1926.

Rorabaugh, W. J. *The Alcoholic Republic: An American Tradition*. New York: Oxford University Press, 1979.

Rosa, Joseph G. *They Called Him Wild Bill: The Life and Adventures of James Butler Hickok*, 2nd ed. Norman: University of Oklahoma Press, 1974 [1964].

———. *Wild Bill Hickok: The Man and His Myth*. Lawrence: University Press of Kansas, 1996.

———. *Jack McCall, Assassin: An Updated Account of His Yankton Trial, Plea for Clemency, and Execution*. English Westerners' Society *Brand Book* 32, no. 1 (Winter). London: English Westerners' Society, 1997–98.

———. "Wild Bill Hickok, Buffalo Bill Cody, and the Grand Buffalo Hunt at Niagara Falls." *Nebraska History* 86, no. 1 (Spring 2005): 12–25.

Rosa, Joseph G., and Robin May. *Buffalo Bill and His Wild West*. Lawrence: University Press of Kansas, 1989.

Roseboon, Eugene H., and Francis P. Weisenburger. *A History of Ohio*. Columbus: Ohio Historical Society, 1996.

Rosenberg, Charles E. *The Cholera Years: The United States in 1832, 1849, and 1866*. Chicago: University of Chicago Press, 1962.

Scamehorn, Howard L. *Balloons to Jets: A Century of Aeronautics in Illinois, 1855–1955*. Carbondale: Southern Illinois University Press, 2000.

Schlumbohm, Jürgen. *Lebensläufe, Familien, Höfe: Die Bauern und Heuerleute des Osnabrückischen Kirchspiels Belm in proto-industrieller Zeit, 1650–1860*. Göttingen, Ger.: Vandenhoeck & Ruprecht, 1997.

Schmaul, Helmut. *Verpflanzt, aber nicht entwurzelt: Die Auswanderung aus Hessen-Darmstadt (Provinz Rheinhessen) nach Wisconsin im 19. Jahrhundert*. Frankfurt, Ger.: Peter Lang, 2000.

Schomaker-Langenteilen, Alwin. *Das Alte Volk von Damme im Kulturspiegel seiner tausendjährigen Fastnacht*. Damme, Ger.: Dammer Karnevalsgesellschaft, 1964.

Secrest, William B. "Bill Hickok's Girl on the Flying Trapeze." *Old West* 4, no. 2 (Winter 1967): 27–30, 68.

——— ed. *I Buried Hickok: The Memoirs of White Eye Anderson*. College Station, Tex.: Creative Publishing, 1980.

Sentilles, Renée M. *Performing Menken: Adah Isaacs Menken and the Birth of American Celebrity*. New York: Cambridge University Press, 2003.

Slout, William. *Clowns and Cannons: The American Circus during the Civil War*. San Bernardino: Borgo, 1997.

———. *Olympians of the Sawdust Circle: A Biographical Dictionary of the Nineteenth-Century American Circus*. San Bernardino: Borgo, 1998.

———. "En Route to The Great Eastern." *Bandwagon* 50, no. 2 (March–April 2006): 28–36; no. 3 (May–June 2006): 24–33; no. 4 (July–August 2006): 32–39; no. 5 (September–October 2006): 17–25.

Sollid, Roberta Beed. *Calamity Jane: A Study in Historical Criticism*. Helena: Historical Society of Montana, 1958.

"The Stella Foote Collection of Western Memorabilia: Treasures of the West." Cody, Wyo.: Brian Lebel's 15th Cody Old West Show & Auction, Lot 263, 2004.

Stevens, Walter B. *St. Louis, the Fourth City, 1764–1909*, 3 vols. Chicago: S. J. Clarke, 1909.

Stevenson, Louise L. *The Victorian Homefront: American Thought and Culture, 1860–1880*. New York: Twayne, 1991.

Stockman, R. L. *North Germany to North America: Nineteenth Century Migration*. Alto, Mich.: PlattDütsch, 2003.

Sturtevant, Charles Gates. "Business Women of the Circus." *White Tops* (January–February 1961): 15.

Taylor, J. N. *St. Louis Business Directory for 1850*. St. Louis: St. Louis Union Office, 1850.

Thayer, Stuart. *Traveling Showmen: The American Circus before the Civil War*. Detroit: Astley & Ricketts, 1997.

——. *Annals of the American Circus, 1793–1860*. Seattle: Dauven & Thayer, 2000.

——. "Great American Riders: 1. Levi J. North, 'America's Own Horseman,'" *Bandwagon* 45, no. 6 (November–December 2001): 16–26.

——. *The Performers: A History of Circus Acts*. Seattle: Dauven and Thayer, 2005.

Thayer, Stuart, and William L. Slout. *Grand Entrée: The Birth of the Greatest Show on Earth, 1870–1875*. San Bernardino: Borgo, 1998.

Thernstrom, Stephan, Ann Orlov, and Oscar Handlin, eds. *Harvard Encyclopedia of American Ethnic Groups*. Cambridge, Mass.: Belknap Press of Harvard University Press, 1980.

Tolzmann, Don Heinrich, ed. *The German Element in St. Louis: A Translation from German of Ernst D. Kargau's St. Louis in Former Years: A Commemorative History of the German Element*. Trans. William G. Bek. Baltimore: Genealogical Publishing, 2001 [1893].

Tryon, John. *The Old Clown's History: In Three Periods*. New York: Torrey Bros., 1872.

Turner, Thadd. *Wild Bill Hickok: Deadwood City—End of Trail*. Hereford, Ariz.: Old West Alive, 2001.

——. "The Shooting of Wild Bill." *True West* 48, no. 6 (August–September 2001): 42–47.

Vail, R. W. G. "This Way to the Big Top!" *New-York Historical Society Quarterly Bulletin* 29, no. 3 (July 1945): 137–60.

Von Baltimore nach Bünde. Bünde, Ger.: Deutsches Tabak- und Zigarrenmuseum, n.d.

Walker, Mack. *Germany and the Emigration, 1816–1885*. Cambridge: Harvard University Press, 1964.

——. *German Home Towns: Community, State, and General Estate 1648–1871*. Ithaca, N.Y.: Cornell University Press, 1971.

Warren, Louis S. *Buffalo Bill's America: William Cody and the Wild West Show*. New York: Alfred A. Knopf, 2005.

Way, Frederick, Jr. *Way's Packet Directory, 1848–1994*. Athens: Ohio University Press, 1983.

Williams. *Williams' Cincinnati Directory and General Business Directory*. Cincinnati: Williams & Son, 1848.

——. *Williams' Cincinnati Directory and Business Advertiser for 1850–1851*. 2nd Issue. Cincinnati: Williams, 1850.

——. *Williams' Cincinnati Directory*. 14th Issue. Cincinnati: Williams & Co., 1864.

Williamson, C. W. *History of Western Ohio and Auglaize County*. Columbus, Ohio: W. M. Linn & Sons, 1905.

Wilstach, Frank Jenners. "Time Widens Wild Bill Hickok's Fame." *New York Times Magazine* (September 13, 1925): 10.

——. *Wild Bill Hickok: The Prince of Pistoleers.* New York: Doubleday, Page, 1926.

——. *The Plainsman: Wild Bill Hickok.* New York: Sun Dial, 1937 [1926].

Wimberg, Robert J. *Cincinnati: Over-the-Rhine,* 2nd ed. Cincinnati: Ohio Book Store, 1988.

The World Book/Rush-Presbyterian–St. Luke's Medical Center Medical Encyclopedia: Your Guide to Good Health, 4th ed. Chicago: World Book, 1994.

Wright, Kathryn. "The Real Calamity Jane." *True West* 5, no. 2 (November–December 1957): 23.

Writers' Program of the Works Projects Administration (Missouri). *Missouri: A Guide to the "Show Me" State.* New York: Duell, Sloan & Pearce, 1941.

—— (Ohio). *The WPA Guide to Cincinnati: A Guide to the Queen City and Its Neighbors.* Cincinnati: Scripps-Howard, 1987 [1943].

Yost, Nellie Snyder. *Buffalo Bill, His Family, Friends, Fame, Failures, and Fortunes,* 2nd printing. Chicago: Sage Books, 1979.

Newspapers

Albany News, Albany, Ga.

Albany Patriot, Albany, Ga.

American Union, Steubenville, Ohio

Anamosa Gazette, Anamosa, Iowa

Arkansas Intelligencer, Van Buren, Ark.

Atlanta Constitution, Atlanta, Ga.

Bainbridge Argus, Bainbridge, Ga.

Battle Creek Daily Journal, Battle Creek, Mich.

Bay State, Lynn, Mass.

Black Hills Daily Times, Deadwood, S.Dak.

Bloomington Daily Pantagraph, Bloomington, Ill.

Boston Daily Globe, Boston, Mass.

Broome Republican, Binghamton, N.Y.

Buffalo Commercial Advertiser, Buffalo, N.Y.

Buffalo Express, Buffalo, N.Y.

Buffalo Reflex, Buffalo, Mo.

Burlington Daily Hawkeye, Burlington, Iowa

Camden Democrat, Camden, N.J.

Canton Weekly Register, Canton, Ohio

Carlinville Democrat, Carlinville, Ill.

Carlisle Herald, Carlisle, Pa.

Cartersville Express, Cartersville, Ga.

Carthage Weekly Banner, Carthage, Mo.

Central Georgian, Sandersville, Ga.

Charleston Daily Courier, Charleston, S.C.

Cheyenne Daily Leader, Cheyenne, Wyo.
Cheyenne Daily Sun, Cheyenne, Wyo.
Chicago Inter-Ocean, Chicago, Ill.
Chronicle, Abilene, Kans.
Cincinnati Daily Commercial, Cincinnati, Ohio
Cincinnati Daily Gazette, Cincinnati, Ohio
Cincinnati Daily Republican, Cincinnati, Ohio
Cincinnati Daily Times, Cincinnati, Ohio
Cincinnati Enquirer, Cincinnati, Ohio
Colorado Miner, Georgetown, Colo.
Columbus Daily Enquirer, Columbus, Ga.
Columbus Dispatch, Columbus, Ky.
Covington Journal, Covington, Ky.
Daily Chronicle & Sentinel, Augusta, Ga.
Daily Courier, Lafayette, Ind.
Daily Express, Lancaster, Pa.
Daily Herald, Newburyport, Mass.
Daily Morning Democrat, Grand Rapids, Mich.
Daily Nonpareil, Council Bluffs, Iowa
Daily Patriot, Harrisburg, Pa.
Daily Picayune, New Orleans, La.
Daily Quincy Herald, Quincy, Ill.
Daily State Gazette, Trenton, N.J.
Daily Sun, Columbus, Ga.
Daily Toledo Blade, Toledo, Ohio
Daily True American, Trenton, N.J.
Daily Zanesville Courier, Zanesville, Ohio
Danville Plaindealer, Danville, Ill.
Dawson Weekly Journal, Dawson, Ga.
Deadwood Black Hills Times, Deadwood, S.Dak.
Deadwood Daily Pioneer-Times, Deadwood, S.Dak.
Deadwood Telegram, Deadwood, S.Dak.
Deadwood Weekly Pioneer-Times, Deadwood, S.Dak.
Delphi Journal, Delphi, Ind.
Democratic Banner, Henderson, Ky.
Democratic Herald, Butler, Pa.
Democratic Union, Upper Sandusky, Ohio
Deutsche National-Zeitung, Berlin, Ger.
Elizabeth Daily Monitor, Elizabeth, N.J.
Evansville Daily Journal, Evansville, Ind.
Evening News, Indianapolis, Ind.
Evening Star, Washington, D.C.

Fall River Daily Herald, Fall River, Mass.
Fort Dodge Times, Fort Dodge, Iowa
Fort Scott Daily Monitor, Fort Scott, Kans.
Fort Wayne Weekly Sentinel, Fort Wayne, Ind.
Der Fortschritt, Jefferson City, Mo.
Galveston News, Galveston, Tex.
Georgia Citizen, Macon, Ga.
Georgia Weekly Telegraph, Macon, Ga.
Globe-Democrat, St. Louis, Mo.
Hancock Courier, Findley, Ohio
Hastings Republican Banner, Hastings, Mich.
Hawkinsville Dispatch, Hawkinsville, Ga.
Hermann Volksblatt, Herman, Mo.
Illinois Journal, Springfield, Ill.
Independent Phoenix, Phoenixville, Pa.
Indianapolis Daily News, Indianapolis, Ind.
Indianapolis Daily Sentinel, Indianapolis, Ind.
Jefferson Radical, Jefferson, Tex.
Junction City Union, Junction City, Kans.
Kansas Daily Commonwealth, Topeka, Kans.
Kennebec Journal, Augusta, Maine
Keokuk Daily Gate City, Keokuk, Iowa
Kokomo Democrat, Kokomo, Ind.
Laramie (Colo.) Daily Sentinel
Liberty Tribune, Liberty, Mo.
Logansport Journal, Logansport, Ind.
London Times, London, England
Louisville Courier-Journal, Louisville, Ky.
Louisville Daily Democrat, Louisville, Ky.
Louisville Journal, Louisville, Ky.
Louisville Morning Courier, Louisville, Ky.
Lynchburg Daily Virginian, Lynchburg, Va.
Lynn News, Lynn, Mass.
Lynn Transcript, Lynn, Mass.
Mahoning County Register, Youngstown, Ohio
Marietta Daily Journal, Marietta, Ga.
Marion Commonwealth, Marion, Ala.
Memphis Daily Appeal, Memphis, Tenn.
Memphis Daily Eagle, Memphis, Tenn.
Mendota Reporter, Mendota, Ill.
Mirror, Leesburg, Va.
Missouri Patriot, Springfield, Mo.

Missouri Republican, St. Louis, Mo.
Missouri Telegraph, Fulton, Mo.
Missouri Weekly Patriot, Springfield, Mo.
Mobile Daily Advertiser & Register, Mobile, Ala.
Monmouth Review, Monmouth, Ill.
Montgomery Daily Advertiser, Montgomery, Ala.
Morgan County Weekly Banner, Versailles, Mo.
Morgan Herald, McConnelsville, Ohio
Morning Telegraph, New York, N.Y.
Muskegon Chronicle, Muskegon, Mich.
Nashville Daily Press, Nashville, Tenn.
Nashville Dispatch, Nashville, Tenn.
Nashville Union, Nashville, Tenn.
Nationalist, Manhattan, Kans.
Nebraska City News, Nebraska City, Nebr.
Neosho Times, Neosho, Mo.
New Castle Courier, New Castle, Ind.
New York Clipper, New York, N.Y.
New York Dramatic Mirror, New York, N.Y.
New York Herald, New York, N.Y.
New York Mercury, New York, N.Y.
New York Sun, N.Y.
New York Times, New York, N.Y.
Newark Daily Journal, Newark, N.J.
Niles Democrat, Niles, Mich.
Niles Republican, Niles, Mich.
Observer, Jersey City, N.J.
Omaha Daily Bee, Omaha, Neb.
Ottawa Republican, Ottawa, Kans.
Ouachita Telegraph, Monroe, La.
Paterson Daily Press, Paterson, N.J.
Pittsburgh Chronicle, Pittsburgh, Pa.
Pittsburgh Daily Gazette, Pittsburgh, Pa.
Pittsfield Sun, Pittsfield, Mass.
Porter County Vidette, Valparaiso, Ind.
Portland Press, Portland, Maine
Portland Transcript, Portland, Maine
Republican Standard, New Bedford, Mass.
Richmond Daily Dispatch, Richmond, Va.
Rome Tri-Weekly Courier, Rome, Ga.
Salem Gazette, Salem, Mass.
Saline County Journal, Salina, Kans.

Salt Lake Desert News, Salt Lake City, Utah
Salt Lake Tribune, Salt Lake City, Utah
Scranton Daily Times, Scranton, Pa.
Sedalia Democrat, Sedalia, Mo.
Sedalia Weekly Bazoo, Sedalia, Mo.
Shamokin Herald, Shamokin, Pa.
South-Western, Shreveport, La.
Southern Banner, Athens, Ga.
Southern Recorder, Milledgeville, Ga.
Spring River Fountain, Mount Vernon, Mo.
Springfield Daily Union, Springfield, Mass.
Springfield Leader, Springfield, Mo.
St. Joseph Valley Register, St. Joseph, Mich.
St. Louis Post-Dispatch, St. Louis, Mo.
St. Louis Republic, St. Louis, Mo.
St. Louis Republican, St. Louis, Mo.
St. Louis Reveille, St. Louis, Mo.
State Capitol Fact, Columbus, Ohio
Steubenville American Union, Steubenville, Ohio
Sun, New York, N.Y.
Sunday Mercury, New York, N.Y.
Taunton Daily Gazette, Taunton, Mass.
Terra Haute Daily Gazette, Terra Haute, Ind.
Times-Picayune, New Orleans, La.
Topeka Daily Commonwealth, Topeka, Kans.
Topeka State Journal, Topeka, Kans.
Tri-Weekly Standard, Bridgeport, Conn.
Troy Daily Budget, Troy, N.Y.
Troy Messenger, Troy, Ala.
Tuscaloosa Blade, Tuscaloosa, Ala.
Valley Spirit, Chambersburg, Pa.
Vicksburg Daily Whig, Vicksburg, Miss.
Vincennes Weekly Western Sun, Vincennes, Ind.
Virginia Evening Chronicle, Virginia City, Nev.
Warrensburg Standard, Warrensburg, Mo.
Washington Star, Washington, D.C.
Waynesburg Messenger, Waynesburg, Pa.
Weekly Ledger, Pleasant Hill, Mo.
Weekly Northern Indianaian, Warsaw, Ind.
Weekly Sentinel, Jacksonville, Mo.
Weekly Tribune, Jefferson City, Mo.
Westliche Post, St. Louis, Mo.

Weston County Gazette, Upton, Wyo.
Wheeling Intelligencer, Wheeling, Va. (now W.Va.)
Worcester Evening Gazette, Worcester, Mass.
Wyoming Stockman-Farmer, Cheyenne, Wyo.
Wyoming Tribune, Cheyenne, Wyo.

Index